For Good and Evil

For Good and Evil

The Impact of Taxes
on the Course of Civilization

Second Edition

Charles Adams

MADISON BOOKS

Lanham • New York • Oxford

Published by Madison Books
4720 Boston Way
Lanham, Maryland 20706

12 Hid's Copse Road
Cumnor Hill, Oxford OX2 9JJ, England

Distributed by National Book Network

Library of Congress Cataloging-in-Publication Data
Adams, Charles, 1930–
    For good and evil : the impact of taxes on the course of
civilization / Charles Adams. — 2nd ed.
        p.   cm.
    Includes bibliographical references and index.
    ISBN 1-56833-123-1 (cloth : alk. paper)
    1. Taxation—History.   2. Taxation—United States—History.
I. Title.
HJ2250.A323   1999
336.2'009—dc21   *98-49954*
                                                          CIP

∞ ™ The paper used in this publication meets the minimum
requirements of American National Standard for Information
Sciences—Permanence of Paper for Printed Library Materials,
ANSI/NISO Z39.48–1992. Manufactured in the United States of
America.

To our children in the twenty-first century—with the hope that they may be creative and develop a tax system devoid of the evils that permeate the system under which we now live.

Contents

Aristides
Father of Just Taxation

He drew up a list of assessments not only with scrupulous integrity and justice, but also in such a way that all states felt they had been justly and fairly taxed. . . . The levy of Aristides was a golden age for the allies of Athens.

—Plutarch, *Life of Aristides*

Foreword

In 1982, Charles W. Adams published a wonderful book entitled *Fight, Flight, Fraud: The Story of Taxation.* I own two copies. I keep one for handy reference in my office, and the other at home (I will replace them with two copies of *For Good and Evil: The Impact of Taxes on the Course of Civilization*). I consult them frequently for anecdotes of tax folly as well as for bibliographical references in my own research. I can honestly say that in the course of fifteen years of professional research and writing about taxation, I would place Charles W. Adams's history of taxation at the absolute top of any reading list on the subject.

Fight, Flight, Fraud was entertaining, informative, and full of lessons about why taxes matter. I delight in telling one and all that the origins of recorded history were inextricably linked to oppressive taxation. Over six thousand years ago, the dawn of history was discovered in the form of clay cuneiform cones excavated at Lagash, in Sumer, which is located in the fertile plain between the Tigris and Euphrates in modern Iraq. And what was recorded on those cones? That Sumerians had more to fear from tax collectors than from their lords or kings. Plus ça change, plus la même chose!

I have lots of other favorite stories. The Rosetta Stone, for example, whose text in hieroglyphics, demotics, and Greek was the key to revealing the stories of ancient Egypt, was in fact a grant of tax immunity. Which is why, of course, it was engraved in stone and not written on papyrus.

Another example is the prosperous island of Rhodes, which charged a 2 percent harbor tax on trade. Rhodes lost 85 percent of its trade in one year after Rome established a tax-free port on the Isle of Delos. Free trade, not war, enabled Rome to overthrow Rhodian commercial supremacy. And Rome itself fell, not to the Huns, but to tax evasion, as wealthy landowners devised one clever scheme after another to escape taxation, leaving the state without resources to defend itself. *Fight, Flight, Fraud* is a gold mine for producers of television series.

Ten years later, Charles W. Adams has brought forth on this continent a new history of taxation. *For Good and Evil* adds both new material and several new chapters to an already impressive body of research and exposition that encompasses ancient civilizations, the Greek and Roman eras, the Middle Ages, the evolving states of Western and Eastern Europe, the Aztecs, and the history of American taxation. One new chapter describes the miracle economies of Japan, Hong Kong, Singapore, Taiwan, and South Korea, which practiced low-tax, supply-side economics decades before Ronald Reagan popularized the term. Another new chapter shows how state constitutions actively protect taxpayers by giving them constitutional controls on taxing and spending. Perhaps the most famous of these is Proposition 13, the brainchild of the late Howard Jarvis, which limits real property tax rates in California to 1 percent of a home's cash value.

Adams also adds a new chapter on "Taming the Monster." He offers several reforms, decidedly pro-taxpayer, to make taxes work for good, not evil. They include making tax extortion on the part of government officials a criminal offense, allowing taxpayers to sue the tax authorities for misconduct, and granting voters recall powers over district directors of the Internal Revenue Service. Perhaps the most important reform is to switch from a regime of direct taxation to one of indirect taxation, to minimize the intrusive powers of the government into the private affairs of individuals.

My favorite recommendation is to scrap the entire U.S. federal income tax system in favor of a 10 percent flat tax without "special" exemptions. This is not a new idea. A 10 percent flat tax is well grounded in several thousand years of the history of Israel, Rome, Greece, and ancient China.

The ten years between *Fight, Flight, Fraud* and *For Good and Evil* were put to productive use by the author. He offers readers several insights learned from the history of taxation. First, good tax systems go bad unless citizens are able to restrain their governments, which have a normal propensity to adjust their spending to their innate voracious appetites, not their wallets. Second, civilization tends to self-destruct from excessive taxation. Third, moderation is an important principle in the design and implementation of any tax system. The principle of moderation includes the choice of tax rates and penalties for evasion, the intrusiveness of tax collection, and the need to treat taxpayers equally by avoiding severe progressivity or regressivity.

Happy reading! And let's hope that our elected, appointed, or, as the case may be, self-anointed rulers take Adams's admonitions to heart.

Alvin Rabushka
Senior Fellow
Hoover Institution
Stanford University
1993

Preface to the Second Edition

Professor Alvin Rabushka advised me soon after the first edition of this book appeared to prepare for a revised edition to keep this study alive as a classic and to make any additions and corrections that would, in time, be required. As a result of that advice I have kept notes on changing events, done new research, and included the input of many readers who have been thoughtful enough to contact me about matters in the text that concerned them and which they believed needed revision. In addition, since the ending of this study deals with current events and not history, it was inevitable that the course of history would deviate from what I had expected, proving the Japanese proverb that the most precious thing in life is its uncertainty.

The most dramatic and surprising event of this decade has been the meltdown of what I called the "Miracle Economies" of Asia. The collapse of their currencies, which damaged their economies, was not anticipated a few years ago. Japan Inc. was not just a world competitor to the Western economies; it was an incredible economic giant that challenged and usually surpassed any competitors. Now it is in economic decline along with the rest of the Asian tigers, and we are reminded that it takes more than a good tax policy to prosper in this world. Good money management and sound banking are as much requirements for sustained prosperity as are good tax laws. My new Asian chapter could well be called "Miracles No More." But I suspect that the Asians will, sooner or later, get their fiscal affairs in proper order, refrain from lend-happy banking, and reassert their dominance in world commerce.

I became especially interested in the critics who complained about my admiration for Elizabeth I and her tax and fiscal policies. It seems Good Queen Bess has a lot of haters in the world who were itching to attack her reign. This motivated me to look further into her fiscal affairs to see if the Elizabeth-haters had good cause. I have not changed my mind; indeed, I find her an even wiser and better monarch than I had originally believed. I had suggested that she was the greatest monarch Europe ever had; I now think she was the greatest monarch bar none!

My view that taxes, not slavery, started the American Civil War was vindicated by *American Heritage* in June of 1996, which said: "The tariff, then nearly synonymous with federal taxes, was a prime cause of the Civil War." I have added and corrected some of the material in that chapter, which the reader should find of interest.

I also became somewhat fascinated with writings about slavery—about tax slavery—which was so prominent with the Founders. Does that kind of slavery still exist? And what did these writers mean? I have ended with a brief look into that. In the nineteenth century we had chattel slavery for the few, the Africans, but have we rid ourselves of that brand of slavery, only to find we have instituted tax slavery for the many?

In looking into the taxes of the ancient world, where taxes began, I had overlooked the Chinese, whose civilization goes back three thousand years. That civilization was known for its great wisdom and sages, and the reader will discover that they were wise indeed in matters of taxation.

Tax reform has heated up substantially since the 1980s, but is there any chance we will rid ourselves of the income tax? We have an administration that likes the income tax "just the way it is." And the mainstream media shies away from the tax reform issue and the tax sins of the IRS except when congressional hearings force them to take note. We got out of Vietnam only after the major networks, and Walter Cronkite in particular, decided it was a senseless and hopeless war. When these same news professionals, who do so much to shape public thinking, finally get on the bandwagon to rid us of the income tax, then perhaps we can expect real change.

This study has now been almost thirty years in the making. It has two main roots: one being my experiences as a tax professional in the trenches, so to speak; the other being a few wonderful years I spent teaching history in a small college with students from the Third World. In the course of that endeavor the role of taxation in many of the important events of history caught my attention. When I sought more knowledge on the matter, I discovered that despite its crucial importance in civilized life, taxation had rarely been studied on its own as a force shaping and directing civilization. This study is designed to set taxation apart and bring it into focus as one of the most powerful forces at work structuring society, today as well as in the past.

It is no surprise that this book does not pigeonhole itself into any of the established academic disciplines. There is no family of American scholars who have devoted their lives to probing into the broad sweep of tax history and the significance of civilization's tax struggles. This study is made to help fill that void.

It is amazing that our great academic institutions have no studies focusing on tax history. We are still in search of the tax historian. We have developed whole new courses and even programs for special interest studies on gays and lesbians, multiculturalism, women's studies, black studies, and ecology, and we can expect to see Latin studies, as that population keeps growing. But taxes, even though they are the fuel that makes civilization run, have never been set apart for study as a force directing and shaping civilization, at least not in this country. In Europe many of the major universities, like the universities of Amsterdam and Lieden, for example, have not only courses on tax history but also endowed chairs for the professorships that are popularized with formal cap and gown ceremonies and with addresses by the newly appointed professors, later printed into booklet form for the academic communities. Perhaps our present tax mess is the consequence of our ignorance of tax history at all levels—at the government level, in our universities, and among our citizens. If history makes men wise, then it is no wonder wisdom is not with us in tax making.

This book deals in part with history, law, economics, politics, ethics, human rights, and the social sciences as a whole. Whenever taxation has touched civilization, we have ventured in for an examination. Limiting our study to a single volume, we have had to simply introduce the reader to a world heretofore explored very little, if at all. We will have to leave it to other scholars to make more comprehensive studies to sharpen our perspective. For me, it has been exciting to explore new territory and unearth new insights into the past and, more important, into our future course.

A book with such a broad scope as this is based to a large extent upon the research and opinions of others. I tried to give the essential facts and interpret them in the light of what others had written. When experts disagreed, I had to make a selection. Some years ago a writer was being praised for his original work. He replied by saying that his work was like a string of pearls, but the only thing that was his was the string. That certainly applies to this study.

Stringing the pearls of civilization's tax story has been a fascinating experience. Our tax story has been deadly serious, of course, but it has also had a lighter side. Consequently, the text that follows is filled with many anecdotes, illustrations, and caricatures that should make this book fun to read.

Introductions appear from time to time to help orient the reader. The narrative is broken for comments and comparisons with modern taxation. There are lessons to be learned from the tax struggles of our ancestors, and parallels are drawn when it seems important to do so. The ancient historians were masters of the art of digression, which is what makes them exciting to read even when the events seem so remote from our times. Digression is necessary if, as the ancient historians believed, history ought to teach. These men believed that knowledge of the past was man's best guide to the future: "It will enable men to act more sensibly and to avoid mistakes" (Michael Grant, *The Ancient Historians* [London, 1970], p. 78).

At the end of this book there are a few hard-hitting chapters that present my analysis and ideas on curing the many faults in the way Western citizens are taxed. Those ideas should form a valuable climax to this study.

I wish to acknowledge the support I received from my fellow professionals, including some of my friends in the revenue service. I want to thank so many readers for their encouragement to bring this study up to date in this revised form, and I want to thank my editor, Jean Donelson, for her skillful editing and for her extraordinary patience with an author who doesn't know when to stop researching and writing. Finally, I wish to thank the many librarians and helpers, at home and abroad, who assisted me with the numerous illustrations that have added spice and flavor to this book. Without these many fascinating tidbits of visual history, many of the insights into our past would have been dulled or lost. In addition, they have also added just the right amount of seasoning to make the main course appetizing.

Introduction

The hypothesis that taxes are a prime mover of history has considerably more merit than many of the other theories of history, some of which are, frankly, crack-pot: super-racism, climate, Divine tinkering, class struggles, life cycles, great heroes, or whatever. There is some truth in some of these theories, some of the time. There have been great and powerful men who have moved civilization, but most of the time no heroes can be found, and the world is led by scoundrels, fools, and second-stringers. Leaders like Moses don't show up very often, especially when needed. Taxes, however, are ever-present, often making a strong impact upon our lives—for good and evil. The prosperity as well as the decline of nations has always had a tax factor, and this we will see time and again throughout history. Human rights have suffered even more than nations—whatever the tax man wants the tax man gets, including our liberty, should he so desire.

Notwithstanding the critical role taxes have often played throughout the course of civilization, this study makes no claim that taxation will provide us with a new philosophy of history. There have been, especially over the past few centuries, many learned men who claim to have uncovered a plot, a pattern, or even a force that directs history. No such assertion is made here. All we have tried to do is to give taxation the status it deserves as an important factor in molding and directing civilization, and as a force for good and evil.

Taxes are a powerful mover of people, more than governments either care to admit or realize. Angry taxpayers can be a lethal threat to a government that institutes oppressive taxation. Taxpayers instinctively rebel: the first warning phase of rebellion is rampant tax evasion and flight to avoid tax; the second phase produces riots; and the third phase is violence. Life ultimately can be catastrophic for any government that pushes its taxpayers too far. When the first phase occurs, governments respond by "cracking down" on defiant taxpayers. In times past, as the British jurist Blackstone observed, the executioner was brought in along with instruments of torture. In modern times, tax makers like to manufacture synthetic felonies to terrorize taxpayers.

The first casualty of what we will call "dumb taxation" has always been liberty; the second casualty has been the wealth and strength of a nation. What we call dumb taxation the Romans called "outrageous burdens."[1] John Adams used the term "ruinous taxation"[2] to describe the British taxes that sparked the American Revolution, and John Stuart Mill used the words "legalized robbery"[3] to describe progressive income taxation. We wouldn't be too far wrong to label all these kinds of taxes as stealing.

We use the term dumb in more than a colloquial sense and more than a synonym for stupid. Dumb also means lacking an essential quality. Historically, a "dumb ship" was a barge because, unlike normal ships, it had no sails. Dumb taxes thus lack an essential quality. Instead of enhancing the strength and prosperity of a people—which they are essentially supposed to do—dumb taxes undermine and even destroy the social order they are supposed to protect and strengthen. Lacking this quality, they are "dumb."

This study will examine many of the major events of history with glasses focused on the tax man, and in doing so we will learn much about man the tax rebel. As we look into the past at the rebelliousness of our ancestors, we can't help but realize what a powerful force taxes are in the course of civilization. Today, except for the People's Republic of China of all places, our rebelliousness is surprisingly, and relative to our ancestors', embarrassingly mild. We have great fear of the tax man—our ancestors had malice aforethought. But as fascinating as the study of man the tax rebel is, the role taxes have played in the major events of history is even more fascinating as we shall see. Indeed, it will seem axiomatic that behind most of the great events of history—the prosperity and poverty of nations, revolts and revolutions, liberty and slavery, and most of all, war—taxes have played an important role that is easily lost sight of in the drama of great events.

The three roots of modern civilization—ancient Greece, Rome, and Israel—involve histories filled with drama centered around taxation. The biblical God, who repeatedly chastised his chosen people, selected taxation as his rod. The words liberty and freedom, which we hold so dear, came to us from these ancient peoples as terms often used to describe a city's tax status.

Taxes played an all-important role in ancient China, where the emperor, to maintain his legitimacy—his Mandate of Heaven—had to keep his tax policy in line with the teachings of the Confucians and the Taoists.

Taxes played critical roles in the Middle Ages and on into the modern world. With the British Civil War and the American and French Revolutions, the tax issue was so all-important that even childhood school books centered on taxation. With events such as the American Civil War, the tax issue that triggered Southern secession and motivated Lincoln's war on the Confederacy is seldom mentioned. The drama of abolition was the great event, but if you were to ask most Southerners in 1861 what was *really* behind the war, an honest answer would have been taxes. The slavery issue was a facade, as was preserving the union.

At the end of this historical study we will try to find meaning and direction from five thousand years of history. If we are to preserve and pass on to our children the liberty and freedom we boast about, which our forefathers passed on to us, we must focus our attention on our tax system and the destructive forces we have put in motion, forces that are far more dangerous than any outside invaders.

"Taxes are what we pay for a civilized society," read the words of Oliver Wendell Holmes inscribed over the entrance to the Internal Revenue Service building in Washington, D.C. But how we tax and spend determines, to a great extent, whether we are prosperous or poor, free or enslaved, and, most important, good or evil.

Part I

Taxes: What They Are and Where They Began

The cartoon on the previous page by James Stevenson from *The New Yorker* magazine is not only funny, it is also profound, because it reveals what taxes are and depicts the way people have felt about taxes since the beginning of recorded history. This same cartoon, with a few modifications, would have produced smiles from taxpayers in ancient Rome, or in many other heavily taxed societies over the centuries. The robbery/tax analogy, which this cartoon presents so graphically, was popular centuries before the Christian era.

The similarity between tax collectors and robbers is also found in the basic meaning behind the word tax, which is exaction. Literally, *exaction* means "to force out." By comparison, its sister word *extortion* means "to twist out." Taxes are not debts, despite the fact that we carelessly refer to them as such. The principle of fair value received—which is the basis for a legally enforceable debt—has no place in a tax dispute. A tax is owed because the government orders it to be paid. Nothing else is required. The essence of a tax is, therefore, the taking of money, or property, or even services, by the government, without paying for it. When a government takes land to build a school and pays for it, this kind of a taking is not a tax.

People instinctively, in all ages, have called tax men robbers because they operate by threats and intimidations and don't pay for what they take. Consequently, the robbery epithet is not as irrational as it may appear. The tax man is, to our emotional systems, a bureaucratic Robin Hood taking wealth where he can find it, and, like Robin Hood, he often does much good with the money he takes. For without revenue, governments would collapse, society as we know it would disappear, and chaos would follow. The tax collector, of course, differs from Robin Hood because his robbery is legalized.

Taxes are the fuel that makes civilization run. There is no known civilization that did not tax. The first civilization we know anything about began six thousand years ago in Sumer, a fertile plain between the Tigris and Euphrates rivers in modern Iraq. The dawn of history, and of tax history, is recorded on clay cones excavated at Lagash, in Sumer. The people of Lagash instituted heavy taxation during a terrible war, but when the war ended, the tax men refused to give up their taxing powers. From one end of the land to the other, these clay cones say, "there were the tax collectors." Everything was taxed. Even the dead could not be buried unless a tax was paid. The story ends when a good king, named Urukagina, "established the freedom" of the people, and once again, "There were no tax collectors."[1] This may not have been a wise policy, because shortly thereafter the city was destroyed by foreign invaders.

There is a proverb about taxes on other clay tablets from this lost

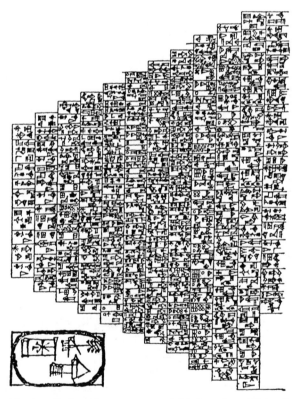

Cuniform writing inscribed on clay cones excavated in Lagash containing the freedom laws of Urukagina that rid the land of "the tax collectors." Encircled are the Sumarian symbols for freedom.

civilization which reads: You can have a Lord, you can have a King, but the man to fear is the tax collector.[2]

Obviously times have not changed. We still fear the tax collector, as evidenced by a recent national cartoon showing a taxpayer urging his accountant to finish his tax audit because he is "running out of tranquilizers."

Ancient tax history has many remarkable parallels in the modern world. In six thousand years, tax collectors and taxpayers have not changed much. Modern computers have little over the all-encompassing surveillance of Egypt's scribes. Our modern sense of tax justice lags behind that of the Romans. Revenue-sharing is not a modern phenomenon; it was developed by the Greeks and functioned without bureaucracy. The ancient Jews battled a form of tax terrorism that makes the Islamic extremists look benign.

From the ancients there is much we can learn, especially in the matter of human rights. Liberty came from the Greeks who believed that tyranny was the consequence of the wrong kind of taxation. The Romans made an addendum to the Greek thesis: In any conflict between liberty and taxes, liberty will give ground.

When we look into our ancient roots, we will have no illusions about taxation and its potential danger to the very civilization it is supposed to sustain. When we tax we are dealing with fire, and without proper controls and care, we can easily burn down everything we have built, and our hopes for a better world can go up in smoke. On the other hand, taxes properly controlled have built great nations and brought much good to their inhabitants. In the ancient world, the right kind of taxes produced the magnificence of Greece and were at the heart of Rome's greatness and even Caesar's success and popularity.

Taxation played a fundamental role in ancient international politics. Empires collided and battled for the right to tax the loser. Peace conferences and treaties centered on the question of how much tax the victors would receive. Small nations revolted or engaged in international intrigue for tax advantages.

In ancient times, taxation was civilization's most important enterprise. Life at all levels was first and foremost a tax struggle. Here is the story.

1

Ancient Egypt: The Ubiquitous Scribes

The scribe is ahead of everyone. He who works in writing is not taxed. Mark it well.

—Egyptian Papyrus, 1200 B.C.

Not long ago the discoveries of Egyptologists made newspaper headlines. Tales of lost tombs, curses, and fabulous treasures excited the imagination then as much as space travel does today. This interest in the secrets of ancient Egypt has never died—there are still sects which believe the secrets of the universe lie hidden in the great pyramids and tombs. This so-called wisdom of the pharaohs may be speculative and occult; more concrete is the message of Egypt's tax story.

Egyptian civilization was highlighted by its enduring length. An advanced form of civilized life was in full bloom along the Nile before 3000 B.C., and it perpetuated itself until the fall of Rome. Twice that civilization fell into disorder, once around 2200 B.C. and again around 1800 B.C., but each time it reverted to its original splendor. In the thirteenth century B.C., during and after the reign of pharaoh Akhenaten, who is remembered for trying to enforce a belief in one God, major changes were made in the tax system. The efforts to bring about monotheism failed, but the tax changes remained and Egypt started on a slow decline over the next thousand years during which time many foreigners ruled Egypt. Nevertheless, the magnificence of Egyptian culture devoured them, and after short periods of assimilation most of them looked, talked, and acted like Egyptians. As powerful as the Egyptian culture was, the Egyptian state never reverted to its greatness. That decline is, most of all, a tax story.

Most of us think of ancient Egypt as a land of cruel masters and oppressed slaves. This is because of the story of Moses in the Book of Exodus. But this story came from a period of unrest for Egypt. Modern translations of hieroglyphic records indicate that life in ancient Egypt was usually bountiful and peaceful. The land was rich, and when the harvest was plentiful, life was good to all. The Egyptian of antiquity was a cheerful person. Men and women were equal; they enjoyed life and they enjoyed each other. In an Egyptian love song a romantic man sings, "If I kiss her and her lips open, I am happy even without beer."[1] Beer, incidentally, was a heavily taxed and state-monopolized beverage. The great pharaohs were often seen arm-in-arm with their queens, the way they wanted to be in the life after death. Workers were not in bondage—the first recorded strike in history was instituted by Egyptians protesting the late delivery of their pay. The temples and pyramids were probably built by workers motivated with love for their gods and pharaohs, like the peasants who built the great churches in Europe and Latin America.

Egypt's prosperity can be traced to the bounties brought to that land by the great Nile River. The annual flooding of the Nile brought continued nutrients to the soil and most often a rich harvest for the people. Ancient Egypt was a land not only annually flooded by the Nile, but perennially flooded with tax collectors. They were called scribes and they ran the society with the same iron-fisted control the Communist party used to run the former Soviet Union. If Lagash in Sumer is to be remembered for its freedom from "the tax collectors," Egypt could be remembered as a land where tax collectors were as numerous as the "sands of the sea," so to speak. Since the word "freedom" in ancient times referred to one's tax status, it is no wonder the word is not found anywhere in the Egyptian languages.

The Egyptians observed the orderly patterns of nature, including the Nile and the path of the sun across the sky each day and during the course of the year. They concluded that the central figure of the universe, the sun, should have its counterpart in the state in the office of the pharaoh. The great pharaoh Sesostris I, who ruled around 2000 B.C., described his office in these words: "For God had made me herdsman of this land, for he knew I would maintain it in order for him." This order was maintained by the scribes, enforcing the pharaoh's taxes, which in turn were built around the annual audit.

The events should be familiar to any modern taxpayer who has gone through an audit. Reluctant taxpayers are compelled to appear for an examination before the government revenue agents with the books and records of the tax bureau. The deputies compel attendance through the use of staves, the ancient equivalent of a tax summons.

Like today, Egyptian taxpayers were not very successful in resisting a tax assessment determined by the scribes. The scribes had their own tax courts and a taxpayer was not even permitted to have an attorney to present his side of the dispute.[2] As we shall discover, tax adjudications were as short on due process in ancient Egypt as they are in the modern age.

The Egyptians taxed just about everything: sales, slaves, foreigners, imports, exports, businesses. Agriculture production was taxed at a hefty 20 percent. This was not just a harvest tax, it included home gardens and crafts—income from every conceivable source exactly like our income tax. To illustrate the tyranny of the scribes in everyday life, consider the tax on cooking oil. The scribes made regular inspections of all kitchens to make sure wives were not using free drippings in place of the taxed oil they were required to use.

Most agricultural land was owned by the state and leased out to peasant farmers subject to the harvest tax, which was not based on the actual production, but on what the production should be. This calculation was based on the amount of land given to the farmer. There is no doubt that Euclid's geometry came from long established practices for measuring land developed by the scribes. Although Euclid was a Greek, he actually spent his life in Egypt and wrote his mathematical treatises while in Alexandria. He was simply systematizing and organizing Egyptian wisdom derived for the collection of taxes.

The scribes' preferred status in Egyptian society is described in a papyrus written around 1200 B.C., during the rule of the great Rameses family. Students asked their teacher for advice on selecting a vocation. Some of them were considering farming. Here is what the teacher told his students:

> Remember you not the condition of the farmer faced with registering the harvest-tax, when the snake has carried off half the corn and the hippopotamus has devoured the rest? The mice abound in the fields. The locusts descend. The cattle devour. The sparrows bring disaster upon the farmer. The grain on the threshing floor at the end falls to thieves. . . . And now the scribe lands on the bank of the river to register the harvest-tax. His assistants carry spears and rods, and they say, hand over the corn, though there is none. The farmer is beaten, he is bound and thrown into a well, soused and held under. His wife is bound in his presence, his children are in fetters. His neighbors abandon him. So the corn flies away. But the scribe is ahead of everyone. He who works in writing is not taxed, he has no dues to pay. Mark it well.[3]

The scribes were not always brutal, however. They were taught that an official of the great pharaoh should act kindly towards the poor and

The tax officials of the pharaoh—everywhere snooping, inspecting, recording, and arresting—even surveyed the nests of pigeons to count the eggs, making sure the pharaoh got his 20-percent cut.

defenseless. Consequently, one ancient text instructs the scribes: "If a poor farmer is in arrears with his taxes, remit two-thirds of them."[4]

Another text admonishes officials to "cheer up everyone and to put them in good humour," or, "if anyone is suffering under pressure of taxation or is at the end of his means, you must let the case go unchecked."[5]

This policy of remitting taxes during hard times was a common practice, originally called "philanthropa" from which our word "philanthropy" is derived. Eulogies to many of the pharaohs recite that they remitted taxes so as not to overburden their people. The three thousand years of Egyptian history are filled with moments of humane and decent tax administration.

The remission of taxes is almost unheard-of in our society. Our laws of debtor relief have no application to tax demands. Most tax collectors can evict a widow with ten children from her humble cottage and sell it. About all the law permits her to keep is the clothes on her back. The humanitarianism expressed in the tax laws of ancient Egypt is nowhere to be found in our revenue codes. (See *United States Internal Revenue Code* Section 6334.)

The enormous endowment of power the pharaoh gave to the scribes

The scribes of Egypt around 2000 B.C., as depicted in scenes from the tomb of Khiti, Lower Egypt.

Levying the tax—a taxpayer in the office of the scribes, pleading for a tax abatement.

Taxpayer in the hands of the tax enactor—a taxpayer in the field being roughly handled by the pharaoh's tax gatherers.

The Bastinado—a delinquent taxpayer, held by two of his friends, is being clubbed with apparent ferocity, but the blows miss as the taxpayer cries loudly. The bastinado was a form of chastisement, rather than punishment—a kind of tax bankruptcy.

created serious problems at times. Corruption is always the inevitable consequence of too much power, especially with a revenue agent, a lesson we have yet to learn. The pharaoh had to train special agents to check corruption in his revenue bureau. Scribes in the field were kept under surveillance by a group of special scribes from the head office. These investigators were to check on all field revenue agents to see if they were using false measures, weights, or accounts to cheat taxpayers. Their primary job was to check out taxpayer complaints.

Shortly after the death of the now-famous young king, Tutankhamen, a strong pharaoh named Haremhab discovered deep-rooted corruption among his special agents. They were illegally sharing tax moneys with the scribes in the field—the very scribes they were supposed to be watching. Haremhab made a secret investigation after hearing rumors of this internal conspiracy. Nine new laws were dictated to crack down on this corruption. A tax-collecting scribe found guilty of over-charging a taxpayer was sentenced to have his nose cut off, followed by banishment to a desolate part of Arabia. This was no idle threat. Ancient records speak of a colony in Arabia of people with deformed faces. Another pharaoh increased the salary of his scribes so they would not be tempted to enrich themselves by cheating taxpayers. This may have only whetted their appetites for more money, human nature being what it is.

We do not know if the Egyptians invented tribute, but they were operating a fairly advanced tribute system long before the time of Moses, and they did so successfully for so long that one wonders how they could have done so. In later times, tribute was an ugly form of colonialism. With the early Egyptians during the zenith of Egyptian power the system operated smoothly and without any revolts, as far as we can tell. The system was "a testimony to the mild and kindly rule, coupled with ceaseless watchfulness, by means of which the Egyptian Empire was built up and maintained."[6]

Tribute, then, starts out in our earliest recorded history as a wise tax, only in later periods around 1000 B.C. does it become ugly, brutal, and oppressive. Yet this is an old story that seems to repeat itself throughout history. We shall learn that tax farming followed the same course of a good tax going bad. In the early modern period, the mighty Spanish Empire collapsed when it turned the excise into a crippling exaction. In the twentieth century our tax makers have followed the same route with the income tax, which started out in the nineteenth century as a smart tax. It makes one wonder, is this the inevitable course all taxation follows?

The earliest forms of tribute were annual lump sums, which scholars called block tribute. It was collected by local officials and delivered to the dominant king in an elaborate ceremony. In return, he made gifts back to the rulers of the tribute cities and usually provided an impressive parade of his might and goodness. Like a godfather he was taking care of his children. Later, in the fourth century B.C., long after tribute ceased to have its benevolence, direct tax assessments with foreign tax agents began. Scribes moved into the tribute territories to assess and collect taxes. This was an inherently oppressive system that required extensive surveillance in the colonial territories. Dissent was crushed by informers and military might. The informers received a percentage of all evaded taxes just as in America today.

There is an allusion to Egyptian colonial informers in the Bible. In the Book of Ecclesiastes, Judea is described as a land full of tears for the oppressed. The Jews at that time were under Egyptian suzerainty, and we gain an echo of the feeling of the Jewish people under Egyptian colonial taxation with the ever-present informers. The spies of the pharaoh were everywhere, we are told, so that "a bird of the air shall carry the voice" (Ecclesiastes 10:20) of the person who cursed the king in secret. It was the king's tax burdens, scribes, and informers that the Jews were cursing. There were no electronic bugs, of course, but the scribes must have had informers planted everywhere so that even secret meetings and cursings were overheard and relayed to the scribes. The informers were rewarded, and the grumbling Jews were punished.

Initially the pharaoh was god incarnate on earth. The flooding of the Nile and the bounteous harvests were attributed to his divine powers. Even in the tribute territories, the rains that came were seen as the result of the pharaoh's putting part of the Nile up in their sky. Religion was the most sustaining force behind the pharaoh's glory and power. Eclipse his power and his empire would fall, and that is exactly what happened. His power was eclipsed not only in the matter of religious belief, but in the matter of taxation. Indeed, the decline of this ancient empire provides support for Paul Kennedy's thesis in his *The Rise and Fall of Great Powers* (1987): The revenue systems become unable to support the empire after it is acquired.

Egypt's collapse as an empire came during the reign of the famous pharaoh, Akhenaten, who tried to rid Egypt of its deeply entrenched system of gods and replace it with the worship of one god, Aten, symbolized by the sun. This endeavor totally consumed Akhenaten as well as his treasury. Unfortunately, his reform movement failed and with it the two-thousand-year-old Egyptian colonial empire. Eventually, for-

eigners would dominate Egypt, and in the next thousand years, Assyrians, Babylonians, Persians, Greeks, and finally Romans would rule.
What did Akhenaten do that brought about such a dramatic and final
demise? Evidence suggests his tax base was cut in half. With this revenue loss, decline was inevitable.

Akhenaten first lost the rich tribute territories in Syria and Palestine.
The Hittite Empire took over because the pharaoh abandoned his empire for reasons no one can fathom. We have letters from his local ambassadors pleading for a modest number of troops and for the pharaoh
himself to visit the tribute cities. These pleas were ignored, which one
Egyptologist attributes to his bureaucracy:

> Gradually, as the Syrian situation grows worse and worse, one comes to
> sympathize intensely with the faithful [ambassador] doing his best . . . in
> such impossible circumstances and destined to so tragic a fate. His very
> rage makes him seem all the more human and likeable, since it is a rage
> against something which the world has raged ever since, yet has still to
> endure—the supercilious stupidity of the little man in office.[7]

Perhaps it was the "little man in office," the Egyptian Foreign Office,
which failed to appraise Akhenaten of the inevitable consequences of
his neglect of the empire; perhaps it was his crazy obsession with his
religious reforms which caused him to lose all interest in his empire and
its tribute. One frustrated ambassador points out that it had been twenty
years since the pharaoh made an appearance, and the faith of the people
in his glory and powers had all but disappeared. Troops were not required to enforce collection, for the vassal states did so out of religious
conviction and faith that the pharaoh's goodwill and blessing would
sustain and protect them. But part of the system required a frequent dog
and pony show—a military parade like the Soviet May Day affair which
showed off the military power of the state for everyone to see. Hitler
loved to do this and there is no doubt he intimidated everyone and may
have gotten his way at Munich with Chamberlain because of the impressive show of force his gigantic parades made to the world.

Akhenaten failed to produce himself or his troops for many years.
His subject territories lost faith, even his local ambassadors had to flee
for their safety. In this vacuum of power it was easy for the Hittites to
take over and for the tribute to dry up forever.

We also have the correspondence from the leaders of these vassal
states complaining about the stinginess of the pharaoh's gifts to them.
The other side of the tribute system was the payments and riches pro-

vided to the rulers who had the obligation to collect and pay the trib-ute—a kind of bribery system, quite legal for the times. Without these handsome gifts any motive from the leaders to collect tribute for this stingy pharaoh would not exist. In a short time, all the rich cities throughout both Palestine and Syria fell under the suzerainty of Hittite, and later Assyrian, rule.

At home the tax wealth was consumed domestically as the new pha-raoh sought to replace all pagan temples and the great architectural con-structions with new faces promoting the new, single god Aten, symbol-ized by the sun. This drained the pharaoh's treasury and may have accounted for his niggardly payments and gifts to the rulers in the trib-ute territories.

When Akhenaten's reforms failed, the new rulers had to tear down his works and even destroy his new capital city. Most of all, they had to tear down the power of the office of pharaoh so it would no longer threaten them. In the future, the pharaoh would have to respect their autonomy and power, and there is no better or more secure way to do so than to take away all taxing power. The temples and the priests be-came tax immune, and future pharaohs were either puppets or co-equals. The pharaoh as the god incarnate for all Egyptians was gone. He was still a god, but he no longer held supreme power on earth over everyone.

Immunity from tax for the temples and priests reached enormous pro-portions, for as much as one-third of all the lands of Egypt were owned by the temples and were tax free. The ancient Greek historian Herodo-tus travelled to Egypt, and in his history he reports that every priest received twelve yokes of land, approximately one hundred cubits by one hundred cubits, tax free.[8] A cubit is the distance from the elbow to the finger tips, about twenty inches. One great temple at Amun in Karnak exerted an authority which rivaled the pharaoh's. This temple alone ruled over ninety square miles of rich farm lands and villages.

The pharaoh Haremhab, who was the first powerful leader after Ak-henaten, granted most of these great tax immune lands to the temples; he even gave them a substantial number of his troops along with cattle and farming equipment. In the end, "his lavish re-endowment of the gods and the priests of Amon, prepared the way for the tyranny of the Amon priesthood, which in the end was the death of Egypt."[9] Was not the tax exemption that went along with this new tyranny the real coup de grace?

The average Egyptian taxpayer didn't benefit much from the rivalry between the priests and the pharaoh's scribes. Once on tax-immune temple lands, workers did not pay a poll tax, nor farmers a harvest tax, but temple religious offerings were just as bad. Tax immunity for reli-

Only the tombs of the pharaoh's chief tax collector rivaled in splendor the tombs of the pharaohs. This wall painting from the tomb of a tax collector at Thebes, 1400 B.C., shows the Syrians paying tribute to Egypt. Within less than fifty years, this scene ended when the one-god pharaoh Akhenaten abandoned his rich colonies in both Syria and Palestine. His immediate successor granted tax immunity to about one-third of all the temple lands in Egypt. These revenue losses appear to have triggered the irreversible decline of this ancient superpower.

gion has continued throughout history. Most of the struggles between the popes and kings in the Middle Ages were over the immunity of the church from the king's tax men.

The temples were not only immune from tax, but the lands and buildings were places of refuge where people could flee and escape from the government, especially the tax-collecting scribes. This right of *asylia*, as it is called, was a kind of substitute for civil rights, and it survives today in diplomatic relations among nations. A Hungarian cardinal lived for years in the U.S. embassy in Budapest, enjoying a kind of asylia guaranteed to all embassies under international law. Foreign nations that conquered and ruled over Egypt for a thousand years were quick to abolish temple tax immunity and put an end to the excessive power enjoyed by the priests, but they did not abolish asylia—probably for good reason. If they were overthrown or defeated in battle, they could always take refuge in the nearest temple and save themselves. The most common user of the right of asylia was the defaulting taxpayer, racing for the temple gates, trying to outrun the scribes in hot pursuit. When the taxpayer won the race and was safely behind the temple gates, did he, one wonders, turn around and stick out his tongue at the frustrated scribes? A lot of taxpayers today would just love to have such an option.

The tax story of ancient Egypt shows what happens in a society burdened with a totalitarian revenue system. The informer, the corrupt revenue official, and—most significantly—the tyranny of all-pervading surveillance are inherent in such a system. Every taxable transaction must be recorded and subject to examination. Consequently, the individual has to submit every aspect of his life to tax inquisition.

Lacking our modern and sophisticated record-keeping, the Egyptians used the scribes to oversee the pharaoh's revenue system. The scribe was the substitute for the banking record, the computer, the tax-identifying number, and the other devices of the modern tax gatherer. In such a system, anywhere, privacy and liberty give way. The scribes were everywhere—snooping, inspecting, and recording. This system of snooping should not be judged too harshly. Our system is basically the same, seeking the same ends, and using the means and tools available at the time. The tools have changed, not the system. For example, in 1975 the United States Supreme Court ruled that federal tax agents have the right to snoop into just about anything by using a John Doe summons. The dissenting opinion of Justice Potter Stewart emphasizes the pervasiveness of our tax system:

> Virtually all persons or objects in this country . . . may have tax problems. Every day the economy generates thousands of sales, loans, gifts, purchases, leases, wills and the like, which suggests the possibility of tax problems for somebody. Our economy is tax relevant in almost every detail. (*U.S. v. Biscaglia,* 420 U.S. 141, 156 [1975])

An IRS agent using a pseudonym wrote: "There is no important piece of information concerning you I am forbidden to seek."[10] Was not this the state of affairs that dominated the tax system of ancient Egypt? Are not our income tax auditors the modern equivalent, in almost every detail, of the ubiquitous scribes of the pharaohs?

16

Painting from a Theban tomb of a "Scribe keeping account of the corn of Amun," from tax-immune temple lands of the priesthood. Here corn is being registered along with a flock of geese, as taxes for the priesthood. It was a no-win situation for the farmers, as they prostrate thenselves before the temple scribes and pay their dues to the priests.

2

The Rosetta Stone Speaks— and Tells a Tale of Taxes

The arrears of taxes which lay on the peoples of Egypt he [Ptolemy V] remitted, an amount immense, how much is not known.
—Rosetta Stone, 200 B.C.

Napoleon started his ambitious military career by trying to conquer Egypt. The British threw him out in no time, but before they did, his soldiers ransacked the tombs and shipped back to France as many relics as they could carry. As these relics were passed around in Europe's high society, Egyptology was born.

Our knowledge of ancient Egypt moved from fantasy to fact with the discovery of the Rosetta Stone. It was unearthed by one of Napoleon's officers near the town of Rosetta in northern Egypt. Napoleon had copies made and distributed throughout Europe. The English eventually seized the stone from the French, and it is now on display in the British Museum in London. It is a slab of black basalt, a hard marble-like rock. It has a message inscribed in hieroglyphic (at the top), demotic, another lost Egyptian script (in the middle), and Greek (at the bottom). With the aid of the familiar Greek the other two lost Egyptian modes of writing were deciphered. The Egyptians were prolific writers, and a great number of Egyptian writings have survived which can now be deciphered, telling the real story of life in ancient Egypt.

Most of us learned of the Rosetta Stone in our first ancient history and geography lessons. This stone is the most important Egyptian archaeological discovery of all time. It is the most significant relic of ancient Egyptian history. Someone obviously went to a lot of trouble to inscribe the Rosetta Stone. Why was the message inscribed in three different languages? Why was stone used instead of papyrus? The message

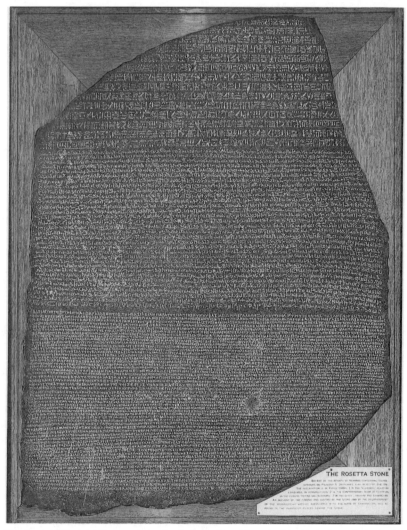

The Rosetta Stone, whose message in three modes—hieroglyphic (top), demotic (center), and Greek (bottom)—was the key to revealing the stories of ancient Egypt, including the reaction to a tax revolt of the boy-king Ptolemy V.

must have been important to have been cut in stone, but why was the message transcribed in Greek?

The Rosetta Stone was inscribed around 200 B.C. during the reign of Ptolemy V, known as Epiphanes. Egypt had been ruled by a dynasty of kings of Greek origin called Ptolemy for over one hundred years. The founder was one of the leading generals of Alexander the Great. After

Alexander died unexpectedly, his generals divided up his empire. Ptolemy grabbed Egypt for himself and became king. A new dynasty was established that lasted until the death of Cleopatra. The Ptolemies were, by and large, good kings, and they tried to carry on the ancient tradition of benevolent dictatorship established by the pharaohs. Greek influence was considerable, but within a few generations the Ptolemies acted more like Egyptians than Greeks.

At the time the Rosetta Stone was inscribed, Egypt had been plagued by a civil war for over a decade. This war started after Egyptian soldiers returned home from a successful military campaign in the east; they found Egypt shackled with new tax burdens. In addition, the tax bureau had been strengthened with tough Greeks who were the best in the business. The revolt of these soldiers turned into a civil war, and to try to restore order the boy-king, Ptolemy V, issued a "Proclamation of Peace." The most important provision was a general amnesty for the rebels. Tax debtors and rebels were freed from prison. Tax debts were forgiven. There would be no more forced conscriptions for the navy. Fugitives were invited to return and take back confiscated property. Finally, there would be tax immunity for the temples and their crops and vineyards, as in the days of the pharaohs. This proclamation was a bold stroke to bring peace to a war-torn nation. It was a capitulation on the part of government to the rebels and the priests.

The great beneficiaries of this proclamation were the priests. At a solemn assembly in Memphis, on the lower Nile, they decreed that an honorarium should be cut in a "stele of hard stone in sacred and Greek letters, and set up in each of the . . . temples at the image of the everlasting king." From this we can assume that there may have been many copies of the Rosetta Stone installed in the temples next to a statue of the boy-king. Why?

The reason is that the tax provisions of the peace proclamation were a road to riches for the priests. Ever since the successive conquests of Egypt by the Assyrians around 700 B.C., then the Persians, and finally the Greeks in 330 B.C., the temples had lost their ancient tax immunities. Now, after five hundred years of foreign rule, tax immunities were being restored. The prospect of economic power and independence for the temples was exceptional. Small wonder that, in honoring the king, the Rosetta Stone emphasized the marvelous tax benefits they had been given. With the right of asylia, which they had never lost, the temples now had a bright and prosperous future. The main stumbling block was the lawlessness of the king's tax men. Having the law on your side—just like today—was not enough to stop some overly ambitious member of the king's revenue bureau. To keep out the king's tax men there was

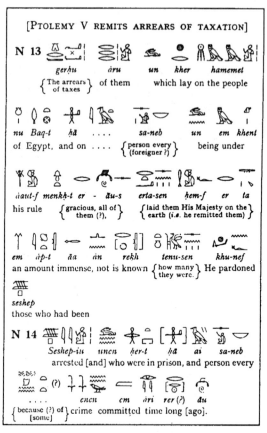

[PTOLEMY V REMITS ARREARS OF TAXATION]

N 13

gerḥu áru un kher hamemet

{ The arrears of taxes } of them which lay on the people

nu Baq-t ḥā .... sa-neb un em khent

of Egypt, and on .... { person every (foreigner ?) } being under

áaut-f menkḥ-t er - āu-s erta-sen ḥem-f er ta

his rule { gracious, all of them (?), } { laid them His Majesty on the earth (i.e. he remitted them) }

em áp-t āa án rekh tenu-sen khu-nef

an amount immense, not is known { how many they were. } He pardoned

seshep

those who had been

N 14

Seshep-iu unen ḥer-t ḥā ai sa-neb

arrested [and] who were in prison, and person every

.... enen em ári rer (?) āu

{ because (?) of [some] } crime committed time long [ago].

Excerpts from the Rosetta Stone translated by Sir Wallis Budge, former head of Egyptian antiquities at the British Museum.

a Greek sign at the entrance to all temples which read: No Entrance to Those Who Have No Business in the Temple.[1]

To bolster the sign, the Rosetta Stone was propped up along with a statue of the king. If there was any question about whether or not a revenue agent had any right to enter the temple, he could then be referred to the Rosetta Stone and read for himself that the temple was off-limits to him. The Greek translation on the Rosetta Stone clarified and supported the Greek "No Trespassing" sign at the entrance.

The fact that the Rosetta Stone is a tax-oriented document should not come as a surprise. A large percentage of all ancient documents are tax records of one kind or another. One of the labors of historians studying ancient material is to sift through piles of tax records in the hope of finding something of interest. Though tax records are generally looked upon as a nuisance, the day may come when historians will realize that tax records tell the real story behind civilized life. How people were taxed, who was taxed, and what was taxed, tell more about a society than anything else. Tax habits could be to civilization what sex habits are to personality. They are basic clues to the way a society behaves.

Behind the grants of tax immunity in the Rosetta Stone is the story of what was really going on in Egypt around 200 B.C. One could interpret these clues to mean that the young ruler had a wise regent who had enough sense to reduce taxation to spur the economy and end civil strife. It may be that the regent was an exceptionally decent fellow who felt sorry for Egypt's overtaxed workers.

This is wishful thinking, of course. Rulers do not reduce taxes to be kind. Expediency and greed create high taxation, and normally it takes an impending catastrophe to bring it down.

The proclamation of peace referred to in the Rosetta Stone means that the pressures of excessive taxation were destroying Egypt. The accumulation of unpaid taxes must have reached an intolerable level. Massive confiscations of private property had proved disastrous for the country: villages were depopulated, farms were abandoned, and critical dikes along the Nile were badly in need of repair. Floods were endangering the whole of Egypt. The release of tax rebels from prison meant that the prisons were full and that the nation desperately needed workers. The amnesty meant that the land was filled with fugitives who had fled their homes to escape punishment for not paying their taxes. In short, the grants of tax immunity set down in the Rosetta Stone paint a pitiful picture of Egypt, and indicate that her rulers were driven to take desperate measures to end the social and economic chaos their excessive tax system had created.

There are numerous other writings of this period that confirm this interpretation. We have discovered that the king was flooded with petitions from taxpayers pleading for relief from harsh treatment by the revenue bureau. Taxpayers in prison asked for a pardon—not because they were innocent, but because the king was losing their valuable services while they were in jail. We have, for example, the petition of a man arrested by the tax bureau when he was urgently needed at the foreign affairs ministry. The king even found his own crops in danger when the tax ministry arrested his royal peasants while they were working on the king's farmlands. Priests petitioned the king about unlawful entries into temples.

Finally, and somewhat puzzling, were a number of petitions complaining about false denunciations by tax men accusing honest taxpay-

ers of evasion. Egyptian taxpayers did not like this attack on their character, even by a corrupt revenue agent. Today, we would probably just
consider the source. Yet even this has a modern counterpart. A person
charged with, but not convicted of, tax offenses usually receives more
publicity than a common murderer.

This flood of petitions from oppressed taxpayers was followed by a
much-publicized letter to all revenue agents, reminding them that the
king and queen wanted fair treatment for all taxpayers. The reference to
the queen in this official proclamation indicates the equal status of
women in Egypt at this time. Not much significance should be attached
to this proclamation, however. The king made his head tax officials responsible for all uncollected taxes. This pressure at the top of the system inevitably passed down to the lowest taxpayer on the bottom. The
king was caught between an empty treasury and rebellious taxpayers.
In such a situation he talked out of both sides of his mouth.

The letter Ptolemy and his queen wrote was basically a public relations stunt, and tax history is full of similar examples. In the interest of
good public relations, governments will make soothing announcements
when there are public outcries from angry taxpayers. Taxpayers are then
assured that tax collectors are supposed to be fair and decent. Whether
they are, however, depends on how much pressure is put upon them by
revenue authorities at the top of the system. An oppressive tax agent is
usually reacting to pressure from above. The truth of this observation
was verified in the 1960s when the Internal Revenue Service announced
in an official public ruling that tax auditors were not to be protectors of
the revenue or advocates for government, but to be fair, impartial
judges. Most any agent will tell you his primary duty is (as he has been
told) to "protect the revenue," exactly what this Revenue Procedure
says he is not supposed to do.

This duplicity of telling taxpayers one thing and then turning around
and directing agents to do the opposite is exactly what was happening
in ancient Egypt. The tremendous pressure put at the top of the system
produced oppression at the bottom—a fact the tax officials must have
known.

Peace proclamations like those in the Rosetta Stone were repeated at
least three times in the next century. The success of the Rosetta Stone
proclamation prompted the government to use tax amnesties as a regular medicine to check civil disorder. In time, the Egyptian government
bestowed quite a remarkable collection of civil rights on all taxpayers.

Scholars have tried to determine what went wrong in Egypt under the
Ptolemies, when an empire that had survived for over three thousand
years simply withered and died. Little resistance was put up against the
Romans when they invaded Egypt. Egypt had suffered no military di-

sasters, famines or plagues. The Nile delta was still the richest farming region in the world. The Ptolemies had been good kings. Egypt could have been the Romans' most difficult conquest, not the easiest.

Some scholars believe all civilizations have a life cycle like plants and animals, and that Egypt simply died of old age. The Greek historian Polybius suggested that the civil war that incapacitated Egypt was caused by the Greek domination in the government. Polybius may have been partially correct, except it was not the Greek element itself which irritated the Egyptians, but Greek tax practices.

The most impressive analysis of Egypt's demise came from the great Russian scholar Rostovtzeff.[2] He believed, after a lifetime of study, that the decay in Egyptian society was the result of lawlessness in the bureaucracy, especially the tax bureau. The king could not restrain it, and his orders went unheeded. Rostovtzeff felt that the continual and unabated tyranny of Egyptian tax collectors produced a nationwide decline in incentive. Egyptian workers and farmers lost their desire to work—agricultural lands fell into disuse, businessmen moved away, and workers fled. Sound money disappeared as a raging inflation destroyed what capital there was. The land became filled with robbers who wrecked commerce and brought fear and despair to the populace. Boating and sailing along the Nile became as dangerous as walking at night on the back streets of New York and Detroit. In the end, thieves were no longer only in the tax bureau—they were everywhere.

The Ptolemies' three-hundred-year rule over Egypt ended after the defeat of Mark Anthony and Cleopatra by Octavian at Actium in 31 B.C. After a short siege at Alexandria, Octavian entered the city and Roman rule began. We do not know what kind of a welcome Octavian received when he entered that great city, but chances are by the time he left he was looked upon with favor for having delivered the Egyptian people out of bondage. In the last century the once kindly and caring Ptolemies were no longer around to control the inhuman Greek bureaucracy that had learned "how the population might be oppressed without too much danger to the oppressors."[3] The throne during this decadent period was dominated by a series of ruthless queens named Cleopatra, who didn't hesitate to murder their rival brothers, sisters, lovers, and even sons.[4]

Octavian, who soon became Caesar Augustus, set about restoring the Egyptian economy. His army became a major construction company. The soldiers were put to work repairing the dikes and cleaning out the canals which had become clogged with mud over the last century. The result was a rebirth of Egyptian prosperity for the benefit of Augustus. He wisely kept Egypt for himself, and even prohibited any Roman senators from visiting Egypt without his express permission.[5]

He must have made some dramatic changes in the tax system, because civil disorder ceased and Egypt became one of Rome's most loyal and peaceful provinces.[6] We have a clue to this in a speech of Herod Agrippa to the Jewish people, urging them to be obedient to Rome's tax demands by appealing to the example of Egypt:

> What occasion is there for showing you the power of the Romans over remote countries, when it is so easy to learn it from Egypt, in your neighborhood? . . . yet it is not ashamed to submit to Roman government, although it has Alexandria as a grand temptation to a revolt . . . and it pays more tribute to the Romans in one month than you do in a year; nay besides what it pays in money, it sends corn to Rome that supports it for four months [in the year].[7]

Roman rule and tax policy followed a pattern in Egypt not unlike the Ptolemies. By the time of Rome's fall, it too became decadent and oppressive, even enslaving the populace. When Moslem armies arrived in the seventh century, it was relatively easy for them to take over Egypt, for they offered the over-taxed Egyptian not just reduced taxation but no taxation if they would embrace Islam. This remarkable episode in history, which happens when the ancient world comes to an end after the Fall of Rome, will be discussed at length.

3

The Age of Terror-Taxation— and the Indomitable Tax Rebels of Ancient Israel

The king of Judah was affrighted at Nebuchadrezzar's threatening; he bought peace with money, and brought the tribute he was ordered to pay.
—Josephus, *Antiquity of the Jews*

The Jews developed the only pre-Christian culture that has survived to our day. Jewish history goes back five thousand years. By comparison, the history of the English-speaking people can be traced through, at most, two thousand years. As a people the Jews have always been small in number but gigantic in their impact on the course of civilization. Setting aside the religious aspect of Jewish history, their economic and political story has been one continuous struggle after another against outrageous taxation.

The tax history of the Jews can be divided into three main periods: The Kingdom of Israel, Judah Stands Alone, and The Scattered People. Jewish taxation ends with the confiscatory taxes Hitler imposed on them as his first solution to the "Jewish problem." Hitler's special Jewish taxes completely destroyed Jewish power in Germany before extermination camps were conceived.

The tax story of the Jews probably began in the Book of Exodus with the enslavement of the tribes of Israel by the pharaoh after the death of Joseph, the son of Jacob. We know the Israelites were a highly respected colony of foreigners living in Egypt, and had received great favors from the pharaoh. Shortly after the death of Joseph a new pharaoh put the children of Israel in bondage, but the biblical account does not answer the question of *how* they were enslaved. The Book of Exodus records the following:

This scene found on the walls of Nineveh shows the people of the Kingdom of Israel being led off into captivity and oblivion, to become the Lost Tribes of Israel.

And the children of Israel were fruitful, and increased abundantly, and multiplied, and waxed exceeding mighty; and the land was filled with them.

Now there arose a new king over Egypt, which knew not Joseph. And he said unto his people, Behold, the people of the children of Israel are more and mightier than we: Come on, let us deal wisely with them; lest they multiply, and it come to pass, that, when there falleth out any war, they join also unto our enemies, and fight against us. . . . Therefore they did set over them taskmasters to inflict them with their burdens. And they built for the pharaoh treasure cities, Pithom and Raamses.[1]

The Jewish historian Josephus, writing nineteen hundred years ago, added this twist to the episode:

Now it happened that the Egyptians grew delicate and lazy, as to painstaking, and gave themselves up to other pleasures, and in particular to the love of gain. They also became very ill-affected towards the Hebrews, as touched with envy at their prosperity.[2]

Both of these ancient writers seem to be emphasizing two points. First, the Jews were a prosperous and growing political minority, and second, the Egyptians, who controlled the political system, were covetous of Jewish wealth. When the pharaoh decided to deal "wisely" with them—the modern word would be "shrewdly"—his objective was to steal the wealth of the Jews and curb their growing power. Just how did the pharaoh do this? We cannot assume he simply ordered the enslavement of the Hebrews and ipso facto they were slaves. The pharaoh was the supreme administrator of Egyptian law, which was divine in origin and not subject to change. He would have had to enslave the Hebrews by complying with "due process of law" or "natural justice" by Egyptian standards of 1700 B.C. Old laws and traditions had to be strictly applied.

Under the legal system of that day a person could be enslaved for being: a criminal; a captive in war; or a delinquent taxpayer or debtor.[3]

The Israelites were not a foreign nation, and there is no reason to believe they were not loyal Egyptian residents paying their 20 percent harvest taxes and production taxes along with everyone else. Since all the Israelites were enslaved there may have been either a gigantic public debt that was not discharged, or rebellion against the pharaoh. As a foreign colony, tribute could be assessed against the entire community as a whole. There was an inherent arbitrariness about tribute. The pharaoh could set the rate so high it could not be paid. Rebellion against such a tax, or mere delinquency, would have permitted the pharaoh to confiscate all Hebrew wealth and enslave the children of Israel. The use of the term "burdens" in the biblical text could be a reference to taxation. Throughout the ancient scriptures, taxes were most often referred to as a burden, sometimes as a yoke.[4] By the use of his power to tax, the pharaoh probably enslaved the Hebrews and set the stage for Moses and the Exodus.

History is full of similar examples—an unpopular wealthy class, without political power, is taxed into oblivion, emigration, or rebellion. Consequently, the most natural and legal way for the pharaoh to deal "wisely" with the Israelites was through crippling taxation.

After Moses led the children of Israel out of bondage, they resettled in Palestine under Joshua. Each tribe received a specific territory, and they had little government, with judges providing what government was needed. We read in the Book of Judges (17:6), "There is no king in Israel; every man did that which was right in his own eyes." In other words, there was no government regulating one's behavior, and that meant there were no taxes for a central government. This social order lasted for about 400 years.

Around 1000 B.C., at the people's bidding, big government was introduced. The people wanted a king, like everyone else had. However, the Prophet Samuel objected to this kind of a political system. God did not want his people to have a king and he told Samuel to tell that to the people. The people still wanted a king, notwithstanding God's will. God then told Samuel to tell the people what life would be like under a king—specifically, their tax life. In the First Book of Samuel the people are given a vivid picture of just what to expect from a king, tax-wise:

> This will be the sort of king who will govern you. He will take your sons and make them serve in his chariots and with his cavalry, and will make them run before his chariot. Some he will appoint officers over units of a thousand and units of fifty. Others will plough his fields and reap his harvest; others again will make weapons of war and equipment for mounted troops. He will take your daughters for perfumers, cooks, and confectioners, and will seize the best of your cornfields, vineyards, and olive-yards, and give them to his lackeys. He will take a tenth of your grain and your vintage to give to his eunuchs and lackeys. Your slaves, both men and women, and the best of your cattle and your asses he will seize and put to his own use. He will take a tenth of your flocks, and you yourselves will become his slaves.[5]

Yet, unmoved by the picture of life under a king and his tax men, the children of Israel still wanted a king, and God tells Samuel to let them have one, and let them suffer the consequences. Samuel then annointed Saul, King of Israel.

The children of Israel in 1000 B.C. seem to have a lot in common with the children of Western civilization in A.D. 2100. We want big government like the Israelites wanted a king, which also meant big government. And like the ancient Hebrews, we too got big taxes, and the consequences that flow therefrom.

Samuel left out the worst part of the big tax scenario—the savage punishment meted out to those who evade. Solomon, who followed David and the first king, Saul, brought that home to the Israelite peoples, two generations later. He amassed enormous wealth through crushing taxation. Jesus' comment about "Solomon in all his glory" referred to his sumptuous courts and harems. One ancient writer gives this account of the man:

> But although Solomon was become the most glorious of kings, and the best beloved of God, and had exceeded in wisdom and riches those that had been rulers of the Hebrews before him, yet he did not persevere in this happy state till he died. . . . He grew mad in his love of women . . . nor was he satisfied with the women of his country alone, but married many wives out of foreign nations.[6]

I believe his madness developed from having a thousand wives and concubines. How he handled so many women is mind-boggling. Apparently, he didn't handle them very well. In the Book of Ecclesiastes (attributed to Solomon), he indicated he could hardly find a good woman in the whole lot.[7] The wives could probably have countered by pointing out that he didn't spend enough time with any one of them to be a proper judge. With that many wives it would take him about three years to make the rounds giving each wife just one night. His "love of women" appears to have been more as a collector than a lover or companion. Still his relationships were hardly platonic for he "laid no restraints on himself in his lusts."[8] Worse still, his foreign wives practiced idolatry and he eventually joined in the practice.

Solomon's wives and glory had to be paid for, and this heavy expense fell on the Hebrew people. Ancient scriptures refer to this as the "yoke" he put upon them. Besides the whips to collect Solomon's taxes, some biblical scholars believe that the tax horror story predicted by Samuel noted in this chapter was in fact written later, and was an account of the tax system Solomon had enforced to build his vast and luxurious kingdom.[9]

When Solomon died, his son Rehoboam was to be his successor. To receive the throne, he was summoned to the city of Shechem, which Joshua selected as the meeting place for the rulers of the tribes of Israel. The tribal leaders asked what his taxes would be, and at the same time, urged him to repudiate some of the heavy taxes Solomon had put upon them, which put them in "servitude." The older wise men of Israel further counselled Rehoboam, "If you speak good words to them they will be your servants."[10] Rehoboam said he would like to think the matter over for three days and then give them his answer. During these three days, the leaders became suspicious because they could see no reason to have to think the matter over. Rehoboam appeared before the people as he said and announced, to everyone's horror, that he would increase taxes, and to the disobedient, instead of using a whip (which the previous rulers must have used for tax compliance) he would use "scorpions," a brutal type of whip with sharp prickles that ripped the flesh.

This was too much: "By these words the people were struck as if by a hammer, and were so grieved at the words, as if they had already felt the effects of them."[11] A well-organized tax revolt erupted on the spot which must have been planned in advance of the meeting. Rehoboam was told he could not be king and that he could only have "the temple which his father had built."[12] To vent their anger even further, they decreed that no descendant of David would ever be allowed to rule over them. Rehoboam didn't realize just how enraged the people were. He sent the chief tax collector (Solomon's) to try and manage the situation and calm the mob. They stoned him to death, probably because they had had enough of him as the head man of Solomon's tax bureau.[13]

Fearing for his life, Rehoboam "got immediately in his chariot and fled to Jerusalem"[14] to take refuge in the temple he had been allowed to keep.

Rehoboam took control of Jerusalem, and the kingdom split, with Rehoboam's rule limited to the small province of Judah. Being a much smaller kingdom, Judah, to keep peace, paid tribute to Israel and its non-David kings.

These Hebrew kingdoms became buffer states between Assyria and Egypt, the superpowers of that day, somewhat like Europe was between Russia and the United States. The latter were locked in a struggle that was partly ideological; in 800 b.c. the struggle was purely economic. Tribute was the prize for the victor.

The Hebrew kingdoms wavered between pro-Assyrian and pro-Egyptian. The prophets advocated strict neutrality. By remaining neutral and paying whatever taxes were demanded, the Hebrew nations would survive. Any alliance with either Egypt or Assyria invited annihilation. A nation that lived by the sword would perish by the sword. This proverb, so popular in ancient Israel, was undoubtedly the word of the prophets arguing for non-alignment with either superpower.

Assyria soon overpowered every city and nation except Egypt. The Black Obelisk of Shalmaneser III shows the king of Israel bowing before the Assyrians and delivering tribute to Nineveh. But this was not a happy arrangement. The Israelites rebelled whenever they could. When the Israelites cut off tribute in 750 b.c., the Assyrian terror-king, Tiglath-Pileser IV, stormed out of Nineveh, pounced on Israel, and demanded one thousand talents of silver (a Hebrew talent was 116 pounds). The subdued Israelites complied and yielded to Assyrian demands for fifteen years. In 734 b.c. they rebelled again in league with all the tribute territories in the Assyrian empire. This time the angry Assyrians crushed Israel and took almost all the Israelites captive. They disappeared from history. A small remnant was left in Samaria. But within ten years they rebelled again, and this time the Assyrians laid siege to Samaria for three long years. Finally, in 721 b.c., the Assyrians breached the walls, captured the inhabitants and led them off into captivity.

The disappearance of the people of the kingdom of Israel has excited the imagination of the Jews and Christians for twenty-five hundred years. They became the "Lost Tribes of Israel." An impressive number of early modern scholars, called "antiquarians," believed the American Indians came from the Lost Tribes. There were prophecies concerning their triumphant return, with highways springing up to provide a royal road for their return from the North country where they disappeared. Most of this folklore has passed away although there are a few religious groups, such as the Mormons, who still adhere to this belief and look for the day when the Lost Tribes will return.

As a matter of historical fact, the Lost Tribes vanished as the result of a courageous but unsuccessful rebellion against unjust taxation. As a "Mighty Mouse" fighting a gigantic superpower, Israel's rebellion and defiance offered hope to an over-taxed world. After Israel was defeated, the Assyrians extended their bondage over the entire known world; even Egypt submitted to the terror-kings. Like a tough Mafia godfather, the Assyrians could write their own tax bill.

The smaller Hebrew kingdom of Judah, with its capital at Jerusalem, obeyed Assyrian demands after the obliteration of the kingdom of Israel. But Assyria's crushing taxes eventually incited rebellion when Egypt promised aid to the impoverished Jews. As always, the prophets advocated obedience and opposed rebellion. Isaiah counselled the Jewish King Hezekiah with these words: "In sitting still and rest shall be your salvation, in quietness and confidence your strength."[15]

In other words, no foreign alliances, and no rebellion.

Compliance with Assyrian demands was intolerable for Hezekiah. He was the one who had to prostrate himself on the ground before the Assyrian king and then oppress his people with outrageous taxation. Neutrality for him meant being the Assyrians' chief tax collector. For this the Jewish people would hold him in contempt. It was only a matter of time before he rejected the advice of the prophets and joined a league of states to throw off the yoke of Assyrian taxation.

By 703 b.c. the new league was in open defiance. The Assyrian king, Sennacherib, soon subdued the rebellious cities. One Jewish fortress after another fell to his advancing armies. The war was lost. Hezekiah sued for peace, but the Assyrians were determined to seize Jerusalem. They surrounded the city which by then was in a state of panic. Isaiah came forth and prophesied that the king of Assyria "shall not come into the city, nor shoot an arrow there, nor come before it with shield, nor caste [lay siege] against it."[16]

Suddenly, the Assyrians broke camp and left—Jerusalem was saved. Prophecy was fulfilled. The Greek historian Herodotus records that a plague of mice (typhus) had infected the Assyrian camp. Whatever it was, it was a close call for Judah, so close in fact that it completely cooled the hot-heads of Judah who were preaching rebellion. Thereafter, taxes were paid.

The Assyrian terror-kings passed into history like a bad dream, leaving a record of ruthless terror-taxation that would qualify them as among the worst imperialists of all times.[17] Every vassal city was seething with anger and bent on rebellion. Eventually, the Babylonians succeeded where the Hebrews failed. In 612 B.C. they led a powerful assault on Nineveh and brought an end to Assyrian power.

Babylon replaced Assyria as the superpower of the East. An ambitious young king, Nebuchadnezzar, went forth from Babylon on a tax collection operation, Assyrian style. When he arrived in Judah the Hebrew king offered no resistance. In the words of Josephus, he "bought his peace with money," i.e., he agreed to pay his tribute taxes, just as in the days of the Assyrians. Four years later the Jews revolted, encouraged by the Egyptians. The Egyptians backed down, as usual, and the Jews found themselves facing Nebuchadnezzar's big battalions alone. The Jews sued for peace, paid their taxes, and entered into a tax treaty with the Babylonians. To prevent further tax defiance, Nebuchadnezzar selected a new Jewish king named Zedekiah. With a king of his own choosing, Nebuchadnezzar thought the situation was under control, at last.

After eight years, Zedekiah renounced his tax treaty with Babylon. When Nebuchadnezzar learned his own hand-picked king could not be trusted, he lost all patience with the Jews. He attacked and destroyed Jerusalem. Zedekiah was condemned for breaking his tax agreement. For punishment his sons were killed in front of him, and immediately thereafter his eyes were put out, Assyrian style. The Hebrew people with their blind king were taken back to Babylon as punishment. The period known as Babylonian captivity began.

Actually, life was not bad in Babylon. The Jews prospered and enjoyed the learning and culture of the Persians. After about sixty years, a new Persian king named Cyrus the Great authorized the Jews to return to Jerusalem. To many Jews the wild frontier of Judah was not as appealing as the cultured life in Babylon—not unlike American Jews who have no desire to return to Israel today with its wars, struggles, and socialism.

The directive to the Jews to return to Jerusalem was not the result of loving kindness. Cyrus was an astute tax man. If he could induce the Jews to rebuild Jerusalem, he could reasonably anticipate adding a thriving, taxable asset to his realm. Not all Jews were keen on returning, certainly not the rich and prosperous. Only a fourth of the 150,000 members of the Jewish community returned.[18]

The history of civilization from 1000 B.C. to 500 B.C. revolved around two superstars, Assyria and Babylon, but the show was stolen by two of the supporting cast, the kingdoms of Israel and Judah. Time and again they battled the terror-tax imperialists. They would not learn from defeats. The Hebrews who survived from the genocidal policies of these terror-kings would rise up again and revolt at the first possible chance.

To the religious mind the defeats and sufferings of the Jewish people

Sargon, one of the terror-kings of Assyria, with his chief tax collector. The equal size of the two men indicates the high ranking of the king's revenue minister, for normally the king would be depicted larger in stature than anyone else.

Nebuchadnezzar's armies breaching the walls of Jerusalem to take the Jews into Babylonian captivity for refusal to pay taxes.

were part of God's plan. To the secular historian, the embattled Jews carried on the longest and most unsuccessful tax revolts in history, spread out over centuries, not decades. The courageous spirit of these Hebrew tax rebels must have inspired hope among the oppressed peoples of the ancient world. Today we remember ancient Israel for the Scriptures, for faith in God and religion devoid of idolatry. Should we not also remember them for their indomitable spirit against unjust taxation?

4

Israel's Final Hour: From Hanukkah's Glory to Goliath's Triumph

He [Joseph] gathered great wealth together, and made vast gains by the farming of taxes. . . . He brought the Jews out of a state of poverty to one that was splendid.

—Josephus, *Antiquity of the Jews*, 200 B.C.

Jewish readers may be surprised to learn that their counterpart of Christmas, Hanukkah, is rooted in the tax struggles of the ancient Hebrews. The story begins when Alexander the Great conquered the Persian empire. His early death was followed by the fragmentation of his empire as rival generals carved out mini-empires of their own. When General Ptolemy was securing Egypt, General Seleucus was taking over Palestine and Asia Minor. Judah was once again a buffer state between two rival powers. The Greeks did not bring freedom to the Jews. Their tribute was simply redirected from a Persian king to a Greek king; even the tax rates remained unchanged, at 33 percent for sown crops and 50 percent for the crop of orchards and vineyards—oppressive by any standard.

Rivalry between these two generals was similar to the earlier struggle between Egypt and Assyria, except the conflict was less barbaric. The Jews were never sure to whom they would be paying tribute on the morrow. There were no tax rebellions; the wisdom of the prophets finally prevailed, along with common sense. For Ptolemy's great library at Alexandria, the Jews prepared a Greek translation of their Scriptures that has survived to this day. To show appreciation for this sacred gift, Ptolemy freed all Jewish slaves in Egypt and paid for their freedom out of his treasury.

Jewish loyalties, however, were inclined towards the Seleucid dynasty, whose kings bore the name Antiochus. When Antiochus the Great was at war with Ptolemy IV (father of the author of the Rosetta Stone), Jewish troops came to the aid of Antiochus and helped defeat the Egyptians. As a reward, Antiochus granted the Jews immunity from tax for three years. Harvest taxes were cancelled for an additional seven years, and at the end of this moratorium, the rates of all taxation would be reduced by one-third. It paid to be on the side of the victor in the ancient world. Just as Third World countries played the USSR and the United States against each other for favors, so the smaller nations of the ancient world offered aid to big colonial powers in return for tax favors.

Unfortunately, this remarkable moment of tax freedom did not last. With tax immunity, Judah was of no value to Antiochus. When his beautiful daughter Cleopatra married Ptolemy following a peace treaty, Antiochus gave Judah to Ptolemy as a wedding present. As a result of this clever maneuver, the Jews lost their tax immunity. Ptolemy was free to write his own bill for his newly acquired territory. For the Jews this was a sad moment. The anticipated freedom and reduction of heavy tribute which had bound them for five hundred years was a fleeting illusion—the Jews were now back in the fold of the oppressed.

This shrewd maneuver should have caused war, especially since the Jewish ruler, a senile old high priest named Onias, flatly refused to pay Ptolemy anything. Ptolemy sent an ambassador to Jerusalem to make sure the Jews had not lost their minds. In no uncertain terms the ambassador informed the Jews that Egyptian troops would occupy Judah and collect tribute by force if payment was not made at once.

Catastrophe was averted when the high priest's nephew, named Joseph, went to Egypt to meet with Ptolemy and the ambassador and persuaded the Egyptians to be patient: "Forgive him, on account of his age; for thou canst not certainly be unacquainted with this: that old men and infants have their minds exactly alike."[1]

Joseph knew he could not collect tribute without his uncle's support. His strategy was to calm Ptolemy's anger, buy time, and devise a plan to pay the Egyptians. Rebellion, though justified, was never considered.

Joseph planned to obtain control of Ptolemy's lucrative tax-farming operations throughout Syria and Palestine. If successful, Jewish taxes could be paid out of the profits. Each year tax-farming rights were sold at auction in the king's court:

> Now it happened that at this time all the principal men and rulers went up out of the cities of Syria and Phoenicia to bid for taxes; for every year the king sold them to the men of the greatest power in every city.[2]

Unfortunately for Joseph, all bids had to be accompanied by sureties guaranteeing the full collection of the tax. Since taxes were in the tens of millions of dollars by our standards, the bidding was limited to the super-rich. Joseph could not possibly tender an acceptable bid. When the bidding for the tax-farming rights for Syria and Palestine stopped at eight thousand talents (232 tons of silver!), Joseph came forth and announced to Ptolemy that all the bidders were in collusion, that eight thousand talents was too low, and that he would bid sixteen thousand talents. The king knew of the collusion, which was standard operating procedure for Greek tax-farmers, and he awarded the contract to Joseph without sureties. To help Joseph, Ptolemy provided two thousand of his best troops.

Joseph's problems were not over. The powerful tax-farmers conspired to frustrate his tax collection efforts, and without sureties, Ptolemy would end up with nothing. When Joseph arrived at the first Syrian city, payment was refused. With two thousand Egyptian troops at his command, Joseph seized the twenty richest citizens, executed them, and sent all their wealth to Ptolemy with a full report. Ptolemy was delighted.

Joseph's reputation spread quickly. As soon as he arrived at the next Syrian city the people "opened their gates, willingly admitted Joseph, and paid their taxes." By the time he had made the rounds of all the cities of Syria, Samaria and Phoenicia, he had enough wealth to pay Ptolemy his full sixteen thousand talents plus an enormous profit to boot. Like his namesake in Genesis, this Joseph also found great favor with an Egyptian king.

For the first time in over five hundred years the Jewish people prospered. In the words of one ancient historian: "He [Joseph] gathered great wealth together and made vast gains by this farming of taxes. . . . He brought the Jews out of a state of poverty and meanness to one that was splendid."[3]

A generation later the Hanukkah story finally unfolds. The Greeks recaptured Judah from Ptolemy and the Jews were once again paying taxes to Antiochus. Within the Jewish community a bitter struggle developed by rival factions for the position of high priest, which controlled vast amounts of gold hidden in the temple acquired since Joseph became chief tax-farmer for Ptolemy.

One Jewish contender tried to gain favor from the Greeks by introducing Greek culture in Jerusalem. Pagan idols appeared and a Greek gymnasium was erected where young Jewish boys and girls ran around naked in sports contests. This shocked the pious Jews. Finally, Antiochus moved against the temple and tried to seize the gold in its holy chambers. For the squabbling Jews this was too much. They united around a young militant family called "Maccabee." A holy war fol-

lowed. Under the leadership of the Maccabees, the Greeks were expelled from the Kingdom of Judah. To commemorate this great victory,
the Maccabees cleansed the temple and lit the oil in the eternal flame in
the temple. There was enough oil in the lamp for one day, yet the lamp
burned for eight days until more oil could be obtained. This was taken
as a sign of God's approval and acceptance of the cleansing of the temple. To celebrate this miracle, the Jewish people at Christmastime take
a candelabrum with eight holders and place a candle in each holder for
eight days until all the candle holders are filled and lit.

After the Jews repelled Greek counterattacks to recover Judah, a
peace treaty was negotiated. We have two letters from the Greek king
to Jonathan Maccabee (Judas's younger brother), who negotiated the
final peace treaty. Nothing is said in these negotiations about religious
practices. The central issue was taxation. In his letter to Jonathan, the
Greek king offered a complete remission of land and harvest taxes,
which he referred to with these words: "Which the king received of
them [the Jews] aforetime from the produce of the earth and the fruit of
the trees."[4]

The "produce of the earth and fruit of the trees" would be the annual
33 percent tax on sown crops and 50 percent tax on orchards and vineyards. For the Jews, the fruit of victory was sweet indeed.

The success of the Maccabean revolt may have been a mixed blessing. Cleansing the temple of idolatry was a good thing, but the defeat
of the Seleucid empire gave the Jews a false sense of power which they
have carried with them over the centuries. The Maccabees re-enacted
the epic of David and Goliath on a national level and gave support for
the fantasy that the Jews could always slay giants with simple weapons
and a pure heart. Antiochus was no giant. He had been a lazy tax collector. His armies were mercenary and they were disintegrating from de-
sertions for lack of pay. The bulk of his armies during the fight with
the Maccabees had been dispatched to Persia to collect delinquent taxes
needed to finance the war. Jewish historians overlook this critical fact.

The victory of little David over Goliath has lived long in Jewish folklore. Unfortunately, the David and Goliath story seldom, if ever, happened in reality. The superpowers of antiquity routinely battled and
crushed the defiant Israelis.

The final and tragic chapter of the history of the ancient Jewish state
is the story of a real Goliath slaying a defiant David. This time the Hebrews did not bounce back, as they had so often in the past. They became a scattered people without a homeland for the next nineteen hundred years. The story lacks heroes; the Jewish state and its leaders had
degenerated into a society of fools.

The Romans arrived in Palestine in 64 B.C. not so much to conquer, but to establish treaties of friendship and mutual assistance with the cities and nations in that region. The Roman general Pompey had just put down the Second Mithridates tax revolt (see Chapter 9) which involved what is today Greece and Turkey. He then moved his legions into this region as a show of force to pacify it for Rome. The leaders of the various cities and countries were "invited" to meet with Pompey at Damascus, which meant that they had better show up with an abundance of gifts, preferably in the form of gold.

There were two brothers contending for the leadership of the Hebrew nation, which at this time was independent and had even gathered in a few small tribute territories of its own. They had a sizeable army and there is no reason why they could not have worked out a very satisfactory arrangement with the Romans, who needed to have a friendly state in Judah while they turned their attention to the riches of Egypt and Persia.

The two brothers came to Pompey and each claimed the right to rule Judah. It was obvious to Pompey that the nation was on the brink of civil war; he advised the brothers to avoid war, and that he would return and settle their differences. In the meantime, he had more pressing business with the Arab kingdom of the Nabateans, who controlled the trade routes to the east and instituted heavy taxes on all commerce. Pompey didn't get very far before he got wind of a revolt by one of the brothers who had gathered together a sizeable army and retired behind the walls of Jerusalem—challenging the Roman general. Pompey was furious. He cancelled his military operations to the east and returned to lay siege to Jerusalem to put down the Hebrew upstart. The walls around the city were eventually breached, his legions entered the city, and Pompey went to see what was in the temple, but left everything untouched, even the gold on deposit. As punishment the Hebrews were made into a tribute territory, which was renamed Judea. Their small colonial empire was taken away as they were reduced to the status of a conquered province with a Roman ruler to oversee their affairs and tribute payments. What followed illustrates the tragedies that beset peoples when they have bad leadership. This foolish defiance had catastrophic effects on the Jewish state. With astute statesmanship they could have been allies with the Romans, kept their small empire, and been tax free. But what might have been has no standing in history.

The Romans put an Arabian in charge of Hebrew affairs who had more sense than the previous Jewish leaders. He cooperated with the Romans and went to great lengths to assist Julius Caesar who took charge of Roman affairs after Pompey. Caesar made this man a Roman citizen and granted him tax immunity for life. For the Hebrew nation, Caesar greatly reduced their tribute burdens and permitted them to rebuild the walls around Jerusalem which Pompey had destroyed. This may not have been a good thing, for it set the stage for the final Jewish revolt that destroyed the nation.

The Jews were not happy with their new leader, especially his son, Herod. Tax gifts to the Romans from the Hebrews were sent as gifts from Herod's family. To make matters worse, Herod murdered a number of Hebrews, which resulted in a murder trial against Herod by the supreme Hebrew judiciary, the Sanhedrin. He was acquitted out of fear, which only encouraged his murderous ways. This was the King Herod who ordered the slaughter of all male infants in Bethlehem shortly after the birth of Jesus. There is historical support for this story independent of the Bible. Herod was paranoid and had his special squads of assassins murder all the members of the Sanhedrin that had tried him. He even murdered his wife and three of his sons, so suspicious was he of any possible threat to his throne. Called "The Great," he died in A.D. 4.

The Romans continued to support the Herodian dynasty over Judea. Along with this local kingship, the Romans sent in procurators to oversee the province, keep the tribute flowing, and check any possible rebelliousness that might arise. When Jesus was asked, "Is it lawful to pay tribute to Caesar?" this was a loaded question, for a negative response would have been treasonous, punishable by death.

Judea was a hard outpost to oversee; consequently, the dregs among Roman procurators were appointed to that region. Roman procurators were a kind of district director of Roman revenue with broad imperial powers. They were supposed to promote peace by respecting local customs and religious practices. Tax collections were local, but corrupt administrators could encourage excessive taxation and share in the spoils. Cicero, in one of his great phrases, refers to one of the most corrupt tax administrations as "that great gulf and quicksand of every vice and iniquity."

After Julius Caesar lightened the tax burdens the Romans had placed on the Jews, Judea had the misfortune to be continually abused. On the eve of the great Jewish rebellion in A.D. 66, Jewish taxpayers had been on a general strike for a number of years, and the Roman procurator, Florus, was on the verge of taking military action. Herod Agrippa, who ruled over Judea as king by Roman appointment, urged the Hebrews to pay their tax delinquencies and avert Roman punishments:

> Granted that the Roman ministers are intolerably harsh, it does not follow that all Romans are unjust to you, and surely not Caesar. How absurd it would be because of one man to make war on a whole people, for trifling grievances to take arms against so mighty a power.[5]

The speech worked. The Jews came forward and paid their tax delinquencies. Florus, however, did not really want this. Rebellion would give him the opportunity to seize the gold in the temple at Jerusalem, which was one of the richest depositories in the Roman world. For centuries, Jews from all over the world paid an annual tax to their great temple. The temple had become a kind of world bank for all Jews. The security of the Jews in this world, as well as the world to come, was residing in the temple. If Florus could provoke a rebellion, he could seize the temple gold and return home with riches to match the greatest in Rome. Otherwise, he was least among Roman provincial rulers.

During the Passover celebration, Florus seized the sacred robes of the High Priest and mocked the religious ceremony, which provoked a riot. As compensation, Florus demanded about a half ton of gold from the temple. This united the divided Jews behind the militant Zealots, who attacked the Romans and drove them out of Judea. The emperor found it necessary to assemble a number of his best legions, led by his best generals, Titus and Vespasian. Not since the tax revolts of Mithridates two centuries before had the Roman Empire seen such an uprising.

Slowly the Roman legions subdued the towns and cities in Judea to recapture the lost territory. When Titus arrived at Jerusalem, with its fortified walls, he tried to make peace with the Zealots to prevent the inevitable carnage. Titus was in love with a Jewish princess of great beauty. She pleaded with him to try and spare her beloved city and its stubborn inhabitants. To please her, Titus offered to call off the siege on two conditions: the Jews would have to recognize Roman hegemony over Judea (which was already an accomplished fact), and pay their Roman taxes regularly. Looking back, the survivors must have wished they had accepted Titus's offer, which, because of the princess, was surely an offer they shouldn't have refused. Taxes were the primary point of contention, as they had been throughout Roman rule; it was perhaps inevitable that the end for ancient Israel would come about this way, as the Jews had been the greatest of tax rebels for well over a thousand years.

The fall of Jerusalem to the Romans was in many ways a reenactment of what had happened seven hundred years before, when Nebuchadnezzar breached the walls and took the inhabitants into captivity, or even earlier when the Assyrians did the same to Samaria. In all these sieges, the deciding factor was the lack of food and the weakening of the defenders by starvation. Jewish historians like to praise the fighting spirit of these defenders and point out that they "almost won." Almost winning a battle or a war means you lost.

The Zealots turned down Titus's benevolent offer. They were convinced they could win, that God would come to their aid as he had done

The menorah, the seven-branched candelabrum of Jewish worship, is one of the spoils of war as triumphant Romans parade through Rome following the destruction of Jerusalem.

in the past (though not always). Like the fools that they were, they suffered total disaster.

Titus returned home in triumph and a great arch can be seen today in Rome which commemorates his great victory. His Jewish princess was at his side as he entered Rome.

The remaining Zealots were not finished. They fled to Masada, a natural fortress on a flat hilltop near the Dead Sea. From that fortress they carried out guerrilla attacks on Roman tax-collecting operations. For the Romans this could not be tolerated, so once again they sent in one of their best generals to take Masada. For two years the Romans laid siege and had to construct a huge earthen ramp to the top of the natural fortress, which can be seen today. When they finally entered, the inhabitants had all committed suicide. Thus ended the last pocket of Jewish resistance in a war that brought an end to the Jewish state in Palestine for two thousand years.

The angry Romans forbade the Jews to rebuild the city of Jerusalem. Most of the lands of the Hebrews were given to Roman soldiers, which turned the Jewish farmers into sharecroppers. Others who kept their lands carried heavy mortgage payments and were not much better off.

Along with the loss of their lands and cities, the Jews were strapped with a new tax, the *fiscus judaicus*, which applied to all Jews throughout the Roman Empire. Previously, as mentioned, all male Jews paid a half-shekel annually to the temple; now all Jews—men, women, and children—paid two drachmas to the Roman temple for the worship of the god Jupiter. This tax was four times as high as the half-shekel tax, and considering the broadened tax base which included women and children, it was oppressive. It set the stage for the next two tax revolts carried out by the succeeding generations. As burdensome as the tax was, it was an outrage to the Jews, who were now forced to finance idolatry. It was only a matter of time before the Jews would rise up again to free themselves from this yoke.

From the Roman position it was a bad tax. The rebellions that followed put a serious drain on Roman expansion and their reputation for invincibility. They won once again, but took a terrible beating. There were no triumphant marches into Rome. Military expansion and campaigns into Persia had to be cancelled, and they never were revived. From then on, the Empire expanded no more and started to contract.

The Jewish uprisings in A.D. 115–117 were world-wide and were far more devastating to the Romans than the revolt in Jerusalem crushed by Titus. No sooner had these rebellions been put down, than the Jews revolted again in A.D. 132–135. In the end, the Jews were forbidden to ever set foot in Jerusalem, and their ranks were infiltrated with spies. The Babylonian Talmud tell the story of three rabbis talking in the presence of a Roman spy during the A.D. 132 uprisings. The first rabbi praised the Romans for providing bridges and beautiful cities; the second rabbi was silent, but the third rabbi said all these things were done to collect Roman taxes. The Romans responded by exalting the first rabbi, banishing the second, and ordering the death penalty for the third.[6]

Four times the Jews challenged the Romans over a two-hundred-year period. Each time they lost, not only in battle, but in their freedoms. Each time taxes got worse, and liberties all but disappeared. In the end, the David-Goliath folk story finally was put to rest. In the eighteen hundred years that followed the last Jewish uprising, the Jews accepted their burdens, their expulsions, degradations, and politically subservient role wherever they resided. They finally complied with the teachings of the early prophets.

The history of the ancient Israelites, from the time of the terror-tax kings in the eighth century B.C. to the destruction and dispersion of the Jewish people by the Romans, was highlighted by a recurring pattern of conflict within the state that has reappeared today. There was a war party and a peace party, each seeking to have its way in international affairs. The war party was clearly responsible for the terrible destruction brought about by resisting the yoke of Assyrian, Babylonian, and Roman taxation, but they have to their credit the freedom and prosperity that followed the military successes of the Maccabean rebellion. When to resist oppression and when to seek peace was the challenge of that age—but is it not also a challenge that has continually faced nations and peoples at all times, in all ages?

5

China: The Mandate of Heaven

China has more than three thousand years of written history, as well as its legendary history. It is surely one of the oldest civilizations on earth. And for most of its history, China has been governed by authoritarian emperors. Under that form of government, there was a continual ebb and flow of taxation policies.

Chinese tax wisdom goes back to Confucius (500 B.C.) (孔子). He set forth a philosophy of taxation that lasted over two thousand years. No doubt it was the tax abuse that had existed for a few centuries of recorded Chinese history that caused this great sage to reflect on the evils heavy taxation had caused. He developed principles of tax justice that would deny emperors a free hand in tax policy. But there was no force to compel compliance by the emperors other than the threat of rebellion.

There was an understanding between the people of China and their philosophers that there was to be an idealistic pattern of governing and taxing. The emperors had a kind of divine right, dependent on the Mandate of Heaven. Confucianism set forth tax guidelines for all rulers to follow, which would maintain this Mandate to rule. If an emperor abused his power and departed from these Confucian ideals, he was not only harshly criticized by China's sages, but the Mandate was withdrawn, and his heavy-handed governing would result in rebellion—the people would stand up and fight and topple his government. Revolution is shown in the Chinese character as 革命, which meant literally, "The Change in the Heavenly Orders." Since the Chinese emperor was "The Son of Heaven" 天子, he was like the pharaoh of Egypt, bound by the laws of heaven, but unlike the pharaoh and Western emperors, he would lose his mandate and heaven would decree his demise if he ruled op-

---

The author is indebted to Takeshi Nishizaki, a Japanese scholar from Yokohama, Japan, for his reasarch that made the Chinese tax history in this book possible.

Confucius, the Chinese sage who set forth the ideal of a just tax system, setting tax rates at 10 percent.

pressively, which usually meant abusive taxation, departing from the Confucian ideal. By overthrowing the emperor the rebels were carrying out the will of Heaven.

Confucianism set forth the ideal tax system, which was set at 10 percent, the same as the biblical tithe and the Roman *decuma*. A ruler should never yield to the temptation to depart from this criteria of tax policy. Even when the dreaded Genghis Khan pillaged Russia he only demanded a 10 percent tax in keeping with the Confucian ideal. Of course it was 10 percent of everything, including people.

Mencius (Meng-tse, ca. 372–289 B.C.) (孟子) was known as the Second Sage, after Confucius. His book, *The Sayings of Mencius*, became a classic, and scholars were required to memorize it completely. It has many tax stories in it, which explains why the tax philosophy of Confucius was so dominant in the political systems of the emperors for over two thousand years. Here is one story from Mencius's book:

Mencius, successor to Confucius. The second sage who further developed the Confucian 10 percent rule into the Well-Field System.

King Hsiian of Ch'i put this question to Mencius:
"Can you explain to me what you mean by the rule of a real king?"
Said Mencius, "Of old when King Wen was keeping peace of Ch'i, farmers paid one ninth of their produce in taxes . . . at the gateways in the markets there was inspection but no taxation; there were no prohibitions relative to fishing in the ponds. . . . King Wen always made certain to care for the four classes (the widows, the elderly, the widowers, and orphans)." [1]

In another of his teachings, his students asked about what the highest caliber of rulers should do about taxes, what a real king should do about taxes. Said Mencius:

1) As for business, tax the locale, but not the gross. [In other words net income, not gross production.]
2) If already subject to a land tax, do not tax production, then all the merchants of the world will be pleased to have stocks in your markets.
3) If at the ports there is inspection but no taxation, all travelers in the world will be so pleased that they will want to travel in your country.

1	2	3
4	<u>9</u>	5
6	7	8

Well-Field Tax System of nine parcels, with the center parcel for tax. Parcels one to eight were for separate farm families, often farming cooperatively.

4) In the case of farm workers, if you do not tax them, all the farm workers in the world will be pleased to work your fields.
5) If workers' dwellings are not subject to a head tax, everybody in the world will be pleased enough to become your subject.[2]

The benefit of the above tax policy would bring peace at home and you would have no adversary in the whole wide world. Such a ruler would be Heaven's Officer, and never fail to be a real king.

Mencius wrote for the Chinese the doctrine of the sacred right of insurrection against bad government, as Thomas Jefferson did for the United States. Mencius regarded all government as coming from Heaven, which meant that all rulers were responsible to God and the people. The aim of government was to promote the happiness and well-being of the people. A heavy tax would not do that. And any ruler that left his subjects in misery deserved to be deposed. People were the most important element of a nation; after them came government workers, and finally, last of all, came the emperor.

Mencius refined the Confucian ideal of taxation by inventing the Well-Field System 井田法 (Ching-t'ien-fa). According to Mencius the economic ideal of kingly government lies in the equal distribution of land, with approximately 10 percent set aside for the government. According to his system each square of *li* is about nine hundred acres (1.4 miles square). Each *li* is cut into nine pieces, with each individual farm containing about one hundred acres of land. The central square is known as "public land" for the state while the eight surrounding squares are for eight families. The farmers cultivate the public land cooperatively for the government. This is their tax.[3]

Later, when there were private owners of large parcels of land, cooperative farms like the Well-Field System were inappropriate. There then developed the Equal-Field System 均田法. Under this system the government lent the lands to a single farmer, or there was private ownership.

In either case the single farmer or owner paid a 10 percent tax on the crop itself.

Of course, as in Western history, some emperors would not follow the heavenly scheme of tax rates. The zeal for big government and big spending infected many Chinese rulers. But they were bucking the wisdom of the great sages, who, not unlike the prophets of Israel, would often see their wisdom cast aside.

Mencius's teachings were often ignored. Emperor Shih Huang-ti, who established the first unified rule over all of China (Ch'in Dynasty, 221–207 B.C.), was a major builder of the Great Wall. To undertake such a monumental building project he increased taxes from 10 percent to over 50 percent and, worst of all, drafted workers for his Wall in the tens of thousands (a tax on labor). A revolt soon followed and he lost the Mandate of Heaven. Within ten years he was deposed.

Legend handed down from this period recounts how the wife of a farmer, who had been drafted to work on the Great Wall, went to visit him at the work site, only to find that he had been sacrificed and then buried in the foundation of the half-finished wall. As the wife cried sorrowfully, the wall crumbled and her husband's body appeared. After mourning her dead husband, she killed herself by jumping into a nearby sea.

After the disastrous rule of the First Emperor, a wise and loved emperor, Ching Ti 景帝 (157–144 B.C.), ruled as a proponent of laissez-faire. This was appropriately called "Governing by Doing-Nothing." He achieved prosperity for his imperial rule by this non-intervention policy and low taxes. His taxes were so low in fact that they departed from the 10 percent Confucian rate and were reduced to about 3 percent. (Today's Libertarians would find Ching Ti to be their man, and the supply-siders would be even more ecstatic.) His granaries were so full because of the low tax rate that his main problem was spoilage.

In the ebb and flow of prosperity and poverty, of high taxes and low taxes in Chinese tax history, it was predictable that China's "Doing-Nothing" emperor would be followed by one of the worst tax tyrants in China's long list of bad emperors. Wu Ti ruled for over forty years from 141 to 87 B.C. The empire became burdened with a spend-thrift emperor whose appetites had no limits. He matched many greedy Western monarchs like Henry VIII or even the biblical Solomon. He spent tax moneys for luxurious palaces and harems for his hundreds of concubines and wives. He spent money for large construction projects and massive gardens, whatever suited his fancy. Soon his treasury was empty, so he did what every rapacious ruler has to do—he increased taxes and created new taxes and then found more ways to drain money from the people's pockets.

Wu Ti increased taxes on merchants fivefold; on manufacturing trades, two-and-a-half times. He introduced taxes on shipping and even on hand-carts. When he became aware that tax evasion was rampant, he instituted a system of tax spying and informers—as in the United States today—with the informer sharing in the tax recovery. When farmers evaded, he confiscated their farms. But that wasn't all. He then entered the marketplace and monopolized salt, iron, and liquor. He then entered the grain market, controlled prices, and thereby purchased cheap and sold high. He turned on the nobles and demanded a payment of gold, and when any noble couldn't make the full payment, he took away their aristocratic status.

This was a rather dramatic example of a good, low-tax system going bad in just one generation, like at so many other times in history, even in our age. In the nineteenth century the income tax was set in peacetime at around 3 percent; in the twentieth century the rates in just about every European country and the United States have risen to well above 50 percent to as high as 90 percent in peacetime—historically an old and common story.

Today, you could say we are very much in a Wu Ti tax and spending era. We may be forced to follow the sacred right of insurrection expounded by Mencius and our Jefferson. Have not our leaders lost the Mandate of Heaven? Is it time for a "Change of the Heavenly Order," Chinese style? The phenomenal growth of tax reform groups throughout the world, not just in America, would indicate change is long overdue in our "Heavenly Order."

The Wu Ti story does have a happy ending. Revolution, though warranted, didn't happen. In his later years Wu Ti repented of his taxation and spending sins. He set a new course for low taxes and low spending, and his successors responded by returning to the time-honored Well-Field System of Mencius, and the Equal-Field System, both focusing on 10 percent taxation and no more. Chinese historians call this the golden age of private ownership. Tax rates were once again reduced to the 3 percent rate and a period of peace and prosperity prevailed . . . at least for a season.

The Confucian tax ideal of 10 percent was deeply ingrained in the religious teachings of China right up to the modern period and there were long periods of prosperity and good emperors who adhered to the Confucian rule of low taxes. Even the second great religion of China, Taoism, was embued with the spirit and philosophy of the Confucian 10-percent-and-no-more tax rule. From one ancient Taoist text we learn of the story of an enlightened sage giving tax advice to a ruler frustrated with inadequate tax revenues:

A king was having a discussion with a spiritually developed one and asked, "What should I do when my government does not have enough money to do all the important things?"

The developed one replied, "Use the ancient time-honored tax method of taking a tenth from the people's production," was the answer.

"Taking two-tenths is still not enough, not to mention one," said the king.

"Decrease the tax, attract people to till the land and invest in your country. This means: increase the revenue by decreasing it. When all people have enough, the government has enough. When people do not have enough, how can the government have enough? Too much tax is self-robbery in that it does not nurture the strength of people to pay the tax."[4]

And Lao Tsu, the revered founder of Taoism, wrote over 2,500 years ago:

The more one governs, the less one achieves the desired result. . . . The more restrictions and prohibitions there are in the world, the poorer the people will be. . . . The more laws are promulgated, the more thieves and bandits there will be.[5]

When taxes are too high, people go hungry;
When the government is too intrusive, people lose their spirit.
Act for the people's benefit. Trust them, leave them alone.[6]

Governing a large country is like frying a small fish; you spoil it with too much poking.[7]

Let us leave China for a contemporary tax story in ancient Greece, and see if the wisdom of the Greeks in *their* golden age measured up to the great sages and rulers in China's ancient days.

6

The Ingenious Greek: Tyranny and Taxes

By the sixth century B.C. the Persians under Cyrus ruled the entire civilized world, including Egypt. The Greek mainland was the only area not subject to Persian taxes. Around 490 B.C. the Persian king Darius sent envoys to the Greek city-states demanding that they submit to Persian tribute. The city-states were all independent and ripe for takeover by the powerful Persians, who could see no reason why Greek riches should not be flowing to Darius along with everyone else's.

The Greeks refused, and the two leading Greek cities, Athens and Sparta, formed defense leagues with the smaller city-states. The Athenian league assessed taxes which were paid into a common treasury, and their armies had common commanders, NATO-style. With this united front, the Greeks defeated the Persians at Marathon. The battle of Marathon was the most important military event in history. Greek culture took control of civilization and has played a dominant role ever since. We still copy Greece's architecture and art, produce her plays, study her philosophy, revere her love of liberty and democracy, and admire her science. There is hardly a scientific idea, political theory, or artistic achievement that is not traceable to a brilliant Greek philosopher, mathematician, or artist.

It seems strange to have made such a big fuss over the five hundredth birthday of Copernicus. He came eighteen hundred years too late. In the third century B.C. a Greek astronomer discovered that the sun was the center of our solar system, and one of his contemporaries, Eratosthenes, went so far as to measure the circumference of the earth to within a few

53

hundred miles. Columbus, on the other hand, miscalculated the circumference of the earth by ten thousand miles. When he landed in the Bahamas in 1492 he thought he was near Japan.

The intellectual achievements of the Greeks were the real wonders of the ancient world. They had an uncanny ability to make brilliantly accurate judgments about the universe with a limited amount of factual data. This exceptional capacity for insight was the Greeks' most pronounced genius.

The Greeks applied their intellect to politics and economics. They invented democracy and established a highly developed system of capitalism. Our ideals and love of liberty are a gift from the Greeks. Before the Greeks came along, all civilization was achieved by despotic governments—civilization and liberty were incompatible. In the recent struggle between East and West, the single most significant difference between the two systems was that the communist system had developed an advanced form of civilized life through the instrumentality of a massive totalitarian bureaucracy. The governments of Western nations exercise less control over their citizens, and as a result many personal liberties are preserved for the people. The Greeks' greatest talent may have been their ability to build a civilized society without a loss of liberty.

Greek democracy and liberty developed out of some bad experiences. Immediately before the rise of ancient Greek democracy, tyrants and Draconians ruled Greece. The Greeks taught the world about the evils of too much political power, but we have not learned very well. Draconians and tyrants still plague civilization and lurk in the hallways of all governments, waiting for a chance to rule.

A tyrant exercises government power oppressively. Whenever excessive power is bestowed on a government agency or official, tyranny will follow. The arsenal of power given to our modern tax bureaus makes them a seedbed for tyrants. Today we inflict savage punishment on tax offenders, often putting them in the same category as vicious criminals. Yet the great sages of our civilization—Adam Smith, Montesquieu, and William Blackstone—all condemned making tax offenses into crimes, blaming government for excessive taxation, which inevitably leads to rebellion, flight, and fraud.

The Greeks fathered the study of history. Greek historians travelled, interviewed witnesses, gathered facts, and wrote the first histories free from folklore. Greek historians did more than present facts, however. They believed history was one of man's most important tools for survival. There were lessons to learn from history, which repeats itself because men behave in a predictable pattern under similar circumstances—politicians with too much power will become tyrants regardless of their good intentions.

Greek historians compared Oriental despotisms with Greek democracy. Why were the Greeks a free people while the Persians lived under despotic rule? The Greeks concluded that private property was a factor. The Athenian people respected property because they respected liberty,"[1] observed Gustave Glotz, professor of history, University of Paris. The perceptive Greek mind concluded that tyranny was the product of the tax system. If liberty were to be preserved, the tax systems of the tyrants should be avoided at all costs. To the ancient Athenian, the tax system was the barometer of the liberty of any society.[2]

To the Greeks, the badge of liberty was indirect taxation. The individual was not taxed directly; what was taxed were some commercial activity such as a sale, import, or use of a public facility such as a road, a bridge, a sea lane, or a harbor. The taxes were justified because the money was needed to cover the costs of maintaining these facilities. A 2 percent harbor tax was justified because the harbors and sea lanes were patrolled by Greek warships to keep merchants safe from pirates. One sea lane which was infested with pirates and difficult to patrol carried a tax rate of 10 percent. There were also taxes on auctions, slaves, and real estate sales. Lodging at inns was taxed. Most taxes fell on foreigners who flocked to do business in Athens.

Tax evaders were taxed at ten times the amount of the evaded tax. Foreigners faced the additional penalty of confiscation. Informers were encouraged for enforcement and they received a reward of 50 percent of the penalty. Fees were also charged for the use of Athenian courts of justice. Foreigners and citizens were treated equally before the law.

Money also played a key role in making Athens the commercial capital of the world. The drachma was the most respected currency in the world. Its silver content was pure. The Greeks guarded its value and purity like the Swiss guard their franc today. In short, good laws protecting property, sound money, safe sea lanes, and low taxes were the foundation of Greek prosperity and liberty.

A number of Greek city-states were ruled by tyrants who were dictators. To the Greek democrat, the tyrant was ipso facto bad. Even if a tyrant were a good ruler his assassination was a virtuous act. Tyrannicide was always justifiable.[3] What offended the Greek democrat the most was the tax system of the tyrants. To him, direct taxation and tyranny were one.

The tyrants resorted to hard policing methods to exact direct taxation. Confiscations, imprisonment, and all kinds of trickery were used. Commenting on these ancient tyrants, one historian has made this observation, which seems to describe many modern political practices:

All these forms of direct taxation rendered the tyrants short-lived, although they attempted to keep their subjects in good humor by the splendor of their courts, by gigantic building operations, and occasional gifts to the masses.[4]

The tyrants should not be thought of merely as ugly dictators. Some were, of course, but a number of them were shrewd politicians, such as Pisistratus of Athens, who ruled before democracy took over (550 B.C.). Pisistratus proclaimed to the people that he was a democrat and benefactor of the poor. He advocated civil equality and a democratic constitution, and became popular with the people. He then seized power and became a tyrant of Athens in the Greek sense, but he used his power with prudence. He built libraries and splendid public buildings. Like all tyrants, he collected a 10 percent income tax, but even then he developed a good press.

Aristotle, who lived two centuries later, tells a tax story about Pisistratus that must have captured the admiration of the Athenian people. Pisistratus travelled around the countryside in disguise to find out what his subjects were really thinking. On one occasion he approached a farmer who was struggling to plant crops on rocky ground. When the disguised Pisistratus asked the farmer what he expected to get from his farm the farmer replied: "Aches and pains and that's what Pisistratus ought to get his tenth of." Pisistratus was so pleased with his frankness and hard work that he decreed that this farm should pay no further taxes and be known as "Tax-free Farm."[5] Pisistratus was deposed twice, but both times he returned with the support of a large segment of the society because of his benevolent policies. His enemies called him a dangerous man and a hypocrite. He preached democracy, but practiced tyranny—a not uncommon trait for political leaders in every day and age.

The direct taxes despised by the Greek democrats included poll taxes as well as the 10 percent harvest tax from tribute-paying vassal city-states. There were also direct taxes on certain despised professions such as prostitution, soothsaying, and medicine. The 10 percent harvest tax was probably an approximation of an ordinary harvest, because the quality and size of the land was carefully considered. If the harvest tax was a strict percentage based on an actual accounting of crop, then land size and condition would be immaterial. Plane geometry, as we noted, was not invented by Euclid, but rather by ancient tax collectors determining land size for harvest taxes. Rivers and floods changed the natural boundaries of farm lands into odd shapes which gave birth to geometry, along with land surveying techniques and laws. Many ancient rulers were praised for their benevolence in not increasing harvest taxes during good harvests. This suggests a fixed tax rather than a tax determined by the actual production. Furthermore, evasion would run rampant unless the state had tax agents on hand as the crops were gathered. Since most crops were harvested at the same time, government tax assessors would have to be at every field on the same day during the common harvest. This would mean the state would need almost as many tax officials as farm owners, which would not have been possible, at least not in ancient Greece.

Even though the Athenians abhorred direct taxation they did not hesitate to use it against outsiders. There was a large body of foreign merchants and workers living in Athens. These foreigners, called *metics*, paid a monthly poll tax, a *metoikion*. It was one drachma for men and a half a drachma for women. A metic was anyone who did not have both an Athenian mother and father. A true, tax-exempt Athenian had to have both parents born in Athens. With the large body of foreigners living in Athens, mixed marriages were inevitable. The Athenian parent would naturally want his or her offspring to enjoy Athenian citizenship. Birth records were sometimes forged. Athenian citizenship not only meant exemption from the poll tax, it also permitted the ownership of land. Only citizens could own land, and land was tax-exempt. If a metic was found to own land or to have evaded his poll taxes, the land was confiscated and tax penalties levied. The informer received 50 percent of the property, as we have noted. The poll tax on metics had humiliating overtones. In Greece, any form of direct taxation was humiliating, and the poll tax was considered the most degrading of all the forms of direct taxation.

The discrimination and special taxes on foreigners have many modern parallels, even the injustices to the half-citizens. In the United States, mixed-blood blacks and Indians in the nineteenth century were treated the same as full-blood blacks and Indians. In World War II, the same was true with Japanese-Americans and Japanese-Canadians. The deportation orders on the Pacific Coast applied to anyone with Japanese bloodlines.

No one was exempt from the *eisphora*, an Athenian wartime emergency tax, but it always retained its special wartime emergency character, which is unusual. Almost all wartime emergency taxes which are productive of revenue continue after the emergency is over. The Greeks are among the few people in history to have successfully limited extraordinary taxes to the emergencies that prompted them.

The machinery for the operation of this tax was ingenious and deserves some comment. All citizens were divided into one hundred groups, equal in number. Each group disciplined itself. They elected a president and two vice-presidents. Every citizen then made a declaration of all his wealth. An assessment was made based on that declaration and the oath that went with it. At this point the tax system developed a unique twist. The three officers had to immediately pay the full tax for all the members of the tax group. These officers would then collect from each member what they had paid on his behalf. Since they were collecting to replace what had come out of their pockets you can be sure they were diligent and skillful in the process. The system was self-administering in every respect. It tended to keep everyone honest, and collections were bound to be prompt. There were no tax-farmers or government bureaucrats in the whole operation.

The eisphora was also assessed against the metics and other foreigners. Since it was a despised direct tax, which was especially offensive to the Athenians, it was cancelled when the war was over. If there was any booty from the war it was used to repay or refund the eisphora.

Unlike a regular tax, this extraordinary levy could not be anticipated. The following words from a fifth century B.C. Athenian, although a bit cynical about life in general, pinpoint the fears of that day about the eisphora:

> Any human being who counts on having anything he owns secure for life is very much mistaken. For either an extraordinary tax snatches away his fortune, or he becomes involved in a law suit and loses all . . . or chosen to finance a play, he has to wear rags himself after supplying golden costumes for the chorus . . . or sailing his ship somewhere he is captured, or in walking or sleeping he is murdered . . . no, nothing is certain.[6]

Tribute was a kind of godfather tax arrangement. It was seldom voluntary. Weaker and smaller cities paid tribute to the larger cities which had the muscle to enforce the tax. The weaker city received protection. The Athenians did not mind tribute taxes as long as they were on the receiving end of the money. Their success at Marathon put them in charge of the defense league of almost two hundred city-states, all of them paying taxes into a common treasury on the island of Delos— hence the name, the Delian League. Not all of these cities joined the League voluntarily. Each city had one vote when the League met in assembly, but Athens controlled the military and financial affairs of the League, which meant they ran everything.

A trusted Athenian general was appointed to oversee the tax system of the League. He was called Aristides the Just. All League cities paid taxes in accordance with his assessments, which were respected and honored. The famous biographer of antiquity, Plutarch, gives this account of Aristides' taxes:

> The Greeks paid a certain contribution towards the maintenance of the war; and being desirous to be rated city by city in their due proportion, they desired Aristides of the Athenians, and gave him command, surveying the country and revenue, to assess every one according to their ability and

The collection of harvest taxes, payable in grain, in ancient Greece. The tax collector, with a military escort, is probably an Athenian, collecting harvest taxes from a small Greek village outside tax-immune Athens.

what they were worth . . . he drew up the list of assessments not only with scrupulous integrity and justice, but also in such a way that all states felt they had been justly and fairly taxed. . . . This levy of Aristides was a golden age for the allies of Athens.[7]

This is a remarkable account, not just because Aristides was a great and just tax man, but because he assessed taxes to everyone's satisfaction, according to ability and worth. Tax equity probably began with Aristides, who can be called the father of just taxation. This is the first historical reference to taxation based on "due proportion," and ability and worth, and these principles are still the ideals of a just tax system. Tax ethics have not advanced beyond Aristides.

The good times of Aristides could not last. He was mortal, unfortunately, and his successors were not so just and not so incorruptible. They even moved the treasury to the Parthenon in Athens where the League's money became Athenian money. The Delian League was now the Athenian League, or perhaps more accurately, the Athenian empire. Tax rates doubled and then doubled again. Corruption from easy tax money was unavoidable. The Athenians spent the money on themselves, raised their standard of living, and built the golden age of Greece that historians praise. It was built with stolen tax money and perpetuated with oppressive tribute taxation. An age of oriental imperialism of tribute and vassals spread over Greece—the very evils the Greeks had fought the Persians to avoid a few years before.

When the Athenians were at the height of their power they had little trouble keeping their tribute-paying city-states in line. On one occasion tribute was reduced because large tracts of land had been given to tax-exempt Athenian farmers and with this land taken off the tax rolls it was only natural to reduce the overall tribute from the city.

Withdrawal from the League was impossible. The island of Melos tried it with disastrous consequences. The Athenians descended on the island with a vengeance. They slaughtered all the men and sold the women and children into slavery. The island was left desolate as a fitting punishment and an example for other cities who may have had similar thoughts. It was a re-enactment of what the Assyrian terror-kings had done a few centuries before in Asia Minor. The freedom-loving Greeks had descended to the depths of the worst tax tyrants of all time. Rivalry and fear of Spartan power may have been other factors in the brutal reprisals against Melos. The Athenians explained the situation to the Spartans in these words:

At first, fear of Persia was our chief motive, though afterwards we thought, too, of our own honor and our own interest. Finally, there came a time when . . . it was clearly no longer safe for us to risk letting our empire go, especially as any allies that left us would go over to you.[8]

No Third World developed in this ancient superpower struggle and neither party desired peaceful coexistence. Sparta started a preventive war to check the growing imperialism of Athens and encroachments on Sparta's sphere of influence. The Spartans justified the war with a fifth century B.C. domino theory, the same theory the United States used to justify its massive involvement in Vietnam. The war raged on for decades; it became the terrible Peloponnesian War. Sparta eventually won, but had neither the will nor the ability to unify Greece. Civil wars continued among the city-states, and Greece went into decline, ripe for foreign take-over.

Ancient Greek philosophers and writers saw the defeat of Athens as the judgment of the gods on Athenian arrogance and imperialism. That analysis is substantially correct—at least the part about imperialism and arrogance. Athens had become an imperial power through the old Delian League by forcing weaker city-states into the League and exacting heavy tribute. As the power and wealth of Athens increased, and with it the Athenian appetite for more tribute and more vassal states, conflict with Sparta became inevitable. The outcome of the war was indeed in the hands of the gods at times. A terrible plague hit Athens, Pericles died, and less capable leaders carried on a hopeless war. Sparta tried to negotiate for peaceful coexistence but the Athenians wanted victory. Power had corrupted their thinking as well as their appetites.

Despite the folly of Athenian leadership in carrying on a senseless war and enslaving her allies, one senses a great loss to civilization when Sparta defeated Athens in the Peloponnesian War. The most honored and revered civilization in the ancient world passed away. Sparta forced Athens to give up her empire and the tribute they paid. These tribute burdens had become intolerable during the war, having tripled after local navies were seized. A number of city-states revolted, and those that didn't knew their freedoms were gone. As the leader of the rebellious city-state of Mytilene said:

So long as the Athenians in their leadership respected our independence, we followed them with enthusiasm. But when we saw that they were becoming . . . more and more interested in enslaving their allies, then we became frightened.[9]

Mytilene, like Melos, paid the supreme penalty with the men slaughtered and the women and children sold into slavery for trying to withdraw from the League and join Sparta.

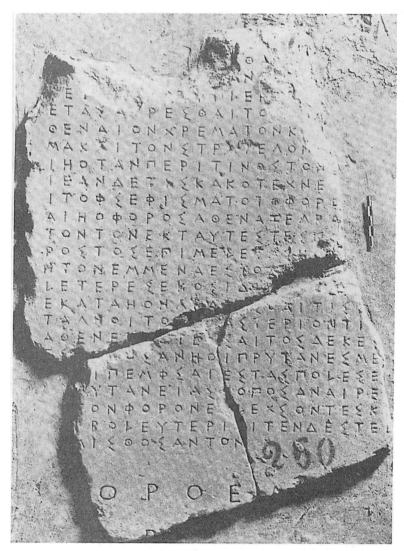

The darker side of Athenian justice. Fragments of an Athenian tax decree from the Acropolis set forth the procedure for tax collection from cities in the Athenian League. Delinquent taxes are to be visited by an Athenian "gang of five." On at least one occasion hostages will be taken to ensure tax collection. Leaders of cities opposing tax collections may be charged and punished for treason.

The Spartans required no tribute from their allies, and many of Athens' so-called allies tried to join the Spartan cause and were hoping for a Spartan victory to gain their freedom. The city-states in the Athenian League were not allies at all, nor was this a league. They had no love, no loyalty, and wished for Athens' defeat. With at least 165 of these city-states seething with discontent and on the brink of rebellion, it is no wonder Athens lost a war it should have won. Athens, after all, had superiority in population, wealth, naval forces—all the ingredients to win, save the loyal support of her empire. They lost that loyalty from oppressive taxation and the bondage required for its enforcement. Greece's story and collapse is an early example of a wise and prudent tax policy—the policy of Aristides the Just—going bad.

During the drama of Watergate, the eighteenth-century historian Lord Acton was quoted a great deal, although the quotes were usually inaccurate. Acton said, "Power tends to corrupt and absolute power corrupts absolutely." The phrase *tends to* is usually omitted, probably because it is not strong enough; *breeds* is more fitting. Power breeds corruption together with a blindness to the corruption itself. The Athenians became oblivious to the ideals of Greek democracy and liberty and to the purposes for which they fought the Persians. Tribute from the weaker city-states around them meant a fat treasury, extravagant public works, and wages for thousands on the public payrolls. Jurors could now be paid, along with the ten thousand rowers in the Athenian navy. Sculptors and architects could be hired to design and build the magnificent Parthenon on the Acropolis at the edge of the city. The tyranny suffered by the weaker city-states was unimportant because of the economic good these taxes did for Athens. This sort of reasoning is still used to justify oppressive taxation.

7

The Ingenious Greek: Public Revenue without Bureaucracy

The rich serve the state with their property by means of liturgies.
—Aristotle, *Politics IV*

The ancient Greek not only invented civilization without despotism; he also invented revenue sharing without bureaucracy. More wealth may have shifted from the rich to the community at large in ancient Greece than in our socialist-inclined democracies. The Greeks did it without government bureaus taxing, directing, and coercing the populace. The Greeks never even used the police power in the process. This may sound incredible, but it is just another example of their ingenuity.

The Greek revenue system was progressive, which means that the richer citizens paid an increasingly larger share of the costs of government and of maintaining society. The farmers were not very prosperous. Greece was poor farming country, but a farmer who had large amounts of land and slaves would generate taxes when his surpluses and slaves reached the channels of trade. Basic subsistence, however, especially among the poor, was not subject to taxation. The poor were also exempt from the eisphora, the special capital levy noted in the last chapter. Commerce bore the weight of most taxation, since Athens was primarily a trading nation. The more wealth a person had, the greater the likelihood he would be involved in commerce and pay more tax.

However, it was not the tax system that extracted the largest amount of wealth from the rich private citizen. This was achieved by the liturgy—the voluntary alternative to progressive taxation.

When a city needed a new public improvement such as a bridge, or perhaps an activity such as a play or festival, the leading citizens were called upon to provide what was wanted. It was not a tax or confiscation

Greek temples that now hold tourists in awe were used as treasuries to protect tax money. The great Parthenon held the tax money of the Athenian League and was financed with tax money stolen from the League's treasury.

of any kind. Called a liturgy, this was a voluntary contribution to the city-state. It was enforced by nothing more than tradition and strong public sentiment. Public amusements, athletic games, and military equipment were purchased by rich citizens and donated to the city. A certain amount was expected of each rich citizen, but most of them gave more than was asked.

Xenophon, a Greek writer and student of Socrates, records a dialogue between Socrates and a rich citizen in which Socrates reminds his wealthy friend:

> I notice that the city is already laying heavy expenses on you, for keeping horses, financing plays, gymnasiums and important functions, and should war break out, I know they will impose on you costs of naval vessels, soldier's pay and contributions so great you will not find it easy to bear.[1]

The rationale of the liturgy was that men of wealth should voluntarily shoulder the expenses of their city. Public generosity through liturgies was their just duty for the unequal share of the riches of the community they enjoyed. By and large the rich did not give begrudgingly. Many of the extravagant public buildings in the classical world were constructed by rich men competing with one another for honor. Socrates in *Xenophon* reminds a rich Athenian of his obligation to the city for revenue sharing: "If ever you are thought to have fallen short in the performance of these duties, I know that the Athenians will punish you just as much as if they had caught you stealing their own property."[2]

Private gifts of warships made the Athenian navy the best and most powerful in the civilized world. They kept the sea lanes around Greece free from pirates. The generosity of the rich Greeks is mentioned in many of the writings of this period, which indicate that many rich Greeks donated three and four times what was expected of them. When occasionally the opposite was true, a wealthy person who had not given freely and generously was held up to public scorn. Public sentiment is a powerful force that is not used in our society as much as it should be. Governments try to manipulate it more than listen to it. The Greeks used it so successfully that progressive taxation was unnecessary.

The closest thing we have to the practice of liturgies is the making of gifts and sacrifices by religious devotees to their religion. In like manner, the city-state was the first love of every citizen. Even the poor contributed their mite. For those who did not have any surplus wealth, there was the alternative of service and labor for the city. These liturgy demands for voluntary contributions of wealth and labor were what the Athenian leader Pericles had in mind in his famous funeral oration, when he spoke of

> those unwritten laws which it is an acknowledged shame to break. . . . We regard wealth as something to be properly used rather than something to boast about. . . . Every one of us who survives should gladly toil in her [Athens'] behalf.[3]

The practice of liturgies created a new sense of private property. Those who had wealth held it in a kind of voluntary trust for the city. Ownership of property involved duties more than it involved rights. This was the Greeks' brilliant alternative to government ownership and bureaucratic control which typified the oriental despotisms of that day and the governments of our day. The rationale was that property, by the natural order of things, was bestowed on those best able to acquire and manage it, but those so endowed were obligated to hold it for the community as it was needed. This system permitted the management of the excessive wealth of the private citizen for the whole community without government bureaucracy—something no other people have been able to do, either before or since the days of the ancient Greeks. Waste and inefficiency that is so inherent in bureaucratic life was replaced by private enterprise for the public good.

The private donor actually managed and directed the public improvement or activity. If a bridge was needed the wealthy citizen actually built the bridge. For his work and money the donor was honored. The city-state government had little to do except to push the project along. Under the system the public received the most from the donor's money. His management talent was free.

Today we shift a great deal of private wealth to the public sector through heavy taxation and government-managed expenditures. The costs are enormous. Worst of all is the spirit of the whole operation. The donors are neither respected nor honored for their benevolence. In fact, the taxpayer, however high the tax he pays, does not know where his money goes. He pays because the alternative is prison and he never pays more than the law demands, if that much. Paying three or four times as much tax as the law demands is unheard-of in our society. Our governments exact taxes with the arrogance of an owner, somewhat like the attitude of Louis XIV as expressed by one of his aides: "All the wealth of his subjects was his, and when he took it he took only what belonged to him." This is the attitude of the despots, which the Greeks understood so well and tried so hard to avoid through the system of liturgies.

Scholars have taken strong positions both for and against the liturgy. It cannot be questioned, however, that the liturgy was the device by which the Greeks achieved civilization without despotism. When a government takes wealth by force and claim of right, it is inclined to trample on the people's property rights and liberties. On the other hand, if private wealth is spent without social conscience on the extravagances of individuals, the less fortunate suffer and are often driven to violence and revolution. The liturgy was a solution to the dilemma of too much versus too little government intervention in the accumulation of private property. The interests of the community and the individual were reasonably balanced. The liturgy respected private property, but it also induced the wealthy to shoulder the main burden of providing for the needs of the community—and the genius of the system lay in the fact that no police power was needed to achieve those ends.

Under a liturgy system there is no place for the games of avoidance and evasion that characterize our tax systems. Loopholes, tax gimmicks, and tax shelters have no place. Every citizen should shoulder his fair share of the costs of maintaining government and providing for the needs of the community. This kind of patriotism is not jingoistic; without it the liturgy will not work.

The Greek practice of liturgies survived the city-states. But when the Romans demanded liturgies from their conquered cities with the muscle of the legions, this was no longer voluntary contribution. Now it was legalized robbery or, to be more sophisticated, the confiscation of private property for government use without just compensation.

It remains to be seen if some sort of liturgy can be used in our modern industrial states. We could begin by having government service carry little or no salary, with the example of unselfish service coming from the top. Government leaders and members of the legislature could serve for a modest subsistence as an example for others. Our youth could donate a year for public service, if for no other benefit than to operate the essential services of government when, as happens routinely in Canada, strikes cripple the economy and cut off services which communities require in order to function. Unselfish voluntary service in the public sector could infect the private sector. Voluntary service could pave the way for voluntary contributions. The two would go hand-in-hand.

The liturgy will probably make little headway until we eliminate the inequities in our tax and military draft systems. Not every young man is obligated to serve in time of military need nor is every person who is able required to pay tax. There are numerous exemptions in our draft and tax laws making it legal to avoid service or payment. Evasion, despite government ravings to the contrary, involves little moral turpitude; conversely, there is little moral incentive for compliance. But the most essential ingredient for the liturgy is strong public sentiment demanding unselfish public service and revenue sharing. Without such a credo we would have to be like the later Romans, falling back on Draconian punishment, thereby defeating the very purposes for which we have government in the first place.

The spirit of the liturgy might even save some of the social services we could lose if taxpayers rise up and block revenue increases or, as in California, roll back assessments. Voluntary public service is the alternative to either higher taxes or reduced social programs. Our society does expect (and receive) voluntary services for all kinds of community programs, as long as they are not government-directed. We volunteer for the Boy Scouts and Campfire Girls, but not for fire service or social work. We will sweat behind a shovel and get blisters using a pick for any number of community service projects, but if we lose our job we will draw welfare rather than accept the pick and shovel to earn a living. In short, we are all willing to eat from the public trough, even when we could get along without doing so. Social insurance or social security could be limited to the elderly who do not have adequate funds to care for themselves.

The liturgy can only operate from a spirit of unselfish citizenship, with each citizen coming forward to give of himself or his substance for the good of the community. It made heavy taxation, and all the evil it breeds, unnecessary. That is just one of many reasons why the Greeks command our admiration.

The Greeks refined another revenue-raising device, called tax-farming, which has a long and fascinating history.[4] Tax-farmers were private contractors who bid at public auctions for the right to collect a certain tax, such as a harbor tax, an inn or hotel tax, or a sales tax. Accurate records were kept from previous years and, barring some calamity, the amount of the revenue could be accurately calculated. The business was risky, but appears to have been profitable. In the city-states, tax-farming proved superior to government tax administration. Just as private contracts for public works are usually less costly to the state, so the private tax man did a better and more economical job of collecting taxes. Private property was well protected in the Athenian courts and we have no historical record of any abuses of the system at the taxpayer level. Incidentally, cities ruled by tyrants had no tax-farmers.

Tax-farming was an extreme phase of capitalism. A government contracting with private citizens to collect taxes is much like hiring a private army to fight a war. These are extreme delegations of sovereign power. Since taxes were low in Greek democracies, tax-farming was not a major enterprise. The geographical area of the city-states was small. Tax-farmers collecting customs could station themselves at the city gates and harbors. The 2 percent tax rate was indirect and was collected from the importers, usually foreigners. Consequently, the abuses that characterized tax-farming in later times did not take place. To the early Greeks it was simply an economical way to collect taxes in a system where tax evasion was not worth the trouble. The most serious abuse of the system was from the tax-farmers. To check corruption the Greeks invented public accountings.[5]

The modest system of tax-farming originally set up by the Greek democratic city-states contrasted strongly with the system of the later Greek kings in the third to first century b.c., who ruled over the entire Middle East. We hear accounts of how the whole world groaned under the terrible oppression of the tax-farmers, and this was before the Romans got ahold of the system. What works well in one time and place may bring disaster when misapplied in other circumstances.

The island of Cos was a typical Greek island under the later Greek kings. Tax-farmers were sent out from the mainland to collect the island's taxes. These tax-farmers were thugs. Even the privacy of a person's home was not secure from them. "Every door now trembles at the tax-farmers,"[6] writes a respectable lady from Cos around 200 b.c. In the later Greek and Roman world no social class was hated more than the tax-farmer. The leading modern historian of that period, Rostovtzeff, describes them with these words: "The publicani certainly were ruthless tax collectors, and dangerous and unscrupulous rivals in business. They were often dishonest and probably always cruel."[7]

The Greek democrats who invented tax-farming would have been astounded to learn that in a few hundred years their simple private collection system was to evolve into a monster of oppression. They would have been even more astounded to learn that tax-farming was to flourish in Western civilization, in many bizarre forms, for 2,500 years, finally going out of business with World War I in the twentieth century. However, today the farming of taxes has re-emerged in many state and local governments, not only to aid in the collection of taxes, but even in the audit and assessment of taxes. An ancient but dangerous practice if history is of any value.

One of the most notable misuses of tax-farming took place in Egypt under the rule of the Ptolemies. When Alexander the Great spread Greek culture throughout the known world around 340 B.C., he did not include in his package the ideals of Greek democracy and freedom from direct taxation. His father, Philip, was from Macedonia, in what is today northern Greece and Yugoslavia. Philip ruled a kingdom far removed from Greek city-state thinking. Around 350 B.C., he subdued the city-states and brought Greece into his kingdom. He died at an early age and his youthful son took over his imperialist ambitions.

Alexander was an emperor bent on ruling a large geographical area through a military bureaucracy with himself as chief bureaucrat. He picked up Greek culture—but not her democratic ideas—and spread it throughout his new empire. Tax-farming was one of the economic tools he acquired from the city-states. Laws were devised to govern tax-farming, and police and military powers were brought into the system. Collecting the largest amount of tax was the primary pursuit of most empires at that time, and tax-farmers with muscle proved to be the most efficient system. Private professional tax collectors far surpassed the best government tax men.

When the Greek Ptolemies set up rule in Egypt they modified the system of tax-farming as practiced in Greece. Greece had tax-farmers because the government had no tax bureaucracy. In Egypt the new Greek rulers inherited the most highly developed tax collecting operation in the world. The Egyptian government had been collecting taxes with great efficiency for two thousand years. Tax-farmers were not needed. Nevertheless, the astute Greek conquerors saw a place for the tax-farmer, not as a collector but as an insurer that all taxes would be collected. The tax-farmer would be a special check on the tax bureau to make sure every last drachma was recovered. His job was to watch over both the taxpayer and the tax collector. He entered into a contract with the king to guarantee the full collection of a certain amount of tax. In case of a deficiency the tax-farmer would personally make up the loss. Scribes would no longer be able to remit taxes for the poor or unfortunate. If all went well, and there was a surplus, then the surplus went to the tax-farmer. In addition, he received a 10 percent basic commission out of his bid—even if there was no surplus.

Tax-farming was a big operation with enormous potential. Normally, tax-farming was done through partnerships and organized companies. It was the big business of that day. The auctions took place in the king's palace under his personal direction. The awarding of the contracts was the single most significant commercial event of the year.

The tax-farmer was not just a private professional tax collector. His side operations were probably more remunerative than the tax collection. Tax-farmers were bankers who loaned money to taxpayers to meet their tax obligations. They acted as merchants for the farmers' products which they taxed. They were grain and wine brokers. Even the merchant fleets carrying the taxed goods to world markets were owned by the rich tax-farmers. In short, the tax-farmers were the Krupps, Rothschilds and du Ponts of the ancient world.

The tax-farming innovation of the Ptolemies was ingenious, to say the least, but it was destructive. This middleman insurer improved the efficiency of the Egyptian tax system. The king now had two independent groups looking out for his revenue. Both were personally liable for any tax deficiencies—tax evasion was impossible. Dishonesty or laxity on the part of government tax collectors would adversely affect the tax-farmer, and as a typical private contractor he was apt to be much more efficient than the state tax collector. The incentive system that so characterizes capitalism gave an added punch to the Egyptian tax system. The loser in this double-barrelled arrangement was the taxpayer, who in Egypt was the peasant farmer.

With the tax-farmer injected into the heavy direct tax system of Egypt, rebellion was inevitable. The moderately oppressive tax system that dominated Egyptian life for 2,500 years now became severe. The civil war that brought about the chaos and collapse of Egypt we noted in Chapter 2 could have been the consequence of the interposition of the tax-farmer into a tax system which now was pushed to the brink of civil war.

The ancient Greek had an uncanny gift for insight into the world in which he lived. There is hardly a theory or great idea that did not take its first flight in Greece. As men they were giants in the ancient world.

Herodotus, the father of history, developed as his main theme the conflict between East and West, which he interpreted as conflict between despotism and freedom. This same conflict and theme is dominant today in the Western interpretation of the conflict between communism and the free world. The Greeks looked deeper into this conflict for clues to determine why the Eastern social system produced bondage. They found that the despotism of a society, or its liberty, could best be measured by its tax system. The Greeks were much more profound than we in the analysis of taxation. We seem to accept any tax adopted by the legislature. Class politics creates tax laws and the legislators can tax just about what they please in any form they desire. Our tax laws are, at best, rough justice. The Greek view was probably expressed in its most refined state in an early-tenth-century encyclopedia called the Suidas. Taxes were tyrannical, and hence illegal, it explained, if they were demanded by "arrogance and compulsion," and they were justifiable when based on "reasonableness and loving care."[8] We have obviously retreated a great distance from these lofty ideas.

The Greek ideals about taxation were short-lived in Greece, but not in Rome. Greek culture and ideas captivated the Romans. Greek tutors were in all wealthy Roman homes. The Romans soon adopted Greek thinking, forbade direct taxation of Roman citizens, and continued the practice for almost five hundred years. Up until the twentieth century, Europe and North America respected Greek ideas on taxation. References to "direct taxation" can be found in the United States and Canadian constitutions. Debate still rages over whether income tax is a direct or indirect tax.

The Greeks put taxation in the field of ethics and required that it be measured by standards of justice. In practice, the Greeks failed miserably. Tax equity or equality was on the basis of class. Only the citizen enjoyed immunity from the hated direct taxes. We should not judge the Greeks too harshly. Those who control governments have always carried a light tax burden; in a democracy it means that those classes who have the votes will overburden those who do not. The high tax brackets of today are for the few, not the many, and in that the Greeks were not much worse than we are. It seems strange that a democratic and free people cannot be relied upon to export their product abroad, or to share it with minorities at home—especially their ideals of tax justice. Perhaps in the Peloponnesian War the gods were punishing Athens, not just for her abusive tribute policies towards the weaker cities of Greece, but for her defiance of the principles of justice which the Greek mind had espoused. Athenian imperialism was especially ugly, because the Athenians knew better.

The bright spot in the Greek tax story was in the administration of tax. Revenue was assessed and administered by the taxpayers themselves, without the intervention of a massive government bureau. And perhaps even more important was the response of the rich to the needs of the community. They shared their wealth with the community, and did not hesitate to see that the city and her people benefited from the bounties nature had bestowed upon them. Was this not the most ingenious of all the achievements of the Greek mind?

Part II
The Kaleidoscopic Romans

The Romans . . . have brought . . . almost the whole of the world under their rule, and have left an empire which far surpasses any that exist today or is likely to succeed it. In the course of this work I shall explain more clearly how this supremacy was acquired, and it will also become apparent what great advantages those who are fond of learning can enjoy from the study of serious history.

—Polybius, *The Histories*

Scholars often referred to Roman taxation as "more or less organized robbery," and Roman tax men as "a band of robbers."[1] But Roman taxation was not always bad. There was a two-hundred-year period at the zenith of Roman civilization when taxes were modest. Some Roman leaders can be praised for extremely humane and honest tax administration—highlighted by the unheard-of charity of paying a large portion of the costs of government out of their own pockets. All kinds of taxes—as well as no taxes—marked the Roman period. Taxation was as vital and unpredictable in the Roman story as were the legions, the Senate and the Caesars. The half-mad Nero once offered to abolish all indirect taxes and make a "beautiful present to the human race."[2] Of all his acts of madness this was the craziest.

The thousand years of Roman civilization are divided by historians into equal halves. The first period is called the Republic, when the Roman Senate was in command. It ended about 30 B.C. with the triumph of Caesar Augustus, the first emperor. The Empire ended with the sack of Rome by the Vandals in A.D. 476. These lines of demarcation are useful in studying Rome's tax story, even though there was a steady evolution of taxation in Roman history which changed color and form at irregular intervals.

To provide the reader with some sort of order and perspective, we have segregated Roman taxation into four periods, ending with the final chapter of this section which looks into the Fall of Rome and adds one more major cause: tax evasion.

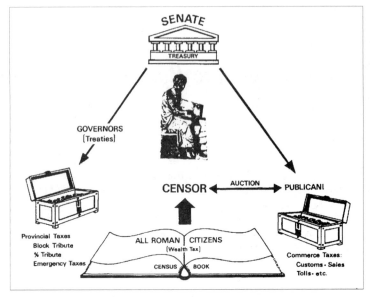

Roman Taxation I: The citizens' war-tax.

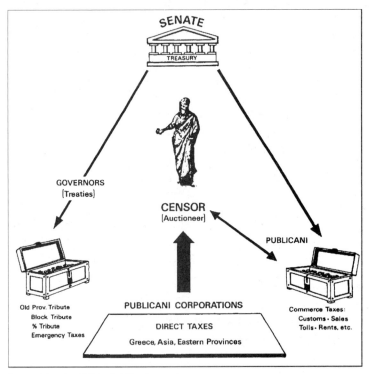

Roman Taxation II: The Publicani carpetbaggers.

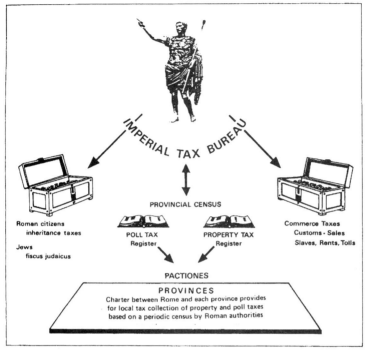

Roman Taxation III: Augustus—master tax strategist.

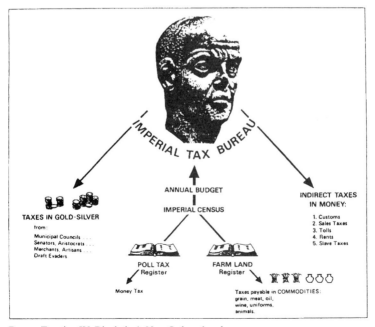

Roman Taxation IV: Diocletian's New Order—bondage.

8

The Early Republic: The Citizens' War-Tax Era

The early Roman Republic required little taxation because it operated with free labor. The army—which is always the most expensive operation in every society—was a citizens' army, composed of property owners who served for one year without pay. They even provided their own uniforms and equipment. This patriotic spirit produced a marvelous fighting force, which defeated all who opposed it and catapulted Rome into the center of the civilized world. This spirit of volunteer free public service inspired all government offices. Even the magistrates served the city without pay. It is difficult to overemphasize the importance of this ancient practice, especially in our age when no one seems willing to lift a finger for the government without a fat pay check. The ideal way to reduce heavy taxation is to instill in all citizens a spirit of unselfish service for the public good. It is not necessary to curtail public programs and services; what is necessary is the curtailment of the spirit of gain and profit that infects public servants and contractors.

Early Rome did not operate tax-free. Some public revenues were needed. They were supplied by a number of indirect commercial taxes that continued throughout Roman history. The earliest taxes in Rome were customs duties on imports and exports. Almost all trade came by ship through seaports, hence the name *portoria* for these taxes. The Romans were pragmatic about taxation. As the Romans acquired new colonies they maintained the existing tax systems. In Spain, customs duty was 2 percent; in Sicily, Africa, and Albania the rate was 5 percent.

Ancient civilization ran on human power more than horsepower. The moral issue was never much of a problem; the economic bond of the slave was recognized by the Jews and early Christians. Slaves, like tribute, were part of the spoils of war.

This relief, from the Louvre, shows a Roman censor taking a census for the assessment of citizens for the war tax.

Taxes touched every facet of slavery. Most slaves were sold at auctions, which incurred a 2 percent to 5 percent sales tax. When slaves arrived in port there was a customs tax. When a slave was freed there was a 5 percent tax on his value. Slaves were given a reduced rate for poll taxes, similar to the United States Constitution which valued a slave for direct taxation at three-fifths of a free-man.

To give the reader some idea of the size of the slave trade, the free port of Delos off the coast of Greece could handle as many as ten thousand slaves at a time. The great commercial facilities on the Isle of Rhodes could handle more. Taxes on slavery were a major source of revenue for all governments. Pirates were the chief slave traders during times of peace. The crew of any vessel seized by pirates was a regular part of the cargo. The task of proving one's right to freedom was extremely difficult once a person was caught up in the channels of slavery.

Private tax collectors were also slave traders. The king of an eastern Roman province complained to the Senate that he was unable to provide men for the legions because Roman tax-farmers had taken his surplus male subjects and sold them. This story is often cited to prove that Roman tax men operated a vast kidnapping-for-slavery operation in the provinces. This may not be a correct interpretation of the records. The king probably pledged his surplus male subjects to secure a loan to pay his taxes. If the loan was unpaid because of a bad harvest, the tax-farmers foreclosed on their collateral, like any efficient banker.

Military expenditures increased as Rome's armies defeated all who challenged them. Even in ancient times military adventures were costly for the victors. The need for greater revenues was met by a patriotic citizens' war-tax, called *tributum*. The word was applied to many types of payments to Rome; consequently, we will avoid its use.

The war-tax was a wealth tax assessed from a census taken every five years. It was the duty of every citizen to come forth and make a declaration of all his wealth. There were penalties for fraud or failure to make a declaration—as with our modern income taxes. One of the penalties was to be sold into slavery by the censor.[1] The war-tax was similar to the Greek eisphora, except that the Greeks exempted the poor, but not foreigners; the Romans exempted foreigners, but not the poor.

Economists like to classify taxes as progressive, proportionate, or regressive. A tax is *progressive* if the rich pay a larger percentage than others; *proportionate* if the percentage is the same; and *regressive* if the poor pay a larger percentage than the rich. Our income taxes are ostensibly progressive because of graduated rates. Sales, customs, and real property taxes are proportionate—the rates are the same for everyone. Poll taxes and license fees are regressive—the fixed amount takes a larger percentage of the wealth of the poor than of the rich.

The war-tax was progressive in a unique fashion. Luxuries such as jewels, expensive women's apparel, and fancy carriages were assessed at ten times their actual value. Other items may have been assessed at two or four times their actual value. Consequently, the low rate of one-tenth of 1 percent was deceptive. For the rich the tax could run as high as 1 percent, ten times the rate assessed against the poor.[2] In addition, the rich were subject to forced loans on top of their basic war-tax. Finally, the tax had a refundable element to it; if there was booty from the war, the booty was used to refund the taxes paid. Small wonder that the early Roman government was dear to the hearts of her people.

Historical records about the war-tax were all written at least a hundred years after its abolition. Cicero expressed contempt for the tax:

When constant wars made the Roman treasury run short, our forefathers often used to levy a property tax. Every effort must be made to prevent a repetition of this; and all possible precaution must be taken to ensure that such a step will never be needed. . . . But if *any* government should find itself under the necessity of levying a tax on property, the utmost care has to be devoted to making it clear to the entire population that this simply has to be done because no alternative exists short of complete national collapse.[3]

Cicero wrote these words when Greek thinking dominated Roman culture. If the tax was so intolerable, why were foreigners exempt? Even widows and orphans paid this tax, and their funds were specifically set aside for the cavalry. The moving force behind this tax was a strong spirit of patriotism, like serving in the legions. In the beginning the tax was probably not despised at all, but paid with pride.

War-tax assessments were made by censors who were the most important men in the Republic, even surpassing senators. They were former senators and consuls, elder statesmen elected to office every five years by the Assembly of all Roman citizens. They had the power to appoint and dismiss senators. These men were not ordinary tax assessors, who normally are not very high on anyone's list of notables.

The ancients frequently used great men to handle tax assessments. The Greeks used great generals such as Aristides the Just. Imagine what would happen today if the senior statesmen in our society were in charge of tax assessments? Winston Churchill might have looked strange as a tax assessor, but this is where he would have ended his illustrious career if he had lived in the ancient world. Taxpayers loved and admired the censors and no doubt the integrity of these great men rubbed off on taxpayers. By contrast, modern tax systems use professional public relations officers to manipulate taxpayers with advertising techniques that utilize fear more than inspiration.

By the middle of the second century B.C. the war-tax was abolished. Thereafter, for four hundred years, Roman citizens living in Rome were immune from direct taxation. Regardless of what Cicero said, the war-tax was abolished because the provinces could now support the legions. Conquered lands became Roman lands and were rented out and taxed. Precious metals flowed into the Roman treasury from captured mines. Grain came from Sicily. Rome became a thriving commercial center and taxes on commerce escalated. Most productive of all, however, were the newly acquired provinces in the east and to the north. It was here, and in all the provinces, that the Romans showed their greatest skill in statecraft, or to coin a better word: tax-craft. The long life of Roman colonialism, as compared to the troubled life of Greek imperialism, was the consequence of newer and more effective means of colonization.

There was an inherent weakness in the tribute systems that prevailed in the ancient world. In solving this weakness the Roman genius in government began to unfold. The absence of direct control over each tribute state permitted rebellions to be organized with ease. The Assyrians

The great Roman lawyer, Cicero, who promulgated the Greek idea against direct taxes: These taxes are an enemy of liberty and should only be introduced after making it clear to the people that no alternative exists short of complete national collapse.

spent most of their energy organizing armies to crush tax defiance in their colonial empire. About all the Assyrians could do to check a tribute state bent on rebellion was to liquidate the inhabitants. This rough policy solved the rebellion problem—as the Jews were to learn the hard way—but it also eliminated future tribute. To correct this defect in the tribute systems of the past the Romans developed the provincial system.

Governors were sent out from Rome with dictatorial powers backed-up by the legions who were stationed in every province. The armies of rebellious provinces were dismantled. This new technique secured Roman exploitation of colonial subjects for hundreds of years. The threat of legions marching out of Rome to chastise a rebellious colony—which was the system of Assyria—was not anywhere as effective as the presence of legions stationed in every province as permanent garrisons.

There was also an element of fairness in the Roman tribute system, unlike the practices of other empires in the past. The Romans usually did not alter the tax system or tax burdens of a newly acquired territory. If poll taxes were customary, they would continue. If there had been a harvest tax based on a tenth of production, then that would continue. Local tax-farmers would not be put out of business. The rationale for paying taxes to Rome was sound: Rome provided legions that brought peace and order to a world fraught with danger. It was only fair for the provinces to pay for the maintenance of these beneficial military forces. Roman tribute was a small price to pay.

Cicero called Sicily the "first jewel of the imperial crown." Sicily was an unexpected dividend from Rome's war with Carthage. Most Roman governors who administered this first Roman overseas colony supported themselves from their own pockets and were "accustomed to bring home nothing from their governorship but the thanks of the subjects and the approbation of their fellow citizens."[4]

A substantial part of Sicily was tax-exempt before the Romans arrived. This was not altered. Tribute, exacted from only those parts of Sicily that had paid it in the past, consisted of a 10 percent harvest tax, a 20 percent orchard tax, and a 5 percent customs tax. The Romans never altered the method of collection. Roman tax-farming corporations were prohibited from taking part in tax-farming auctions. A Roman magistrate conducted the auctions and limited the bidding to local tax-farmers. Cities bid for the right to collect their own tribute. That way the commission from tax-farming went to support the city.

Rome almost lived on the grain from Sicilian harvest taxes. Cicero, quoting Cato the Wise, referred to Sicily as, "the nation's storehouse, the nurse at whose breast the Roman people is fed."[5] The delights of having a rich, loyal colony brought home to the Romans the wonders of colonialism and whetted Roman appetites for more territories. The system looked foolproof. In theory it was.

Not all Roman governors were benevolent rulers. Thanks to Cicero's zeal for writing we have elaborate details of his prosecution of Verres, a governor who fleeced Sicily with oppressive taxation which he then stole from the Senate. He encouraged his friends to purchase tax-farming contracts at high prices and then demanded a kick-back. He kept the 5 percent customs taxes for himself by falsifying tax records. The successful prosecution of Verres was one of those rare moments in history when political corruption is fully exposed for the world to see.

The Extortions Court which tried Verres was established to punish corrupt governors, who collected more tax than the treaties authorized or who embezzled tax moneys. Unfortunately, the court was not very effective. It was said that a governor had to extort three fortunes from his colonial subjects—one for himself, one for the army, and one to bribe the Extortions Court when he returned home.

The war with Carthage also brought Spain into the Roman colonial empire. But Spain, unlike Sicily, smoldered with rebellion for 150 years. Trouble started when Roman armies lived off the populace and collected tribute, in block form called *stipendium*. Cicero called this tribute "the fruits of victory or a punishment for engaging in war against us."[6] The Roman practice of supporting troops off the land in Spain was the root of Cicero's remark that a town suffered nearly as much when a Roman army took up winter quarters as when it was taken by storm.[7]

At first, under conquering general Scipio, Roman armies in Spain lived off the land. Supplies promised from the Senate did not arrive because of corrupt tax-farmers. When Scipio made an urgent appeal for help, the Senate hired three tax-farming companies to send supplies to Spain. The tax-farmers purchased dilapidated old ships and loaded them with worthless cargoes; the ships sank soon after they left the harbor. The tax-farmers then applied to the Senate for money to replace the lost ships and cargoes, falsely representing that the ships were sound and filled with valuable cargoes for Scipio.[8]

While grain was the prize from Sicily, silver and gold were the fruits from Spain. In ten years, from 206 B.C. to 197 B.C., 130,000 pounds of silver and 4,000 pounds of gold were taken from Spanish mines and shipped to Rome. This precious metal formed the basis of the Roman monetary system for centuries to come.

Finally, these colonial harvests excited the ambitions of many Romans, who wanted to repeat the colonial process in other lands. Nothing will propel a nation down the road of imperialism more than a rich harvest from a successful colonial operation. The United States, in 1898, abandoned an entrenched policy of anti-colonialism, when Cuba, Puerto Rico, Guam, and the Philippines were acquired in the Spanish-American War with less than seven hundred casualties.

9

The Publicani Drive the Republic to Ruin

The whole world groans under the Publicani.
—Roman writer, second century B.C.

In the second century B.C., Roman businessmen not of aristocratic rank rose to dominate the Roman state. The Senate was reduced in power. These businessmen were the carpetbaggers of the ancient world, arriving in newly conquered provinces closely on the heels of the legions. Tax-farming was their principal endeavor, but the riches they acquired from tax-farming soon permitted them to dominate trade, banking, and shipping; in short, all economic life. In the provinces their operations achieved brutal and grotesque forms as these colonial exploiters became the "ugly Romans" of the ancient world.

The publicani, as they were called, rose to power through the Tribal Assembly of the Roman people. The aristocratic Senate excluded commoners. The Assembly could not pass laws; it could only veto laws that trespassed on the rights of commoners. Around 130 B.C. the Assembly started creating law. But this activity only lasted a few years, and most of its laws were soon annulled. Two reforms did survive: the distribution of free bread to the rabble of Rome; and a new tax system in the rich Greek and other eastern provinces. A *decuma*, or 10 percent harvest tax, would replace the tax treaties of the Roman Senate. This harvest tax would be collected exclusively by the publicani under five-year contracts, auctioned by the censors. The contracts were large. Part of the price had to be paid in advance, which gave the Roman government cash, up front. When the publicani started to collect the decuma, the Roman government had already been paid and had to enforce their demands. The large contracts required the pooling of funds, and this pro-

87

duced the world's first corporations, called *societates publicanorum*. A legal distinction was made between shareholders and management. Senators could own shares, but they could not participate in management. Our modern corporate laws follow a similar pattern. Shares in these corporations were sold in the Forum in Rome, which became the world's first Wall Street. The yields of publicani stocks were excellent. When a company had financial troubles it was easy to lobby a decree through the Senate reducing the publicani contract. Publicani stocks were the best investment of the day—"a sure thing"—the glamour stocks of 100 B.C.

Publicani exploitation of the provinces went unchecked. "The publicani are a nuisance," or "It is the duty of every honest administrator to oppose them,"[1] were common expressions of that day. In later times (A.D. 14), the Roman historian Livy condemned them: "Where the publicani are, there is no respect for public law and no freedom for the provinces."[2] But the government could not get rid of them. Government revenues depended on them and no alternative method had been developed. Cicero emphasized this problem in this letter to his brother Quintus, governor of the province of Asia:

> However, to your good will and careful policy the great obstacle lies in the publicani: for if we oppose them, we alienate from ourselves and the State an order which has deserved exceedingly well of us and which has been linked to the State by our efforts; if on the other hand we comply with them in every case, we shall allow the complete ruin of those for whose welfare and interests we are bound to have regard.[3]

These arguments to support the publicani and tolerate the evil they foster are still with us. Throughout history, whenever a tax develops that is productive of revenue, but oppressive to taxpayers (like the income tax), the tax will continue. The financial needs of the state override most constitutional, moral, and cultural ideals.

The Fall of the Colossus of Rhodes

The island of Rhodes is one of the largest Greek islands in the Aegean Sea. It lies off the coast of Turkey. After the fall of Athens in the fourth century B.C., most of the commerce of the east moved to Rhodes, which was far from the war zones of Greece. Rhodes became a Switzerland of the ancient world. Banking and commerce flourished as Rhodian merchants discovered the wisdom of neutrality. The kings and courts of the entire ancient world honored the businessmen of Rhodes, who were hard neutralists in international politics.

Business and commerce is drawn to peace and stability. War repels trade. Even today, the great loss to Lebanon is her once-thriving financial community. If peace were to come tomorrow, the bankers would not return. Switzerland's great secret to financial success is her policy of staying out of wars and maintaining neutrality at all costs. This is the climate which commerce has sought since the days of antiquity.

Rhodes was also in a key geographical position. To reach Rome and Greece from the east, it was necessary for many ships to stop at Rhodes to take on supplies or to dispose of their cargo. All vessels paid a 2 percent harbor tax based on the value of their cargo, even if the cargo remained on board. Free ports were unknown at the time.

The prosperous Rhodians dazzled the merchants of the world by constructing a bronze colossus over one hundred feet high, which became one of the Seven Wonders of the Ancient World. Legend says that this huge statue of Apollo stood astride the entrance to the main harbor, and ships sailing into the harbor passed between Apollo's legs. Modern scholars dispute this and believe the colossus stood at one side of the harbor like a lighthouse.

An earthquake toppled the colossus into the harbor around 225 B.C. We do not hear much about Rhodes after the Romans moved into the region sometime later. What caused the fall of this great commercial center? Was it the aftermath of the earthquake or the onslaught of Roman military power? Actually, it was a force even more powerful. The story of how the commercial men of Rome toppled this commercial colossus is one of the most fascinating tax stories of antiquity.

During the time of Rome's wars with Macedonia, the Rhodians had the good fortune of receiving favors from Rome. The Romans wanted Rhodes as a buffer state between them and Persia. To strengthen this position, Rome turned over to Rhodes a number of tribute territories bordering on the Persian empire. It was a good arrangement for both countries.

Unfortunately, the Rhodians had an anti-Roman political group in power when Rome was struggling with Philip of Macedonia. The Rhodians took a neutral position and offered to mediate a peace treaty between Rome and Macedonia. The Romans looked upon this neutrality as an act of treachery for an ally they had richly rewarded. The Rhodians misjudged Roman power, and when the Romans defeated the Macedonians, they were confronted with an angry and embittered Rome. The Rhodians quickly dispatched to Rome their most pro-Roman diplomats to try and prevent a military confrontation.

The Roman Senate was not forgiving. They took back the territories they had given Rhodes. Roman publicani saw this as an opportunity to overthrow Rhodian commercial supremacy in the east. They persuaded

the Senate to establish a rival free port on the Isle of Delos to challenge
Rhodes. Greek businessmen were invited to operate the free port. The
Romans built new harbor facilities and set up commercial services to
rival those of Rhodes. Most important of all, the new port would be tax
free. Goods could come and go without paying the 2 percent harbor tax
the Rhodians had charged. The trade of the east immediately bypassed
Rhodes and went to Delos. In one year trade declined by 85 percent.
Annual tax receipts which normally ran about 1,000,000 silver drachmas declined to 150,000.[4]

The commercial colossus of the east had fallen because merchants
found an easy way to avoid a 2 percent tax! The Romans did with taxation what an earthquake could not do. The Rhodians had miraculously
recovered from the earthquake, but from the rival free port there was no
recovery. The Switzerland of the ancient world was destroyed when the
Romans established history's first tax haven.

Yet the Romans made a serious error when they destroyed Rhodes.
The Rhodians were a powerful force for peace and economic prosperity
in the east. The 2 percent harbor tax was used to maintain strong naval
forces to keep the shipping lanes free from pirates. The Rhodians did
not hesitate to use their naval strength to check any maritime powers in
that region who tried to curb trade or charge excessive taxes to use the
sea lanes. The Rhodians were the first advocates for freedom of the high
seas. They were as astute in commerce as the Romans were in war. The
Romans needed their influence and power in the east.

Roman publicani did not see this. They only saw the Rhodians as
commercial rivals to be eliminated, if at all possible. They failed to see
that once Rhodes declined, pirates would take over the east, crippling
trade and almost achieving the status of nationhood. This disruption of
shipping and commerce would eventually compel the Senate to endow
General Pompey with extraordinary military power to destroy the pirates. In the end, the general and his successor (Caesar) would destroy
much more than the pirates—the Republic itself would succumb to their
power.

The ruthlessness with which the publicani exploited the provinces
was bound to incite rebellion—that was obvious. But what was not obvious was the fury of the rebellion and the devastation it would bring to
Roman civilization.

Mithridates the Great

Mithridates the Great ruled a small country in what is now Turkey.
He had an extraordinary ability to arouse discontent among unhappy

taxpayers and organize a rebellion of unbelievable magnitude. He planned a secret attack for a certain day in 88 B.C. which involved most of the cities of Asia and Greece, including Athens. Ancient historians tell us that on the first day, eighty thousand Roman publicani were put to death, and twenty thousand Romans and pro-Roman Greek businessmen were slaughtered at the free port of Delos, which never recovered. These numbers may be a gross exaggeration.[5] Rome was shocked. When news reached the Forum there probably was a panic in publicani stocks, like Wall Street's 1929 crash.

Mithridates' main appeal was to exterminate the publicani and grant five years' tax immunity to every city that joined his rebellion. It was not hard to gather support. The big question was whether or not he could defeat the Roman legions. His cause was strong, but what about his army?

The success of Mithridates called the Senate to action. They appointed a loyal, anti-publicani general, Sulla, to raise an army and restore Roman authority in the east. With superb leadership Sulla succeeded after a four-year struggle. At home, the publicani were stripped of power and the Senate was restored to its key position in government.

When the revolt was crushed Sulla ordered the leading citizens of the revolting cities to meet him at Ephesus. There would be no reprisals or "acts of barbarism," said Sulla, "I shall only impose upon you the taxes of five years, to be paid at once, together with what the war has cost me."[6] To enforce this tax Sulla established a division of "special agents" with extraordinary powers to collect these exactions. Their special power was called *imperium* with *lectores*. (A lector had the power to scourge and behead, which was enough to make any taxpayer cooperative.)[7]

Up to this time in history we have seen self-assessment tax collection, private tax collection, army tax collectors, and regular government tax men. Sulla's "special agent," as he was called, was a highly skilled specialist with the arrogance of a bureaucrat and the power of a military executioner. Taxpayers lost all inclination to evade this combination of power. Special agents have emerged time and again in the course of history, surviving in the modern age as "fiscal police," or simply "special agents," using the title first given by Sulla over two thousand years ago.

Mithridates fostered two more rebellions before he finally disappeared from history. One of them was a relatively minor disturbance in Bithynia on the north coast of Turkey, but the story is worth telling.

When the king of Bithynia died he left his entire kingdom to the Roman Senate. The Bithynians had been loyal to Rome during the first revolt of Mithridates and they enjoyed tax immunity. The gift of the

Silver tetradrachma bearing the portrait of Mithridates, Rome's most formidable tax rebel. He challenged Roman colonial taxation in Greece and Asia, and his revolts came close to overthrowing Roman rule in the eastern Mediterranean region. He obtained strong support for his struggle against Rome by offering cities that joined his cause a tax moratorium of five years.

kingdom to Rome seemed like an appropriate way to show appreciation to the ever-so-generous Senate.

The king did not realize the legal implications of this provision in his will. As a new Roman territory, Bithynia would no longer have tax immunity. It now had the same legal status as land that had been for-feited to Rome as punishment for rebellion. Bithynia was open for new taxation or rental in whatever form the Senate desired. This blunder by the king's lawyer was probably history's worst example of estate planning.

Roman publicani soon arrived to extract revenue with their usual arrogance. The surprised population revolted and called upon Mithridates for help. Roman legions eventually arrived to quell the rebellion, and

Mithridates took to flight. We have no record of any reprisal taken against the rebellious kingdom, nor do we have any indication of what happened to the inept lawyer who drew the will.

Other cities lost their tax immunity to the publicani. When the Roman Assembly granted the publicani the exclusive right to collect 10 percent harvest tax in the east, this decree, in effect, annulled a number of senatorial charters and treaties which granted tax immunity. Protests from these cities were ignored. From that time forth the publicani were constantly pressuring the Senate to renege on its treaty commitments. Cicero condemned the practice with these words to the Senate: "What a disgrace to our government! On this occasion even a pirate could have improved upon the Senate's good faith."

The senators answered Cicero by arguing that they needed the money and were justified by expediency. To this Cicero replied: "But will people forever incorrigibly see advantage in what is wrong? Governments cannot do without the splendid reputation and good will of their allies. So how can unpopularity and infamy possibly be to their advantage?"[8]

Cicero's condemnation of the Roman Senate for overriding its tax treaties would apply today to the United States, which does the same thing and for the same reasons. U.S. Senator Paul Sarbanes (Maryland), like the Roman senators, excuses this for even more outrageous reasons. He reasoned that since other countries are on notice the word of the U.S. government in its tax treaties is no good, how can they complain?[9] The remarkable similarity between superpower Rome breaching its tax treaty commitments and the United States doing the same thing, for similar reasons, two thousand years later, should fascinate those who are intrigued with unusual examples of history repeating itself.

The tax immunity granted by the Senate in its treaties did not mean complete freedom from Roman taxation. An emergency 2 percent wealth tax could be assessed to support a Roman army passing through any tax-free locality.

The publicani started in decline when Sulla began using special agents to collect his punitive taxes in Greece. Thereafter, hostility developed against them in all the provinces. An Asian governor named Gabinius refused to sit in judgment on any lawsuits involving publicani. A tax agent or collector without police power is not much more than a solicitor for donations. Gabinius would not even tolerate publicani presence in any city he visited. After the example of Sulla he put the government back into the tax business, but not with special or regular tax agents.

The publicani had become lazy and started to subcontract tax collection to the cities to be taxed. The city would then collect the tax and pay it to the publicani who would then pay Rome and retain a large profit as middleman. It became apparent to Gabinius that the publicani were not necessary anymore.[10] In the past the publicani engaged in the difficult job of actually assessing and collecting taxes—that is what they were being paid to do. Now, by using subcontracts they were becoming useless middlemen, leeching on the tax process by reducing the government's revenue and increasing taxpayers' burdens. In short, the publicani were becoming obsolete. Gabinius sensed this and started to cancel publicani subcontracts with the cities. Immediately thereafter he would negotiate the same contract with the city, eliminating the publicani and benefiting everyone else.

The Roman Republic died in the course of the great civil wars that erupted after Sulla. These wars were fought between rivals for a strong man to succeed Sulla. The Republic had no place for an emperor, but the political crises of that era created a vacuum of power which fostered dictatorship. Constitutional checks are ineffective against tyrants when people want or believe they need a dictator. Roman generals were returning home with the blind loyalty of their soldiers. They were Sulla's soldiers or Caesar's soldiers first, and Roman soldiers second. The rich spoils of war they enjoyed came from their commander, not the Roman Senate.

These semi-private armies in an era of chaos made the establishment of a military dictator inevitable. Cicero summed up this sad state of affairs shortly before his brutal murder, after the death of Caesar:

> Rightly are we being punished. For if we had not allowed the crimes of many to go unpunished, this one man would never had dared to act in such an outrageous manner. A few people have inherited his estate but many scoundrels have inherited his ambitions. . . . And so in Rome only the walls of her houses remain standing . . . our Republic we have lost forever.[11]

Cicero's remarks were even more prophetic than he could have imagined. Strong men, kings, and generals would direct the course of civilization—not just through the Roman era, but for the next two thousand years. Democracies and republics would not play a dominant role in civilization until the nineteenth century A.D.

Two powerful generals followed Sulla—Pompey and Julius Caesar. As we noted, Pompey was sent to the east to defeat the pirates who seized control after Rhodes declined. To finance his armies, Pompey instituted heavy taxation on the provinces in the east—a poll tax on all men and slaves, a household tax, and military requisitions for everything he needed. To aid in these exactions he established "special agents" after the example of Sulla. He seized publicani money as a "loan" even if the money was tribute for the Senate. When Pompey finished, Cicero described Greece in these words: "Cities which had been flourishing in the past now lay before my eyes in ruin." Cicero had a special reason to be bitter. His own funds on deposit with the publicani in Ephesus were seized by Pompey as a "loan."[12]

Julius Caesar replaced Pompey and adopted a new tax policy. He believed the road to provincial peace was modest taxation, not plunder. Vanquished cities were not to be crushed with taxation after the manner of Sulla and Pompey. Caesar purchased loyalty with reduced taxes and refunds. In Asia he remitted one-third of the taxes collected by the publicani the previous year. He learned from Gabinius and started to negotiate tax agreements with the cities. The Jews were jubilant over Caesar's new system. Said Josephus: "Caesar, consul, hath decreed, that the Jews shall possess Jerusalem, and may encompass that city with walls . . . and that the tribute they pay be not let to farm, nor that they pay always the same tribute."[13]

Caesar's system was flexible—the agreed amount of tax was subject to renegotiation if the harvest was poor. Because of this benevolent tax policy the Jews filled Caesar's military granaries at Sidon. For the first time in over 150 years Rome's relations with her rich eastern provinces were peaceful—but then came the Ides of March, 44 B.C.

The murder of Caesar darkened the tax story of the east once again. Brutus went from city to city seizing everything he could lay his hands on. Cities that resisted were sold into slavery. In Rhodes all the ships in the harbor were taken; everyone was ordered under penalty of death to surrender all personal silver, gold, and jewels. Special agents seized the wealth of Roman citizens and publicani residing in that region. This repetition of Sulla's harsh methods is an ancient example of Adam Smith's observation, "There is no art which one government sooner learns from another than that of draining money from the pockets of the people."[14]

Mark Anthony was even worse. After he defeated Brutus, he demanded a double tax from every city that supported Brutus, to which one cynic replied: "If you can take a tax twice in a year, you can give us summer twice and the harvest twice." The people of the east remember Anthony as "a reckless and hard-hearted robber,"[15] who stripped Greece of money, slaves, livestock, and grain. When the battle of Actium was over, the victorious Octavian went to Greece to establish his authority. He was so aghast at the pitiful state of the people that he gave them all of the grain he had on reserve for his military forces.

The grain Octavian gave to Greece was no doubt welcome and desperately needed, but the peace he brought to the world was his greatest gift of all, along with a reduction of taxes and the final elimination of the Roman publicani. But this was not without a price. All representative government passed away. Caesars would rule for the next fifteen hundred years. And for this tragedy, who and what was to blame? The tax system of the publicani.

10

Augustus: Master Tax Strategist

The splendid alter built to the "Augustus Peace" on the field of Mars was a symbol of the fact that peace had overcome war and was not the prominent feature of Augustus's rule.

—Rostovtzeff, *Roman Empire*

If we were to try to select the most outstanding Roman of all time, Caesar Augustus would be a likely choice. In an age dominated by war, he chose peace, and he achieved the most lasting peace ever enjoyed by the human race. He also dismantled the five-hundred-year-old war-prone Republic and put a stop to further Roman imperialism. When divine titles and the crown of emperor were offered to him, he rejected this glorification and accepted the simple title of First Citizen. The political achievements of Augustus, as well as his lasting peace, were products of his astute management of taxation. Augustus may have been the most brilliant tax strategist of all time.

Augustus destroyed the power of the Roman Republic by redirecting the cash flow of the tax money. In the past it had gone to the Senate; in the future it would go to the First Citizen. It was believed until recently that taxes from the older senatorial provinces were under the control of the Senate, but recent scholarship indicates this was only a formality. The traditional revenue chests for the Senate were available to Augustus as if he were the owner.

Augustus did not change the format of Roman government. The Senate was still the sovereign ruler of the state, but Augustus was emperor in fact, if not in law, and he overpowered the Senate at every turn. He brought peace and order to a war-torn Republic. The military spirit of his legions, which forged the best fighting force in the world, became the spirit of the new Roman government—and like it or not, it worked. Perhaps the period of Pax Augustus (Peace of Augustus) is support for

Aristotle's observation that the best form of government is the absolute monarchy, where the monarch is wise and just.

The most important change in administration came with the rise of a tax bureau under the control of Augustus. Starting with Pompey and Caesar, the power of government shifted to the military because tax revenues shifted from the Senate to the generals. The riddle of why the Senate declined and how the Republic died is solved by the answer to the question of who controlled the tax money. The Senate's revenue wells dried up in the civil war. When the war ended, it was the First Citizen who had the money to run the state, that is, to provide bread and entertainment for the mobs in Rome, provide pensions for the army, make public improvements, and see to every other municipal need.

Until recently we did not know how Augustus cut off the cash flow to the Senate. In Republic times governors rendered an accounting to the Senate of the tribute they collected, and it was deposited in special money chests under the control of the Senate. Strong generals, however, accounted to no one but themselves. Pompey and Caesar collected tax moneys and used them as they saw fit. The main reason Caesar eliminated the publicani in the east was not to please a colonial people but rather to seize the Senate's money. Under the auction contract, the publicani were responsible to the Senate; Caesar was responsible to no one once the publicani were removed.

Egypt gives us another clue to what happened. When Augustus seized Egypt from Anthony and Cleopatra, the richest lands in the world were in his hands. This great country became his personal estate. Its grain from harvest taxes would feed Rome. Gold from Ptolemy's treasury was minted into a coinage, with the image of Augustus. The Senate was on the outside looking in.

Wealth from the older senatorial provinces was also under the control of Augustus. He did this by appointing a personal revenue representative to take charge of tribute and taxes. As soon as the publicani were eliminated he followed the practice of his father and negotiated tax agreements with the cities and provinces. Governors could be replaced at his will, and taxes were no longer under their control. Senatorial provinces, like senatorial money chests, became a matter of name only.

The publicani passed away with the Republic—not because of their bad behavior but because the government could negotiate its own contracts, called *pactiones*, with provincial cities for local collection of tribute. This was an ancient example of job elimination by new techniques. With respect to indirect taxes—customs, sales, rents, etc.—the central government replaced most of the publicani by appointing energetic businessmen, called *conductores*, to collect taxes on commerce. At first

Caesar Augustus, the first emperor of Rome, was probably the most brilliant tax strategist of all time.

they received a commission, but after a time they worked free like all patriotic, independently wealthy citizens in the public service.

In the Republic, provincial tax obligations were set out in a charter between the province and the Senate. The existing system was seldom changed; it was simply redirected to work for the Romans. Tax-farmers were injected into the system to look out for Roman interests. This produced a hodgepodge of taxation spread out over the empire. The publicani were about the only common denominator for the system.

To develop a more uniform system, Augustus decreed that the entire empire should be appraised for tax reform. A great census would be taken to register everybody and everything. This census is recorded in the New Testament:

> And it came to pass in those days, that there went out a decree from Caesar Augustus, that all the world should be taxed. . . . And all went to be taxed, everyone to his own city.
>
> And Joseph also went up from Galilee, out of the city of Nazareth, into Judea, unto the city of David, which is called Bethlehem: (because he was of the house and lineage of David). To be taxed with Mary his espoused wife, being great with child. (Luke 2:1–5)

The King James version uses the word "taxed" which means to be registered for tax. Joseph and Mary were simply being registered with their property for future tax assessments.

The registration ordered by Augustus did not mean that taxes were to be controlled by the central government. To the contrary, the census involved a decentralization of the tax system. Individual taxpayers throughout the empire would never again face Roman tax men. Tax collection was to be a local matter, administered by local people. The census let the Roman government know how much wealth and how many people were in the empire. With this information Rome could make a more equitable assessment against every city and leave collection methods for local administration. Previously, Roman publicani created a direct link from taxpayers to the central government. The new system of Augustus took the Roman government out of the process of assessing and collecting taxes on an individual level.

The primary innovation of the new system was an adaptation of the final publicani practice of subcontracting. The emperor's revenue representative would negotiate a contract, or pactiones, with each city using the census as the basis for negotiations. There was no resistance to this new system devoid of publicani. Says historian Rostovtzeff:

> The cities were glad to get rid of the exactions of the publicani. They had had their full measure of suffering in dealing with those sharks, and they

were therefore willing to help the state in collecting the taxes of their districts.[1]

The cities were free to tax in any manner they liked. We continue to hear of publicans and harvest taxes of a tenth or a fifth. Local governments could use local tax-farmers if they wanted to. Matthew, the apostle, was a local publican, or tax collector. He was apparently at his tax office, collecting customs, when Jesus called him (Matt. 9:9).

The new tax system promoted decentralization of all government. Carpetbaggers from Rome began to disappear. If there was a problem involving Rome and the local populace, it was most often handled by local city governments. This process of decentralization may have been the key to the success and long life of Pax Romana.

An inheritance tax was instituted by Augustus to provide retirement funds for the military. It was assessed at 5 percent on all inheritances

Caravaggio's *The Calling of St. Matthew* (1597). Christ gestures to Matthew, a simple local tax man, seated at a tax table with his companions counting money. A shaft of light calls Matthew for a new life, out of darkness (Matt. 9:9).

except for gifts to children and spouses. The tax was productive because many rich Romans left their estates to friends and adopted children. Modern inheritance tax laws are derived from the system of Augustus. The British and Dutch made reference to the inheritance tax of Augustus when they adopted their systems in the seventeenth century. Exemptions or reduced rates are common for gifts to children and spouses.

A sales tax in Rome supplemented the inheritance tax. The rate was 4 percent for slaves and 1 percent for everything else. When the Romans grumbled about these new taxes, Augustus threatened to re-establish the old citizens' war-tax. After Augustus died, the sales tax rate was cut in half. In A.D. 40 the sales tax was abolished altogether by Caligula with a flourish of trumpets. Sometime later it was revived, but we have no record of the time or the emperor who reimposed it.

Tax-farming by Roman Publicani Corporations was not completely abolished by Augustus and the early Roman emperors. Tacitus, a Roman historian who wrote around A.D. 100, gives an account of Roman senators who persuaded Nero in A.D. 58 to abandon his idea of abolishing all indirect taxes (customs) because of the "many companies" established during the Republic which were still farming these taxes, and that it was necessary to preserve them in order to "balance income and expenditures."[2] The Romans had budget problems just as we do. Unfortunately, we do not know anything about these publicani. They probably operated in the western regions, far removed from the civil wars and turmoil in the East, which brought an end to the publicani in the eastern Mediterranean.

As an alternate means of tax reform, Nero made a number of improvements, which brought cheers from the senators:

1. Tax regulations, heretofore confidential, would be made public.
2. There would be a one year statute of limitations on the recovery of tax defaults.
3. All Praetors in Rome and Governors in the provinces must give "special priority" to cases against tax collectors.
4. Merchant ships would be exempt from property tax assessments.

There were also "other excellent provisions," says Tacitus, "but they were soon evaded."[3] We have no information on what these provisions were, or how or why they were evaded. The Romans had a long history over many centuries of trying to reform their tax system, which so frequently misfunctioned. One recurring policy was to crack down on errant tax men.[4]

Unlike our practice, in Rome's better days taxpayers' interests were of prime consideration. Sometime around A.D. 35 the Emperor Tiberius

Three Roman tax collectors and four taxpayers. On the table: a tax book, a basket of coins, and a pile of coins. One taxpayer looks away; the second receives a coin, perhaps change from his tax payment; the third with finger raised to lips shares thoughts with the fourth, perhaps about the pile of gold.

received a request to increase provincial taxes. We do not know what increase was requested, but Tiberius replied that the governors should "have my sheep shorn, not skinned alive."[5]

The Roman press joined in the attack on oppressive tax men. Here are the words of one Roman writer of that day:

> The rulers of the cities must stop breaking the necks of the cities by continuous and heavy taxes. . . . They choose on purpose the most merciless of tax collectors, full of inhumanity. . . .
>
> Recently a man was appointed tax collector among us. When some of those who were supposed to owe taxes fled . . . he carried off by force their wives and children, their parents and the rest of their families. The tax collector did not release them until he had tortured their bodies with racks and wheels and had killed them with newly-invented devices of death.[6]

The above incident may not have been as brutal as reported, but the important point is that the press, the emperor, and the people were no longer willing to tolerate abusive revenue agents. Assaults on revenue agents were so frequent that soldiers had to accompany most tax men— not to assist in collection but to protect them from assaults by taxpayers. In the British Museum there is a fragment of a papyrus (Papyrus No. 10, 171) which indicates that misbehaving tax men were punished by crucifixion on the very spot of their misdeed.

Finally, informers were hired to spy on corrupt revenue officials. The penalty for excessive tax collection was fixed at ten times the excessive tax, 40 percent of which went to the informer. These harsh measures against corrupt tax officials were important in bringing peace to the provinces and sustaining Pax Romana. Taxpayer contentment was unquestionably more important than revenue collection, unlike modern practice.

Tax moratoriums were frequently used if harvests were poor. The emperor would declare a moratorium and defer tax collection for a few years. Here is an edict of Hadrian (A.D. 135) to Egypt (Oslo Papyrus No. 786):

> Since I have been informed that this year again, just as it did last year, the Nile has risen rather insufficiently and incompletely. . . . I have deemed it necessary to bestow a benefaction on the farmers. . . . May good fortune attend! Know that the money tax due for this year shall be distributed . . . over five annual payments. . . . The mode of paying semi-annually is allowed those wishing to do so.[7]

Taxes were also reduced for a village if any farmer fled. A notice of flight was filed by the villagers:

To . . . village secretaries . . . my brother . . . fled abroad possessed of no
other taxable assets. I therefore submit this memorandum requesting that
he be entered on the list of fugitive paupers from the current sixth year of
Tiberius.[8]

The frequency of tax moratoriums and equitable adjustments were
also important safety valves for maintaining taxpayer contentment. The
revolts under Mithridates had taught the Romans that angry taxpayers
were a greater threat to peace than the barbarians of the north. Never in
history had a government made such a conscientious effort to make its
tax system palatable to taxpayers. Pax Romana was to a large extent a
tax-pax-Romana.

In the second century A.D. the emperors were flooded with petitions
for a complete remission of tax delinquencies. When it became clear
that these taxes could not be paid, Hadrian, in A.D. 118, and Marcus
Aurelius, fifty years later, announced from the Forum with the blare of
trumpets that taxes would be cancelled. To make the decree irrevocable,
Praetorian guards burned the tax records in the presence of the emperor.

Historians consider the two hundred years from Augustus to Marcus
Aurelius (30 B.C. to A.D. 180) as the high-water mark of Roman greatness. Gibbon said it was the greatest period of peace and prosperity ever
enjoyed by the human race. Roman cities spread across Europe for a
thousand miles. They were nice places to live in with well-paved streets,
large fresh-water aqueducts, market places, and little crime. Sports
arenas, temples, gymnasiums, and amphitheaters were the pride of most
cities. Pirates and robbers disappeared. Small wonder that historians of
the past have praised the grandeur of life during this time.

Pax Romana was not always peaceful. Ugly and oppressive Roman
administrators caused revolts that required strong military action. In
A.D. 60 in the British Isles, Boadicea, queen of East Anglia, led a revolt
that slaughtered every Roman soldier for a hundred miles. London was
seized and 80,000 people were killed. Roman historians describe Boadicea as possessing "greater intelligence than often belongs to women."
She assembled an army of 230,000:

> She was very tall, in appearance most terrifying . . . around her neck was
> a large golden necklace . . . she now grasped a spear . . . and spoke as
> follows.
>
> "For what treatment is there of the most shameful or grievous sort that
> we have not suffered since these men made their appearance in Britain?
> Have we not been robbed entirely of most of our greatest possessions,
> while for those that remain we pay taxes?
>
> "Besides pasturing and tilling for them all our other possessions, do we
> not pay yearly tribute for our very bodies? How much better it would be

The emperor Hadrian (or Trajian) announcing the cancellation of all tax debts, at the Forum in Rome.

to have been sold to masters once and for all than possessing empty titles of freedom, to have to ransom ourselves every year? How much better to have been slain than to go about with a tax on our heads!"[9]

Even the Roman historians, who placed little value on the female psyche, had to admit, that "for a woman" she was very intelligent. Unfortunately, her male generals did not measure up to the Romans, and they were defeated by a small but well led Roman force, resulting in Boadicea's death.

After Boadicea's defeat a special commission was set up by Nero to make a study. The commission blamed corrupt Roman administrators. New leaders were appointed by Nero. Peace followed and Britain settled down to a long period of quiet Roman rule.

Ten years later, in A.D. 70, a revolt in France was also triggered by corrupt Roman administration. After the revolt was crushed, the Roman general Cerialis (who also defeated Boadicea) spoke to the French people:

> The tranquility of peoples cannot be had without armies, nor armies without pay, nor pay without taxes. . . . There will be vices as long as there are men. But they are not everlasting, and they are compensated by the interval of better times . . . let the lessons of fortune in both its forms (good and bad) warn you not to prefer rebelliousness and ruin to obedience and security.[10]

As with the revolt in Britain there were no reprisals. Roman political wisdom once again dictated that rebellious taxpayers should be pacified with a policy of conciliation and reason.

The reader should note the contrast between the exhortation of Boadicea to her people to resist Roman taxation, and the speech of General Cerialis to put up with bad taxes and leaders. These two speeches represent the argument for rebellion and the argument for peaceful tolerance of bad tax laws. Throughout civilization's five thousand years of written history, this has been the dilemma for all oppressed with bad taxes, and there is no easy answer for the taxpayer.

The great era of Roman peace passed away with the death of Marcus Aurelius in A.D. 180. By the time Marcus came to power the decay of the empire was irreversible. His *Meditations* are full of gloom as he struggled to save Rome. If there ever was a philosopher-king with the qualifications set down by Plato it was poor Marcus. If unselfish service is the key to good government, then Rome should have had no troubles under Marcus. When his treasury was bare, rather than increase taxes he spent a number of months auctioning off his vast personal fortune to pay for the cost of running the government. Marcus saw taxation as the

Boadicea, famed for leading her English troops into battle in her chariot, challenged them to overthrow the Roman rule in England and free the land from Roman taxation.

root of Rome's troubles. He sent advisors to the provinces to persuade local government to spend less money and collect fewer taxes. When he made peace with the tribes along the Danube he did the absolutely unprecedented: he granted them immunity from Roman taxation. Marcus accepted the barbarians' plea that taxes were an affront to their liberty.

Marcus was obsessed with the idea that taxes were too high. When his soldiers demanded extra pay after a great victory, he made this famous reply: "Anything that you receive over and above your regular pay must be exacted from the blood of your parents and relatives."[11]

All over the empire Marcus was confronted with demands for lower taxes. When minor relief was granted to some cities, one Roman senator spoke these passionate words at the Senate:

> I move, therefore, that our special thanks be expressed to the two emperors, who by salutary remedies, disregarding the interest of the fiscus, have restored the shattered state of the cities and the fortunes of the leading men, which tremble on the verge of utter ruin.[12]

Taxpayers and soldiers were at the brink of rebellion, and Marcus and his empty treasury were caught in the middle. His cancellation of tax debts helped cool angry taxpayers, but it only intensified the revenue deficiencies of the government. The great period of Pax Romana came to an end because the finances of the empire were in a shambles and no amount of benevolence could correct the economic defects in the revenue.

Perhaps the most tragic error of all was Marcus's selection of a successor. Throughout the period of Pax Romana the emperor chose a successor from the most capable men in the empire. The Roman empire was not a monarchy until Marcus. He appointed his son Commodus as his successor. The son had none of the great qualities of his father, confirming the Japanese proverb, "Great men have no seed." Great leadership may have saved Rome, but greatness was one quality Commodus did not have. After he was murdered by one of his closest advisors, a pattern of cruelty, murder, and incompetence enveloped the imperial throne as Rome fell under military anarchy for the next century.

11

Diocletian's New Order

The story of its ruin is simple and obvious; and instead of enquiring why the Roman Empire was destroyed, we should rather be surprised that it had subsisted for so long.
—Gibbon, *Decline and Fall of the Roman Empire*

If we were living in the third century A.D. we would probably have lamented the terrible decline and impending fall of the Roman Empire. The two hundred wondrous years of Pax Romana had evolved into chaos. One military coup after another befell the imperial throne. The average life of each emperor was about three years, or until a new military strong man offered more money to the soldiers. This merry-go-round of emperors was like an auction sale with the soldiers selling their loyalty to the highest bidder. The emperor Septimius Severas (A.D. 193–211) summarized the situation in his dying words to his sons: "Live in harmony, enrich the soldiers and scorn all others."[1]

The survival of the Roman Empire was probably because of the strength of her cities. The intensive decentralization under Augustus shifted the strength of the Empire to the cities. When the central government was in chaos the welfare of the people in most of the Empire was not in jeopardy.

As might be expected, the tax system of Augustus broke down. The tax moratoriums, burning of tax records, and the auctioning of the emperor's personal wealth all attest to the failures of the system. Even so, the real collapse came in the third century when the government in Rome accelerated its policy of devaluing the currency to the point where the Roman denarius became practically worthless. By the time of Septimius (A.D. 210) the silver content of a previously pure denarius was 50 percent; sixty years later the silver content was 5 percent. Naturally, prices soared. A bushel of wheat which cost ten denarii in A.D.

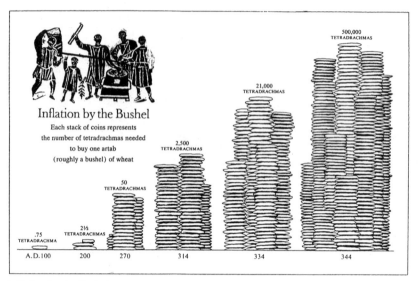

Inflation by the Bushel

Each stack of coins represents
the number of tetradrachmas needed
to buy one artab
(roughly a bushel) of wheat

Inflation by the Bushel.

200, cost two hundred denarii seventy years later. In A.D. 344, a bushel
cost two million denarii.[2]

The tax system of Augustus was based on a stable currency. Provincial taxes were payable in denarii which kept depreciating. New appraisals could not keep up with inflation. In order to survive, the government fell back on four somewhat obscure revenue devices: the gold
crown, the liturgy, the inheritance tax, and military requisitions.

1. Gold crown or *aurum coronarium*. In the days of the Republic the
   provinces adorned victorious Roman generals with gifts of gold
   crowns. Caesar on one occasion received 2,992 such crowns
   weighing 22,414 pounds. The treasure was immediately melted
   down and minted into gold coin with Caesar's image. From this
   the gold "crown" was born which has survived to this day in the
   coins of the monarchies of the world.

   Gold crowns became an enforced obligation when the emperor
   needed them: the birth of a son, a military victory, or any other
   real or imaginary event was enough to trigger this tax. Finally, it
   became an annual affair fixed at 1,600 pounds, allocated among
   the cities of the empire.
2. The liturgy came to life as another enforced obligation. The ten
   leading men in every city, called *decurions*, were drafted into a city
   council which was responsible for the needs of the government.

3. The inheritance tax was made universal. The emperor Caracalla in A.D. 212 granted Roman citizenship to everyone so they would come under Augustus's inheritance tax law. Rates were increased to 10 percent, and there were no exemptions.
4. Military requisitions, called indiction, provided the legions with their basic needs. This is the most arbitrary form of taxation because it falls on the unlucky victim who happens to be nearby and has what the army needs.

These four inflation-proof devices permitted the government of Rome to survive. Rome's runaway inflation was similar to what happened in Germany in the 1920s. The denarius, like the mark, was rendered worthless by a government that used printing press money to meet its demands. The Germans used paper; the Romans used copper. As a solution the Roman government ignored the denarius. Taxes would be paid in things a government needed. After all, this was the way taxes were before money was invented.

Businessmen in the private economy had abandoned the denarius long before the government had done so. The denarius was just one of many ways to pay for something. When fiscal systems collapse, men instinctively turn to these primitive but trustworthy mediums of exchange. In 1980, when inflation was raging, investors turned to gold and silver as anxiety grew within our society over the prospects of worthless money.

As the denarius faded away these new systems of revenue set the stage for dramatic changes within the Empire. A leader was needed to put these new revenue devices in a permanent, workable form. That leader was Diocletian. Like Augustus he reorganized the Empire and restored order to Rome—but, unlike Augustus, he centralized and nationalized the state to achieve his ends. Augustus achieved peace by dismantling the army, decentralizing the state, and reducing taxes. Augustus was a patron of laissez-faire. Diocletian moved in the opposite direction—centralizing the state, accelerating tax rates, and nationalizing everybody and everything. Roman citizenship after eight hundred years was to finally lose its liberties—not to an alien power, but to the very government that was supposed to protect it.

On the eve of Diocletian's reorganization, the empire was in a state of complete disorder. The government was collapsing from a worthless currency. The soldiers refused to accept the debased coinage as pay, and tax collectors refused to accept it as payment. Law and order broke down, the seas were infested with pirates and the roads with robbers. There were terrible peasant revolts, and farmers were driven from their homes by "voracious tax collectors" who refused to accept the emperor's money as legal tender. The government, whether the army or civil servants, fell back on forced requisitions and forced labor. They had no other choices. In A.D. 245, an Arab leader named Philip petitioned the emperor for help, complaining of these illegal seizures:

> We are suffering . . . illegal exactions beyond all reason. . . . Soldiers, powerful men from the cities, and our own officials leave the highways, descend on us, take us from our work, seize our plough and oxen and illegally extort what is not due to them. . . . our resources are exhausted and the lands deserted.[3]

Historians often condemn Diocletian for having doused the torch of liberty the Greeks and Romans passed on to civilization. But this indictment may not be altogether fair if the salvation of the Roman Empire is of importance. Martial law is not only an accepted tool to govern an unruly state, it is the only tool known. Diocletian was simply using the best known method to combat disorder: compulsion.

Diocletian tackled inflation with military commands. He ordered prices to remain stable under penalty of death. To Diocletian's surprise prices kept rising. When price controls failed to work he fell back on the indiction in a modified form. The government would use an equitable system of requisitions to replace the denarii. Money would no longer be accepted as legal tender for tax obligations. Wheat, barley, meat, wine, oil, and clothing would be the commodities in which taxes would be paid. In short, why not have taxpayers make their payments in what the government needed? Why use money at all? Said Rostovtzeff:

> It was much simpler to leave aside the work of centuries [Rome's tax system] and to introduce the most rough and primitive system of assessment which had ever existed. Every soldier could understand it, although any fool could see that in this case what was simple was not fair and just.[4]

To set up this system of taxation in kind, Diocletian started where Augustus started: he made a census. When the censors came around—as they did every few years—the people knew taxes were in the making. In the past, lands were re-evaluated and the tax rolls brought up to date. This time things were different. In the first place, all of Italy would be required to take part. There would be no more tax immunity. Romans living in Italy were to lose the freedom from direct taxation which they had enjoyed for almost five hundred years.

After the census was taken the Roman government started the long and tedious job of valuing farming operations, based on what the farm *should* produce rather than what it did produce. Old monetary terms like the denarius were replaced with units of production called an *iugum*. In Syria a schedule of land classification has been found. An iugum was 12.5 acres of prime land, 25 acres of second class land, and 37.5 acres of third class land. Can you imagine the disputes that arose over whether or not a farmer's land was first, second, or third class? In time, all kinds of variables and adjustments were developed. What started out as a fairly simple tax idea turned into a Frankensteinian monster when applied to reality. But this system should not be judged too harshly, at least not by us. Compared to our income tax laws, Diocletian's system was simple.

Diocletian's system gave birth to a monstrous bureaucracy. The statement appears in many ancient texts that the number of tax agents was greater than the number of taxpayers:

> The number of those receiving pay was so much larger than the number of those paying taxes and that because of the enormous size of the assessments. The resources of the tenant farmers were exhausted, fields were abandoned, and cultivated areas transformed into a wilderness.[5]

The fourth-century writer Lactantius goes on to say that the courts were swamped with tax litigation:

> Very few civil cases came before all of these, but only condemnations and frequent confiscations, and there were not merely frequent but perpetual exactions of innumerable things, and in the process of taxation, intolerable wrongs.[6]

Farmers started to abandon their farms if they did not like their classification. The new system was endangered by the fundamental right of all Roman citizens to move about the Empire as they pleased. Freedom of movement had been a right of citizenship since Rome was founded on the Tiber a thousand years before. This freedom distinguished Roman farmers from the Royal peasants of Egypt. Unfortunately, Diocletian's new tax system could not work unless everybody stayed where they were. Land taxes could not be paid unless farmers stayed on their lands. So to make the system work, the thousand-year tradition of freedom of movement of Roman citizens was destroyed. All farmers, their children, and their children's children were bound to the land forever. Totalitarianism was the final order of Diocletian's new order for Roman farmers. This is not unusual. In time the reader will discover that civil liberties are adjusted to a tax system; the tax system is not adjusted to civil liberties.

Since it was not possible to store surplus for future years, the system produced history's first governmental budget. Foodstuffs would spoil so the tax rate was limited to the current needs of the government. Each year the central government would order all Roman administrators to submit to Rome their needs for the coming year. The total estimate would then be divided up, pro rata, among the tax units of the Empire. On September first the government would announce its tax rate for each iugum. This was harvest time. No farmer knew in advance what his tax would be. Enforcement became a matter of life and death for the state. Taxes must be collected or soldiers would rebel and plunder the countryside. Tax delinquencies could not be tolerated. It was not just taxpayers who were under compulsion, but tax collectors as well. The primary tool of enforcement for the whole system, taxpayer and tax collector, was the death penalty.

Here are the words of an Egyptian edict introducing the tax:

> Diocletian and Maximian . . . having learned that the levies of the public taxes are being made haphazardly, so that some persons are let off lightly and others overburdened, have decided to root out this most evil and baneful practice for the benefit of their provincials and to issue a deliverance-bringing rule to which the taxes shall conform. Accordingly, the levy on each iugum according to the classification of the land. . . . The magistrates of every city have been ordered to send out to every village and every locality a copy of the divine edict together with the schedule. And also the collectors of each revenue are reminded to uphold the tax law with all their might; for if any should be revealed to have transgressed, he will risk the death penalty.[7]

The most fascinating aspect of the above edict is the preamble, which sounds as if Diocletian is about to introduce a reform law to remedy imperfections and lighten tax burdens. Modern governments do the same thing. New tax laws which increase taxation through "reforms" usually come with proclamations of glad tidings for taxpayers.

Constantine, who followed Diocletian, brought Christianity to the Roman world. He may also have given the world the first income tax on commerce. The production taxes of the ancient world bypassed the merchant since he did not produce anything. In A.D. 306, Constantine instituted a general tax on commerce and industry, a direct tax which few escaped. At Antioch a cobbler whose only asset was a knife is listed among the taxpayers. The tax was paid every four years, apparently based on the value of the commercial operations. Gibbon said the tax was "extremely rigorous in the mode of collecting," and often taxpayers were "compelled by the impending scourge to embrace the most abhorred and unnatural methods of procuring the sum." Which means that many taxpayers had to sell their children into slavery in order to raise the necessary funds. Why? Because the tax was payable in gold and silver, the regular commercial tender for slave sales. Gibbon's analysis of this tax, in 1788, is peculiarly applicable to modern income taxes on commerce:

> The secret wealth of commerce and the precarious profits of art and labor are susceptible only of a discretionary value, which is seldom disadvantageous to the interest of the treasury . . . the payment of the imposition, which in the case of a land tax may be obtained by seizure of property, can rarely be extorted by any other means than those of corporal punishments.[8]

What Gibbon is trying to point out is that land taxes are only enforced with liens, whereas income taxes require the use of corporal punishments in addition to liens. No one is punished by fines or imprisonment for refusal to pay land taxes, while our income tax system depends on the threat of imprisonment as a primary means of enforcement.

Roman tax men may have used racks and scourges to collect this tax. Torture of some kind would have been necessary to drive parents to sell their children into slavery. Constantine is reputed to have prohibited the use of torture for tax collection, which suggests that the practice was not uncommon. In place of torture Constantine proposed the use of a "spacious and airy prison as a place of confinement," thus instituting the first record of imprisonment for tax evasion. This "free and open confinement" was really a kind of house arrest. Seventeen years later, even imprisonment for tax evasion was abolished. In a revised decree repealing imprisonment, Constantine said, "It shall suffice for a delinquent tax-payer to be summoned to the necessity of payment by the seizure of pledges" (A.D. 353).[9] It is not surprising that imprisonment was first used to enforce a kind of income tax on commerce. Actually, imprisonment was humane for the times. Diocletian used capital punishment routinely. Many Christian martyrs executed during this period may have died for tax rather than religious crimes. The decrees punishing the Christians contain words such as, "we ordain that their property be confiscated to our treasury," or "see that their property is attached to our treasury and that they are committed to the mines of Phaeno."[10]

The estates of senators were tax-immune, but in order to be a senator a special tax, called a *gleba*, had to be paid annually. It was payable in units of eight, four, and two, probably in pounds of gold but we are not sure. A senator who could not pay the minimum tax was required to resign from the Senate.

Finally, there was a tax to avoid the draft of animals or men into the legions. Since a draft is basically a tax of labor, the tax to avoid the draft was a tax for tax immunity. Gold was the required means of payment; consequently, only the rich could afford legalized draft avoidance.

Constantine added to the gold supply when he became a Christian. He seized the gold in all the pagan temples in the Empire and melted it down for a coinage and thereby, along with the taxes in gold coin, put Rome on a gold standard. Gold has remained the basis for all sound revenue systems since that time, despite arguments by modern governments to the contrary. Compare the value of the Swiss franc with other currencies since Nixon took the dollar off the gold standard. All Swiss francs are backed by a fixed percentage of gold, a practice ridiculed by the go-go fiscal whiz-kids in London, Ottawa, and Washington, but in the minds of the investors and bankers of the world, gold has always been the basis of sound currencies.

The bondage of farmers was finally extended to workers and artisans. The cobbler and all his descendants were to make shoes forever. His sons were to marry cobbler's daughters. The final product was the complete enslavement of Rome's economic classes—they became castes to make the tax system work:

> The emperors of the fourth century, and above all Diocletian, grew up in the atmosphere of violence and compulsion. . . . They took their duties seriously, and they were animated by the sincerest love of their country. Their aim was to save the Roman Empire, and they achieved it. . . . They never asked whether it was worth while to save the Roman Empire in order to make a vast prison for scores of millions of men.[11]

12

Rome Falls: Was It Tax Evasion?

*A dangerous vicious circle comes into action. Increased state expenditure
on the army, the bureaucracy, in welfare state commitments brought about
a continual unbearable tax pressure. Tax pressures grew heavier and the
tendency to evasion—illegal or legitimate—on the part of high officials
and large landowners, was increased . . . and was the end of the state.*

—Aurelio Bernardi, *The Economic Problems of the
Roman Empire at the Time of Its Decline*

In the early months of 1942 headlines in American papers read:
"Wake Island Falls," "Corregidor Falls," "Singapore Falls." These
headlines stunned the Allied world during those dark days of World War
II. Had London fallen, too, it would have had the same shattering effect
achieved in A.D. 476, when a barbarian king named Odovacar seized
Rome.

It was not the first time the city had been sacked by raiders. Odovacar's occupation of Rome was significant because of its political implications. For hundreds of years the focal point of Western civilization
has been centered in Rome, the Eternal City. After A.D. 476 Rome would
cease to be all that important. New stars were rising.

The much-touted Fall of Rome has been dramatized by writers for
centuries. It has been said that each new generation inquires into the
causes that led to the collapse of Roman power. We ponder the death of
Rome as some great calamity which was not only shocking but ominous
for mankind.

Roman civilization did not end with the Fall of the Roman Empire.
When the city of Rome declined as a unifying and dominating political
force, the great civilization of these people made a new departure. Even
today, Roman civilization is very much alive. We still think and act like
Romans in the way we govern ourselves, make war, and collect taxes.

119

It is absurd to suggest that Rome is gone, like Egypt. Only the political power of the city is gone; all the rest merely underwent a metamorphosis. Caesars have roamed the earth for the last fifteen hundred years. There has hardly been a moment in history when we have not been without at least one of them.

It has been suggested that Rome fell because of depopulation caused by disease, wars, soil exhaustion, over-taxation, or even sin. The list of causes bringing about the decay of the Roman Empire is a long one, including such things as too much wealth, class warfare, race suicide— the adulteration of the Roman race by inferior races—social leveling, poor generals, and the influx of barbarians. You can pick whatever cause you like and point to that as the cause of the empire's collapse. In the fifth century A.D. the empire had undergone many changes from the early days. There was a bundle of causes, and no single factor can be pointed out as the sine qua non of Rome's fall.

In the eighteenth century the discoveries of Newton and other early scientists made an impact upon the study of history. It was believed that the causes controlling the motion of the planets had counterparts in the historical process. The French philosopher Montesquieu, whose political ideas influenced the founding fathers of America, expressed the thinking of that day in these words:

> There are general causes, moral and physical, at work in every monarchy, which elevate and maintain it or work its downfall; all accidents are the result of causes; and if the chance of a battle—that is, a special cause—has ruined a state, there was always a general cause at work which made that state ready to perish by a single battle.[1]

Montesquieu had the Roman Empire in mind when he made this observation. The deeper social and economic causes of the Fall of Rome will always be subject to debate. The immediate causes, on the other hand, are not obscure.

The English historian Edward Gibbon took up the challenge of that day when he wrote his monumental *Decline and Fall of the Roman Empire*, a book that is still in print. Today, scholars and historians shy away from what they call "Gibbon's problem," as if it no longer concerns us. Historians are supposed to stick to factual matters and avoid such ivory tower pursuits. Historians who do not are considered radical and, their scholarship is sometimes branded as specious.

To the list of "causes" of the demise of Rome, one more subject must be added: tax evasion. The immediate cause of the Fall of Rome to the Vandals was rampant and uncontrolled tax evasion within the Roman state. If the Roman government at that time had had sufficient revenues to maintain an adequate military force, the marauding band of barbarians would not have been able to enter the Italian peninsula, let alone sack Rome. The city of Rome fell because it could not defend itself against a third-class military force. There was sufficient wealth in the social order to have raised and sustained a strong military force, but such a force did not exist—because the tax evaders had all the money.

The problem began with Diocletian and his great social and economic reforms. These reforms produced a greatly enlarged military and civil bureaucracy for Rome. In the century that followed, Rome flourished. With a military force of over half a million men, there was little chance for the success of an Odovacar, or anyone else, for that matter. Rome was unquestionably invincible and capable of defending itself against any invader. Diocletian's reforms had made Rome strong. The army's strength had doubled and doubled again, but so had the revenue demands of the state. As tax demands increased to support the monstrous bureaucracy, the natural instinct in men to avoid heavy taxation moved the economy of Rome into the direction of tax evasion.

Throughout most of the fourth century the bondage of Diocletian's tax system turned tax collectors into slave masters. Emperor Constantine's chief tutor describes how tax assessors summoned peasants to the town square and applied torture and made children give evidence against their parents, wives against their husbands, and servants against their masters; they extorted by blows exaggerated tax returns which they then made even higher by placing children and old men on the tax rolls of small farmers.[2]

Besides his own tax burdens, the small independent farmer lived in fear of having his neighbor's taxes passed on to him because of collective tax responsibility. If farmlands were abandoned, tax men transferred those lands to adjacent farmers along with the tax bill that went with them. For the small farmer, private ownership became intolerable. To obtain relief, small farmers found they could transfer their lands to the nearest military chief or large landowner and rid themselves of tax obligations. The peasant farmer was better off. Tied to his land, he would still live in the same house, farm the same land, use the same animals. Only the tax picture had changed. The tax man would now have to deal with his master, who had the wherewithal to handle any Roman tax man.

To check the flight of small landowners, the Roman government passed laws prohibiting the merger of small farms into larger estates. But big landowners had no trouble avoiding this law by bribes and an assortment of legal tricks. If nothing else, big landowners could purchase small farms at forced tax sales, or simply offer to pay any delinquent taxes to the government if a merger were legitimized.

Large landowners evaded their taxes through a variety of legal and illegal devices. Bribery was used to obtain low assessments. Most important were tax amnesties. Shortly before the Fall, tax amnesties were granted for the years A.D. 401, 411, 434, 445, 450, and 458—which would indicate that the Roman fiscus was not collecting much tax. These amnesties were highlighted by a public burning such as, "We command that the documents of superfluous tax assessments be burned," or "In order that the very memory of delinquent taxes may perish from the earth."[3] Amnesties usually covered accumulated delinquencies. Big landowners would simply stall the tax collector and use their influence to lobby another amnesty through the Senate. At the same time the *gleba*, or tax on senators, was abolished along with sales taxes and inheritance taxes. Lobbyists for tax avoidance were hard at work tearing down the revenue system.

We first came upon the *decurions* in the early days of the Empire when the ten richest men in every city were appointed to a city council, a *curia*, to look after Rome's revenue system. Later this group became a kind of municipal senate, expanding to the richest one hundred men in every city. Besides tax collection they were responsible for the military draft, government mail, grain transportation, and any other needs.

Artist's conception of the burning of tax records at the Forum. Rome's final demise was partly caused by the evading of tax obligations by the rich and powerful, who were able to have the government cancel their debts, followed by a burning of their records, at the Forum.

The curia, along with the small farmers, were the backbone of the Roman state.

Like the small farmer, the revenue burdens of the curia became intolerable, and they also took to flight. Rich decurions could buy a seat in the Senate and enjoy perfect tax immunity for all time. The less affluent had a more difficult task. To avoid taxes, some of them became officers in the legions, others became clergymen or joined the Roman civil service. Many probably joined the ranks of the peasant farmers.

The government tried to check the flight of the decurions by a series of laws ordering them back to the city councils from whence they came. There was a twenty-year statute of limitations in this new law. A decurion who had taken flight could remain in his new post only if he had been there for at least twenty years.

As might be expected the great race to evade taxes brought an end to the liturgy. The rich no longer shared their wealth with the community. The process of redistribution of wealth reversed itself. Furthermore, the race and struggle for tax evasion produced a class of corrupt senators whose wealth was based on their ability to abuse the tax system and corrupt public officials. This was not the wealth of energetic and creative entrepreneurs who were skilled in commerce and agriculture, but rather the wealth of men skilled in bribery, fraud, and political manipulations.

Without the burdens of taxation or public charity, these big landowners built enormous villas that were autonomous, lavish, and fortified, and a prison house for thousands of farmers who had become serfs. These tax evaders were as corrupt and mean as the Roman state they were tearing down. The ugly Rome of Diocletian split into a myriad of little Romes, each with its own Caesar, legions, and slaves. Rome was like a mother cancer cell that passed its vicious propensities on to its children. Even the term vicious may be an understatement. Salvian, the bishop of Marseilles at the time of Rome's fall, describes the decadence, cruelty, and evil the tax system had created in a once humane society that loved liberty. Even assuming some exaggeration, Salvian's picture of Rome on the eve of the Fall is of a society lacking all sense of civilized decency. Any individual with any degree of humanity fled to the barbarians.[4] In time the Roman aristocrat with his powerful villa became the medieval lord with his manor. The medieval world was only a step away.

A number of able emperors tried to correct abuses within the revenue system to stem the flight of taxpayers. Informers were outlawed. Oppressive tax agents were to be burned alive in public. Governors were to make special audits on the reports of tax agents. In A.D. 320, Constantine initiated a decree decriminalizing the tax law:

> In connection with the payment of taxes due, no person shall fear that he will suffer, at the hand of perverse and enraged judges, imprisonment, lashes of leaded whips, weights, or any other tortures devised by the arrogance of judges. Prisons are for criminals. . . . In accordance with this law, taxpayers shall proceed with security.[5]

Not only were taxpayers' sins decriminalized, but the later published *Theodosian Code of Laws*, under Constantine, decreed that "If any person shall complain in court that payment has been unduly exacted of him or that he has sustained any arrogance and if he should be able to prove this fact, a severe sentence shall be pronounced against such tax collector."[6]

The laws the Roman emperors adopted to correct revenue abuses were impressive, but the evil to be corrected was the revenue system itself. As a result, the legislation was as severe in form as it was inefficient in substance.

The policies of Julian (A.D. 360) were an exception to the punitive methods used by other emperors to solve Rome's revenue problems. Julian's approach was extraordinary for any age. To reduce government spending he discharged masses of government workers. Tax rates were reduced, and most important, tax immunities, exemptions, and amnesties were cancelled, since these practices did not benefit the small peasant farmer. Thousands of small tracts of land were sold to poor farmers.

For the soldiers, Julian refused to increase their pay, but he did make certain they were paid on time. He tried to improve the garrisons on the frontier by enlisting better troops, and he died leading them in battle trying to improve their morale.

For the decurions in the cities he decreed that the gold crown tax, the *coronarium*, be made voluntary as it was originally. To reduce military expenditures he sought new weapons and military hardware so the number of military personnel could be reduced without weakening the strength of the army. He even sought the advice of scholars and asked for their opinions on how to reduce the costs of government. Julian saw Rome's problems as economic and financial, centered in an erroneous policy of excessive spending and taxation. When Julian's local administrator in Gaul (France) demanded the right to increase taxes because (as he asserted) land and poll taxes were inadequate, Julian responded that "he would rather lose his life" than increase taxes. Julian then conducted his own investigation and concluded that the regular taxes were more than enough and he refused to permit any new taxes. The contemporary historian, Ammianus, who reported this event, commented: "And so it came to pass then and thereafter, that through the resolution of one courageous spirit no one tried to extort from the Gauls anything beyond the normal tax."[7]

Had Julian lived, it has been suggested that he might have saved Rome. As it turned out, his successors soon abandoned his constructive programs and reverted to the policy of coercion to solve Rome's revenue problems. The two remaining escape routes for the small taxpayer from the state's outrageous taxation were closed. The ancient right of asylia, which had protected abused taxpayers since the days of the pharaohs, was denied to taxpayers by a Christian emperor in A.D. 392. A few years before, another Christian emperor made it illegal for a small free farmer or merchant or worker to renounce one's liberty in order to place oneself under the patronage of a great landlord, and thus avoid taxation. Bondage to the tax man (tax slavery) was to many worse than bondage to a lord (chattel slavery).

Shortly after Julian's death the army was reintroduced to collect taxes. The expenses of a military tax bureaucracy were high, and to meet this cost taxes were doubled, with the 100 percent increase going to pay the military collectors. Zosimos, a Greek historian living in Constantinople, in his *Historia Nova*, describes the horrors that evolved to collect the five-year gold and silver tax on small merchants:

> As the fatal time approached, all the towns were seen in tears and grief. When the tax period arrived, the scourge and the rack were used against those whose extreme poverty could not support this unjust tax. Mothers sold their children, and fathers prostituted their daughters, obliged to obtain by this sorry trade the money which the collectors of the [tax] came to snatch from them.[8]

In the early Republic, the small citizen farmer served as a patriotic duty without pay. He was the best fighting man in the world for centuries. In the last century of the Empire the quality of the legions changed. The frontier garrisons were composed of either misfits from Italy or barbarians who were concerned with securing their own territories, not with protecting the Empire. Conscription was used as a tax dodge. Farmers were taxed on the number of workers on their land. When new conscriptees were needed, farmers would send off their misfits or purchase worthless slaves to satisfy the government's demands. This way they kept their best workers, eliminated their bad ones, and reduced their taxes. The government eventually made it illegal to buy up slaves to satisfy conscription obligations.

The better troops had enough influence to be stationed at home. It was the misfits who were sent off to fight border wars. They were so inept that one ancient writer lamented what a pity it was to watch them fight, "knowing how much they cost."[9] The decline in the power and moral strength of the legions had been going on for two hundred years.

Tacitus observed in the early second century, "Their strength was corrupted by luxury in contrast to the ancient discipline and maxims of our forefathers, in whose day valour formed a better foundation for the Roman state than money."[10]

The prevalence of crippling taxation prior to the Fall of Rome has led many historians, in all ages, to suspect that Rome, like so many great empires, taxed itself to death. Recently, the tax theory of the Fall has become unfashionable among many scholars—perhaps because of our own tolerance for heavy taxation. No one likes to think we are writing our own obituary when we draft modern tax legislation. If our civilization is to be destroyed, we like to think it will happen Hollywood-style—a cataclysmic event like an atomic war, an ecological blunder, or some other dramatic happening. Certainly not something so simple and dull as everyday taxation.

A few modern scholars still hold to the tax theory as the cause of Rome's fall. A prominent Cambridge scholar summarized Rome's predicament this way:

> The army could not be enlarged because the land could not stand further depletion of manpower; the situation of the land had deteriorated because taxes were too high; taxes were too high because military demands were increasing.[11]

Other European scholars agree. There was discovered among the unpublished manuscripts of the late A.H.M. Jones of Oxford, a leading economic scholar of Rome, a treatise entitled, "Over-taxation and the Decline of Rome," which has been published along with his other studies of the Roman economy. He saw high taxation as an important cause of Rome's demise, citing the Christian historian Lactantius, "The resources of the farmers were exhausted by outrageous burdens of all taxes, the fields were abandoned, and the cultivated land reverted to waste."[12] Why? Because the taxpayers had fled. Many to the lands of the barbarians. As one group said, "We will flee to some place where we may live as free men."[13] The contemporary scholar Salvian of Marseilles, France, wrote in A.D. 440 that the justice and humanity of the Goths (French barbarians), greatly exceeded that of the Romans—government as well as citizens. He saw the coming collapse of Rome with the real weakness to be crushing taxation, the cruelty of the ruling classes, and the rapacity of the government. He noted at that time that the treasury of Rome was bare. "Where are the riches of Rome? The imperial finances are in a state of indigence and the treasury reduced to misery."[14]

A modern Italian scholar actually pinpoints tax evasion as the critical cause. He pointed to a vicious cycle of disappearing taxpayers in one form or another coupled with a growing and increasingly costly tax bureaucracy to fight evasion. When the peasants were taking flight, the wealthy classes were, through legal and illegal means, evading their taxes. This flight of small taxpayers coupled with the evasion of big taxpayers

> showed itself in the course of the fifth century. The bankruptcy of the enormous State at the same time as the small privileged groups, while they evaded taxation, heaped up riches and created around their villas economic and social microcosms, completely cut-off from the central authority. It was the end of the Roman world. It was the beginning of the Middle Ages.[15]

One of the newer theories suggests Rome's demise came from a soaring death rate which caused the population of peasants to decline.[16] The peasants were dying from malnutrition for not having enough to eat— sort of like the millions of peasants who died in Stalin's Russia in the 1930s. The Roman peasants didn't have enough to eat after the tax man took the lion's share. What most scholars have seldom analyzed is that behind so many of these "causes," taxation can be found. Whether death from starvation or flight to the Goths, taxation played its part. Even the decline in humanity—the viciousness and cruelty among Romans towards each other—was but a reflection of the government's viciousness towards all citizen taxpayers.

The undermining of liberty was also crucial. The people of the Empire had great traditions of liberty, from the Republic, reflected in the writings of Cicero, to the laws of the Empire, found in the Justinian *Digests*, which said, "Liberty is a possession on which no evaluation can be placed."[17] And again, "Freedom is beloved above all things."[18] The goddess of Liberty appeared on Roman coins. Ancient histories refer from time to time to the Temples of Liberty in which the goddess is a central figure, but these references were all during the time Roman citizens were tax immune.[19] When Diocletian and later Roman emperors shackled Roman citizens with tax bondage, the coins and temples had long since vanished. The goddess reappeared in America on coins, and the giant Statue of Liberty in New York harbor was not just a gift from the French, but a concept from the Romans.

In the final analysis, Rome's Fall may have been grounded on psychological factors most of all. After Rome's sack in A.D. 476 by the Vandals, there was no popular movement to revive the Empire. Succeeding emperors tried and failed for lack of grass roots support. Patriotism, sacrifice, and love of country, which Montesquieu saw,[20] was missing—having been choked to death by Diocletian's tax system. People from all walks of life no longer needed or wanted the government of Rome anymore, and her citizens simply did not care if she survived—The Eternal City was no longer first in the hearts of her people.

Part III

The Middle Ages

Most Roman taxes disappeared in the West by the eighth century A.D. The early kingdoms of medieval Europe did not have the expertise to operate the revenue systems of the Romans. The old Roman land tax did have some usefulness if a king wanted to exterminate someone. The undesired person would be appointed land tax collector and sent out to collect delinquent land taxes. That unfortunate fellow seldom returned. In the seventh-century *Chronicals of Fredegar* (a primary source for our knowledge of the early medieval period in Northern Europe), we learn of a Frankish queen's scheme to liquidate a rival, which records, "So that Berthold would die all the more quickly, they sent him to certain cities and districts in the kingdom for the purpose of collecting taxes."[1] Berthold did not die, however, for he went forth with three hundred armed men for protection.

Indirect taxes and tolls multiplied and provided feudal lords with what revenues they needed. These taxes, however, stifled commerce, and the decline of civilization in the West may have been the fault of the tax system as much as the overemphasis on the world-to-come.

Byzantium and Kievan Russia became the new centers of civilization. They also emphasized the other world, but their taxes on commerce were light, and money was welcome. Trade, which was almost nonexistent in the West, was active and healthy in the East. This explains why the Eastern Roman Empire lasted an extra thousand years.

When Islam burst forth on the world in the seventh century A.D. the promise of reduced taxes in a decadent Roman world may have had greater appeal than the promise of a paradise to come. Islam ceased to spread when converts were not offered a tax break. Just a coincidence?

In the medieval world tax customs petrified into fixed sacred demands on the government as well as the taxpayer. As the modern age began to emerge these revenue systems were inadequate. Kings desperately needed more wealth, but kings who created "unheard-of taxation" invited rebellion. Kings had to search for new ways to raise revenue outside the local Christian populace. They turned on the Jewish community

129

Peasants paying toll for passing a bridge. From a fifteenth-century glass painting in the Cathedral of Tournai, Belgium.

and fleeced it until there was little visible Jewish wealth left. They stole from the church whenever possible. Eventually, when all other avenues were exhausted, the concept of new taxation "by consent" was discovered as a means around the prohibition against "unheard-of taxation."

Kings who obtained taxpayers' consent to new taxes had to grant something in return. This bargain for taxes became fundamental to the process of government, and with it our forefathers purchased their liberty with taxes—and bequeathed it to us.

13

Islam: Death or Taxes for the Infidel

In the name of God, the Merciful and Compassionate. Become Moslem and be saved. If not, accept protection from us and pay the poll tax. If not, I shall come against you with men who love death as you love wine.
—Moslem general to the Persians, A.D. 633

Shortly after the Roman Empire died in the West, a new and exciting religion burst forth on the world. It had the vitality of youth and a theological simplicity that has made it the envy of most Christians in all ages. Armed with the Koran and the sword, the armies of Muhammad swept through the Middle East, North Africa, and Spain. They seized a large portion of the territory of the Roman Empire, but unfortunately they squabbled among themselves, and their vast empire fragmented and split into separate kingdoms and caliphates.

At first, the Muhammadans came as liberators and brought relief to the inhabitants of an over-taxed and enslaved Roman world. As a result, the Moslem armies were often outnumbered on the field of battle but victorious. Most territories did not put up much of a fight.

In Persia the new believers were the Zoroastrians; it was from this religion that the astrologers or wise men came to give homage to the infant son of Mary in Bethlehem. The Zoroastrians were, however, burdened with heavy taxes and it was not too difficult for them to accept the religion of Islam.[1] But the largest body of new believers came from Christianity. For over 250 years Christianity was the state religion of Rome, hence the Roman Empire—the empire the Moslems expanded into—was Christian. Nevertheless, the Christians were shackled to the old brutal Roman tax system. The first great caliph said to them, "All who would accept his religion and pray his prayers, would be relieved of the poll tax."[2] This was not an offer to choose between Christianity and Islam; it was really an offer to choose between bondage and free-

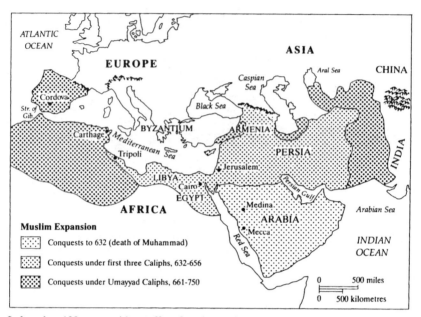

In less than 120 years, with an offer of tax immunity, Islam spread very quickly, expanding into India in the East and coming to a halt at the Atlantic Ocean in the West. The main loser was Christianity, which was tied to the oppressive Roman tax system. No religion, before or since, has spread so far, so fast. Was the tax immunity, rather than religious ideology, the cause of this miraculous conversion?

dom. It is easy to understand why Christianity lost. One early historian at the time made this observation: "Because of the heavy *Kharaj* [tax] and grievous burdens, many of the rich and poor denied the faith of the Messiah [Christ]."[3]

Once in power the Moslems struggled to establish an effective government. They lacked the genius of the Romans—especially the genius of Augustus—who taught the world for all time to come that an effective ruler must have a tight grip on the public purse. The Moslem rulers were supreme autocrats, more so than Augustus, but they made the fatal mistake of farming out taxation to local generals and governors. As can be expected, these rulers drained off most of the tax blood of the empire and reduced to a trickle the flow to the central government. The empire of the Caliphs withered from tax anemia as the Islamic world broke up into sub-empires of sultans, *visiers*, and local tax chiefs.

The heart of the Islamic world was centered in the eastern portions of the Roman Empire. They took over the territories in Iran (Persia), Iraq, Syria, Palestine, Egypt, North Africa, Spain, and some bits of Europe itself. The land tax and poll tax were solidly entrenched in all these territories, thanks to Diocletian and Constantine. The Moslems did not make any dramatic changes to these taxes, but they did humanize them a bit and ease the burdens that were so oppressive to so many. The spirit of Moslem tax policy is well illustrated in the story written by a Moslem magistrate in an introduction to a book on the land tax which the Caliph had asked him to compile.

"See to it that you collect all the land tax [Kharaj] that is owing from them. Beware lest you let them off anything, beware lest they see any weakness in you." Then he said, "Come to me at noon." So I went to him at noon and he said to me, "I only gave you the advice which I gave you in the presence of your charges. . . . but take care, when you come to them, not to confiscate their property, do not strike them, nor make them stand on their feet to collect taxes. Do not sell any goods belonging to any of them to cover any part of the land tax, for you are commanded to collect only their surplus. If you disobey my commands, God will punish you." . . . Then I took my departure, and I acted as he had commanded me, and when I returned, I had not reduced the yield of the land tax at all.[4]

A similar policy of common sense was introduced when the Moslems took over Egypt. At that time the heavy land tax was payable only in gold and silver currency. Taxes were assessed against whole communities and there was a poll tax as well. The Moslem ruler, Amr, turned the collection and allocation of taxes over to the local native officials. Taxes could be paid in anything the peasants desired. It need not be gold or silver but could be in kind. Land covered with clover was exempt if Arabs were permitted to graze some of their cattle on these lands for a short season in the spring. The poll tax of two dinars a year, with exemptions for hard times, was limited to non-believer tradesmen.[5]

The humanity in the tax policy of the Moslems was of utmost importance. The Arabs brought peace and gentleness to an overtaxed world. They liberated the old Roman world from decadent, oppressive, and corrupt taxation. Nothing illustrates this better than the tax refunds they made to Christians and Jews in Palestine in A.D. 636. At that time the Moslems had conquered most of the lands of Judea, but their forces were overextended, and a large body of Roman troops was on the march from Antioch. At a war council the Moslems decided to evacuate most of the conquered territories. After this decision was made the Moslem leader called in the chief tax collector and gave him these instructions:

You should therefore refund the entire amount of money realized from them and tell them that our relations with them remain unchanged but that as we are not in a position to hold ourselves responsible for their safety,

Gold dinar, annual head tax for nonbelievers. This dinar is on display at the Kuwait National Museum. The inscription on the left reads: "There is no God but God alone. He has no associate." On the reverse side it reads: "In the name of God this dinar was struck in the year eight and seventy" (the Islamic calendar began in A.D. 622, when Mohammed took to flight from Medina).

the poll tax, which is nothing but the price of protection, is reimbursed to them.[6]

Accordingly, the entire sum collected from the Christian and Jewish communities was refunded to them. This affected the Christians to such a degree that tears trickled down their faces and, one and all, they passionately exclaimed: "May God bring you back to us." The effect on the Jews was still more marked. They cried out with vehemence: "By the law and the prophets, the Roman emperor shall not take this city as long as the spark of life scintillates in our bodies."[7] It's too bad the Jews and Moslems today don't feel that way.

The Moslems used taxation to bring converts into the faith. The spread of Islam has been attributed to the sword and many historians harp on the Moslem cry of "Death to the infidel." The Koran (9:29) certainly justifies that course of action. In practice, the Moslems acted quite to the contrary. Slaughter was not the normal modus operandi of even the most fanatical Moslems. Vanquished people were given three choices: death, taxes, or conversion to the faith. With these options it was not necessary for conquered people to lose their heads or their religion.

The Moslems modified Roman poll taxes by reducing rates and limiting their application to non-believers. This new tax policy probably brought more converts to Islam than either the sword or the Koran. Joining the faith became an absolutely safe and sure way to avoid taxation. In time a shortage of revenue developed because of a shortage of infidels. We have the record of an Egyptian ruler pleading with the caliph to permit him to reinstate the poll tax on converts. Because of drastically reduced tax revenues he had to supplement his treasury with 20,000 dinars from his personal wealth.[8] Conversion had become a serious loophole in the tax system. This is an early example of the over-use of a tax avoidance device. Finally, Moslem rulers had to close the loophole, even if it meant annulling an important public policy. Spreading the faith was the noblest pursuit of all Moslems, but when pitted against diminishing tax revenues, this noblest of endeavors had to give way. In any contest between God and taxes (like the contest between liberty and taxes), even God must give ground.

The poll tax, or *jaliya*, assessed against non-believers was based on a pact between them and the Moslem authorities. That pact was called the *dhimma*; it was similar to the pactiones of Augustus.[9] This contract spelled out the rights and duties of the parties. The primary duty of the non-believers was to pay his jaliya, not to strike Moslem men, and to keep his hands off Moslem women. He had to be a good Samaritan to Moslem travelers. If he did all these things, then he was assured of safe conduct and security in the Moslem world. He could practice his own religion, travel unmolested, and live and work how he pleased.

The tax rates for the jaliya varied from time to time and from place to place. The earliest accounts indicate that the tax was fixed. In Egypt it was two dinars per adult male infidel. In other, less prosperous places, the payment of one dinar was most common as illustrated by this early account of the introduction of the poll tax in Tiflis in A.D. 642. (Tiflis is currently Tbilisi, the leading city in the former Soviet Republic of Georgia.)

In the name of God, the Merciful and the Compassionate. This is a letter from Habib ibn Maslama for the inhabitants of Tiflis, in the land of Hurmuz, giving safe-conduct to you, your children, your families, your convents, your churches, your religions, and your prayers, on condition that you accept the humiliation [?] of the jizya at the rate of a full dinar for every household. You must not join separate households together in order to reduce the jizya which you pay, nor may we separate what is joined in order to increase the jizya which we receive.[10]

In other words: No tax evasion on your side and no tax oppression on our side!

When the Moslems first moved into Persia, the leader of the Arab forces sent an advanced notice to the Persians to become Moslems, or choose between death and the poll tax. For most Persians the poll tax demanded by the Moslems was less burdensome than the established taxes. Only those in power stood to lose because they paid very little tax. A century later, when the Moslems were mopping-up the remaining Persian strongholds, a harder line was taken. By that time there was a sizeable Moslem population which had been discriminated against because of their religious beliefs. The Moslem conquerors set out to correct that situation. Here is an account of the introduction of the poll tax in one Persian city in A.D. 739:

> Indeed, Bahramsis [the Persian King] used to favor the Magians; he favored them and protected them and loaded their burdens [of taxation] onto the Muslims. Ashbdad son of Gregory used to favor the Christians, and Aqiva the Jew used to favor the Jews and do the same thing. But I favor the Muslims; I shall favor them and protect them and load their burdens on to the polytheists.
>   By the following Friday, 30,000 Muslims came to him who were paying a jizya poll tax, while 80,000 polytheists had been relieved of their jizya. He imposed it on them and removed it from the Muslims. Then he organized the kharaj and imposed it where it belonged and levied it in accordance with the terms of the armistice.[11]

The reference to the Jews being favored with tax exemptions is probably directed at the Jewish kingdom of the Khazars, north of Persia, which was established at this time. The Khazars followed the Moslem practice of taxing non-believers (Christians and Moslems). This practice caught hold in Western civilization and lasted a thousand years. It is a relative of the Greek practice of taxing the metics (foreigners) as opposed to locally born citizens. This religious relative of the metoikion was used by all religious groups in Western societies as a primary revenue source and as a stimulus to conversion. Tax devices are economic inventions and once a nation discovers a new revenue technique that is highly productive, other nations will quickly follow suit. William Pitt's income tax and Harcourt's estate duty are modern tax inventions that may have revolutionized the world more than the theories of Einstein.

The poll tax in Persia was quite different from the poll tax in Egypt, perhaps because Egyptian economics was based on land and the land tax was the principal source of taxation. Persia was a trading nation, so commercial taxes were most important. The poll tax in Persia was revised to fall heavily on commerce. Merchants paid an annual poll tax equal to 10 percent of the value of their stock in trade. The tax also fell on peasants and artisans; it was designed to tax the commercial wealth of the nation on a proportionate basis, that is, on the taxpayers' ability to pay. There were minimum rates for the poor and maximum fixed limits for the rich, which permitted a wealthy merchant to pay the maximum and avoid an audit and appraisal.

The Moslems continued the Persian practice of stamping a tax receipt in indelible ink on the neck of the taxpayer. Jewish historians object to this practice because it was humiliating, which it was, but it did have some virtues. The indelible tax receipt on the taxpayer's neck was an excellent tax record. It assured the taxpayer against double payment and it was his personal passport for safe travel. A lost or misplaced tax receipt could create serious problems. Archaeologists have unearthed a letter from one unfortunate Jewish traveler who was stranded because he had lost his tax receipt. The letter is a plea of desperation to his family to send him another tax receipt so he could return home. The tax receipt was the passport for the non-believers in the Islamic world. Without it the traveler could be in great peril.

The story of the conquest of Iraq sheds further light on the lack of order and uniformity in the poll tax. When the Moslems moved into Iraq they attacked the headquarters of the Roman governor and ignored the other cities. They wisely reasoned that if they could take the capital city and oust the Roman ruler the whole country would fall into their hands. They laid siege to the city, and one night the Roman governor and his followers fled to the mountains. All that was left was a native Arab population.

In the peace treaty negotiated with the remaining Arab people, the Moslems were most gentle. They first offered them a treaty in which the tax was to be no more than they were able to pay. The local Arabs weren't about to submit to such an uncertain tax system. The early record states that, "The townspeople knew that they had in their possession property and income that would disappear if they agreed to pay according to their capacity. They therefore refused anything but a fixed sum."[12] When the Moslem commander saw how determined they were and the strength of their defenses he accepted their terms, and the city fell under the Islamic rule.

Other parts of Iraq neighboring on the border with Persia were treated differently. When the country first fell into Moslem hands, the poll tax was set at one dinar plus a quantity of wheat, oil, and vinegar. The successor Moslem rulers were impressed with the ease with which wealth could be amassed through taxation, so they greatly increased the tax. Here is an account (A.D. 637–641) of how they did it:

> Finding the taxes taken insufficient, he counted the heads of the population. Assuming that everyone worked with his hands, he made an estimate of his annual earnings, deducted what they spent on food, condiments and clothing, and deducted feast days throughout the year. He then found that

everyone had four dinars left. He therefore fixed this poll tax for all of them, treating them all the same. . . . He then taxed the lands in proportion to their nearness or farness. He levied one dinar on 100 jaribs (about three acres) of cultivated land if it was near, and the same amount on 200 jaribs if it was far. He also levied one dinar on 100 shoots of vine olive trees if near, or 200 olive trees if far. He called far that which was a day's journey or more, and near, that which was less than a day's journey.

Syria and Mosul were taxed the same way.[13]

At some later date a progressive tax was instituted in Syria and Egypt. The rates were four, two, and one dinar depending on one's ability. This three-tier system prevailed for over five hundred years. The rates changed from time to time, but the three-rate system continued in about the same proportions. In these areas the tax was levied on all males over the age of puberty (fifteen years). There were exemptions for government and military workers, priests, hermits, the sick, and probably for anyone caught up in hard times.

It is difficult to make generalizations about the land tax (kharaj). Some authorities insist that it was abolished for believers just like the poll tax and that the words were often used interchangeably. There is no question but that the land tax applied to everyone after the first century of the Islamic era. The mass conversion of native populations to Islam drained off a large percentage of all taxpayers. The Moslem poor tax and tithes were not sufficient to maintain the realm. The greed of the sultans and caliphs demanded that all sources of revenue be exploited to the utmost, so religious tax immunity passed away and the land tax once again came down on the peasants. Heavy taxation became the order of Islam as the day of a new age of tax gentleness passed into darkness.

The Islamic world reached its limits when it took over Spain. The Pyrenees Mountains were a barrier they could not successfully penetrate. Historians have said that the mountains were too formidable. It is also quite probable that it was not the mountains at all. Islamic imperialism bogged down in Spain because in that region its tax system became most corrupt. Here is an early supply-side account of the cause of the failure of Islam in Spain:

Ja'far ibn Yahya said, "The land tax is the tent pole of the realm. How great it becomes by justice, how mean by oppression.

"The quickest way to ruin a country, the disuse of the cultivated land, the destruction of the subjects, and the cessation of the land tax is by tyranny and extortion. A ruler who burdens his taxpayers until they cannot cultivate the land is like one who cuts off his own flesh and eats it when he is hungry. He grows stronger in one part and weaker in another, and the pain and weakness he brings on himself are greater than the ache of hunger which he remedies. He who taxes his subjects beyond their capacity is like one who coats his roof with earth from the foundations of his house. He who makes a habit of cutting the tent pole will weaken it and bring down the tent. If the cultivators become weak, they cannot cultivate the land, and they leave it. Then the land is ruined, cultivation is weakened, and the tax diminishes. This leads to the weakening of the army, and when the army is weakened, enemies covet the realm.

"I heard some of the old men of Spain, from the army [jund] and others, who said that the Muslims were victorious over their enemies and their enemies were weak and inferior as long as the tax-paying peasants were treated kindly. . . . the land was distributed and assigned to the army in the form of 'iqta. They exploited it and dealt kindly with the peasants and cared for them as a merchant cares for his merchandise. The land flourished, there was plenty of money, and the armies were well-supplied with equipment and provender and weapons beyond what they needed. So it was, until in his last days Ibn Abi Amir reintroduced a fixed monthly pay for the army, took the money by force, and sent tax collectors to the land to collect it. They devoured the subjects and misappropriated their money and exhausted them, so that the subjects fled and could not cultivate the land. The revenues brought to the Sultan diminished, the armies became weak, and the enemy grew strong against the lands of the Muslims and seized many of them. The Muslims remained inferior and the enemy victorious." [14]

The foregoing account explains why Islamic imperialism stalled in the West. It was written a thousand years ago and the modern suggestion that the mountains were a formidable barrier does not enter the picture. The Moslem imperialistic machine became corrupt and oppressive and stunted the growth of Islam.

Another cause of Spanish discontent with Moslem taxation may have been the introduction of a 5 percent excise tax, perhaps the world's first excise. Unfortunately, we know practically nothing about this tax until it emerged in Imperial Spain some centuries later.

The chief spiritual and temporal ruler of Islam was the caliph, successor to Muhammad and oriental despot. Muhammad did not have such an office in mind when his simple austere religion was preached in the world with its message of universal brotherhood. The caliphs and sultans were hardly brothers to the common Arab.

The caliphs developed an extravagant appetite for magnificent courts, enormous harems, gold overlay, silver, and jewels. The wealth from easy taxation corrupted them beyond all imagination. In their lust for riches the caliphs made the fatal step of farming out tax collection to their local governors (sultans) and generals, for a 20 percent override, which left 80 percent for the local ruler. The disease of extravagance infected these local tax chiefs as much as the caliph. In time they developed courts and riches to rival the caliph.

The first fatal defect in the structure of the Islamic empire was its tax system. Lack of control over taxation turned the caliph into a spiritual figurehead with little temporal power. Without effective audit control the local sultan kept most of the tax money for his personal extravagance and the caliph's 20 percent was probably less than 5 percent.

Corruption wrought by too much tax wealth was the second fatal defect in the Islamic world. Tax discontent spread throughout the empire as greedy sultans demanded more and more taxes from their subjects. Islamic armies no longer brought liberation from oppressive taxation. They evolved into adjuncts of local tax chiefs and brought cruel physical suffering to the local population, infidels and believers alike. Equality was introduced into the tax system—not an equality of fairness for all, but rather the equality of oppression to all. This negative kind of equality infected much of the communist world in this century.

In Egypt the local sultan tried to increase taxation by 5 percent and triggered a major revolt. In reply to his request for more taxes, one courageous advisor told the sultan that he could not ask for more taxes from the people when the "wife of the sultan wore on the day of her son's circumcision a dress worth 30,000 dinars, and that is only one dress and one wife!"[15] Incidentally, a dinar was originally a gold coin of considerable value in the Moslem world. The one dinar annual poll tax was not a small sum, so the 30,000-dinar dress must have rivalled the sumptuous apparel of the richest monarchs of Europe and the emperors of Rome.

A heretofore ignored aspect of Moslem history, and perhaps the key to Islam's phenomenal growth, was the use of taxation as an inducement to conversion. Moslem tax policy was the greatest proselytizing tool the religious world has ever known. Christian writers of the past have influenced our histories and explained Moslem growth—and excused the collapse of Christianity—as the consequence of a misunderstood Islamic death sentence for non-believers. Scholars now recognize that that was not the real story:

> The pressures upon them to convert came not from the "sword" as Christian polemicists used to maintain, but rather from the purse: Christians and Jews paid a special tax from which Muslims were exempt.[16]

Most Arabs and converts of that day were Christian; many were illiterate and could not be expected to read and understand the Koran—but none of them were so illiterate that they couldn't understand the simple mathematics of no tax vis-à-vis the land and poll tax assessed against the non-believer. Christianity all but vanished from the Islamic world.

After a few centuries all of this changed, and believer and non-believer alike were caught in the tax vice of greedy sultans. The annual burden of one gold dinar easily moved upward to four dinars. One Moslem minister argued that a capital tax of two-thirds of the value of all the assets of Christians and Jews alike would be good for the empire. In the end, a 25 percent crop tax and fairly heavy capitation taxes shackled everyone. As taxes went up and spread to the believer, the expansion of the empire went down. This was hardly a coincidence.

Besides the heavy increase in the tax rates and in the tax base (everyone becoming taxpayers), the manner and method of collection took on more oppressiveness. The jaliya was collected in a way to humiliate the Jews and Christians. In Egypt we have the fragment of a papyrus which says that the non-believer must bow before the tax collector as he pays his tax and that he is then to be given a blow on the neck, and a guard standing beside him is to "drive him roughly away."[17] The Moslems had led the world right back to where it was before they had arrived on the scene. Only the names had changed. Moslem tax men ended up rivalling the worst of the Roman Empire. Perhaps this picture of Moslem tax chiefs (*visiers*), written centuries ago, best illustrates the end product of their tax system:

> They were cruel rascals, inventors of a thousand injustices, arrogant and presumptuous. . . . They were the scourges of their age, always with a causeless insult ready in their mouths. Their existence, passed exclusively in oppressing the people of their time, was a disgrace to humanity.[18]

14

Medieval Taxation: When Taxpayers Had God on Their Side

God will surely punish anyone who reinstitutes an old tax, for that very day, the son of the man who reinstituted the land tax caught a fever and three days later died.

—Pope St. Gregory I, *Dialogues*, circa A.D. 600

After Rome collapsed, small farmers and artisans continued to surrender to large landowners and military chiefs, only at this time the process was motivated by anarchy and lawlessness that prevailed in the countryside. What started as a movement to exchange tax slavery for chattel slavery became a way of life for survival in a feudal world.

The feudal system was based on contract. Initially, little revenue was generated by the feudal contract, which was a three-party arrangement with God as the third party. Tax provisions in feudal contracts were unalterable. The King of Tours, for example, made a covenant that he "would not burden the people with new taxes" (much like a modern politician). A count in his kingdom levied a new poll tax without the king's knowledge. An early chronicle records, "the king was horrified" and feared the wrath of God for having broken his covenant. The king destroyed the new tax roll, refunded all the taxes paid, and repented of his sin.[1]

The King of Tours actions were understandable. Taxpayers in the Middle Ages had God on their side. Today, we are supposed to have the Constitution on our side, but, looking back, I think the taxpayers in that day had a superior arrangement. They had a kind of divine supply-side economics. One of the religious teachings in the medieval world was that the king who taxed excessively incurred sin, and would be punished by God. The King of Tours was looking out for his prosperity when he

Medieval taxation was often based upon a covenant between rulers and their subjects, with God as an important third party. Excessive tax collections were sins against God. To punish this sin and to purge themselves of guilt, rulers such as William the Good of the Netherlands executed errant tax men. This graphic portrayal of such punishment, *The Administration of Justice by William the Good*, is the only surviving masterpiece of the seventeenth-century Dutch painter, Nicolaas van Galen. It is in the Town Hall, Hasselt, Overijssel.

refunded the excessive tax, for the other aspect of this belief was that the king who taxed modestly and justly would be blessed with sons, wealth in his domains, and riches in his treasury.[2] Isn't this what the supply-siders are telling us the laws of economics will do? In the medieval world it was the laws of God that would create the prosperity, but is there really a difference?

The count who levied the unauthorized poll tax that upset the King of Tours probably came out much better than a tax collector under William the Good of the Netherlands, who collected excessive taxes from the people in his domain. William had the tax collector beheaded. A painting from one of the great Dutch masters of this execution can be found today in the city hall in Hasselt, Overijssel, in the Netherlands.

Harsh and punitive measures against new or excessive taxation had their origin in the Edict of Paris of A.D. 614, sometimes likened unto Magna Carta. This was a treaty between rival kings in the Frankish kingdom which spread over most of northern Europe, covering France, the Low Countries, and Germany. There was a large national assembly to reorganize the kingdom. What is significant is the following provision in the edict against all new taxation:

> Everywhere, where a new tax has been wickedly introduced and has incited the people to resistance, the matter will be investigated and the tax mercifully abolished.[3]

The strong medieval prohibition against any "unheard-of tax," or an *exactio inaudita*, had its roots in this edict, which could be described as medieval Europe's early constitution. Thereafter, any charge that a tax was *exactio inaudita* was sufficient to defeat most any tax. The effectiveness of this prohibition no doubt had its strength in the position God played in medieval charters and covenants.

One of the last kings of the Frankish kingdom was named Dagobert. Twenty-five years after the Edict of Paris, a saint of this period tells a story that indicates the force the edict had in medieval life, especially when you realize that Dagobert was one of the most powerful kings to rule over most of western Europe. The saint tells us that Dagobert was motivated by greed and ordered a ruffian to "do much wickedness," i.e., levy taxes. Without an ounce of mercy he imposed a head tax on the people in Bourges (about one hundred miles south of Paris), a measure which was "contrary to customs." The rest of the story is recorded as follows:

> The inhabitants, filled with repugnance, hurried in a great multitude to the man of God [the saint], begging him with lamentations and confused cries to please help them. Moved by pity, but unable to act on their sobs and tears, Sulpicius [the saint] commanded a three-day fast and begged divine Providence to help his oppressed people. Then he sent one of his clerks to the king to ask for royal grace in all humbleness with tears and lamentations, to render his assistance against the wicked deeds. Horrified, the king [Dagobert had died and a new king was on the throne] ordered the levy to be discontinued and the already-compiled tax books to be abolished immediately. And the people of Bourges, relieved of this assessment, still live today in their former freedom.[4]

This is the last record we have of a head or poll tax being levied in this period of medieval history. The few surviving writings from this period contain limited information upon which scholars cannot agree. Montesquieu in his *The Spirit of Laws* (1751) gives us some insight into this period.[5] It was a strong anti-tax period which equated liberty with taxes, a concept that dominated the thinking of the founders of America. A chronicler from this period summed up their belief: a man is free only if his name does not appear on a tax roll.[6] With this kind of thinking, kings that needed revenue had to resort to voluntary contributions. Not only were new taxes out of the question, even old Roman direct taxes on land or persons were not to be tolerated.

God's hand was not only found in the medieval tax documents, he even brought forth miracles to protect taxpayers from unauthorized exactions. In *The Miracles of Saint Benedict*, A.D. 875, written by a monk at the Abbey of Fleury, the following story is recorded:

> This very sacred monastery [Fleury] had received from the Frankish kings the right, written in a formal deed, to have four boats sail on the Loire every year, exempt from whatever taxes were to be given to the treasury. At the time of the above-mentioned count [Raho], one of these boats had sailed as far as Nantes to take on a load of salt. On the way back it had called in at the cities and harbors that lay on his travel route and, thanks to the protection of the royal charter, had not encountered any trouble. It finally reached Orleans. The toll collectors of this city detained the vessel and demanded that the captain pay the toll. The captain referred him to the exemption granted by the king. However, the toll collector took no notice of the royal charter and, as payment to the treasury, impounded the boat and its load of salt and entrusted it to the harbor master so that it would be put under embargo along with other vessels. This happened on a Sunday. However, at the third hour of the day when everyone was attending mass, our boat, under guard along with the other impounded boats in the harbor, suddenly lay outside the harbor, without the intervention of a human oarsman; it reached the middle of the Loire, where the current is the strongest. And sailing upstream, it reached the water gate that is still called "The Gate of Saint Benedict" and berthed there.[7]

Initially, money was not abundant in the feudal system. Every lord sustained himself from his own domain. Kings had the added advantage of receiving side moneys from the system: fines, guardian fees, tolls on commerce, and a special payment when a vassal's oldest son became a knight or his daughter married. Kings and lords were marriage brokers and received a fee for their services. One English noblewoman paid four pounds and a mark of silver (eight ounces) "that she may not be married except to her own liking."[8] Another nobleman gave the king 20,000 marks to marry Isabel, Countess of Gloucester.[9] Isabel obviously had the right assets. What is not so obvious is why one English lady gave the king two hundred hens "for permission to sleep with my husband Hugo de Nevill for one night."[10] One wonders what that was all about.

Medieval revenues were not designed to finance large military operations. The history of civilization at this time focuses to a large extent on the struggles of medieval kings for money to fight wars caused by the collision of expanding kingdoms.

Kings and rulers also had to deal with God in the matter of church taxation. Churches were exempt, and this included church lands. Monasteries and abbeys spread throughout the countryside, and they often had vast and rich land holdings which could not be taxed. And as we observed, tolls for bridges and roads were often exempt for the clergy, which prompted many English merchants to travel through northern Europe disguised as pilgrims or clerics on religious excursions. Thus the religious tax exemption that survives today, which is often misused by phoney religious impersonators, is an evasion scheme as old, at least, as the Middle Ages.

Thus the rulers in medieval Europe were frustrated by a limited supply of taxpayers and by the impropriety of instituting new taxes against their subjects. As they looked around for new sources to tax, the only source of abundant wealth that did not have God on its side, i.e. outside the law, was Jewish wealth. Without God's protecting hand, and with an inflexible tax base, the Jews were fair game for the rulers of Europe. In fact, they were the only easy game in town.

Finally, all persons and property within the lands and holdings of the church were like the Egyptians of three thousand years before, subject to taxation by the church rulers—especially the Bishops and Archbishops. These clerics possessed great power and influence in medieval Europe. Their power was based on solid taxing powers equal to if not exceeding the taxing powers of the kings and nobles.

15

The Jews: On the Road to the Final Solution

Wherever and whenever one casts his eye on the Jewish communities of the Middle Ages, the observer always finds the Jews in the clutches of extortionate tax collectors.
—Israel Abraham, *Jewish Life in the Middle Ages*

In the Middle Ages the Jews played a crucial role in Western civilization. Modern capitalism and banking probably developed out of Jewish money and commercial practices.[1] In addition, the Jews carried the torch of learning and knowledge through this difficult period. The wisdom of the ancients—whether Hebrew, Greek, or Roman—was preserved through the Dark Ages by the Jewish community. The learned men of that period were found in the synagogues, not the monasteries. While it may be a surprise to most readers, the medieval Jewish society was classified by education, not wealth; the Jews were scholars first and merchants second. The education of Christians was restricted to religious dogma and produced a grotesque distortion of reality, and for those who ventured outside accepted dogma there was the prospect of being burned at the stake.

The Jews provided the personnel to administer most governments. They were the only people with a balance in their education. Christians, even the so-called educated ones, were usually incompetent in commercial matters. Worldly wisdom was an exclusive prerogative of the Jewish community.

The Jews prospered with the monopolies they enjoyed in banking and commerce, and this made them natural targets for taxation. Every Christian ruler collected special taxes from the Jews throughout the medieval period. This practice continued throughout most of Europe

149

until the time of Napoleon. Bad taxes that are productive of revenue die hard.

Special taxes against the Jews began with the *fiscus judaicus* of the Roman Emperor Vespasian in A.D. 72. This special Jewish tax was abolished by Julian in A.D. 326, and shortly thereafter he sent this letter to all the Jewish communities in the Roman Empire.

> In times past, by far the most burdensome thing in the yoke of your slavery has been the fact that you were subjected . . . to contribute an untold amount of money to the account of the treasury. Of this I used to see many instances with my own eyes, and I have learned of more, by finding the records which are preserved against you. Moreover, when a tax was about to be levied on you again I prevented it . . . and threw into the fire the records against you that had been stored in my desk. [Julian then tells how he put to death Roman officials who tried to enforce the Jewish tax.]
>
> And since I wish that you should prosper yet more, I have admonished . . . that the levy which is said to exist among you should be prohibited, and that no-one is any longer to have the power to oppress the masses of your people by such exactions.[2]

While Julian's successors abolished most of his reforms, they did not revive the special tax on Jews. Julian had the wisdom to destroy all the records pertaining to this tax, as well as all the tax collectors. A special procurator administered this tax along with a specialized staff which was outside the regular tax bureaucracy. When Julian exterminated the proponents of this tax, the special procurator and his key personnel were probably the first to go. Extermination has always been the most effective way to rid society of an undesirable political group. In the twentieth century the communists have used this technique with great success.

Special Jewish taxes were reintroduced in A.D. 813 by Louis the Pious, the son of Charlemagne. It was a modest revenue device at first, but like all taxation without representation, it quickly escalated. Once discriminatory taxes are assessed against a despised minority, it is only a matter of time before they become oppressive. Taxation without some concrete form of restraint knows no limit. The Jewish tax story is a marvelous illustration of that principle. One medieval historian summarized the Jewish tax situation with these words: "Wherever and whenever one casts his eye on the Jewish communities in the Middle Ages, the observer always finds the Jews in the clutches of extortionate tax collectors."[3]

The Jews became a scattered people after the Romans dismembered their country in the first century A.D. The term "wandering Jew" described the Jewish people after that time. More often than not, the wandering Jew was looking for a home after having been fleeced of bag and baggage by some voracious tax collector and sent on his way. They wandered because of the extortionate tax systems that drove them into exile.

In the ancient world the Jews were primarily farmers. In medieval times their lives were centered in commerce and banking. This shift in Jewish enterprise stems from their ostracism from farming and trades and crafts by the medieval Christian communities. By law, the Jews were compelled to perform the socially undesirable jobs in society. They were the tax collectors, the executioners, and the money-men of the community. All loathsome pursuits were passed on to the Jews. In addition, land ownership is always insecure in the face of oppressive taxation. Land can be seized with ease by the tax collector; gold and jewels can be hidden in the ground. Commercial paper is even safer. When the Jews were expelled from Spain, there were so many Jewish farms on the market that one could be bought for a piece of linen. In France, after the Jewish expulsion in A.D. 1306, one man acquired over fifty Jewish houses for a pittance. The local count and bishop demanded that the man share his good fortune with them. The lucky purchaser gave the Count five thousand livres (one livre was originally a pound of silver), two of the houses, and a plot of farmland. The bishop also received a large sum of cash.

It soon became obvious to the Jews that they must not put their assets in land. The safest way to hold wealth during precarious times is in a movable form and preferably in a small size that can be hidden. Tax collectors, monarchs and thieves can be thwarted when wealth is hidden in the ground. Most of the buried treasure of the Middle Ages was probably Jewish. The movement of Jewish enterprise into money and banking served both sides. It filled a vital economic need for the Christian community, and it served the security needs of the Jewish community.

The wandering Jew became a kind of tax rebel, but he was not the violent kind, like his ancient forefathers. He seemed to have learned from the failures of his rebellious ancestors. Better a shrewd taxpayer than a dead tax rebel. Perhaps there was a survival instinct, telling the Jews to handle their oppressive tax burdens in a peaceful manner. Historically, the ancient kingdoms of Israel and Judah were destroyed by unsuccessful tax revolts. The Jews learned to be shrewd rather than militant, and with that shrewdness they survived.

Avoidance of taxation was not always a wise policy. When the caliph of Baghdad offered to eliminate all special Jewish taxes, the leading Jewish banker in the community opposed such a drastic tax reduction with this reply: "Through the tax the Jew ensures his existence. By eliminating it, you would give free rein to the populace to shed Jewish blood."[4] Jews were often tolerated because they were valuable property and they performed needed services. The Jews survived because they were a quick source of easy cash for the rulers of most communities. The Jews sensed this and paid their taxes as protection money and a ticket for survival.

Yet even when the Jews paid their taxes there was the danger of extermination. When taxes reached outrageous levels, about all they could do was appeal to the conscience of the king, but when taxation is in issue, even today, the sovereign's conscience is like a piece of Swiss cheese—full of holes!

There was a whole bundle of Jewish taxes to support the Christian community. Poll taxes were most onerous, along with wealth taxes and arbitrary tallages that were assessed whenever the government was short of funds. Religious customs were taxed: marriages, burials, wines, Kosher food, and religious paraphernalia. There were coronation taxes, naval taxes (in Spain the Jews had to provide the anchors for all new vessels), protection taxes (for the military), taxes for public amusements (to pay circus performers), special taxes for the Jews when they used roadways, bridges and even when they entered and left Christian marketplaces and fairs. The Jews were called upon to shoulder the financial burdens of the Crusades, and they were compelled to finance church constructions. In brief, whenever money was needed, the Jews were the primary target of the tax system.

Despite these heavy burdens, the Jews were capable of living with them and even enriching themselves. They became the bankers and moneymen of Europe. Interest rates usually ran around 20 percent. To avoid the charge of usury they often had to structure a loan in the form of a sale, lease, or profit-sharing venture. While interest was illegal, borrowers had no choice but to pay it if they wanted a loan. The sinful and illegal status of interest is bound to have increased Christian and Moslem hostility toward the Jews.

The Jews are not to be pitied for their outcast and oppressed status in the Middle Ages. They were the freest people in the world at that time. By being outcasts from the Christian society they were not subject to the bondage and depressing rigidity of feudalism. Heavy taxes were the price they paid for the liberty they enjoyed.

The internal revenue system of the medieval Jews was an ancestor of our modern progressive tax practices. Three basic systems were developed to distribute equitably the tax burden of the Jewish community. Medieval Jewish taxes were somewhat like Roman tribute—the local Jewish community was expected to assess and collect the revenue on its own. In time, three effective methods were developed.

The first method can be called *paternalistic*. A wise member of the Jewish community was appointed to assess each person in a manner that seemed just and fair. The wealthy were expected to shoulder a larger share of the tax debt than the poor, who were usually exempt along with rabbis, doctors, and teachers. Like the liturgy the system was progressive. We might call this the Aristides system, because a respected elder statesman allocated tax burdens among all taxpayers according to their ability to pay.

The second method involved a *tax expert* or accountant. The tax bill of the community was divided upon accounting principles. Everyone paid his share, calculated by mathematical precision, after being interviewed by the tax expert. If the total income and wealth of the community was worth one thousand talents and the tax bill was one hundred talents, then each person paid 10 percent of his wealth toward the taxes owed. The system was proportionate.

The third method we can call *declarative*. Everyone made a declaration of his worth and the tax bill was then divided up, proportionately, among all taxpayers based on their declarations. A tax expert was not used. It was an honor system.

Our modern revenue systems for income taxation are a combination of all three. The taxpayer starts by making a declaration and paying the appropriate tax. Thereafter a tax expert looks at the declaration and performs an audit if the declaration looks in error. In addition, we add the progressive feature of the paternalistic method, except that the ability to pay is determined by arbitrary standards, established by our tax makers.

Shakespeare may never have seen a Shylock, the leading fictional Jewish character in literature. In *The Merchant of Venice* his human qualities were unique in an age dominated by anti-Semitism. He could bleed, cry, laugh, and have all the joys and pains that Christians experience. Shakespeare humanized this Jewish character for an English audience that had little if any contact with Jews.[5] In A.D. 1290, the Jews had been expelled from England by a Catholic monarch; they returned, four hundred years later, after Shakespeare's time, with the permission of a Protestant king.

The English were one of the first to expel the Jews. Once they had done so, most other European leaders followed. When the Jews were in England, the king set up a special tax bureau to handle Jews. There were special tax rolls and a Parliament of the Jews to guarantee and assist in the collection of a number of Jewish taxes.

Regular Jewish taxes consisted of religious taxes, commercial taxes, poll taxes, and death taxes. The poll tax was graduated—wealthy Jews paid more than poorer ones. The death tax was one-third of the estate. But the tax that crippled the Jewish community was the tallage—an arbitrary assessment against the Jews invoked by the king at will. It was

Preserved in the Public Record Office, London, this drawing comes from the Jewish tax
rolls of England for the year 1233. A strange illustration for tax records, it shows a
wealthy Jew, Isaac of Norwich, portrayed with three heads. His wife is shown below.
Demons are depicting the suffering he will receive. Norwich was one of the principal seats
of the Jews in England. Thomas Wright, in his *History of Caricature* (London, 1864, p.
176), says that one of the clerks in the king's court drew this caricature on one of the
official tax rolls where it has been preserved.

often a wealth tax, calculated on a fixed percentage of Jewish wealth,
such as one-third or one-tenth. It could be a fixed sum, like Roman tribute. It was morally justified because the Jews acquired their wealth by
"sinful means," i.e., by banking and money lending. Legally it was justified because the Jews were deemed to be the property of the king, like
his royal serfs and peasants. The king was simply taking what was his.
When a churchman suggested that the king force the Jews into the
church, the king scoffed at the idea by pointing out that if the Jews
became Christians he would be "rid of valuable property and given only
a subject in return."[6] As Christians they would be protected against arbitrary tax levies, and by medieval tax-limiting charters between the
king and his Christian subjects.

In England a Jewish Parliament was established to approve any Jewish tax that the king demanded. The main purpose of the Parliament was
to make the leading men in the Jewish community insurers for the full

collection of the tallage—a revival of the old Roman decurion system. If the king became impatient and wanted to speed up the collection process, he would imprison the richest Jews and their families in the Bloody Tower. Once the kings of England discovered how easy it was to assess and collect the tallage from the Jews, the Crown's revenue needs were solved. Christians settled down to an era of little tax while the monarch fleeced his Jewish tax-serfs of their wealth. Unfortunately, the greed of Henry III and his successors knew no bounds of reason. King John, for example, ordered a wealthy Jew, Abraham of Bristol, to pay him ten thousand marks (a mark was eight ounces of silver). When the man refused, John ordered his tax collector to extract one tooth every day until payment was made. After seven days, and seven teeth, the assessment was paid. After that, Abraham committed suicide. For sixty years the Jewish community was plundered until the Jews were a destitute people. King Edward, in 1290, ordered the Jews to leave England, partly because they were no longer "valuable property." The main reason may have been because of the Christians. The clergy, barons, and commoners made an enormous tax offering to the king. Early records state that to all Christians the expulsion "was very pleasing." For the next 365 years Jews were ostensibly forbidden on English soil. Their final exodus was described by a Jewish historian in these words: "Expulsion must have come as a relief to the oppressed people, whose sorrows were past all endurance." There may have been little relief by the expulsion order, despite what this Jewish historian says. The order provided for the confiscation of every item of property and land the Jews possessed, and further decreed that if any Jew were found in England at any time after the date set for expulsion, they would be hanged. He did allow them to keep enough money for passage out of England, but they were robbed of all their funds at the ports of embarcation.[7]

The Jews may not have been as destitute as Jewish historians contend. A Jewish underground economy, like today, was in full operation in medieval Europe, secreting Jewish wealth out of oppressed countries to safer depositories.

While new taxation may not have been available to the French king because of the medieval prohibition against an unheard-of tax, the English device of expulsion would accomplish the same thing, and do a more thorough job than taxation. In the name of God, angels, and saints, the French king, Philip the Fair, expelled the Jews from France, ostensibly for oppressive money-lending policies. With the Jews gone, to whom would the French borrowers make payment? Like a good sovereign Philip appointed royal guardians to collect the loans made by the Jews. With the Jews gone, the money quite legally passed to the Crown. Philip must have been proud of his ingenuity—he had surpassed his rival across the Channel without the use of a tax and in a much shorter time.

The scheme did not work well. The Jews were good businessmen who kept their customers happy in the interest of good business management, while the king's debt collectors were ruthless thugs. Finally, in 1315, because of the "clamour of the people," the Jews were invited back with an offer of twelve years of guaranteed residence, free from government interference. The Jews returned but the king's successor did not honor his commitment. In 1322, the Jews were expelled again.

The Jews fleeing from England, France, and central Europe found favor in Spain. For two-and-a-half centuries the Jews lived peacefully in Islamic Spain under the Moors. Their welcome turned sour after the Christians took over and expelled the Moslems. In 1492, only a year after they had been granted a lucrative contract to collect taxes for Queen Isabella, expulsion was ordered. A wealthy Jew, influential with the Queen, offered a large sum of money to cancel the expulsion order. When news leaked of this offer, Jew-haters likened the deal unto the thirty pieces of silver paid to Judas Iscariot. The Crown had no choice but to renege. There were hundreds of thousands of Jews in Spain. The exodus that followed was as horrible for the Jewish people as the Holocaust in Hitler's Europe. The King of Portugal offered his land as sanctuary for a head tax of one ducat plus 25 percent of the wealth of the immigrating Jews. Six months later he threw the Jews out of his country and, naturally, kept the tax.

The road to Dachau stretches back five hundred years. Hitler's solutions to his "Jewish problem" were not new. Since the Middle Ages the Jews in German-speaking Europe had been taxed and exterminated in a manner far more ruthless than what had taken place in the rest of Europe. The *fiscus judaicus* started with the Romans and ended with the Nazis. But the Nazis only revived a long-standing revenue device that had become deeply embedded in German society.

Long before Hitler, the Jewish poll tax had become the Poll Tax of Shame. It was levied and collected in an abusive and rude manner. The ghetto arose primarily as a convenience to the tax collector. Collective tax responsibility is meaningless unless the taxpayers are consolidated into a taxpaying entity of some kind. The isolated part of the city set aside for the Jews was a tax district. In order to leave the ghetto, the Jew had to pay a special toll. The Jewish community was told to organize and collect its poll taxes and tender the final aggregate sum to the state.

Ghettos, which were originally tax districts, were frequently fleeced by Christian mobs. When German rulers needed large revenues they did not need to increase taxation; they would issue an expulsion order, often coupled with an extermination order of burning. In the fifteenth century, expulsions, burnings, and property seizures spread from Vienna to Berlin, Frankfurt, Bremen, Dresden, Leipzig, and throughout Bohemia and Saxony. Oppression was so bad in Saxony that it has been called the Protestant Spain of the Jews.

The events in Germany were significant because they did not subside. By the seventeenth century, the Jews were accepted in France, Britain, and the Low Countries. But in German-speaking Europe, anti-Semitism continued with lootings and with increasingly oppressive laws and special taxes, which continued well into the nineteenth century. When Hitler came to power and looked for a solution to what he called his Jewish problem, he did not have to reach very far back in time. The Nuremberg decrees of the Nazis which took away citizenship from the Jews can be traced back to 1343 when a German emperor, Louis IV, called the "Bavarian," did the same thing. The confiscations of property under the guise of taxation, the blaming of the Jews for the ills of society, and the aspersion that the Jews were "devils" was reflected in medieval as well as Nazi teachings. Even the "final solution" has a medieval counterpart. The genocidal solution was attempted around 1298 by the *Judenschlachter* (Jew killers), led by a butcher named Rindfleisch. They slaughtered the Jews in the city of Rottingen, which in itself was nothing new, as periodic killings on a city basis were not infrequent. But what was unique about the *Judenschlachter* is that they then went from city to city throughout medieval Germany, exterminating the Jewish inhabitants. A contemporary chronicler declares that 100,000 Jews were put to death: "Ultimately, only a few handfuls of impecunious and vagabond Jews remained in northern Europe."[8] Exactly what Hitler tried to achieve.

It must not be assumed that the Jews paid all their oppressive taxes with complete honesty and faithfulness. Among the great unsolved secrets of this period are the techniques and methods by which the Jews evaded these exactions. The devices the Jews used to hide and protect their wealth may never be known. But hide it they did. The commercial paper of our age, which the Jews invented in the medieval period, was used to frustrate fraud, thieves, and tax collectors as well as aid commerce.

The innumerable schemes devised to steal Jewish wealth were equally matched by schemes on the part of the Jews to protect their wealth. We know that in the 1930s a great deal of Jewish wealth slipped across the borders of Germany into Swiss banks, as Hitler set out to steal Jewish wealth through tax techniques that were over five hundred years old. The Swiss banks came to the aid of the German Jews in the 1930s, but what was the Swiss counterpart in the late Middle Ages? It

Napoleon in his imperial robes grants to European Jews relief from special tax exactions that had been their burden for over seventeen hundred years, since the *fiscus judaicus*.

is likely we will never know the whole story. The secrets and techniques were obviously never published and they have been lost from history. One allusion to Jewish evasion practices comes from Bohemia in A.D. 1336. The king fined the Jewish community for concealing its wealth. Furthermore, the Jewish Talmud regulations of this period required treasures to be "buried in the soil."[9]

Special Jewish taxes continued on the continent until the time of Napoleon. For all his sins, he was the great champion of tax equality for the Jewish people, who should have a warm place in their hearts for the Corsican general. Like Julian in Roman times, Napoleon rid every country he conquered of the *fiscus judaicus*. But unlike Julian, his reforms did not always last. After the defeat in Russia, as the Grande Armee retreated back to France, the old Jewish taxes returned. As soon as Napoleon's troops had withdrawn and the rumble of cannon died out, the central Europeans, especially the Germans, reinstated the Jewish taxes. When Hitler came to power, he simply reinstated them once more. Bad taxes are hard to kill, especially when they are directed at a wealthy but unpopular minority.

16

Medieval England: How Englishmen Purchased Liberty with Taxes

With occasions of his wars he pilleth them with taxes and tallages unto the bare bones.

—King John, prior to *Magna Carta*

Women have played a remarkable role in England's tax struggles. We noted how Boadicea battled the Romans and lost the revolt to rid the English of Rome's tax burdens. In the Middle Ages, long after the Romans had left England, we read of the legend of Lady Godiva. The chronicler Roger of Wendover (died 1236) relates how the countess Godiva appealed to her husband to remit the heavy taxes he imposed on Coventry. Fed-up with her nagging, he promised to comply if she would ride nude through the town. She let her hair down so only her beautiful legs showed, mounted a horse, and rode through the town. The taxes were remitted. Today, Godiva's ride is reenacted in pageants in Coventry.

In the early Middle Ages the Vikings pounced on English villages along the North Sea coast, plundering and slaughtering the inhabitants. You can still find an old English prayerbook with the passage, "Guard us from the Northmen."

To defend against the Viking menace a special land tax was devised called the *danegeld*, payable at the rate of two shillings for every hide of land (100–120 acres). The system was unpopular and a number of tax collectors were killed trying to collect the danegeld in Worcestershire. By the time of William the Conqueror (A.D. 1066), the tax was being replaced with a land tax on ploughed land only, called a *carucate*.

The famous Doomsday Book contained a complete survey of all the lands and personal property in England. William the Conqueror had the book compiled for the taxation of his newly acquired England, but re-

"He took away the tax, And built himself an everlasting name" (Tennyson on Godiva).

The *danegeld* was a tribute tax paid by the English to buy peace from the marauding Danes. It was a humiliating tax, usually assessed at two shillings per hide of land.

volts crippled tax collection from the beginning, and in time English kings ceased to use this remarkable census.

> [T]here was no single hide nor yard of land, nor indeed one ax nor one cow nor one pig was there left out, and not put down on the record. . . . Other investigations followed the first . . . and the land was vexed with much violence arising from the collection of royal taxes.[1] (Eleventh-century chronicle)

Knights were required to spend forty days a year in the service of the king, providing there was a genuine need for their services. In time, a money payment developed in lieu of services. Forty days was hardly sufficient to carry on a military venture in Scotland or Normandy. The tax in lieu of service was called the *scutage*, or shield.

The most arbitrary medieval tax was the feudal tallage, limited to the domains of a lord; it could not pass through the ranks of the feudal system. The king could levy a tallage on his own domains (which included all Jews), but he could not levy a tallage on the domains of a baron, duke, or other nobleman. The tallage was sometimes called a land tax, but it was also a capital tax on personal property. It could come as a poll tax. The closest thing we have to a tallage today is the plenary power legislatures have to tax. Tallage was used in a generic sense, referring to any arbitrary and oppressive tax. One medieval historian, Geoffrey of Monmouth, records the use of the tallage, "to help the cristen men of Jhersalem to pay cruel tallages that the turkes had sette upon them."[2]

When the king had special needs that could not be met by his regular revenue devices, he went to the Great Council of Barons and asked for an *aid*. The barons would debate the request and if it seemed reasonable they would vote an aid for the king. But they would often exact something in return.

The aid was the forerunner of national taxation. If the Great Council approved an aid it passed through the ranks of the feudal system to the lesser nobles and vassals of the realm. Aids had the potential to reach the wealth of the entire nation.

Charters restricting taxing powers were common throughout the medieval period. Magna Carta, meaning "great charter," was not a new or novel document. King John had terrible financial troubles. The pope had excommunicated him for seizing church lands; he had been expelled from northern France by the French; and finally, his brother, Richard the Lionheart, needed an enormous sum for ransom following his kidnapping while returning from a crusade in the holy land. John increased the customary scutage for knights from one to two marks. In 1204 he increased the rate again by half a mark with the consent of a council of knights at Oxford. In 1210 and 1214 he increased the scutage to three marks without authorization. Tallages, which were supposed to be occasional, became perpetual. One writer wrote in 1211, "With occasions of his wars he pilleth them with taxes and tallages unto the bare bones."[3]

Even these taxes were not enough. John tried to introduce a novel fine of from three to ten marks against knights who refused to join his forces. He passed this fine through the medieval system to lesser knights who served barons and dukes. This was a daring, ingenious, but desperate attempt to tax the whole realm without going to the barons for an aid.

The barons confronted John on the plains of Runnymede outside London and compelled him to sign Magna Carta, which would stop his con-

King John is confronted by his rebel barons at Runnymede, June 15, 1215. He agrees to place his royal seal on Magna Carta, which prohibited arbitrary government, especially in matters of taxation.

tinual disregard of the tax customs of the realm. The key provision was, "No scutage or aid, save the customary feudal ones, shall be levied except by the common consent of the realm." John's attempt to stretch the revenue devices of the realm had failed, but not entirely. Extra taxation could be collected with consent. In time the consent concept expanded. A rising class of wealthy commoners were called to meet in a House of Commons, to approve taxation for commoners in the same way the Great Council approved taxation for the nobility. The king now became a politician. When extra revenue was needed, he did not need to steal it or arbitrarily increase taxation, he would call together his two councils of taxpayer representatives and present a case for more taxation.

In the beginning, consent did not mean that the barons would vote with a majority binding the minority. No baron was bound unless he consented. This is illustrated by an early case in 1217, two years after Magna Carta. The Bishop of Winchester was brought before the King's Court for not collecting an aid for the king. The court acquitted the bishop because he was absent from the council when the vote was taken.[4] No one could consent on his behalf. It would be some time before consent meant majority rule, which was another victory for the king. Unanimous consent is a hard principle to work with, especially in exacting taxes.

One of the most important and overlooked chapters in Magna Carta is the provision for merchants, creating free trade in an era of crippling tolls and duties. Merchants were never sure of their right of free passage in and out of England and, especially, free passage within the country. Merchants were often taxed relentlessly by local authorities and by the king's tax men as well. Magna Carta protected trade from internal tolls and duties and prohibited excessive tolls at seaports:

> Let all merchants have safety and security to go out of England, to come into England, and to remain in and go about through England, as well by land as by water, for the purpose of buying and selling, without payment of any evil or unjust tolls, on payment of the ancient and just customs.[5]

The United States and Canadian constitutions adopted this principle of internal free trade. Commerce moving within the nation cannot be taxed. Freedom to travel in and out of the country cannot be curtailed. The Russians find it difficult to understand why the West emphasizes this basic human right. Magna Carta is the source.

When the king asked for an aid (all aids were for war), the Great Council was concerned with two things: Was there a real need? If so, was the request reasonable? For a war to be necessary it had to be a just, defensive war. England was a Christian nation and the shedding of human blood required justification. An offensive war was illegal; taxes for such a war would be improper. In short, a lawful tax requires a just expenditure.

When the king asked the Council for a scutage from the lesser knights of the realm for a war in Flanders, the barons refused with this explanation: "For neither they nor their predecessors nor their forefathers ever did service in that land." About the same time the pope gave the Crown some lands in Sicily. The king again asked for an aid to secure these lands. The Council again refused for the same reason.

When the king asked for an aid to recover lands in Normandy, the barons asked, "Was not Normandy the same as Sicily and Flanders?" The king was learning that a good politician had to be a good debater. He answered the Great Council with the domino theory: If Normandy is not secure, French kings could easily invade England. The recovery of the king's estates in Normandy was actually a defense of the common realm because these lands protected England from invasion. Like good politicians the barons compromised and began approving limited aids for the king's military operations in northern France. The concept that taxes for military purposes must be for "defense" developed at this time in England. It will reappear again in the Netherlands, Imperial Spain, and the U.S. Constitution.

The constitutional doctrine that developed was expressed by Henry of Ghent, a Parisian legist, whose writings on legal theory appeared from 1272 to 1296. The king could not levy extraordinary taxes except upon "evident utility, evident necessity and dire emergency."[6] The lawfulness of a tax was determined by its expenditure. An extraordinary tax for war had to meet the foregoing standards. We no longer subscribe to that view although a number of Vietnam protesters went to prison for refusing to pay income taxes which financed a war founded on dubious constitutional grounds. Furthermore, the Vietnam debacle may have happened because the Great Council of the United States (Congress) did not adjudicate the issue of "evident utility, evident necessity and dire emergency" of the war. They accepted the domino theory even though Vietnam was on the other side of the world. If Congress had made a full and open investigation of that terrible war the false assumptions made by the presidency might have been uncovered.

The king also learned that lobbying a tax law through Parliament was not always a good thing. An aid for an offensive operation against the Scots produced a rebellion in Cornwall. The Cornish people lynched a number of tax collectors because the war was not for the defense of the realm, but rather was an offensive war which could not be lawfully financed with extraordinary taxation. In the end the people were the final judges over taxation and their opinions could not be ignored. Parliamentary consent was not, necessarily, the consent of the realm.

The debate and bargain for taxes between the king and his Great Council eventually gave birth to parliamentary government. The king needed revenue, but revenue depended on the reasonableness of the king's request. Even then, Parliament learned to grant taxes in return for favors from the king. Tax moneys had to be bargained for and this bargaining process became the essence of politics. Liberties and rights were granted by the king in return for money.

To ensure a continuation of rights and benefits from the king, Parliament realized in the beginning that taxation should only be granted for short periods, rarely more than one year. The rights of Englishmen would be secure as long as the king was denied the power to tax permanently. Each year the process of debate and bargain for taxes would repeat itself.

English government after Magna Carta was based on the separation of powers, but not the separation of powers the Americans espouse so vociferously. The king could spend, but not tax, Parliament could tax, but did not spend. As long as power to tax and the power to spend were separated, the rights of Englishmen would live forever, especially the right to be free from oppressive taxation. Today the principle of the separation of powers means something quite different. Our current runaway taxation is the natural consequence of our abandonment of that ancient English practice. We live in a pre-Magna Carta world in which we—like the subjects of King John—can be "pilleth with taxes and tallages unto the bar bones."

Part IV

Russia, Switzerland, Spain, and Germany

Russian history has fascinated and puzzled Westerners for centuries. The Russians are referred to as the "mysterious slavs," and their history, said Winston Churchill, was "a riddle wrapped in a mystery inside an enigma."[1] The puzzle, however, is not so incomprehensible if Russia's tax story is understood. The Russian political psyche developed out of the tax brutality of the Golden Horde and the early Moscow rulers. Later, Peter the Great put Russia on a course to superpower status by reorganizing a tax system that had crippled economic growth for centuries. He gave the Russian people the option either to pay poll taxes or enter state service. The communists, after destroying the ruling classes, simply took away the first option.

The Swiss, like the Jews, are a small people who have influenced civilization in a way out of proportion to their size. No nation today can make monetary or political changes without taking into account the reaction of the bankers of Switzerland. Currencies rise and fall with the opinions of "the gnomes of Zurich." Canada's currency took a serious fall shortly after the election of the separatist party in Quebec—because Swiss bankers felt uncomfortable about the future of the Canadian dollar. If Quebec separated and the Canadian confederation fell apart, what would become of the Canadian dollar and foreign debt obligations of the Canadian government?

No modern nation has ever matched the power of Imperial Spain, not even the British Empire. The collapse of Spanish power in the seventeenth century has perplexed historians for three hundred years. Analysts of that collapse keep returning to Spain's tax troubles as the root of the decay that brought about Spain's demise.

For hundreds of years Germany was a bundle of small princedoms under the Holy Roman emperor, but because the emperor could not tax he was a mere figurehead. Modern Germany was eventually forged by Prussian military power. The Prussians succeeded where the emperor

167

failed, largely because taxing power went along with their military rule. The war department in Berlin was as much a tax bureau as it was a military staff, acting as chief tax collector for Prussian rulers. When analyzing the Prussian takeover of the German states, Prussian taxing power should not be overlooked. In a word, taxing power is the guts of sovereignty.

A sixteenth-century manuscript from the Lenin Library, Moscow, shows Ivan I ("Money-bags") as the Khan's chief tax collector, punishing a delinquent taxpayer, Boyar Abencius.

17

Russia: The Tax Road to Serfdom and the Soviets

She was wiser than all men.
—Russian Chronicles on Princess Olga, A.D. 1000

Russia's road to nationhood had little in common with the rise of the nation-states of Western Europe. When the West was enjoying a rebirth of Greek and Roman culture in the Renaissance, the Russians were under the yoke of the most ruthless tax collector since Sargon and the terror-kings of Assyria. Genghis Khan and his Golden Horde swept through the heartland of the slavs and annihilated an advanced form of democratic and civilized culture. The Mongol Khans brought a form of oppression to the Russian people that has lingered to the present. Moscow rose to dominance because her princes became the Khan's best tax collectors. Then it was an easy step for the prince of Moscow to move from chief tax collector for the Khan to chief of everything over everybody.

In the Middle Ages, Russia had the good fortune of being outside the Roman Empire and was free from the forces that fostered feudalism. The Russian peasant could move about the countryside and contract his services to the landowner who offered the most attractive price. The Russian peasant, unlike his counterpart in the West, was free.

Traditional Russian history begins when the Vikings moved into Russia and took control of Kiev, Novgorod, and Pskov, key trading cities on the Kiev Waterway dominated by the great Dnieper River which flows into the Black Sea. In a short time slavic culture absorbed the Scandinavian Rus. Of these three leading cities, Kiev eventually dominated, probably because of the tax policies introduced by Princess Olga around A.D. 950. Early Russian chroniclers called her "The wisest of women," and "wiser than all men,"[1] a title she justly deserved. Before Olga's tax reforms, the princes of Kiev, Novgorod, and Pskov would embark on an annual winter visit to the smaller towns and cities to collect taxes, in what was a very inefficient system. Olga divided the countryside into tax districts, each with a district director of taxes who was responsible for all revenue and who lived in the district all year. With this greatly improved system, Kiev easily rose to dominate the Waterway and became the leading city in all of Europe. In A.D. 988, Olga's grandson, Prince Vladimir of Kiev, embraced Christianity, rejecting Islam and Judaism ostensibly because Russians didn't want to give up their vodka or submit to circumcision.

Olga ruled Kiev as regent for her minor son, Svyetislav. When he became of age she not only passed the ruling authority to him, but her wisdom with respect to taxation, political power, and prosperity. Most of the Kievan region, especially to the south along the borders of the Dnieper to the Black Sea, was ruled by the Khazars, a Jewish kingdom. The Khazars' power was based on a 10 percent tax on all trade along the Dnieper, Don, and Volga Rivers. This tax naturally clashed with the ambitions of the new Kievan rulers who now had a district director tax system capable of expanding throughout the Ukraine all the way to the Volga. Olga's son, Svyetislav, ordered the villages and traders along the rivers to "pay nothing to the Khazars."[2]

One by one the cities and villages controlled by the Khazars fell to the Rus until the Khazars were destroyed. Thus Russian control over the slavic peoples began when they expelled the ruling Jews over a 10 percent tax. It is quite possible that Vladimir joined Christianity, not so much for his vodka and foreskin, but for tax incentives and support against the Khazars. When he embraced Christianity he knew Constantinople would be on his side. Furthermore, this was an age when co-religionists received a tax break. Vladimir had selected his new religion for more down-to-earth reasons than previously believed.

We do not know much about the Khazars. They assessed a special poll tax on all non-Jews and brought order to the steppe lands of Russia. After their destruction, the steppe was taken over by bands of Tartars, whom the Russians could not pacify. In time a military stalemate developed which neither side could win. This stalemate is the basis for the Russian opera, *Prince Igor*, which tells a romantic story of a Russian prince who goes to war against the Tartars. The story ends in peaceful coexistence.

The vacuum of power in the steppe was eventually filled by the Golden Horde. Under the leadership of Genghis Khan, a sea of Mongol warriors, living on mare's milk, subjugated the inhabitants and then turned on the Rus. They demanded 10 percent of everything now, and

10 percent annually thereafter. This was not the same kind of tax the Khazars had levied. The 10 percent paid to the Khazars was a pittance compared to the 10 percent tax of the Mongols. The Russians were to learn a lesson about tax systems that taxpayers everywhere including today should not forget—never judge a tax system by its rates alone.

Thriving Russian cities along Russia's waterways were reduced to ashes. The savage Viking Rus were no match for the Horde. Terror swept over the countryside and whole villages surrendered at the sight of a single Mongol horseman. As a rule, however, the Russians fought valiantly for their homeland, as Hitler was to learn. The modus operandi of the Horde was simple. When they came upon a city they would send in an ambassador with an ultimatum: pay or die. In the city of Ryazan (about one hundred miles from Moscow), the prince replied to the usual Mongol summons to surrender a tenth of everything (population included): "When there is none of us left, all will be yours."[3] And so it was. Ryazan was one of the cities obliterated.

The Mongols were only interested in taxes and recruits for their armies. They showed no interest in Russian culture, or any culture for that matter. Under the Mongols Russian civilization slipped back into a dark age at the very time the West was moving out of its dark ages into the Renaissance—the rebirth of ancient Greek and Latin culture. "The Mongols," said the great Russian poet Pushkin, "did not bring Aristotle to Russia."

The shattering of Russian culture by the Mongols was achieved with taxation. During the two hundred or more years of Mongol rule there were three distinct phases of their tax system.

In the beginning the Mongols farmed out tax collection to powerful Moslem merchants from Baghdad. The Mongols were warriors, and tax collection was beneath them. The Moslem tax-farmers were slavers as much as tax collectors. Defaulting villagers were quickly seized and shipped to the slave auctions in Baghdad. In 1262 a number of Russian cities revolted and slaughtered the Moslems to the last man, inviting almost certain reprisal and death. History, however, like anything involving human nature, is never certain. The great Russian prince Alexander Nevsky persuaded the Khan to take no reprisals, but rather reform his tax system. As a result, Moslem tax-farmers were removed from the system. The Khan divided Russia into a number of military-financial districts governed by a Mongol tax director called a Great Baskak, supported by a garrison of Mongol warriors.

A census was taken which included all lands, peoples, and a registry of young males for recruitment. The system was Roman in form, but Assyrian in spirit—a spirit that still continues in the Russian social order.

This picture appears in a modern history book used in Russian elementary schools. A Russian peasant bows before a "Great Baskak" (Mongol tax collector) during the second phase of the Mongol tax system.

A dual system of government also developed. Local Russian princes took charge of everything except tax collection and military affairs, which were under the Khan. The Great Baskaks were the district directors of Tartar revenue, collecting seven basic taxes: annual and extraordinary tribute, sale and customs, raw land taxes, a plow tax, a poll tax, and a draft evasion tax.

The third and final state of Mongol taxation carried seeds of destruction. The Khan made the common, but fatal mistake of relinquishing control over tax collection. The Great Baskaks were replaced with Russian princes. On the surface the system looked good. Local princes would run the tax systems, eliminating the need for Mongol garrisons. For the Khan the new system provided easy revenue at a much-reduced cost.

An obscure prince of an unheard-of Russian town caught the Khan's attention with his unusually successful tax collecting methods. The town was Moscow and the prince was Ivan I, nicknamed "Moneybags" for his extraordinary talents as tax collector. Ivan persuaded the Khan to commission him to collect taxes from delinquent Russian cities. Moneybags's fame spread along with the demand for his services. The Mongols probably asked, why not let angry Russian taxpayers deal with

Ivan? Why should brave warriors degrade themselves with tax collection when Moneybags could do it so much better? Whatever the reasons, the Mongols appeared anxious to assign their tax-collecting duties to the Moscow prince.

Ivan took full advantage of his new role in the Khan's tax system. Without the Baskaks to keep a watchful eye on revenues, the prince had an opportunity to keep much of the tax money for himself. The profit was enormous. The Khan did appoint an annual receiver, called a *Moscovskii Doroga*, to take custody of the payments due to the Khan, but the Doroga was far removed from the tax-collecting process. Ivan was brutal, but not in an indiscriminating way. The Tartars had used a sledgehammer approach of punishing delinquent cities—everyone would suffer: men, women, and children. Ivan did not abuse the peasants, but rather, he punished the nobles and city rulers.

His success impressed the Khan so much that he was appointed chief tax collector for all Russia. Moscow became the clearinghouse for all Mongol taxes, and the unheard-of city would be unheard-of no more.

With huge profits from surplus revenues and shrewd bargaining with the Moscovskii Doroga, the prince of Moscow started to acquire adjacent principalities and lands. He had revenues to obtain the best warriors. Cities that could not be bought were easily conquered. His wealth attracted the rulers of the Church of Kiev. Like Augustus of Rome, the prince obtained control of Russia by controlling the tax system. The step to Tsar (Caesar) was as easy for him as it was for Augustus. His revenues enabled him to build the Kremlin, which was the only fortress in Russia capable of withstanding a Tartar siege. Russia's other princes, some willing and some not, soon rallied around Moscovy.

With large tax revenues at his disposal, Ivan and his successors prepared to free themselves from Tartar rule. The Russians made the Tartars fight for tribute. Slowly Mongol control (tax collection) of Russia faded. It wasn't until the sixteenth century that the Mongol grip on Russia was finally releasd by the efforts of Ivan IV, called "Ivan the Terrible." The power base established by his fathers through taxation had built up to the point where he could expel the Mongols, once and for all. He initiated this expulsion by first repudiating all tax obligations to the Tsar when the Moscovskii Doroga made his annual visit to receive tribute. Ivan built the beautiful St. Basil's Cathedral to commemorate the event. "Tsar of all Russia" would be his new title and the princes of all Russian cities would receive their commission to rule from him by bowing on their knees before the mighty Tsar. Local assemblies of taxpayers who directed Russia's princes in the days before the Mongols would never return. Autocracy would prevail at all levels. The new system which Ivan set up "was madness, but the madness of a genius."[4]

Ivan the Terrible repudiates his tax obligations to the Khan, asserting Russian independence and causing a shock for the Tartars' tax receiver, the *Moscovskii Doroga*. Control of the tax revenues gave Ivan control of Russia.

Ivan the Terrible established a special branch of agents with extraordinary power apart from the regular government; hence the name *oprichnina*, meaning special, separate, or apart. These special agents had their own courts and operated in a world of their own like Stalin's NKVD.

Ivan's special agents took a loyalty oath to the Tsar: They would only associate with fellow oprichniki; they wore black clothing, rode a black horse with saddlebags showing a dog's head and a broom. The broom symbolized a clean sweep over the Tsar's enemies; the dog meant faithfulness to their master. They were indiscriminately ruthless in their operations. The diary of one oprichniki records, "I did no harm to anyone today, I was resting."[5]

The oprichnina were concerned with revenue as much as with the tsar's enemies. The tsar needed revenue from the nobles more than homage. The oprichnina confiscated lands of the nobles and transferred them to new owners, or themselves, with new revenue and service obligations to the tsar. When the oprichnina were disbanded, this pattern of revenue and service to the tsar soon applied to all nobles and all lands. With the oprichnina, Ivan was not just rooting out traitors, but rather reorganizing the revenue structure of the state.

Ivan the Terrible and his special revenue agents, the *oprichnina*. In this woodcut, Ivan holds the head of a boyar and leads a group to their death while three *oprichniki* divide up the spoils. They were as much ruthless revenue agents as security police—separate and apart from the regular governmental agencies, like modern tax police.

The road to serfdom in Russia and Rome was similar. In both places overtaxed peasants accepted bondage or chattel slavery to a large landowner as a way to avoid tax slavery. The bondage of serfdom was less oppressive than the bondage of the tax system.

In Russia serfdom came slowly. There was no Diocletian who revolutionized the tax system one year and put everyone into serfdom the next. In the beginning, peasants became de facto serfs when they became tenants of farmlands. The landlord gave them land, a house, livestock, and farming tools. A mortgage was executed by the peasant which was due and payable each November. After paying a one-third crop rent, interest on the mortgage, and taxes to the Tsar, nothing was left to pay off the mortgage. The collateral for the mortgage was the peasant and his family—human collateral, which was bound to the landlord until the debt was paid off. In the normal course of events the debt could never be paid off, which is the way the system was intended to operate.[6]

Landlords developed an interesting tax avoidance scheme. A new landlord would pay off a peasant's debt and refinance the peasant on his own land. Poll taxes were based on a census which was conducted about every five years. Before the census was taken, new serfs would not be taxed—they were not on the census rolls. The Russian government eventually had to pass a law preventing this practice.

The Russian people had bad luck with their tsars. Most of them from the death of Ivan the Terrible in 1584 until the reign of Peter the Great in 1682 were just plain stupid. Peter the Great was one who was not. He was seven feet tall, a human dynamo of a man, and he was gifted with a clear sharp mind. Once Peter became tsar, the Russian state started to move.

Peter is often remembered for his crudeness. After he visited England, Parliament felt compelled to pay a large sum of money to restore the shambles of the house he occupied in London. It took six months for the stench to finally leave the place. Peter ate with his fingers, belched and farted in public, and indulged in other gross behavior. His guests were drowned in booze—so much so that once in a while someone actually died from excessive intoxication or wandered out drunk into the Russian winter and froze to death. He wanted Russian ladies to look sexy like Western women. He ordered them to wear low-necked evening dresses. And if they refused to drink, he and his friends would hold their noses and pour wine down their throats.

As a leader, Peter was something else. His visit to the West made him determined to remake Russia on Western standards not unlike Russian leaders today. At the time he came to power Russia was in decline. Peter reversed the course of Russian history by remaking the tax system, stimulating economic growth, and decentralizing the state. Before Peter's reforms, homes and farmlands were being abandoned. There were hordes of people who did not work, paid no taxes, and drifted aimlessly. Taxes were paid on plowed land, Tartar-style. There was little incentive to acquire new farming equipment, and old lands that were not productive were abandoned. There was also a household tax on each farming family. Shrewd peasants would band together and share a common dwelling. Duplexes and triplexes were built to take advantage of the one-dwelling, one-tax loophole. The tsar's tax collector responded by considering each outside door as a separate household. The peasant responded by boarding up one of the doors. This meant that families would not expand and develop new lands or construct new farmhouses. Idleness and unemployment prevailed. The plow tax and the household tax had crippled the country.

Peter corrected the tax system by abolishing both of these taxes and instituting a single poll tax on all males. Free peasants paid a higher rate than serfs. This poll tax was called a soul tax. Peasants found it difficult to understand how the state could tax a soul, since the soul was a spiritual thing. Of course, like all taxation, it was not necessary for the taxpayer to understand; it was only necessary that he pay. This new tax did not thwart incentive. A peasant who worked hard and acquired new farm equipment and housing could keep the extra revenue he made. In this regard, Peter has been said to have captured the spirit of Adam Smith.[7]

To Peter's surprise these new tax laws did not produce much revenue. The number of males on the tax rolls was only a fraction of the number of males able to work. Many peasants avoided registration by bribing the tsar's assessors. Peter decided to make a new census. He learned there were hordes of unemployed, unregistered drifters in every town and monastery. Idleness was a way of life for a large segment of society.

Peter now tackled the problem like Diocletian. Everyone would be a worker or a taxpayer. The unemployed had four choices: pay the poll tax, become a serf and be tax-free, enter government service (military or civil), or be a galley slave. Most of the drifters had a choice between being a galley slave or a serf. Serfdom was obviously the better choice. To the government serfs were not tax-free, the serf's lord had to pay a poll tax on all his serfs. The peasant was relieved of personal tax liability, but for that benefit he gave up his freedom.

The ranks of the serfs began to swell because landowners were compelled to accept anyone who sought serfdom. Each new serf, wanted or unwanted, came with a tax bill around his neck which the lord had to pay. Landlords demanded and received greater power over their serfs. Russia became a land of serfs and masters, with every master a serf to the tsar. The greatest autocracy of the modern world was born to ensure the collection of taxes, the same as in the late Roman Empire.

Peter had the army take over the revenue bureau. Three times a year a military-trained tax collector visited each landowner to audit his affairs and count the number of souls for the poll tax. Landowners suspected of cheating on their taxes were stretched out and broken on a wheel. In ancient times Russian tax men would cut off a nose or ear, but Peter was more sophisticated. Stretching a person out on a wheel and breaking his back was clean and modern—no blood or mess to clean up. Petty tax evaders were struck across the shin bones with a rod. With a small bribe the taxpayer could insert a shield within his pants for protection and thereby proclaim his innocence without flinching.

Peter did not stop with a soul tax. He found ways of taxing everything, including the church. If he needed metal for cannon he would steal as many church bells as were necessary and melt them down for guns. He taxed food of all kinds, rents, clothing, horses, hats, boots, lodging, mills, fisheries, beehives, cellars, chimneys, water, and public baths. On the personal side he taxed births, marriages, burials, beards, the unbaptized, and those who were not members of the Russian church. The only tax he missed was a death duty. It is hard to understand why he did not tax estates or inheritances. All trade going in and out of the country was taxed. There were stamp taxes on commercial paper, and legal documents had to be prepared on special paper sold by the government at ridiculously high prices. There were state monopolies on salt, salt fish, tobacco, and a number of items that were all sold at excessive prices. In short, there was an inconceivable jumble of taxes on just about everything and everybody. The above summary is by no means exhaustive.

To supervise this jungle of taxes, Peter organized a special tax think-tank which he called the Senate. It was composed of ten super-bureaucrats who were also responsible for developing new ways of raising revenue. Peter's military ventures were costly. He was always short of money and he continually prodded, threatened, and pressured the Senate to raise more of it. Here are some of his admonitions to the Senate:

Money is the heart of war. Do ye gather in all that ye may.

The closer one shears a sheep the more wool one obtains from its back.

In order to obtain as much as possible, one should demand the sheerly impossible.[8]

Peter had little patience with private capital, like the rulers of the Soviet Union before perestroika. But seizing private wealth was not as easy as enslaving human wealth. Russian gold slipped out of the country for safer and more lucrative investment opportunities in Amsterdam, London, and Paris. Private capital has no national allegiance—it always seeks the safest and most profitable sanctuary. Peter passed laws forbidding the export of capital, like modern exchange control, but it is impossible to evaluate the effectiveness of these laws. The diligent have always found ways to evade even the toughest tax and exchange control laws. Since Peter first introduced exchange control, up to the present day, professional couriers have smuggled gold out of Russia with little risk of detection.

Russia had little attraction for either domestic or foreign loans. Peter was unable to borrow money from anyone. He modernized Russia with cold-blooded bondage and taxation. He did not incur much debt because he never had the opportunity to borrow. There was little faith in Russian credit then as now. Only during the last days of the tsar did the world have much faith in Russian credit, when piles of tsarist bonds were sold over the world's stock exchanges. Today the descendants of those gullible investors use these old tsarist bonds to paper their bathrooms. To the surprise of everyone, in the late 1980s the Soviet government offered to redeem these bonds.

The Cossacks were to the Russians what temple asylia was to the ancient world. All peasants knew—and their masters knew—that if taxes or serfdom was too oppressive the peasant could always join the Cossacks. When Peter introduced his new reforms turning everyone into taxpayers in one form or another, an estimated 100,000 peasants fled with their belongings (and some of the belongings of their masters) to the land of the Don Cossacks. Each departing peasant's name was taken off the poll tax rolls, for Cossacks were tax-immune. For Peter this was intolerable; he was losing recruits and taxpayers. Peter had no choice but to send his military regulars to subdue the Cossacks and bring them under his control.

The Cossacks were an important safety valve against rebellion. The ambitious and rebellious peasants who had joined the Cossacks in the past would have been leaders of peasant revolts had they stayed at home. When Peter closed the Cossack door of escape, he opened the door for rebellion at home. This was his most dangerous legacy to his successors.

After Peter's death peasant uprisings became almost monthly affairs. A small riot would bring a detachment of troops. By the time the troops arrived the ranks of the rioters may have expanded to hundreds, armed with pitchforks, rocks, and farm tools. By sheer force of numbers they would often subdue a small military force. Finally, at about the time of the Boston Tea Party, an aggressive Cossack named Pugachev raised an army of over ten thousand angry serfs and Cossacks. He was marching on Moscow when he was captured and executed.

Catherine the Great tried to wipe Pugachev from the minds of the Russian people. The village where he was born was burned and the inhabitants were relocated in a new village with a new name. Catherine made it a criminal offense to speak his name. Talk of reform became dangerous, not just because of Pugachev, but because of the revolutionary fever that was gripping the world after the American and French Revolutions.

The Russian government repressed reform for almost a century after Pugachev. Finally, at the time Lincoln was freeing the American slaves, Tsar Alexander II freed the serfs. Freedom from serfdom did not end the taxes that produced it, but rather the emancipation eliminated the powerful middleman aristocrat and the extraordinary profits he took from the tax system. With the master gone, the tsar had to assume full responsibility for tax collection. The Russian serf came out much better than his counterpart in the American South because he was given land, usually the very land his family had farmed for centuries. The blacks in America were given nothing, so that economically many of them were worse off with freedom. This important distinction does not mean that the Russians were more humane than the Americans. The Russian peasant had to pay taxes and without land he would have been unable to do so. He also had to make payments to his former master. The land he was given provided the means to pay those obligations.[9]

There were three main types of serfs in Russia. The tsar had a vast body of Crown serfs who were the envy of all others. Crown serfs were never a problem. The tsars treated them well, often relieving them of taxes and many other dues and obligations.

There were two systems of private serfdom. Obrukny serfs paid an annual *obruk* to their masters that was twice the poll tax. This left their masters with a 50 percent profit. Obrukny serfs were taxed on a village basis. To pay their collective obruk they organized themselves into village councils, elected leaders, and held much of their land in common. Collective farms and recent co-operatives in the Soviet Union operate in a similar fashion.

Bartschina serfs caused the most trouble. They had their own farms but worked from three to seven days a week on the lands of their masters. During planting and harvest time some masters required them to work from dawn to dark, seven days a week. No time was left for their own farms. This oppression incited rebellion and strikes. Peasants who refused to work were beaten, put in irons, or compelled to wear a spiked collar. Others were dunked in a river, head down, until they almost drowned. The Bartschina serfs also achieved a level of communal collectivization in the way they farmed the lands of their masters. In short, serfdom, the ultimate means of tax control, formed the groundwork for Soviet collectivization of agriculture.

Russian serfdom should not be judged too harshly. It was more humanitarian than modern slavery.[10] Every state keeps a close watch on its primary source of revenue. What is taxed must be under control. If the tax is critical, then the controls must be effective. Land was the source of Russia's wealth. Serfdom was simply a tool to protect and ensure the collection of revenue.

Today most governments acquire their revenue from income. Income is paid in money; money moves through banks. Consequently, our banking institutions are placed under strict surveillance to ensure tax compliance. Serfdom in Russia was a device to do the same thing. We have lost our freedom and privacy in banking for the same reason the Russian peasant lost his freedom. The Russian state, like our own, was merely looking after its revenue.

The influence of Russian culture on civilization has been much more significant than we realize. At the end of the Middle Ages the Russians protected Europe's rebirth in the Renaissance by absorbing the Mongol invaders at the cost of great destruction to themselves and an advanced form of democratic life. The Russians put an end to the growth of Napoleon and his dream of being Europe's emperor. Mankind was saved from the Nazi plague by the sacrifice of millions of Russian citizens.

Russia's greatest mission, however, may have been her role as a guinea pig for a Western ideology, conceived and popularized in Britain, Germany, and throughout Europe. It was forced upon them against popular support and even Russia's strong spiritual tradition. It was the ultimate form of taxation in which the state took everything in the economic order and gave back to the people what the state thought they needed. Their example and life under communism has shown the world the horrors and inhumanity of such an enforced system. In the words of a modern Russian historian, "Sacrifice in the name of the world has been Russia's real historic mission.[11]

18

The Swiss: From William Tell to No-tell

In the view of the Swiss people, the freedom of the individual takes precedent over the fiscal interests [of the state], even on the risk that this freedom is sometimes misused.

—M. Bonvin, Swiss Federal Council, 1967

Most people who visit Switzerland feel envy for the Swiss. They have the most sensible and stable democracy in the world, coupled with a genius for keeping out of wars. Tax history would be incomplete without a look at this remarkable country. The Swiss, like the ancient Greeks, see a direct connection between democracy, liberty, and taxes. Americans and Britons who study Swiss society soon learn that the Swiss have a concept of liberty the British and Americans had in the eighteenth century, i.e., that liberty is centered in one's pocketbook.[1] We have drifted far from that early concept, but the Swiss have tenaciously held fast to the belief that liberty, to be real, requires privacy, especially financial privacy.

The capital of Switzerland and its executive branch of government differ from the rest of the world. The story is often told of the American visitor to Bern, Switzerland, who learns from his guide that Switzerland has a president, but who also learns, to his surprise, that most Swiss people do not even remember his name. The life-style of the president is even more surprising—he often rides to work in a street car!

Democracy in Switzerland is ancient. We do not know how long these forest and mountain people have been governing themselves. During the Middle Ages, when the Swiss were a part of the Holy Roman Empire, they paid light taxes to the emperor. At the same time, Swiss villages were ruled by democratic assemblies that have survived to this

The Swiss Confederation, established to resist Hapsburg taxation, proved its worth in 1315 when its freedom fighters defeated the Austrians at the Battle of Mortgarten Pass.

day. Their officials were elected by the people and Germanic law governed the community.

In 1240, the communities of Schwyz and Uri were released from taxation by the Holy Roman emperor. A few years later the powerful Hapsburg family in Austria refused to recognize the independence of the Swiss, and in 1273 they sent in tax gatherers and overlords to collect full feudal dues. The Swiss were not willing to submit to full Hapsburg taxation, and rebellion followed. During this struggle the legend of William Tell was born. William Tell refused to acknowledge the Austrian Hapsburgs and their gang of tax collectors. For this defiance he was ordered to shoot an apple from the head of his son with a crossbow.

The admiration and homage the Swiss have for the legendary William Tell is not for his skill with a crossbow, but for igniting a successful revolt against the oppressive tax policies of King Rudolph of Hapsburg and his successors. The key political event took place in 1291 when three forest communities formed a league of mutual assistance against Austrian tax aggression. Soon other communities joined the league and Switzerland was born. The crucial military event was in 1315 when Austrian troops were sent into Switzerland to enforce Hapsburg demands. The united Swiss infantry, which was outnumbered almost ten to one, inflicted a crushing defeat upon the Austrians in the battle of Mortgarten Pass in the mountain approaches to Switzerland.

The Austrians made two further attempts to subjugate the Swiss, seventy years later, but both invasions failed. After that, foreigners stayed clear of Switzerland, and except for a brief rule by Napoleon, the Swiss have remained independent. Not all was peaceful within Switzerland, however. The country was plagued with religious strife during the Reformation and the cantons (provinces) fought each other, off and on, for three centuries.

The present Swiss confederation began in 1815 following the defeat of Napoleon. In the treaty at the Congress of Vienna, Swiss neutrality was formally recognized by the powers of Europe with these words: "That the neutrality and integrity of Switzerland and its independence from any foreign influence are in the true interests of European policy as a whole." This provision has formed the basis for Swiss neutrality. In 1848 the Swiss adopted a constitution which established a confederation of Swiss cantons with very limited federal government. What is unique is the absence of a large federal bureaucracy. The cantons administer most federal laws.

In 1820, the fiscal wisdom of the Swiss came to the attention of John Taylor, a senator from Virginia and an early leader in the politics of that day. By comparing the Swiss to the French and the Italians, he observed that when a government is poor, the people are rich; and when a govern-

The legend of William Tell occurs frequently in the art of Switzerland. Tell, remembered for igniting a revolt against Austrian taxation, was forced to shoot an apple from his son's head for defying Austria's tax overlords.

ment is rich, the people are poor. While Italy and France were indeed very rich countries, it was not so with their masses. But Switzerland, being a poor country with limited resources, had the freest and happiest people in Europe and a government on a tight pocketbook, free of debt.

When the Swiss adopted their constitution in 1848, they rejected the United States' concept of a president because it had a "dictatorial tendency"; furthermore, their "democratic feelings revolted against any

personal pre-eminence." These were remarkably prophetic statements
for a time when U.S. presidential power was in its infancy. The dictatorial tendency which the Swiss foresaw over 150 years ago has been
brought out by history. Few can argue that the American president has
as much, if not more, power than any executive officer in the free world,
even the former Soviet Union. The Vietnam War was instituted and carried out by the U.S. presidency. The most critical problem facing the
U.S. form of government today is the "dictatorial tendency" of the presidential office. Perhaps if the U.S. president learned to ride to work each
morning in a street car, like the Swiss president, the problem would not
be so difficult.

Switzerland is often said to be the only real democracy in the world.
The English-speaking peoples have what is called representative government, giving members of the legislature the last word on almost
every major issue facing society. If new taxes are put in force or if tax
rates are raised, this is a legislative matter. Taxes are very much a consequence of lobbying, class politics, and "influence." Normally, when
one segment of society is burdened with new taxes, another segment
benefits from a reduction. Tax burdens and benefits shift from one class
to another depending upon how much (or how little) each class influ-
ences the legislature.

In Switzerland the final decision on revenue is made by the voters.
Unlike the Canadian or U.S. legislators, the Swiss legislator cannot vote
himself a salary increase. Salary raises must be submitted to the Swiss
people. If increases are to be made in the tax rates, the voters have to
approve. The Swiss people keep an extraordinary check on the taxing
power of their government. In 1975 the Swiss government submitted a
referendum to the voters for an increase in the income tax rates. The
voters turned it down cold. When one prominent Swiss citizen was
asked what this meant, he said, "The government will have to live on
what it has—like the rest of us." In 1991, Swiss voters turned down the
government's request for a VAT, but the government eventually won
after submitting the VAT to the voters three times. In the end, the Swiss
people approved the tax, but the point here is that in Switzerland taxation is the people's business.

The Swiss practice of submitting all revenue matters to a vote of the
people embodies the wisdom of separating the power to tax from the
power to spend. Once these two powers reside in a single governmental
agency, the power to spend will invariably override restraints against
tax. We have already pointed out how English government was originally established to perpetuate the principle of the separation of these
two powers, when the king, as the great tax spender of the realm, was
never given the power to increase or to institute new taxes.

United States revenue authorities look with frustration at Swiss bank secrecy. They cannot see much virtue in it, let alone what it has to do with liberty. About all they see is the opportunity for Americans to evade taxes. And now, after a prolonged effort, the Swiss have caved-in to the American tax authorities, agreeing to provide information for tax fraud cases, and even, as in the Imelda Marcos criminal case to extradite her partner, Kashoggi—one of the world's richest people—for a crime that did not exist in Switzerland. The Justice Department got its way, only to end up the laughing stock of the cadre of lawyers specializing in international matters, when a jury acquitted everyone. Switzerland didn't look so noble either for caving-in to American pressure. One of the Swiss prosecutors told me in confidence when I investigated this matter, "The problem is, you Americans make everything criminal."

Since childhood we have been taught to love liberty. Our relatives and neighbors have died in its defense. We have been taught to give our lives if need be for the defense of freedom. It is a sacred cornerstone of the national heritage of almost all Western nations, certainly of the English- and French-speaking nations. Our flags, bills of rights, and constitutions all stand as symbols and bulwarks of a free society.

At no time, however, have we been told that our banking has anything to do with liberty. Our courts confirm this judgment. Our bank accounts are open to revenue authorities who can snoop into them without our awareness if that is the way the government wants it to be. An example of this happened recently when a banker asked one of his customers, a lawyer, how the lawyer's tax problems were coming along. (Bankers always want to know about the financial health of their customers.) The lawyer replied that he did not know he had any tax problems and wondered why the banker asked the question. The banker revealed that six months earlier tax agents had examined the lawyer's records for the past few years. Needless to say, this would never have happened in Switzerland without the taxpayer's knowledge and a court order.

Bank secrecy is an ancient rule of Germanic law. It has been maintained for centuries as a matter of custom and tradition. In the 1930s it was put on the Swiss statute books with harsh criminal penalties to discourage the Nazis from piercing its veil. With the Nazis gone, other countries with high tax laws or tough exchange control laws have tried to penetrate Swiss banking privacy. These banking laws are said to be a shield for law-breakers and a nuisance to the world. It was noble, of course, to assert bank secrecy to protect German citizens from Hitler, but times have changed, it is said. After all, most Western nations are not in Hitler's camp.

The Swiss have reacted soberly to the assaults on their banking laws.

They do not want their laws used to protect common criminals, but they are not about to classify breaches of the revenue laws of most countries as "common crimes." Currency restrictions are normally the consequence of financial misfeasance on the part of governments. A government has the power to print money and when it does so without financial reserves, it is robbing its citizens no less than the thief who demands your money or your life. The tax and currency laws of Nazi Germany had nothing to do with the military aggressions of later years. Furthermore, Hitler's tough exchange control laws have been copied by many countries today.

The Swiss believe the British and Americans are shortsighted, failing to see that broad surveillance and snooping by government destroy individual liberty. All totalitarian states, communist and fascist, are characterized by intensive and unrelenting spying and snooping into the lives of their citizens. In a free society the power of the government to spy on its citizens is strictly limited, restrained, and controlled. All other differences between a free society and despotism or totalitarianism are secondary.

The Swiss take the position that an individual's liberties are safe only when the liberties of every man are protected.[2] Consequently, bank secrecy in Switzerland is for the Swiss themselves, and outsiders benefit because the Swiss extend it to everyone who uses their banking facilities. The tragic thing in the world today is that we fail to realize the consequence of our present naked banking. In the words of one prominent Swiss apologist:

Banking secrecy is a major component of the wall of discretion that must protect the individual with his privacy if liberty is to be defended with success against the dominance of the state. This, and no less, is what is at stake. The frightening thing is that it should be necessary to state it.[3]

Banking privacy in Switzerland is not absolute. It can and will be lifted by the Swiss courts upon a proper showing. In the Clifford Irving-Howard Hughes hoax, the banking privacy of Mrs. Irving was lifted in a matter of hours when it was established that Mr. Hughes had not endorsed the check made out to him and which she cashed. It is not difficult to unveil Swiss secrecy upon a proper showing. What Swiss banking privacy really means is that the state has no right to go on a fishing expedition and snoop into the financial affairs of its citizens without just cause.

English Common Law is not alien to that principle. The doctrine that a man's house is his castle, and that not even the monarch has the right to intrude, is fundamental to English law. In each castle there was a private treasury which was—first and foremost—to be protected from the king's snooping. This is what the concept was all about. Once the king knew how much money a man had there was the likelihood that he would try to figure out some way to steal it. As modern banking developed, the English lost sight of the fact that the private treasury in the castle moved to the private banker for commercial reasons and for safety—not to open it up to a snooping king. If a man's treasury in his castle was beyond the surveillance of the king, then so should his treasury at the bank be similarly protected.

In the hearings conducted by the Irwin Committee on Watergate, John Ehrlichman, President Nixon's czar of domestic affairs, was asked about the government's right to snoop into a psychiatrist's office to gather information about the mental affairs of the man who was behind the leak of the Pentagon Papers. Mr. Ehrlichman thought it was proper. Senator Irwin asked him about the ancient rule of law that even the king could not invade a man's castle, Mr. Ehrlichman replied that times have changed. You might say that Mr. Ehrlichman was only half wrong. If the government had wanted to snoop into this man's financial affairs (as opposed to his mental affairs), there is no question but that revenue agents could have snooped to their heart's content with an IRS summons. With respect to one's financial affairs, Mr. Ehrlichman was right—times have changed.

There is a saying in Switzerland that the people want to be as free as their fathers. The Swiss are among the few people in the world who have come close to that wish. Most of us have surrendered the bulk of the privacy and liberty we inherited from our fathers to the ever-expanding tax bureaus of our ever-growing governments. In most countries with long traditions of freedom the people look back in history with envy to the freedom of their fathers—to the time when castles were beyond the surveillance of the king.

19

The Collapse of the Hercules of Europe

The sun never sets on the dominion of the king of Spain and at the slightest movement of that nation the whole world trembles.

—Sixteenth-century historian

No nation in history better illuminates the thesis of this book than Imperial Spain. This great empire, which has never been equalled, was devastated by rebellious taxpayers from all ranks and in all possible ways. Voluntary taxpayer compliance, to use a modern term, was almost unknown. Spanish taxpayers resorted to violence, they took to flight in every possible direction, and finally, they developed a system of tax fraud and evasion which, in some circumstances, may have taken 90 percent of tax revenues from the government. Taxation was at the heart of Spain's decline, but it was bad taxpayers as well as bad taxation that brought about the collapse of this once-mighty power.

The Spanish Empire came into being from a sequence of important royal marriages. At the time of Columbus, the marriage of Ferdinand and Isabella united the two major provinces of Spain, like a union of England and Scotland. Their daughter followed the same pattern and married into the great Hapsburg family of Austria. The son of that marriage, Charles V, became emperor over most of Europe. At the same time Spanish explorers brought most of the New World into the empire. For more than a century Spain was more powerful than any other European state since the Romans. Her overseas empire was the largest the world has ever known.

In the seventeenth century this vast empire started to disintegrate. The English like to think the defeat of the Spanish Armada was the cause. That view is good for Anglo-Saxon egos but it is not good history. Two-thirds of the ships in the Armada managed to sail back to Spain. Furthermore, the Armada was defeated by the "Protestant Wind" more than English seamanship.

The Duke of Wellington remarked that, "Spain was the only country in the world where twice two did not make four."[1] What really makes no sense is how a nation with the greatest military and naval forces in the world, with vast riches arriving every month from the New World, with control over most of the world, could collapse for no apparent reason. In the history of Imperial Spain, two plus two did not make four.

The most hated of all Spanish taxes and the most productive of revenue (the two usually go hand in hand), was the *alcabala*, a 10 percent excise on the transfer of all real and personal property. The Moslems invented this tax and brought it to Spain in the Middle Ages. Queen Isabella, in 1504, called for the abolition of the alcabala in her Last Will.[2] The famous Spanish cardinal, Jimenez, pleaded with Charles V to abolish this tax.[3] Like our modern income tax, the alcabala produced so much revenue it could not be abolished; indeed, it expanded to include food, and the rates increased. It became "the most lucrative of all taxes . . . hence the tenacity with which many generations of Castilian kings clung to this disastrous impost."[4]

The alcabala had a depressing effect on industry and trade. The same goods, as they changed hands, paid this tax many times over and priced Castilian goods out of the market at home and abroad. A terrible imbalance of payments developed as foreign goods (usually smuggled) underpriced Spanish goods on local markets. Gold and silver flowed out of the country as fast as it arrived from the Americas.

The empire of Charles V was a loosely knit bundle of provinces with a healthy zeal for their "ancient liberties and customs," which is a sophisticated way of saying there would be no new taxes. The provinces would be loyal to Charles, they would fight for him, but taxation for offensive wars, not for defense of the taxpayers' homeland, would not be acceptable. Charles soon realized this and when he needed more money he looked to his home province, Castile, for more revenue. Charles assumed his local subjects would support their local king in all his military adventures—but he assumed wrong. Taxation only for defense was deeply rooted in European thinking everywhere.

Revenue measures required the approval of the *Cortes*, a body of taxpayer representatives like the English Parliament or French Estates General. Nobles and churchmen were tax-immune, so their vote was unimportant. Deputies from the towns and commoners were all-important—their consent was required for the taxation of their constituents.

When revenue was needed the king would summon the Cortes and send one of his ministers to deliver a speech from the throne. They would respond with a petition for things they wanted from the Crown, such as a new bridge, a road, or the change of some law. Eventually the king would grant the petition and the deputies would approve the taxes. This procedure had all the appearances of good parliamentary government, but in practice the Cortes did as the king asked.

On one rare occasion when the Cortes turned down the finance minister's request, the king marched into the Cortes and ordered the ministers to approve his request in thirty minutes. The deputies remained steadfast and the rebuffed king left in a rage. By evening martial law was imposed on the province. The deputies quickly assembled and approved the king's demands. There was little genuine debate and bargaining in the Spanish system.

The king usually avoided clashes with the deputies by offering them lucrative pensions, offices, and "benefits." This was not bribery but just the fringe benefits of public office-holding, as happens today. In 1520 Charles set off a major revolt in Castile by over-doing the pension routine in order to obtain new taxes. Angry taxpayers turned on their deputies and demanded political changes to end the corruption in the Cortes.

The events in northern Spain at Segovia give an idea of the savageness of this revolt. A mob of local taxpayers brutally murdered their deputy without allowing his request for last sacraments from the parish priest. These angry taxpayers did not want their deputy to obtain forgiveness for his last sins—especially the sin of burdening them with unwanted taxation.

Charles eventually crushed the rebels and by all appearances the revolt failed. Nevertheless, the revolt taught the monarchy a lesson—taxes still had to be tolerable for the taxpayer, regardless of what their corrupt representatives might do.

Charles established a "no new taxes" policy after the revolt in Castile. Nevertheless, he was able to triple revenues by ruthlessly enforcing existing tax laws and rates—an ominous lesson for those who believe they can restrain a government hell-bent on spending through legal means. Charles established a Council of Finance and ordered the council to "apply the screw" to uncooperative taxpayers ("uncooperative" is still a word of art for those in the revenue bureau). Applying the screw was not a figure of speech in that day; it meant using the tools of the Spanish Inquisition to collect revenue. Tax agents were also made judges and executioners in any tax dispute. In the end, the legal system became an instrument for obtaining the maximum amount of revenue with the least regard for the rights of taxpayers. Even this has its modern counterpart.

After Charles died, his successors reduced the Cortes to a rubber-stamp operation. *Servicios*, the special grants like an English aid, were granted every year in the millions of ducats; previously they were in the hundreds of thousands and then only for extraordinary needs.

Spanish taxpayers did not sit still and accept their burdens. Since they had no legal recourse, and the Cortes was corrupt, they turned to extra-legal defenses—they went against the system (violence), underneath the system (evasion), and away from the system (flight). In their endeavors they were successful; the world has never seen, before or since, such defiance. When they finished, the empire of the Hercules of Europe was a shambles.

In the early seventeenth century a Spanish writer called attention to the depopulation of Castile by flight to avoid tax: "In place of wondering at the depopulation of the villages and farms, the wonder is that any of them remain."[5] Many historians point to the plague, the expulsion of the Moors and Jews, as the cause of this depopulation, but a healthy social order could have replaced these temporary setbacks in population growth. On the other hand, the flight of taxpayers was not a short-term affair. Year in and year out, for decades, thousands upon thousands of Spanish peasants and workers left for tax-exempt places and jobs. This continuous drain was the primary cause of Castile's population decline. Where did the taxpayers go?

First, most of them fled to the New World. A French spy wrote these words in Madrid to his government in Paris:

> The galleons left on the 28th of last month; I am assured that in addition to the persons who sailed for business reasons, more than 6,000 Spaniards have passed over to America for the simple reason that they cannot live in Spain.[6]

The Americas were a sanctuary from the Spanish tax system, especially the alcabala. These lands offered opportunities for adventure, tax-free noble status, and riches. Two hundred years later even Bismarck, the great German leader, touched on the flight of Spanish taxpayers. He opposed German colonies because Germany "might end up sending her best blood overseas as Spain had done."[7]

Second, a great number of taxpayers with some education joined the tax-immune civil service. This was especially disastrous for the Crown because it not only lost a taxpayer but gained another mouth to feed. "There are a thousand employees," said one Spanish writer, "where 40 could suffice if they were kept at work; the rest could be set to some useful labor."[8] As the government's army of civil servants expanded, the labor force plummeted.

Unnecessary civil servants are leeches on the tax system, and Spain, like Rome, had more leeches than taxpayers. "The stupendous fabric," said Gibbon, speaking of Rome's bureaucracy, "yielded to the pressure of its own weight"[9]; Spain had the same problem.

Third, taxpayers with money and influence became nobles or *hidalgos*. Every commoner dreamed of achieving noble status. A stigma of dishonor was attached to labor and taxpaying. A Spanish novelist of this period had one of his characters express the attitude of that day with these words: "Any no-good wretch would die of hunger before he would take up a trade [and pay taxes]."[10] Once a Spaniard became a hidalgo, like all good aristocrats he disdained work—idleness was the mark of a good nobleman, and many of them lived at starvation level rather than take up a productive trade.

Fourth, poor overtaxed peasants with no education, money, or influence often joined the nearest band of gypsies after the tax system reduced them to abject poverty. This was accomplished through a medieval death tax which required a peasant family to give their lord their best cow when the head of the family died. It was customary for the lord to give the cow back, but the Crown claimed this tax and appointed tax-farmers to collect it. Since the tax men were also judges over tax disputes, they interpreted this tax to apply to every death in a peasant family. Short life expectancy and infant mortality brought disaster for the peasants. When the last cow was taken, the peasant family lost its main tool of production and had no choice but to join the nearest band of gypsies.

Tax Revolt in the Provinces

In time the depopulation of Castilian taxpayers turned the attention of the Crown to the provinces, which were immune from the alcabala and paid little tax. Their defiance to Spanish taxation took the form of violence.

The Netherlands was the center of world commerce; Amsterdam was the most important city in Europe. Freedom of the high seas was a Dutch legal invention designed to rid the North Sea of English tax collectors. The monarch of England looked upon the North Sea as an English lake subject to taxation by the king, who was "Lord of the Seas." On one occasion Dutch ships were rounded up and assessed license fees for fishing in the North Sea.

The Netherlands were part of the vast Spanish Empire, locally ruled by a regent for the Crown, Margaret of Parma, a daughter of the Emperor, Charles V. In 1566, violence erupted in the Netherlands over religion. This Protestant-inspired turmoil gave the Spanish Crown an excuse to intervene with a Spanish-style Inquisition. A prominent group

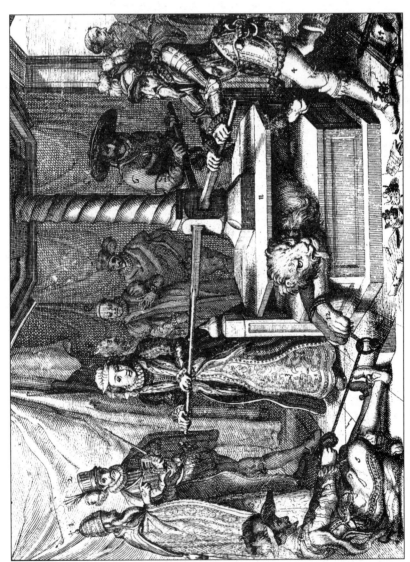

An allegorical print depicts the Dutch lion crushed in a huge press, turned by Alba and Margaret of Parma. Bystanders include the pope and Philip II, emperor. The allegory of taxpayers being crushed in a huge press is as popular today as it was four hundred years ago.

of Dutchmen petitioned the emperor for moderation. The Spanish Crown called the petitioners "beggars." The name stuck, riots followed, and a disastrous civil war started which lasted almost eighty years.

The emperor selected the Duke of Alba to lead twenty thousand of his best troops to restore order. He gave this stupid and cruel man authority to institute the hated alcabala, which would replace a locally administered income tax the Dutch had been grudgingly paying to the Crown. On top of the alcabala was a 1 percent capital tax and a 5 percent real property transfer tax:

> But Alba mov'd with no Rumours, terrifi'd with no Threats from a broken and unarmed people, and thinking no Measures nor Forms were any more necessary to be observed in the Low-Countrys . . . demands a general tax of the Hundredth part of every man's Estate in the Low Countreys to be raised at once: and for the future, the Twentieth of all Immovables, and the Tenth of all that was sold.[11]

Alba summoned the Estate General of the Dutch people for authority to levy the "tenth penny" as the Dutch called the alcabala. The Dutch, like the English, had no intention of granting the Spanish Crown the right to levy a permanent excise, which violated their ancient liberties. They compromised by approving the 1 percent capital levy with a medieval-type aid of two million gelders, payable over two years. At first, Alba accepted this compromise, but eventually, at the insistence of the Crown the alcabala was instituted, to be collected by force through a Council of Blood. Dutchmen who rebelled were lynched and their bodies were hung on posts at the entrance to their dwellings. A prolonged civil war followed dominated by guerrilla warfare. Even Dutch women took up arms.

The alcabala was instituted to relieve the Crown of the financial burden of maintaining Spanish forces in the Netherlands. Money had to be sent from Spain to Amsterdam through the English Channel. These ships were often seized by just about everyone. First by the Dutch, then the French, the Huguenots, and finally by Queen Elizabeth. Dutch children in school are taught a patriotic song.

On one occasion, as we shall learn Elizabeth stole the silver in a Spanish galleon that tried to avoid capture from Dutch raiders by seeking safety in an English port. An enraged Emperor would eventually turn on this gutsy queen with the Spanish Armada.

The rebellion in the Netherlands put a serious drain on Spanish finances, but most important, it put the Crown on notice that encroachments on the ancient tax customs of provincial people would invite rebellion. The Crown did not dare try to institute new taxes in the other

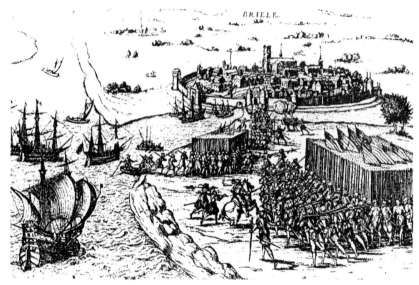

The Dutch "beggars" soon turned out to be more than a match for the Spanish. The "tenth penny" was their battle cry. Within a few years the entire Netherlands was in revolt against the tax. In 1572 the beggars captured the port city of Brielle, as shown above. They then began preying on Spanish galleons, which were bringing silver and troops to put down the rebellion. Dutch seamanship proved superior to that of the Spanish, and while Queen Elizabeth got the blame for pirating Spanish galleons, the Dutch were by far the main culprits.

Today in the Netherlands preschool children are taught a Dutch verse about the most famous admiral in the fleet of the beggars. While it does not rhyme in English, it does in Dutch: *Piet Hein, Admiral, his name is short, but his deeds are long, he captured the silver fleet.*

provinces for almost fifty years even though New World trade was in a sharp decline and Castilian taxation was drying up.

A government study in 1619 concluded that the provinces must pay more taxes and share the revenue burdens of Spain's unwieldy empire. The provinces received this advice with horror, much like an appeal to share one's tuberculosis. Heavy taxation had wrecked Castile; why should other provinces suffer the same fate? Was not the emperor bound to respect the ancient liberties and charters of all provincial peoples? "It was up to the sovereign ruler to persuade the province that the aid revenues served the province's own interest and that they were being spent on defensive wars."[12] Were not these taxes for military purpose, not connected with the defense of their homelands?

Some token help was offered, but new taxation was rejected. In response, the Crown decided to use the Spanish bayonet to enforce new provincial taxation. The Basques were selected as the first victims. This

Medallion. One side depicts the struggle against the "tenth penny": an upright sword with one coin on its point, nine coins on the right. The other side exalts the nobles willing to wear the beggar's pouch for the beggar's cause.

small province of sheepherders was no Netherlands and could not possibly resist new taxation, but resist they did even though their cause was hopeless. Shortly thereafter the Crown triggered a war in Catalonia that many historians believe mortally wounded the empire. This revolt was triggered by taxation in its most odious form—the quartering of troops without means of support. When pleas by the Catalan people were rejected by the Crown, an angry populace killed the viceroy and turned on the Castilian troops quartered in their country. Eventually, after a ten-year civil war, the province was recovered, but the cost was enormous. This war came at a time when Spain needed all her reserves for crucial military battles against the Dutch, French, and English. As it turned out, Spain's last reserves were spent at home fighting tax rebels. The overseas empire could not defend itself.

When the civil war in Catalonia was raging, the Crown instituted a 5 percent alcabala in Portugal, contrary to the charter between Portugal and Spain. A ruthless Portuguese quisling was appointed to collect this excise. Angry Portuguese attacked the palace, seized the governor, and escorted him to the border; the ruthless tax administrator was lynched, and the Portuguese people have been independent ever since.

Excises on food set off revolts in Sicily and Naples. In Naples the revolt started when a Spanish tax collector trampled on a basket of figs owned by a defiant fruit peddler. A mob formed, led by a fish peddler, which routed Spanish infantry and burned the houses of the tax collectors. The viceroy called a truce and agreed to cancel the new excises. Within a year, however, Spanish naval fleets arrived to restore the food excise by force.

The collapse of Spanish power abroad from tax rebellion at home permitted the British to seize Jamaica and many other Spanish colonies. The Dutch took over the East Indies. From that time forth the rich fruits of Spanish imperialism became ripe plums for easy picking. Stealing the colonies of Spain became an international sport; in time, the pickings were so easy it was not considered sporting to take them. The last of Spain's empire fell to the Americans in the Spanish-American War—a war many European powers considered decidedly unfair on the Americans' part.

The Spanish men of commerce engineered what was probably the best system of fraud and evasion that history has ever known. The revenue loss from evasion can never be calculated, but the amounts could have been ten times what the government actually collected. There was a tax evasion underground that included almost all tax collectors as well as all taxpayers.

Spanish businessmen transformed Atlantic commerce into one massive smuggling operation to evade the Royal Fifth, a 20 percent customs tax on silver and goods from the colonies. All trade had to enter certain ports of entry in Spain to clear customs. There was also a tax at the port of departure and a convoy tax as well to pay for the escort vessels. In 1600 the convoy tax was 6 percent; in 1630 the tax was 35 percent. This increase of six times in thirty years could mean that tax evasion increased that much.

Silver bullion was the government's primary target. Besides the Royal Fifth, the government confiscated bullion when it was short of money and gave the owners government bonds. Furthermore, silver was subject to exchange control and was registered when it arrived in Spain. Free silver, which was unregistered, was in great demand. Merchants granted large discounts for purchases made with free (smuggled) silver.

Bullion evaded tax through a number of devices. Silver from Peru was consigned to nonexistent persons in Panama and then transported across the Isthmus and loaded on ships for Spain. Since the silver supposedly stayed in Panama, it never appeared on the ship's register. Smuggling into Spain was easy; naval commanders of the escort vessels unloaded the bullion at small fishing villages far from the ports of entry. Sometimes silver was loaded at night just before the ship embarked for Spain, after the ship's register was closed. Other silver was understated on the register, then understated again at Spanish customs with the appropriate bribe. No one will ever know how much silver was really shipped to Spain during the early 1600s. For example, in 1600 silver worth thirty million pesos was shipped to Spain. By 1650, when smuggling was in full swing, only three million pesos-worth was shipped, according to customs records.

It could be argued that silver shipments declined from exhausted mines in the New World. There is truth in that, but shipwrecked galleons that have recently been salvaged by scuba divers in the Caribbean have unearthed enormous quantities of silver bullion. Evidence of customs evasion comes from trade records for the famous Mexican dye, cochineal. Revenues from this dye declined like bullion imports did during this same period, while other sources indicate the amount of dye in production in Mexico was not declining at all and was destined for Europe.

The Crown tried to stop smuggling in every manner conceivable. They tried the death penalty. This did not scare anyone, so they went to the other extreme and offered a pardon for confessed smugglers if the smuggler would promise to be good. The Crown promised to stop silver confiscations. All these efforts failed because "the habit of fraud was too deeply engrained."[13]

The evasion system of Imperial Spain survives today. The present Spanish government publicly admits tax evasion is a serious problem for the revenue. Throughout Latin America businessmen find the bribe an indispensable tool in doing business. The current laws in the United States against bribes and kick-backs confront a standard operating procedure that is four hundred years old. It is doubtful if real progress can be made against this system. At some place in the transaction of business and taxes, a bribe will be given—and if the Americans won't pay it, someone else will, in some form or another.

Oxford's leading scholar on Imperial Spain said:

> Spanish industry was strangled by the most burdensome and complicated system of taxation that human folly can devise. . . . The taxpayer, overburdened with imposts, was entangled with a network of regulations to prevent evasion. . . . He was thus crippled at every step by the deadly influence of the anomalous and incongruous accumulation of exactions.[14]

This historical indictment of Spanish taxation has an application to our tax system—certainly the "most burdensome and complicated system of taxation that human folly can devise." Historically, we are not alone.

As oppressive as Spain's tax system was, was it not Spain's taxpayers, rather than its tax system, that wrecked the empire? Was the 10 percent alcabala in the Netherlands, or the 5 percent alcabala in Portugal, really so intolerable?

There are probably no objective standards to determine when a tax is intolerable. The American Revolution clearly established that proposition. Taxes must be measured by subjective standards—by what a people are willing to accept. Spain's troubles began when her taxpayers launched a triple-barrelled attack on the system in every conceivable manner. Spain's tax story illustrates, above all else, what can happen from massive taxpayer discontent. Spain's troubles probably started when the Council of Finance decided to "turn the screw" on Spanish taxpayers; when revenues were not spent for defense. There is probably nothing more dangerous for a government to do than crack down on taxpayers who defy a rotten tax system. When the Spanish government finally came to its senses and realized the system was bad, it was too late—disobedience had become a way of Spanish life that could not be changed.

Thomas Jefferson touched upon this problem when he wrote a letter to James Madison suggesting that a country needs a rebellion every twenty years or so, and that the government should not punish the rebels too severely because they are pointing out sicknesses the government needs to look after.[15] Applying this to taxation, massive taxpayer noncompliance or even anger with a tax system should be a warning to governments that something needs to be corrected. Ignoring the symptoms could be like ignoring the danger signals of a serious illness. The Spanish government (like most governments) interpreted tax defiance as a call to arms to enforce obedience. The resulting crackdown was about as effective as putting gasoline on a smoldering fire.

A full century before Spain's collapse, there were a remarkable number of wise Spaniards who urged reform, going back as far as Cardinal Jimenez shortly after the discoveries of America. Their utterances and efforts came to naught. As Gonzales de Cellorigo put it around 1600, while helplessly watching Spain's decline, "Those who can, will not, and those who will, cannot."[16]

20

How Cortés and Pizarro Found that Taxes Were the Chink in the Armor of the Aztec and Inca Rulers

The story behind the conquest of Mexico is one of the most fascinating and romantic tales in history. It has all the earmarks of a Hollywood motion picture: a tall, handsome and daring commander, a group of gallant men, a beautiful and clever woman, palace intrigue, and all the rest. The military story is unparalleled in history; if it had been written as fiction it would have been held up to ridicule. The militant Aztecs, numbering over a million strong, could not possibly have suffered defeat from 508 soldiers, 16 horses, 14 cannon, and a few greyhound dogs.

Until recently historians offered the Quetzalcoatl story to explain Cortés's incredible feat. When Hernán Cortés landed in Veracruz in 1519, the Aztecs are supposed to have thought he was the bearded god returning, and before they knew otherwise, Cortés seized control of the empire and killed Montezuma II. Modern historians discard this theory. Long before a single Aztec warrior faced the Spaniards, Montezuma was aware the Spaniards were enemies, not gods. Soon after Cortés landed he desecrated Aztec temples, something a god would not do. The Spaniards made it clear to Montezuma they were after the tax spoils of his realm. To understand the full story we must go back and look at the Aztecs before Cortés.

The Aztec empire was called the Triple Alliance, being a union of three great cities, with Mexico City as the hub of the empire. This alliance was formed two hundred years before Cortés arrived. The Aztecs conquered the weaker cities of Mexico and organized them into tax-rendering vassal states. No attempt was made to rule over them or to develop any cultural or social relations. They were, first and last, tax-

203

paying assets of the realm. The Aztecs, like the Assyrians in the eighth century B.C., used terror and military power to collect taxes and control their empire. It was the New World's age of terror-taxation. The similarity between Assyrian and Aztec tax methods has been noted by leading anthropologists.[1]

Aztec imperialism followed a simple pattern. Merchants would be sent out from Mexico City in disguise to acquire goods from cities that looked like worthwhile prospects for plunder. These merchants would return with these goods for examination plus information about the defenses and armies of the city. If the city was rich enough, and if the prospects for conquest were promising, a huge war party would be assembled and sent forth to attack the city.

The Aztecs were masters of camouflage and they attacked by stealth, usually scoring a decisive victory. The rulers of the defeated city would sue for peace, a conference would be held, and the peace terms resolved. The city rulers could keep their positions of leadership, except that they would now be tax-paying vassals of the Aztecs. Every eighty days an Aztec tax collector would arrive to receive the taxes specified in the treaty.

There would be no army of occupation, but a district director of Aztec revenue would be stationed in the region to keep a finger on the pulse of the community. Except for this tax director, and a few assistants, no other Aztecs would remain behind. The district director would report regularly to the emperor: "The task of this local tax-gatherer was not to act as governor of the province, but more as a kind of imperial agent to ensure payment of the amounts stipulated."[2]

At the conclusion of the peace treaty the Aztecs would be lavishly entertained, loaded with presents, and with the first tax installment they would depart for Mexico City, accompanied by numerous prisoners for sacrifice to the gods.

Defiance against Aztec taxation was common, just like it had been in Assyria. The system suffered the same defect in the New World as in the old—without troops stationed in the subject territories rebellion and defiance were inevitable. Consequently, the Aztecs were continually fighting small brushfire tax rebellions that plagued the empire. Since there was no army of occupation to back up the tax gatherers, the Aztec empire was continually on the brink of rebellion.

A typical outbreak occurred in 1458 in the city of Cotaxtla (near Veracruz). The Aztec district tax director and all his assistants were killed. A surprisingly patient emperor sent in a group of special agents to threaten and intimidate the rebellious city, but the city put these agents to death and then dressed their corpses in sumptuous robes, set them before a feast, and prostrated themselves before the dead agents. Addressed as lords, they were asked why they did not eat. When news of this reached Montezuma I, he went into a rage and proclaimed: "It is resolved that the people of Cotaxtla shall be utterly destroyed, and that no memory of them shall remain." Eventually the Aztecs reconquered the city, but Montezuma changed his mind about making reprisals; instead, he invoked the usual tax penalty for rebellion, i.e. double the normal tax. Like most wise tax men he decided to protect the revenue, not destroy it.

The Cotaxtlans were enticed into murdering Montezuma's revenue agents by the Tlaxcalans, who were the most defiant and successful of all the Aztec tax rebels. Fortunately for Cortés they lived midway between Veracruz and Mexico City, for without the Tlaxcalans it is difficult to see how Cortés could have succeeded. No Aztec ruler had been able to subdue them, and after years of successful defiance they understood Aztec military strategy in every detail and drove Montezuma to tears. In the end, about all the Aztecs could do was set up an economic blockade which prohibited the Tlaxcalans from trading with the empire.

There were other rebellious cities on the edge of the empire and occasionally the emperor's big battalions achieved indecisive results on the field of battle. Aztec conquests may have been the result of bluster and show rather than solid military strength and power.

Cortés landed near Veracruz in Aztec tax-paying territory. He soon met the local Aztec district tax director, named Tindile, and even though there was no visible display of power, Cortés realized Tindile was the local strong man.

Tindile watched Cortés and kept the emperor informed of his every movement. He reported that the Spaniards had strange beasts (horses and greyhound dogs), unlike anything the Aztecs had ever seen. Besides these beasts, the bearded white men had sticks that spoke with fire, cannon that roared like lightning, and huge sailing ships that dwarfed the small vessels of the Aztecs. It would be like having invaders from outer space land on the Earth with superior space equipment, weapons, and strange animals. Montezuma was filled with fear and wonder. These were no ordinary men. It seemed prudent to present them with lavish gifts and hope that they would go away. As we know, the rich gifts only whetted Spanish appetites for more. From the moment Cortés feasted his eyes upon a Spanish helmet Tindile had filled with gold, there was no stopping him. This was perhaps the most fatal move Montezuma had made. Cortés now knew that the stories of Aztec gold were true.

Cortés was not blinded by his lust for gold; for five months he camped at Veracruz and studied the situation. A quick assault on Mexico City would have met certain disaster. In a direct pitched battle the odds would have been at least a hundred or a thousand to one. On the positive side, Cortés had the hardware to deliver a mortal blow with this small, but superior fighting force, if he could effectively position himself.

One day when Cortés was walking along the beach near Veracruz he met five Indians who were embittered by the yoke of Aztec taxation. It was a momentous discovery for Cortés—he had found his answer—taxes were the chink in Montezuma's armor.

Following this lead Cortés went to visit the city of these discontented taxpayers. As soon as he arrived at the city, some of Montezuma's tax men appeared. Cortés noticed that when the Indians heard that Montezuma's men were coming, they "lost color, trembled with fear, and hurried away to receive them."[3] Cortés arrested Montezuma's tax men and after roughing them up, he released two of them so they could return to Montezuma and tell their story (the Indians wanted to kill all of them on the spot). Cortés knew that the Aztecs would return to punish these Indians and thereby force the Indians to look to the Spanish for protection and enter into an alliance for their own safety. When news of this defiance reached Montezuma, there was no question, from that time forth, that the Spaniards were rivals and enemies. To further irritate the Aztecs, Cortés desecrated the idols in the Aztec temples.

No sooner had these Indians joined forces with Cortés than he started his drive for Mexico City. On the way he entered the lands of the Tlaxcalans, the one foe the Aztecs could not subdue, but the Tlaxcalans were no match for the Spanish. After a few skirmishes they sued for peace and added their strength and wisdom to the Spanish assault. Montezuma was in a state of shock when he learned of the ease with which the Spanish subdued the Tlaxcalans. He invited Cortés to Mexico City, hoping to prevent a Spanish-Tlaxcalan alliance. He then changed his mind and ordered them not to come. Nothing, however, could deter Cortés from his objective—he had learned much from the Tlaxcalans who pointed out defects in the Aztec military system and weaknesses in the empire. Cortés was a leader of rare genius and incredible courage; by exploiting the tax discontent of Montezuma's vassal states he could achieve victory over impossible odds. Yet, had he failed to see that taxes were the chink in Montezuma's armor, he may have never left Veracruz alive.

The Spaniards destroyed most of the culture of the Aztecs. They attacked pagan worship and human sacrifices with a fury equal to their lust for gold. As a result of this mass destruction the key to understanding the civilization of ancient America was lost. One aspect of Aztec culture was permitted to survive, however. To exploit the riches of Mesoamerica, Aztec tax records were meticulously preserved. We know in detail the amount of taxes Montezuma collected from each city and

yliyocan.

Hernán Cortés joins forces with the friendly natives of Tlaxcala for his assault on Mexico City. His interpreter, Doña Marina, stands behind him. The Tlaxcalans had sucessfully evaded Aztec taxes and conquest for centuries and contributed both psychologically and militarily to the Aztec defeat.

from the empire as a whole. Each year Montezuma received seven thousand tons of corn, four thousand tons of beans, and no less than two million cloaks, to name some of the basic items.[4] So effective was the Aztec tax system that not even the dates of payment were changed by the Spanish. Two hundred years after Cortés, the Indians of Mexico were still paying taxes every eighty days, exactly as they had done for centuries before Columbus.[5]

The tax story of the Indian empires did not end with Cortés. Within a few years another Spanish conquistador, lusting for gold and silver, led an assault on the empire of the Incas. Francisco Pizarro conquered another great empire composed of millions of Indians by exploiting the tax discontent of the tribes held under one gigantic bureaucratic pyramid of tax collectors, with the emperor at the top as the Son of the Sun.

The Inca Empire was divided into four provinces that spread over the western slopes of the Andes from Bolivia to Peru to Equador. Each province was divided into a myriad of tax districts on a pyramidal structure: units of 10,000 taxpayers, then sub-units of 5,000, then 1,000, then 500, then 50, then 10 at the bottom. Unlike the Aztecs who exacted products and commodities from their conquered subjects, the Incas were more centralized, and exacted labor from all taxpayers—labor for agriculture, public works, mines, warriors, runners, metal workers, weavers, and any other needs of the emperor. Like the scribes of Egypt, the tax men paid no tax. Since the emperor was a god, rebellion among the Incas was unlikely, but not so with the conquered non-Inca tribes.

This massive empire of exploited taxpayers was ripe for rebellion, and Pizarro, like Cortés, was the man of the hour. Once again we witnessed the conquest of a mighty empire of millions by a small force, even smaller than Cortés's: two hundred men, horses and cannon. As with the Mexicans, taxation was the chink in the armor of the Inca Son of the Sun, Sapa Inca.

In the end, the conquered Inca Empire exchanged one despotism, with rigid but known tax demands, for another system of exploitation and despotism, with unlimited demands. In each instance it was the nobles, whether Inca or Spanish, who exploited the taxpayers and made ruthless demands for the wealth of the empire. Perhaps it was worse under the Spaniards, for while the Incas were tax-slaves under their emperor, under the Spanish they were chattel slaves used to channel the gold and silver of the realm into the pockets of their European masters.

21

Taxes Forge Modern Germany

In 1524 astrologers and mystics in Germany foretold of impending troubles. The alignment of the planets in the sign of Aquarius indicated that there would be a great flood, as in the days of Noah. Strange monsters were reported to have appeared and some suggested that the great flood would be composed of peasants, overthrowing their masters.

The first peasant disturbances had begun some fifty years earlier when a young mystic, Hans the Piper, announced that the Virgin had appeared to him and told him to go forth and preach: There should be no princes or priests; everyone should be a brother to his neighbor, earn his bread with his own hands, and possess no more than his neighbor. All taxes, duties, tolls, rents, and other exactions should be abolished. The forests, streams, and lakes should be open to everyone.

In his last appearance Hans told the men to return in a week, armed with weapons and prepared to go forth with the Virgin as their leader. The next week, over 34,000 peasant men returned, but the Piper was not to be found. He had been seized by a local bishop and burned alive as a heretic. Other peasant leaders followed the Piper but they too were arrested and executed. To check further disorder German nobles prohibited peasant assemblies, including weddings and popular merry-making festivals. Angry peasants reacted in 1524 by refusing to work or pay taxes. Tradition says the great Peasant Revolt began in the Black Forest when a noblewoman made an exaction of labor on a holiday. Since the peasants were forbidden to celebrate she could see no reason why they shouldn't work. The peasants formed a league, adopted flags, and issued a document called the twelve articles, which called for the abolition of new taxes and the reduction of old ones. Thereafter, angry peasants swept through the countryside in mobs lynching any nobles they could find and devastating castles and churches. Unfortunately for the peasants these mobs were disorganized; they had common grievances but not common leadership.

A 1517 engraving portrays a German peasant paying his taxes with eggs. The slaughter with which German nobles responded to peasant revolts left the country depopulated for over a century.

Martin Luther was on the scene when these uprisings took place. He first supported the peasants:

> We have no one to thank for this sedition save ye princes and lords. . . . Moreover in your worldly pursuits ye do naught otherwise than to flay and extort taxes that ye may satisfy your pomp and vanity, till the poor peasant cannot and may not bear it any longer.[1]

A month later, Luther changed his mind after observing the destruction and death wrought by the peasants. He wrote a new pamphlet entitled, *Against the Murderous and Thieving Bands of Peasants*, and called on all decent Christians to "crush them, strangle them and pierce them . . . even as one would strike dead a mad dog."[2]

Shortly thereafter the tide of battle turned against the peasants. Their slaughter reached proportions almost unknown in history. Germany was depopulated for over a century.

Luther and his noble friends failed to consider the economic consequences of their genocidal policy. Without peasants, who would plow the fields, harvest the crops, or provide labor to support the nobles? When the last member of one peasant family was led off for execution, his pleas for mercy fell on deaf ears until he told his executioners that his death would leave no one to harvest the crop. The lord promptly freed him. Eventually, economic realities prevailed over fanaticism, and the slaughter stopped.

Germany emerged from the Middle Ages as a bundle of little kingdoms. Every few miles there was a new prince with a new domain. The Holy Roman emperor ostensibly ruled over these principalities, but he was only a figure-head and had no sovereign powers.

Shortly after the peasant revolts, the Hohenzollern family in Berlin started to acquire more and more German territories. This family had produced the leaders of the Teutonic Knights, a powerful crusading order, whose presence was felt in all of Europe and even into Russia. Order and discipline governed these knights, and the Hohenzollern family applied these traits to their growing political domains, which included small bits and pieces of territory from the borders of Russia to the Rhine. The story of the formation of the German state over the next three hundred years is the story of the expansion of these bits and pieces into a unified, geopolitical Germany. With adroit diplomacy at the right

A coach stopped at toll gates, early nineteenth-century Germany. Before unification in the nineteenth century, Germany was composed of a number of small princedoms, each with its own laws, money, and taxes. The tax system crippled commerce, primarily because of the toll gates that were erected at all borders, bridges, and even roads within each principality. Merchants and travelers were stopped every few miles to be questioned, searched, and taxed. Small wonder Germany was an insignificant power before unification. This is why Germany was a latecomer among Europe's leading empire builders.

time, with the good fortune of being on the side of the victors during the Napoleonic Wars, with superior discipline and tactics, the Prussians exercised an influence in Europe far in excess of their size. The Hapsburgs and French were political giants, yet in the end the Prussians won and drove these superpowers from what is today modern Germany.

The first notable Prussian ruler was Prince Frederick William of Brandenburg (1640–1688), called the Great Elector. He was one of the body of electors who elected the Holy Roman emperor to his figurehead office. Incidentally, the Electoral College in the United States was derived from this German institution, which was still in operation in 1787 when the United States Constitution was adopted.

The Great Elector tried to repopulate Germany by inviting Jews and outcast French Huguenots to come to Germany and receive special tax privileges and favors. He organized a small but brilliantly trained army and rented it out to the highest bidder. When the army was not in the field it was put to work constructing canals and public buildings. Soldiers were used to administer the affairs of state and to operate the tax system. Prussia, it was said, was not a state with an army, but an army with a state. The story of the German people, their achievements and their tragedies, is tied closely to Prussian militarism.

The Peasant Wars convinced German aristocrats that the serfs were not to be trusted. These landed gentlemen, called junkers, held poor quality lands and they had limited resources to defend themselves against invaders from without and rebellious peasants from within. The Hohenzollerns offered their military forces as security to the junkers in return for the right to collect an excise, like the Spanish alcabala. Germany was one of the few places in Europe where the excise tax was introduced without any trouble. The tax was administered by the war office in Berlin, which was as much a tax bureau as a military staff. The Prussian alcabala succeeded because of the efficiency and discipline of army tax administration. When Peter the Great had his army administer the soul tax, he was copying Prussian ways. The difference, however, was that Russia's army tax men were notoriously corruptible—the Prussians were not. Berlin became a "Sparta of the North"; its army tax men were ordered to "ein plus machen," i.e., make a profit.[3]

The great-grandson of the Great Elector, Frederick the Great, injected an element of moderation into Prussian rule, perhaps because his father had Frederick's best friend beheaded in his view when the two of them went AWOL from army service. Frederick turned his military forces on the Goliaths of Europe with remarkable success. When Napoleon visited his tomb he told his aides, "Hats off, gentlemen—if he were still alive, we should not be here."[4]

Frederick the Great was a true benevolent despot, except with respect to the Jews. He adopted detailed anti-Jewish regulations which even went so far as to forbid marriage so the Jews would not have children. Special collective Jewish taxes were instituted after the pattern of the Middle Ages; some Jewish properties were confiscated. The anti-Semitism that so characterized Nazi Germany found strong support from this great national hero; his special Jewish taxes and laws survived until 1850. Hitler did not have to go back more than eighty years to find a format for Jewish oppression.

Frederick inherited a full treasury from his frugal predecessors, but he soon dissipated it by trying to reduce taxes and increase government spending. One of the first things he did was to abolish heavy taxation and proclaim himself "King of the Poor," and then undertake a number of expensive programs to improve the lot of German peasants and workers. This drained his treasury and compelled him to reinstate the taxes he had cancelled. Frederick could never quite accept the hard rules of economics, especially the self-evident truth that high government spending requires heavy taxation, sooner or later, in some form. Frederick's zeal for benevolence backfired. If he tried to improve the quality of life for the poor, he had to raise revenue to achieve that end—but this required increased taxation, which fell back on the very people he was trying to help. Furthermore, Frederick's military adventures, though successful, kept his treasury bare. Low taxes were not possible in a world dominated by military operations.

On one occasion when Frederick was away on a military campaign his enemies seized his treasury. This loss was more upsetting than a battlefield defeat. In desperation he issued leather money, hoping to fill the void in his finances until hard cash could be obtained. But the most incredible of all his revenue undertakings was the reopening of tax rolls

Frederick the Great's French tax-farmers on their way to Berlin to take over from his army tax collectors. Effective though corrupt, the French professionals were later said by Frederick to have "plundered Prussia to make their pile," but he retained their services to his death.

back to the year A.D. 1221! This was possible because taxes were collected from towns, not individuals. If a town had failed to pay its annual taxes a century before, Frederick could demand payment from its current inhabitants.

Actually, this maneuver is not as far-fetched as it may appear. We have no statute of limitations when a taxpayer fails to file a return. In some situations, the responsibility for unpaid taxes passes to the heirs of a dead taxpayer. Frederick was doing on a village level what we do on an individual level. When a government needs money—no matter how enlightened it may be—there seems to be little concern for the moral principles that govern non-tax affairs. The statute of limitations was designed to compel creditors to bring law suits when recollections are fresh and evidence is not stale. Tax claims require the same kind of evidence as any other claim for debt. Why should stale tax claims be outside long-established principles of sound jurisprudence?

One of the most delightful stories in the entire history of taxation came from Frederick's troubled times. During one of his cabinet meetings Frederick asked his finance minister why his treasury was so low when his subjects were paying so much tax. Where was all the money going? To explain the problem, the finance minister asked for a piece of ice. He handed it to the minister farthest from the king and told him to pass it to the next person, on up to the king. By the time the ice reached Frederick all he received was a wet hand.[5] The lesson the finance minister taught the king ranks in wisdom with the parables of the Bible. Most taxes are consumed by the bureaucracies of the government. It is a wonder Frederick even received a wet hand.

The Prussians collected three basic taxes. Rural areas paid a land tax based on a percentage of the value of the expected harvest. An appraisal took place before the harvest, and if there was a last-minute crop failure the result would be disastrous. Like the ancient harvest taxes of Egypt and Rome, the tax was not abated.

Inhabitants of towns paid an occupation tax, a kind of license fee to carry on their trade or business. Nobles were not tax-exempt unless they served in the military. Even church lands paid taxes.

Most revenues came from excises and customs. Frederick made an innovation in his tax administration by replacing army tax collectors with French professionals (tax-farmers).[6] The Frenchmen were tough, and perhaps corrupt. One of Frederick's ministers said these Frenchmen had reduced the German people from "comfort to utter misery—by the damnable efficiency of the tax collectors." Another critic said Frederick was not always looked upon as the father of his country, but as a tyrant who employed "foreigners to screw out of his subjects the money needed to implement these plans [i.e. military adventures]." Frederick was not blind to the oppressiveness of his French tax men. He told the Frenchman who was head of his excise bureau that his men were "rogues who steal whatever they can lay their hands on," and that they had "plundered Prussia in order to make their pile."[7] (The slang words "screwed" and "making a pile" are of considerable antiquity.) Notwithstanding all these ravings and rantings, Frederick kept his French excise collectors until his death.

When Frederick died he left a sizeable treasury and a first-rate military force, and he accomplished this with a country that was second rate in resources and population size. He was undoubtedly one of the finest European leaders in the eighteenth century. Few can compare with him in energy, dedication, creativity, and success. As the George Washington of Germany, he left his mark on his countrymen for all time.

Part V
The Ancien Régime

In the Middle Ages the French king was not much more than a medium-sized baron. Many nobles in France were larger and more powerful than the king of France. The English king, on the other hand, started as the absolute ruler of England with William the Conqueror in 1066.

The childhood game of king-of-the-mountain is useful in understanding European political history. England's monarchy started at the top of the mountain and slowly moved down its slopes until it reached the bottom, where it exists today as a mere figurehead of state, with no power. The French king started at the middle of the mountain, moved to the top and remained there until his head was chopped off in the French Revolution. Taxation was a critical factor in the movement of these two monarchies up and down the mountain.

No Magna Carta was necessary in France for the simple reason that feudal contracts granted freedom from taxation to most nobles; furthermore, French kings respected these contracts and would not dare institute an exactio inaudita (an unheard-of tax).

Tax restraints on the French monarchy also applied to lords. The *taille*, like the English tallage, was hated as much in France as in England. Many charters between lords and commoners prohibited this most arbitrary power to tax. In Flanders, the local count invited weavers to come and live, upon the express condition that there would be no taille. The weaving industry that developed from this taille immunity still survives as the dominant industry in Flanders today. The attitude of the French people towards the taille is illustrated in this preamble to the medieval charter for the city of St. Denis (near Paris):

> [the taille] is inordinately bad and hateful, in that it kept them in constant fear, and so, not daring to display their goods, they made little gain. Wherefore, not only were the outsiders afraid to settle in the town, but the natives were impelled to go elsewhere.

The charter of St. Denis specifically abolished the taille if the inhabitants would pay a fixed poll tax each year. The hatred the French people had for the taille became a critical factor in the course of French history up to the time of the defeat of Napoleon. Of equal importance was the zeal of the French people for tax immunities. Not even Napoleon, during his most critical times, could alter that zeal. Many Frenchmen lived without taxation. It was a prerogative of political power. In the French Revolution it was only natural for the overtaxed peasants and workers to expect tax immunity as the fruit of victory and a gracious benevolence from their emperor. Napoleon could defeat the armies of the world; he could re-arrange the nations of Europe at will—but he could not move the French peasants from this illusion.

Philip the Fair, the French king who expelled the Jews and seized their wealth, started France down the road to royal absolutism, primarily through his lawlessness. After fleecing the Jews he utilized the same process to steal money from the rest of France's bankers. He then turned on the church and when the pope threatened excommunication he sent a band of thugs to kidnap the pope to establish the papacy on French soil where it would be more cooperative toward his tax plans. This period of "Babylonian captivity," as it has been called, was instituted by the king of France to assure his right to tax church property.

Philip finally succeeded in increasing taxes on the nobility by commuting knight service into an annual tax like the English scutage. On top of this bastardized scutage he added a capital levy, but he was unable permanently to enforce this tax.

Philip's most difficult problem was with heirship. He had a daughter and a grandson, which should have solved the problem, except his grandson was in England and was the Crown Prince. On Philip's death the Kingdom of France passed to the king of England. No Frenchman could accept this.

There are moments in history when sound legal principles produce outrageous results. This was such a moment. When that happens, lawyers can be counted upon to find a solution. In France they unearthed a seven-hundred-year-old Frankish law which prohibited a woman from becoming a monarch. They then stretched this to mean that her son could not be a monarch either. This reasoning was ridiculous because under long-established principles of primogeniture any man can inherit a kingdom through his mother. Nevertheless, it was enough to wrench the French monarchy from the clutches of the English.

The English were not as interested in the French kingdom as they were in their feudal lands along the coasts of France. Parliament responded, as we have noted, with a modest grant to the king to raise an army to recover these lands. The battles that followed started the Hundred Years' War, a war England lost even though it won most of the battles.

This sympathetic cartoon shows the abused French peasant farmer, gaunt and tattered, feeding his livestock, toiling in the field, and paying all his profits to the tax man.

Two important events brought victory for the French—Joan of Arc and a new French tax system. Joan rallied the French people behind a new king who had good reason to be unsure of his claim to the throne (he was a nephew of Philip, while the English king was a grandson). At the same time, the Estates General, a kind of parliament of France, also supported the wavering king and granted him the power permanently to levy the taille against much of the wealth of France. England's short-term tax armies were only good for a battle or two, while French armies had a solid financial base to endure defeats and eventually drive the English from French soil. This was the tax that beat the English. (Four hundred years later, in the second Hundred Years' War, the tables were reversed. By this time Britain had developed a tax to beat Napoleon.)

With his new tax power the king of France was the envy of the monarchs of Europe. He was also granted the power to levy a sales tax and a tax on salt, but it was the taille that provided over 80 percent of his revenues. Looking at this new grant of taxing power from the standpoint of the French people, it eliminated the need for parliamentary debate and bargain. The Estates General was not needed any more. Royal absolutism, though not as absolute as it claimed, was nevertheless the consequence. The French monarchy could now easily move to the top of the mountain while the king of England was clearly on his way down.

During the Hundred Years' War, overtaxed peasants revolted in France and England. In France the revolts erupted in 1348 when tailles were increased beyond endurance to raise funds to ransom the king and a number of his nobles. A ransom of over one million gold crowns was actually paid. The revolt was led by a peasant named Jacques Bonhomme, and it was called the revolt of the Jacquerie. As usual the peasants were massacred (about twenty thousand), but not before the "Isle of France was a desert."

For the next two hundred years peasant uprisings over taxation brought devastation and death throughout Europe. These revolts are significant because the peasants never had a voice in taxation, though they bore most of the burdens. The Parliament of England and the Estates General in France had no seats for representatives of the peasants. Constitutional struggles between kings and their subjects over taxation did not concern the peasants. When taxation became too oppressive for them they voiced their discontent through the only means available: violence.

22

The Devil's Tax System

So there is only one way of escaping taxation and that is to make a fortune.
—Pierre-Samuel du Pont de Nemours

The revenue system that finally evolved out of the taxing powers granted to the French monarch in the Hundred Years' War was everything a good tax system should not be. A French writer of that period said that if the Devil himself had been given a free hand to plan the ruin of France, he could not have invented any scheme more likely to achieve that objective than the system of taxation then in operation.

It was a system that produced the greatest amount of viciousness between man and man, and man and state. It was a great evil, but not without parallel to other times and places. The tax system of the ancien régime was not unique, any more than the corruption in Nixon's regime was unique; it was simply a high water mark in bad taxation. It teaches us much about taxation and the evils bad taxation will produce, not only in the injustices of government, but in the atrocities angry taxpayers are inclined to commit.

When the Crown tried to introduce a wine tax in Bordeaux in 1635, angry taxpayers shouted: "Death to the gabeleurs! Kill the gabeleurs!" and they meant it. (French tax collectors were called *gabeleurs*.)

The name ancien régime refers to the social and political order of France before the French Revolution in 1789. Historians have often remarked that it is not easy to understand this period of history. The French monarchy is said to have been absolute. Historians often spend whole chapters comparing the absolutism of the king of France with the limited monarchy in England. The best illustration of that absolutism is the remark made by Louis XIV concerning complaints about excessive taxation. Louis said that since everything belonged to him, he was only taking what was his. Actually, the French monarchy was anything but absolute. The mere suggestion by the Crown of a need for tax increases was enough to produce a revolt and end the life of some innocent tax collector. There were revolts of major proportions that were incited by groundless rumors about new taxes. To combat these rumors the government would send out high-ranking officials with impressive documents to assure and reassure the people that the rumors were false. If that was not enough, the Crown threatened the death penalty for anyone guilty of spreading such rumors. Behavior of this sort on the part of government is more an indication of panic than absolutism. There is no doubt, however, that Louis XIV did boast about his absolute power, but it is doubtful if even he believed it. One thing is certain, the French people didn't believe it. The so-called absolutism of the French monarchy was only a facade.[1]

The taille (usually a land and wealth tax), became an ordinary annual assessment after the Hundred Years' War, fluctuating with the king's military needs. It could have been an equitable form of taxation if it had been applied to the kingdom as a whole. Unfortunately, the nobility and clergy and even some of the cities and provinces were exempt or had reduced rates. For some it was a land tax; for others it applied to all wealth. This inequity prompted one finance minister to blame most of the ills of the kingdom on the taille, which he said left one-tenth of the people beggars, five-tenths next to beggars, three-tenths overtaxed workers, and one-tenth in modest comfort.

By the eighteenth century, the taille was called the "peasant's tax" because most everyone else had found some way to avoid it. During the French Revolution, when the taille was finally abolished, the famous Pierre-Samuel du Pont de Nemours (who later fled to America to found the great Du Pont financial dynasty) told the French National Assembly: "One will hardly believe that in order to become noble it is sufficient to become rich; and to cease to pay taxes it is sufficient to become noble. So there is only one way of escaping taxation and that is to make a fortune."[2]

For over two hundred years the French monarchy tried to reform the taille, but it was simply not powerful enough to reconstruct a more equitable system. About all it could do was tinker with the existing system and retreat whenever resistance was too formidable. Louis XIV came close to modifying the taille with his poll tax, which classified everyone into twenty-two categories. Each category paid a rate of tax based on the amount of wealth normally associated with that category. This graduated form of wealth taxation was designed to reach the taille-immune, but with the aid of able lawyers evasion was easy. When Louis XIV died the poll tax was quickly repealed.

Some tailles were administered by local governments, but most were under the national government. The country was divided into twenty-four districts, each with a district director called an Intendant, the strong man or "special agent" of the system: "Intendants were employed . . . to supervise tax assessments and collection by the tax bureau or to spy on the judicial work of local judges and tax agents."[3]

The excise was called the *gabelle*, which was levied on just about everything that moved, including food. On wine there were five kinds of excises: a tax on the vine, a tax on the harvest, a tax on the manufacture, a transportation tax, and a tax on the sale. The poor drank cider.

Wine tax collectors made daily rounds to check on the wine inventory of tavern keepers. A hidden cache was normally buried in the cellar and sooner or later the inspector would discover the untaxed wine. This discovery would be silenced by a bribe. The Frenchman of three hundred years ago drank his wine despite the intolerable tax burdens placed upon it.

Related to the excise are stamp taxes, which usually come in the form of government seals and special paper for commercial transactions. The 5 percent excise was matched by a 5 percent tax on commercial transactions. Where seals were not used the government required special paper for deeds, contracts, bills, and notes. The paper could only be purchased from the Crown.

Unlike England, import duties were not a large source of revenue. Smuggling along the borders of France could not be effectively checked. Consequently, customs were levied at the entrances to cities and towns. These internal customs were called *octroi*. In Paris, as the city expanded, the customs gates were soon surrounded by houses which provided an easy route for evasion. To prevent smuggling into the city, a Paris wall was constructed inside the city, reminiscent of the Berlin Wall of recent history, and hated just as much. One of the first things destroyed in the French Revolution was this wall with its customs houses.

Even though the king of France had considerably more revenue than his rival across the Channel, like all kings of this period he was short of cash—the need for new revenue was insatiable. In time, the king and his finance ministers developed an art for acquiring what was called extraordinary revenue. They concocted schemes that have fascinated financiers and economists for three centuries. We could say they were the world's first successful alchemists—not in making gold out of base metals, but in doing even better, making gold out of paper!

The ministers in charge of the king's go-go money schemes soon overshadowed the regular tax ministry. Without their fiscal gamesmanship the government would have collapsed. The French monarchy in the seventeenth century was bankrupt until these financial whiz-kids saved

The burning of the Paris *octroi*, or city customs tax houses, during the French Revolution.

the Crown, which opted for revenue gimmicks as an alternative to either bankruptcy or fiscal responsibility. Until the French Revolution, the Crown pursued a pot of gold created by fiscal chicanery.

Borrowing money was not easy for a government in a society that forbade the lending of money at interest. But in that day the French were not seriously bothered about morality, especially when it interfered with their way of life. As the great German poet Goethe said, "What serves the moment . . . seems right to the French."[4] Private businesses in France had been borrowing money for some time with the skill of legal craftsmen. Loans were made in the form of sales with lease-backs. A borrower would sell whatever property he had to a lender, who would pay cash for this "property." The property was never physically transferred, however, because the borrower (seller) would immediately rent it back from his lender-buyer. This rental payment was really an interest payment on the money the borrower received from the phony sale. Finally, in the very same document, the borrower would agree to buy his "property" back for the original sum. This was the repayment of the loan.

French tax-farmers, called paper money men, creating "money"—not unlike today's central bankers.

The Crown had trouble with this arrangement because of its bad credit. To solve this problem, straw men were used to front for the government. These straw men were high-ranking ministers and tax-farmers who became guarantors if the government defaulted. Large fortunes were made by these "financiers," as they were called.

The government's financial paper was not initially sold on the open market. It was acquired in wholesale lots for speculation, at a large discount, in the same way that investment banking firms buy up blocks of new stock issued in the United States and Canada. The financiers then resold the paper at a lesser discount. France developed a busy Wall Street, the Rue Quincampoix, with all the ups and downs of "the market," including their own 1929-type crashes as well.

The common people of France, as in Spain, had a zeal for aristocratic status. The Crown sold offices and titles for a substantial fee. In time, the government created an enormous inventory of "offices" for sale. In reality, these sales were interest-free, perpetual loans to the government. Consider for example, the sheep and cattle farmers in Brittany who produced hides. The Crown took notice of this enterprise and created an office of inspector of hides. All hides had to be inspected, for a fee. The annual fees provided a nice profit for the inspector who was permitted to keep everything he collected. He could hire deputies to do the work and never even needed to leave Paris. The price paid for this office was directly related to the expected return. The losers, of course, were the farmers. The inspection served no useful purpose; it was simply a tax on the hide business.

If an office brought in more fees than was expected for the price paid, the Crown would divide the office and sell a second office. If an office holder wanted to increase his salary or his fees, the Crown would do so providing he paid for the increase. The ratio between the salary increase and the cash payment to the government was the "prime rate" of that day; i.e., if the interest rate was 5 percent, then the office holder would have to pay one hundred livres for every five livres annual pay increase. The salary increase was really "interest" on a new perpetual loan.

Some offices, especially judgeships, created noble status which the office holder wanted to pass to his heirs. The government would accommodate this for an annual fee, called a *paulette*, which was also used to keep judges in line. If a judge irritated the government by ruling unfavorably too often, the finance ministry would respond and withdraw its paulette.

The French practice of office-selling, and its corruption, had a profound effect on the founding fathers of America. The Constitution has two separate provisions prohibiting the sale of offices and grants of nobility. The last thing wanted in the Americas was government based on office-selling, referred to in the Constitution as "emoluments."

The importance of tax-farming in the ancien régime cannot be overemphasized. Tax-farmers were to the ancien régime what the Federal Reserve Board, the Bank of England, and the Bank of Canada are to their respective countries. They had the power to create money and to provide the government with enormous amounts of credit. They were the national bankers of France, in an informal way. Paper money issued by them was backed by taxes to be collected and kept the government afloat. That system in France has its counterpart today—our national debts are backed by future taxes, not gold.

Tax-farming in France began in the Middle Ages. Lords did not have the machinery or the inclination to collect taxes. Private tax collectors, usually Jews, paid the lord a fixed sum in advance for the right to collect tolls and customs. This instant cash is what made the tax-farmer so desirable. Furthermore, tax bureaucracies of kings and nobles were usually corrupt as well as inefficient. Only in an emergency, when tax-farmers offered insufficient revenues, did the king collect his own taxes, and then only as a temporary expedient.

As the kingdom of France expanded, its tax-farmers formed large national corporations. The country was divided up into tax-farming districts. The standard contract was 10 percent down, plus periodic payments over six years, represented by notes from the tax-farmers. The Crown could assign these notes to pay its debts. Holders of these notes accepted them at less than face value because payment was not due. The amount discounted depended on the date of payment. Holders had three choices: (1) they could keep the notes till maturity and collect the full amount; (2) they could negotiate them, also at a discount, to pay their own debts; or (3) they could take them to the tax-farmer and obtain cash at a discounted rate. These notes were simply the zero-coupon bonds of that day.

The credit of tax-farmers was sound. Was this process really any different than the money we use today? Basically, this paper money was an assignment of future tax receipts. Our governments operate on the same principle. With tax-farming contracts running six years, the French government had that much credit available. Again, not unlike today.

The risks in this elementary national banking system were tax revolts, wars, droughts, plagues, or anything else that might bring about a failure of the tax harvest. The most serious danger to the system was the lack of controls. At times, the government issued assignments against tax receipts that did not exist and the tax-farmers honored these assignments. This kind of fiscal irresponsibility frequently drove the system to the edge of bankruptcy.

Tax-farmers were put out of business for a season after the death of Louis XIV. The regents for his infant great-grandson Louis XV, blamed the tax-farmers for the financial troubles of the régime. To correct these troubles they brought in a daring fiscal innovator from Scotland named John Law. Law organized a national bank, issued a new kind of paper money, and put the tax-farmers out of business by cancelling most excise taxes. Government debt paper could be exchanged for stock in Law's bank or used to pay taxes. Tax-farming assignments were not needed nor were they available with excises cancelled.

To provide a basis for the bank's credit, Law obtained the exclusive rights for all trade from Louisiana and Canada, the New World lands filled with gold and riches—at least that was the rumor, and during speculation fever a good rumor is as effective as the real thing. No one had seen the gold, but that did not matter as long as the rumor persisted.

Law was the man of the hour for France. His bank issued notes without regard to anything other than public acceptance and government need. It was not long before Law's notes were everywhere. In the beginning, Law redeemed his notes for gold and silver, but this made drastic reductions in his meager cash reserves so Law stopped redeeming his notes (like President Nixon did). Most of the redemptions were made by tax-farmers who helped precipitate his collapse by making a run on the bank. Eventually an overly confident public realized that his notes and the shares in the bank were only paper and the gold in the New World was only a hope. The "assignments" of the tax-farmers began to look good; they had been backed by taxes, the real gold of the Kingdom of France—solid, dependable wealth, produced by the sweat of the French people.

Law's bubble burst, his system collapsed, and he fled into exile. His rise and fall became a classical story of economic history. There were many defects in his system, but from a tax point of view, he freed government expenditures from tax receipts and cancelled a number of excise taxes. The combination proved disastrous; with reduced tax revenues and unrestrained expenditures, the country was simply flooded with paper—worthless money. His system was doomed from the start even if there had been no speculation fever.

French tax-farmers were reluctant to pick up the pieces of Law's debacle. For a number of years the Crown had to collect its own taxes, using the personnel of the tax-farmers. Eventually, the revenue system returned to the tax-farmers and they remained in control until the revolution in 1789.

Tax-farming passed away with most of the ancien régime in the French Revolution. The leaders were herded together, tried en masse for treason, and beheaded by the guillotine. They were condemned for fleecing the French people out of 300 million livres. When they were unable to produce a quick, satisfactory accounting the guillotine was put in operation. No tears were shed when their heads flopped into the basket.

The ultimate irony of their downfall and beheading came some years later when their widows and orphans sought a return of the property the government had seized to pay the alleged 300-million-livre debt. When a final objective accounting was rendered, the French courts acknowledged that there never was any indebtedness; instead, the state was indebted to the tax-farmers for 8 million livres. The seized property was returned to the heirs. The government could not restore the heads that had dropped into the basket, and as for the office of tax-farmer, it had passed from French history for all time. The unique institution, which played such an important role in the tax systems of Western civilization for almost three thousand years, finally succumbed in Europe to the guillotine and the mobs of Paris.

23

Many Revolts—One Revolution

They raised a clamour and confused threats against all the lives of the gabeleurs, using this word to include all the collectors of His Majesty's taxes. They tore to pieces an unfortunate surgeon whom they suspected of being a gabeleur. After stripping him naked and cutting off one of his arms, they made him walk around the fair, and then finished him off.
—Peasant tax revolt, Blansac, France, 1636

This savage account of the behavior of angry French peasants repeated itself time and again throughout the seventeenth century. A teen-aged clerk from Paris who kept books for a tax collector was torn apart by these same peasants. His flesh was cut into strips and nailed on cottage doors to remind other revenue officials what was in store for them.

Unlike the peasant revolts in Germany, the upper and middle classes of French society often encouraged and aided the peasants. French tax revolts had no social overtones; they were pure and simple tax revolts. When the peasants shouted "Kill the gabeleurs," they also shouted "Long live the king without gabeleurs." They were opposed to new taxes, increases in tax rates, changes in collection methods, and any new revenue device. In brief, they wanted the revenue system left the way it was. In Germany the peasants killed any member of the upper classes they could find; in France they only killed tax collectors.

Tax rebellions in France were typical of this age of tax rebellions. The French, like the Spanish, had more trouble fighting tax rebels at home than they had fighting each other abroad. The rebellions at home were related to the wars abroad. These wars required revenues far in excess of the miserly amounts provided by the medieval tax systems that were still in force. Kings had to raise new revenues, but when they did, rebellion followed. This was the iron law of seventeenth-century taxation.

Tax rebels were not revolutionary at this time. They could even be

A revolting peasant is put to death, as so often happened during the many tax revolts in seventeenth-century France.

called reactionaries. A petition to the king of France by the peasants of Brittany illustrates the temper of the times:

> We are ready to pay taxes that were in being sixty years ago, and we do not object to paying anyone what he has a right to receive, and we are not arguing against anything but the new edicts and charges. [And they] beg his Majesty to look upon them with compassion and to relieve them.[1]

The fiscal leaders of the ancien régime had to have the attributes of a magician, a thug, and a firefighter. Like magicians they had to be able to create revenue by fiscal hocus pocus, like pulling a rabbit out of a hat. At the same time, they had to be skilled with the use of brutality against the weaker members of society—uncooperative taxpayers. The tax objective of the state—"what the traffic would bear"—was the amount of tax that could be extracted one step short of causing a major revolt. The government, of course, misjudged repeatedly, and when it did, the internal revenue system became a fire brigade rushing out to extinguish brushfire rebellions. Knowing when to fight and when to conciliate was the mark of statecraft. The rulers of France did a remarkable job in that regard until 1789.

Economists in the ancien régime believed that the best medicine to cure poverty was heavy taxation. Indeed, the poorer a region, the heavier it should be taxed. Increased taxation, said these experts, would increase productivity and benefit everyone; consequently, taxes were the appropriate tool to combat poverty. The poor were like grass—the more they were cut down, the stronger they would become. We should not ridicule this logic too severely. In 1947, the U.S. Treasury espoused this idea to justify high progressive peacetime taxes.[2] In the nineteenth century the dogma of the rich and powerful was Social Darwinism. Nature's survival of the fittest meant that the strong and rich could abuse the poor—this was nature's intent. At the same time the Marxists taught that the extermination of the capitalist class would bring Utopia for oppressed workers.

Overtaxed peasants in France did not accept the view that they were like grass and should be cut down for their own benefit. They protested routinely with murder, mayhem, assaults, arson, and other forms of violence. Ten years after a tax revolt near Bordeaux the finance minister confessed to the Queen that it was safer for a French soldier to walk through a Spanish village (France was at war with Spain at that time) than it was for a French tax man to "pass from province to province, even to leave one's home." This violence against his majesty's tax men was the consequence, said the minister, of the "ravages and violence of the king's tax men."[3] If life insurance had existed then, it is doubtful that tax collectors could have received coverage at any price.

Normandy gives us a good example of what tax revolts were like in the ancien régime. In the first place, they were all local. If the wine makers in Bordeaux revolted and forced the Crown to reduce taxation, that reduction would only apply to Bordeaux; the wine makers in Burgundy and the rest of France would not be benefited. They would have to fight their own battles.

Normandy, located on the English Channel, is where the D-Day invasion took place in 1944. For centuries this province has been in the center of many of Europe's military conflicts. This had a natural tendency to make the province subject to heavy military taxation. There was no province in France taxed more, nor more set on rebellion, than Normandy.

One of the major rebellions of this period started in Normandy over a false rumor of an increase in salt taxes. In response to this rumor the salt makers organized, adopted a flag, raised an army, and rallied the rest of the populace with these verses about the king's tax men: "Men made rich by taxes . . . who sell their fatherland . . . and run to fetch the excise."[4]

For decades a special committee operated in the province to spy on all newcomers. Anyone suspected of being associated with taxation could be lynched. Many innocent strangers were put to death. Local judges had a long history of refusing to convict tax evaders or to register the appointment of new tax officials. Even the intendant was disloyal to Paris. On one occasion a company of special agents were about to attack a group of salt-tax evaders camped in a forest near a small village. Just before the attack was to begin the village bell started to ring alerting the smugglers. The leader of the special agents complained to the intendant and demanded that the culprit be punished. The intendant agreed. He then ordered the villagers to remove the bell and bring it to the town square where it was given a public lashing to everyone's delight.

The authority of the Crown over this region was finally restored, but only after prolonged military occupation, public hangings, and the transfer of all tax cases from local courts to Paris. Normandy settled into a prolonged "cold war" tax rebellion which heated up from time to time. Twenty years later (in the 1660s), the Crown misjudged the surface calm and tried to increase the taille. Violence erupted once again and the army returned to restore order. Like so many other French provinces, Normandy operated on the brink of rebellion; but Normandy, like all the rebellious regions, never threatened the Crown, only its local revenue. The French people wore blinders; they were unable to see the suffering and injustices meted out to their neighbors. Because of this, the monarchy was secure, no matter how rotten it was. This blindness may stem from the peculiarities of the French political mind; splinter parties dominated France three hundred years ago almost as much as they have during most of the twentieth century.

The only rebellion that endangered the Crown was the famous revolt of the Fronde in Paris. This revolt started in 1648 after the high court refused to register a number of new revenue measures. Mobs appeared in the street at this time and peppered Crown administrators with rocks, hence the name *fronde*, or sling shot.

The registration process of new tax and revenue decrees was somewhat like the American principle of judicial review. New laws had to

Andre Vincent's painting of Mathieu Mole, president of the French High Court, facing the Parisian mob during the Fronde revolt. Angry French taxpayers demanded immediate tax relief—a *taille* (land tax) reduction for the peasants and a drastic cut in tariffs on goods entering Paris for the merchants.

be registered in the courts for enforcement, but laws that were unconstitutional were refused registration.

The French system of judicial review developed a peculiar twist. The king could cure the defect in any law by personally appearing before the high court and ordering the judges to register the decree, but in 1648, the king was only ten years old. Now what?

The boy-king's mother was his regent. She was not even French, but Austrian. Her chief finance minister was Italian. The three of them marched into the high court in a solemn assembly and ordered the court to register the rejected tax and revenue measures. The attorney general was with her and presented the matter to the high court. As he ended his address to the court, he made this startling comment:

> For ten years the country has been ruined, the peasants reduced to sleeping on straw, their furniture sold to pay taxes; so that to maintain luxury in Paris, millions of innocent persons are forced to live on bread made of bran and oats, hoping for no protection except in their weakness, and owning but their souls, because no means has been devised to sell these at auction.[5]

Two days later the judges ruled against the young king and his mother: a regent could not order the registration of laws declared unconstitutional. The high court then proceeded to exercise considerable authority over the Crown: tailles were reduced by 20 percent; the number of intendants was cut from twenty-four to six; and there would be no new taxes and no offices for sale. Tax-farming of the taille would also be prohibited.

These revenue reforms could have been the beginning of the end of royal absolutism, except that they were temporary in nature. The court's new power would end when the king came of age (fourteen years). And that is exactly what happened. When Louis became fourteen he marched into the judges' chambers and ordered them to register all his decrees in a week. He turned to the president of the court and ordered him to keep his nose out of the affairs of state. It was then that he made the famous statement, "I am the state." Finally, he changed the name of the court from sovereign court to supreme court. Only the king held sovereign powers. As an adult monarch he could order the judges to do what he liked. Is not this what the judges had decided when he was ten years old? In 1648 the judges had committed the fatal error of lawyers—win the case at hand and the long-range consequences be damned.

Louis XIV had two remarkable finance ministers. Colbert was the most famous, but his successor, Vauban, was the most courageous. They both made gallant but unsuccessful efforts at reform. Colbert tried to substitute indirect taxation for taille reform, but Brittany and Bordeaux, both taille-exempt, revolted over his new excises and stamp taxes. They understood, too well, that Colbert was trying to circumvent their taille immunity. The rebellion in Brittany was so fierce that the Crown had to hire Swiss mercenaries to restore order.

Vauban proposed a 10 percent income tax in place of taille reform. Because of the Crown's heavy expenditures, said Vauban, the income tax was the only way to save France, unless you were "either stupid or wholly malintentioned." This last remark was directed at Louis XIV,

Louis XIV, in his classical portrait, celebrating his victory over the Fronde, the name given to the tax revolt by mobs using the fronde, a sling shot with which they peppered the Crown's tax men with rocks. His most famous statement upon assuming the crown at age fourteen was "L'État, c'est moi" ("I am the state"), meaning that since everything belonged to him, when he taxed he was only taking what was his. With rates of tax for income and wealth running from 80 to over 90 percent in our time, the modern state makes the same assertion, but without the arrogance of the sun-king.

who dismissed Vauban. Vauban had made a special study of exemptions and discovered there were seventeen different ways to achieve tax immunity. Each loophole had a political power base to ensure its success. The only principle behind the taille was "that of paying more the poorer you are; so that a man with 4,000 to 5,000 livres of income from loans may pay 10 to 12 crowns, while another man in the same village making cheese with 300 to 400 livres of income may pay 100 crowns." Vauban's sharp criticism of the king put him in exile and his books in the fire. If he had been king, the course of French history would have been changed.

During the rule of Louis XV the French government put Vauban's income tax into operation, but each year the returns declined as more and more techniques to evade the tax were developed. The 10 percent tax was followed by an improved 5 percent version but evasion killed this tax as well.

In 1750 a taille reform plan was adopted, which removed taille exemptions from church lands, noble lands, and tax-exempt provinces like Brittany. Unfortunately, the king scuttled these reforms, as well as the finance minister who proposed them, after there was an assassination attempt on the king's life. There was another glimmer of hope in the final days of his reign when he stripped the high court of the power to veto tax reform. With the obstructionist court out of the way the road was open for reform by decree, but Louis XV died, and his inexperienced grandson restored the court's veto power.

On the eve of the French Revolution, when Louis XVI came to the throne, it was clear the tax system could only be reformed through revolution. The proponents of this view were not finance ministers, but intellectuals who frequented the coffeehouses of Paris. They published the famous *Encyclopedia* in thirty-five volumes. Voltaire, Rousseau, Montesquieu, and others focused on the social injustices of the tax system:

In the matter of taxation, every privilege is an injustice. (Voltaire)

He who only has the bare necessities of life should pay nothing; taxation on him who has a surplus may, if need be, extend to everything beyond necessities. He may urge that on account of his rank what is superfluous for a man in a lower position is necessary for him, but that is untrue, for a nobleman has only two legs like a cowman, and each only has one belly. (Rousseau)

Those who say that the poorer the people, the larger the families—the heavier the taxation placed upon them, the greater their effort to pay it— blaspheme against the human race. They ought to experience the bitter destitution to which they condemn their fellow citizen in order to determine how false and atrocious is their attitude. (Mercier)

To levy taxes on essential foodstuffs is cruel to the highest degree. Man's right to existence is above all social laws. Has he lost it by the establishment of laws?

By squeezing the destitute of their bare subsistence the state deprives them of all strength. Of the poor man it makes a beggar, of the workman an idler, of an unfortunate a rogue, and thus leads through starvation to the gallows. (Raynal)

Copies of the *Encyclopedia* were in most every town and city in France. The common man may not have been interested in the subtleties of political philosophy, but he was aware something was terribly unjust about the tax system. Oppressed taxpayers began to think beyond the tax man to the tax-exempt classes as the cause of their burdens.

The tax-exempt classes and provinces had support for their preferred position. Taille-immune provinces had medieval charters that guaranteed their "ancient liberties"—which meant taille-immunity. Their ancestors had fought and died for their right to be free from this oppressive tax. Within the system, exemptions were purchased with hard cash. The judges, for example, paid for their immunities; it was only natural for them to fight for what they purchased. Tax immunities were to these people what constitutional rights are to us.

The final effort at reform came in 1789 after the high court once again vetoed tax reforms which took away the ancient liberties of the tax-immune. The court reasoned that only the Estates General, an assembly of all classes of French society, could authorize the tax reforms the king sought. The court was aware that the Estates would reject the king's reforms since there were three chambers in this great assembly, each with one vote. The clergy (tax-exempt) and the nobles (also tax-exempt) would outvote the commoners and end tax reform for all time.

To counter the court's plan, the king doubled the size of the commoners so they could challenge the tax-exempt clergy and nobility. With this skillful move the meeting of the Estates General promised to produce a tax struggle of major proportions. How would this stalemate be resolved? As we know, the tax issue was soon buried in the violence of the French Revolution that followed.

A 1780 engraving portrays the lack of uniformity in taxation in the ancien régime. The clergy and nobility crush the commoners, who bear the heavy taxes of society. The uniformity clause in the U.S. Constitution was designed to prevent this from happening within the factions of U.S. society.

Part VI

After Magna Carta

In England at the time of Magna Carta, the principle of parliamentary supremacy over taxation appeared to be well established. In the centuries that followed, England's tax struggles shifted from king v. Parliament to Parliament v. taxpayers. A third factor emerged in tax-making—taxpayer acceptance and approval. English taxpayers revolted against taxes they did not like. Some revolts were violent, but most were of the "cold war" type, or what could be called national conspiracies at all levels. Taxpayers, assessors, and sheriffs refused to cooperate regardless of what Parliament had approved. Parliamentary consent was not necessarily taxpayer consent.

English peasants revolted during the Hundred Years' War, soon after the French Jacquerie uprising. In 1379 Parliament considered a graduated poll tax with rates running from ten marks for a duke down to forty shillings for a baron. After a prolonged debate Parliament adopted a simple poll tax of one shilling for every man and woman over the age of fourteen. Under the first proposal rich nobles would be assessed a sum which bore some relation to their wealth, but the final law placed the main burden on the poor. In addition, the tax was farmed out to private contractors, French-style, and it was "levied with insolence and severity. The patience of the people was at last exhausted. They flew to arms."[1]

The revolt started when the chief justice of the Court of Common Pleas went to Brentwood with three of his clerks to investigate alleged frauds on the poll tax rolls. An angry mob seized the judge and his clerks. The judge barely escaped (he had the fastest carriage), but his clerks were not so fortunate. They were beheaded by the mob and their heads were hoisted up on poles as a protest against the poll tax. Violence spread throughout England. Tax records were burned. The Archbishop of Canterbury was killed and the king saved his own life by promising to help the rebels. Once the king felt secure he turned on the peasants, seized their leaders, and beheaded them.

Peasant revolts are not noted for success. (Karl Marx made a big point of that.) But this revolt was very successful so far as the peasants were concerned. Future poll taxes for centuries to come excluded the peasants or taxed them at nominal rates. The last thing Parliament or the Crown wanted was another peasant revolt.

Parliament began experimenting with income taxes after the disastrous poll tax, but with no success. These early income tax laws had teeth, with fines and imprisonments, but English taxpayers and sheriffs conspired against them. In 1449 a gentleman named Cade organized a rebellion in Kent which ended with the beheading of the king's chief tax minister. Finally, in 1472, Edward IV made what was the last attempt at income taxation with a 10 percent assessment to finance 13,000 archers for a campaign in France. Strong taxpayer resistance forced the Chancellor of the Exchequer to appear before the Parliament and admit defeat. Parliament, said the chancellor, should stay with the "fifteenths" and "tenths," which was a tax the English taxpayer was "most easy, ready, and prone to payment."[2]

The "fifteenths" meant one-fifteenth of the assessed value of a taxpayer's personal property, usually livestock and goods. The "tenths" meant one-tenth of real property rentals. No one was "doubly taxed." In actual practice the tax evolved into a grant of £30,000 for all of England. Each tax district was obliged to pay a fixed amount to the treasury. There were no audits or appraisals. The same amount was paid by a family for generations. Assessments and collections were performed by local people. The Crown had to wait up to two years to receive payment. The English liked this tax because everyone knew exactly what his tax would be, and generally consented to the final figure. There was no undue pressure for payment, and most important, the king's tax agents were excluded from administration.[3]

Later, concurrent with the "fifteenths" and "tenths," came a "subsidy," which was fixed at £80,000, almost thrice the fifteenths and tenths. Values in the "Queen's Subsidy Book" were based on tradition and appearances. In John Lyly's play *Mother Bombie* (1594), a character, speaking of the old times, says, "I may tell you that he that had a cup of red wine to his oysters was hoisted in the Queen's subsidy book."[4] The chances are his tax valuation was ridiculously low, and by modern standards would be criminal fraud. Yet this was the system the English were willing to accept and the Crown learned to live by it. When Sir Walter Raleigh complained to Queen Elizabeth that values were a hundred times greater than reported on her subsidy books, she did not object.[5] There was, in her words, "a tradition of evasion in the realm." She was not about to upset that tradition, or any other tradition with respect to taxation. Not all monarchs were that wise.

Henry VIII came to the English throne at the end of the fifteenth century. He was nicknamed Bluff King Hal. From a tax standpoint we could call him Heister Hal because he pulled off the biggest heist of all time—he stole the assets of the Catholic Church throughout England.

An aggressive monarch like Henry VIII was bound to have revenue problems, especially with England's stingy Parliament. When he went to France in 1544 he crossed the Channel in a ship with gold sailcloth. Yet for all his extravagance, there were no serious tax revolts during his reign.

Henry started his search for revenue with the tax system. He was unsuccessful with the poll tax. The traditional "fifteenths and tenths" was not enough, so he worked with the subsidy. He doubled the rates, prompting one minister to say that there was not that much gold in all of England. When the subsidy failed to give him what he wanted, he issued a supplementary subsidy without the approval of Parliament. Taxpayers refused to pay, commissioners refused to assess, which left Henry with the option of backing down or going to war. Henry decided not to provoke the issue. He penitently promised never again to ask for revenue the English people did not want to give him. This does not sound like Henry, especially when it came to money. "Bluff King Hal" had other, deep laid plans.

Henry's attention turned to the church. Every month large quantities of gold and silver left England for Rome. The pope received more wealth than Henry did and he did not have to battle Parliament. Henry received a piece of the tithes of the church, but the lion's share went south.

Merchants also objected to the flow of silver and gold to Rome. England had no silver or gold; the limited amounts of these precious metals in England came from trade. The outflow to Rome seriously handicapped English merchants and businessmen. Henry capitalized on this discontent and in 1529 Parliament prohibited the payment of tithes to Rome with these words: "intolerable exactions of the pope of Rome of great sums of money whereby the subjects of the realm, by many years past had been, and yet were greatly decayed and impoverished."[6]

Charles V of Spain is blamed for the pope's rejection of Henry's request for an annulment of his marriage to the Spanish princess, Catherine of Aragon. This was a factor, but Henry's assaults on the pope's revenues may have been more significant. Henry may even have planned for the rejection of his annulment. He cut off church revenue shortly before he asked for the annulment. He was in no position to expect the pope to grant him such a special favor. The stakes between Henry and the pope were not the annulment, but rather, the largest bundle of wealth in England—the lands and income of the church. Henry was not called "Bluff King Hal" for nothing.

Henry seemed to be waiting for his excommunication. Parliament responded and proclaimed Henry supreme ruler of the Church in England. This permitted him to execute the greatest heist of all time. Henry started selling monastic lands and he redirected tithes and offerings to his coffers. With these lucrative revenues, new taxes were not needed.

24

Why Queen Elizabeth I Was Called "Good Queen Bess"

I would rather the money [taxes] was in the pockets of my people than in my treasury.

—Elizabeth I

The Russian chroniclers of A.D. 1000 had to acknowledge that Princess Olga was "wiser than all men." Five hundred years later, another woman ruler was obviously "wiser than all men" as well. Is it really possible that women make better rulers than men? The stories of Elizabeth and of Princess Olga would seem to prove that.

If epithets were formally given to English monarchs, Good Queen Bess would certainly have been called "Elizabeth the Great." Many historians have indeed used those words. She inherited an England that was mediocre at best. The England she left was fast becoming a superpower and would dominate the world for four hundred years. By the end of the twentieth century, English law and political practices became the format for a hundred new nations born in this century. It was English parliamentary style government the world's new nations wanted, not the American presidential system. Presidents have historically tended to become dictators, prime ministers have not. Most new nations therefore opted for the prime minister format.

Elizabeth's greatness was even acknowledged by her successor, James the First, who gave us the King James version of the Bible. But he had no reason to praise Elizabeth. His mother, Mary Queen of Scots—Elizabeth's aunt and rival for the throne of England—was beheaded by Elizabeth's government with the Queen's consent. Nevertheless, when James came to the throne after Elizabeth's death, he said that she was "as one who in wisdom and felicity of government surpassed

Elizabeth's earliest known portrait, made when she was twelve years old. Her love of learning and books is evident by the book in her hand and the others on display. Elizabeth was raised by Henry VIII's last wife, who sensed Elizabeth's genius and encouraged her love of learning.

all the Princes since the days of Augustus."[1] Why would he say this, knowing what had happened to his mother? He could hardly be charged with bias. He said it because it was true then, and still is. And when it came to her fiscal affairs and tax policy, it is true even more so, *a fortiori* as the Latin statement goes.

Elizabeth outwitted every ruler in Europe as well as the most powerful men in England. She chose intensely loyal and able ministers and assistants, who could never quite predict her behavior. They remained captivated by her genius. Even her tax policy was unprecedented, and still is. Never before nor since has a ruler behaved toward taxation the way she did—she decided to be loved by her subjects, and she repeated that time and again throughout her reign. She said she would accept whatever revenue they were willing to give her. It was Elizabeth, and not the many other leaders of the past after her time, who said, "To be taxed and to be loved is not given to man."[2] This remark is even common today as governments increase tax burdens upon the people, meaning, that the government will not be liked when it taxes its people. So, it's a no-win situation for the government. What Elizabeth had in mind was that she would be loved; therefore she could not burden her people with taxes. She would accept whatever tax moneys were willingly provided, and adjust her rule to the moneys available. Toward the end of her reign, when offered new taxes, she declined, saying, "I would rather the money was in the pockets of my people than in my treasury." As far as I know, no other ruler in the history of civilization has ever made such a statement. Governments, including the American government most of all, have an insatiable appetite for money, and will resort to any scheme to acquire it, even destroying a Bill of Rights or a Constitution if necessary to fatten their spending pot.

Toward the end of her reign, when her treasury was on the short side, she said, "I will end as I began, with my subjects' love." Her taxes were unbelievably low for her time, and while some histories state that she was insolvent at her death, a more careful study of the fiscal records will show that while she was about 400,000 pounds in debt, she had receivables of well over one million pounds from the Netherlands and the King of France, plus uncollected tax revenues due but unpaid. When you look at her complete balance sheet, she was indeed in good fiscal shape. Elizabeth inherited a bankrupt government from her father while her successor, James I, was soon in very good fiscal condition. His problem was that he, too, had a big spending problem, and soon was in financial trouble. Frugality was a trademark of Elizabeth's government, but not of her successor's.

One of the first things Elizabeth did was to eliminate the use of an oath on tax returns. Today, that is the "penalty of perjury" clause found on just about every tax document. This policy of Elizabeth's was carried on for some time, and the idea lived on well into the nineteenth century. Even our Supreme Court at one time showed respect for the idea, but as spending demands increased and the need for compliance overrode all considerations, we, and most nations, have not only brought in the oath, but a sledge hammer to boot. Said one of Elizabeth's early biographers, "Yet Her Majesty in her time remitted the usual manner of assessment by oaths of the assessors, so as the taxation of men's values was voluntary without any inquisition by oath or other coersion."[3]

The reference to "other coersions" shows that Elizabeth made little effort to strictly enforce taxation and grants given her by Parliament. England under Elizabeth had by far the lowest taxes in Europe. Sir Francis Bacon summarized the good fortune of the English taxpayer:

> He that shall look into other countries and consider the taxes, tallages, and impositions, and assizes, and the like that are everywhere in use, will find that the Englishman is the most master of his own valuation, and the better in the purse on any nation in Europe.[4]

When Elizabeth came to the throne and was faced with her father's enormous debts, it took her fifteen years to pay them off, and even this required borrowing on a large scale. She had to seek out foreign lenders, and for additional collateral, she was able to persuade the City of London to act as surety for her obligations. But in time she balanced her budget, paid off the Crown's debts and established a solvent realm. With her frugal ways, she soon became a creditor nation making large loans to the Dutch to support their struggle for independence from Spain. She even made large loans to the King of France, as he, too, was an enemy of the Spanish. To further aggravate the Spanish, she commissioned privateers to raid on Spanish silver fleets, Sir Francis Drake being the most notorious. But her privateers ranked about fourth behind other European raiders who made off with bigger hauls with much less fanfare. The Dutch and the French plundered Spanish shipping far more than did the English, yet it was the English whom the King of Spain complained about most bitterly, and who called Elizabeth a pirate.

Elizabeth was more than a thorn in the side of the Spanish emperor, who was certainly the most powerful monarch Europe ever knew. On top of all her support for Spain's enemies, she had the gall to steal a Spanish galleon loaded with silver. One of Philip's silver galleons was on its way to the Spanish Netherlands with pay for Alva's starving troops, on the verge of rebellion and mutiny. The ship was being chased by Dutch raiders and slipped into an English port to escape capture. When the Spanish emperor demanded the release of the silver ship,

Elizabeth infuriated the emperor even more by saying that she understood the silver really belonged to some Italian bankers and she would hold the silver while sorting out the matter. In fact she would even use the silver and consider this a loan from its rightful owner.[5] This must have driven the emperor up the wall with rage, for here was a woman, no less, swiping his silver with a cock-and-bull story about Italian bankers owning the money.

In time, the emperor had had enough from this upstart English woman, so he assembled the largest naval force in history, the Spanish Armada, to set sail and conquer England, and thus get this thorn and this "woman" out of his life and his empire.

Elizabeth turned to Parliament for help. She said her "chiefest strength and safeguard was the loyal hearts and goodwill of her subjects."[6] When she issued ship-writs for ships, sailors, and guns, her writs were filled beyond expectation. Parliament granted her four "fifteenths and tenths," plus two subsidies, most of which were collected in two months, not the usual two years. This was unheard of in English history. And remember this was achieved at a time when she had dis-

Queen Elizabeth Leading the Dutch Cow, an allegorical, sixteenth-century painting of Philip of Spain riding the cow of the Netherlands, his spur drawing blood. The Duke of Alba is seen milking the cow (the tenth penny) while it is fed by Elizabeth.

mantled the compulsory and oath aspect of tax administration. With help from the weather, called the "Protestant wind," the Armada was defeated and limped back to Spain. England was saved, and from that time forward the English have almost always been one-up on the Spanish. The defeat of the Armada was the beginning of the end of Spanish world domination.

The world may never have had a Shakespeare had it not been for this remarkable woman. Against the opposition of London's leaders, she gave the development of the arts, and especially drama, her protection. She was a patron of the arts and in turn was celebrated by poets, writers, musicians, scholars, and painters. They owed their golden opportunities to the triumph of her rule.

In her last speech to the Parliament, just before she died, Elizabeth told the country, "This I count, the glory of my crown; that I have reigned with your love."[7]

She showed her love in more ways than in taxes. In an age of war, she avoided war in every possible way—for to the common people war meant not imperial glory as it did to rulers, it meant dark graves for sons in far away lands, cold and watery graves for seamen—and for families, mourning for dead sons, husbands, brothers, and friends. Elizabeth was a ruler in tune with the common people who, just like today, see no great value in national destiny and domination over foreign lands. They want security in their homes, adequate food and housing, education, and peace. Elizabeth identified with their wishes and obtained their love for doing so. American presidents in this age would do well to learn from her. They have been all too willing to sacrifice the youth and manhood of the nation for international glory and pursuits. As one recent historian observed about Elizabeth, "She reaped a great advantage from being a woman, she was not tempted by the idea of military glory."

It is a wonder England survived on the meager revenues from Parliament. Yet Elizabeth's England did more than survive, it was on its way to becoming a superpower. Some years later a historian remarked with amazement, "the solvency of her government has been held 'the miracle of the age.' "[8] It was no miracle at all, just smart taxes and spending management. Hers was the only European government that did not go bankrupt.

It wasn't just Elizabeth's tax and spending management that uplifted English commerce, there was also the important management of the currency—English money and its value. Her harebrained father depreciated the value of the pound by cutting its value in half, exactly as Roosevelt did in 1932, but that is another story in another time. Henry VIII decreed that a pound would only be worth half as many shillings as in the past. The shilling was a silver coin, the basic coin of the realm. By decreasing the number of shillings in a pound, Henry gained quite an increase in his money supply from his innumerable creditors, who would now only receive half as much coinage for every pound sterling he owed them. But that was not all. He then melted down the silver shillings and added about 40 percent base metals, so the shilling was only about 60 percent silver. It was this fiscal folly that prompted one of Elizabeth's advisers, Sir Thomas Gresham, to advise the Queen on the value of sound money, hence came Gresham's Law: "Bad money drives out good." Elizabeth called in all the bad coinage debased by her father, and reissued good silver shillings. But to do so she had to use up her treasury and borrow an enormous sum from the City of Antwerp to replace the bad money with good money. She then increased the number of shillings in a pound to the pre-Henry VIII days.

Elizabeth's policy of sound money for the realm made the English shilling the most sought after coinage for many centuries to come. The merchants could deal with her money in confidence, thus acting as a boon for trade and commerce. Sound money and good laws for commerce have always been an essential ingredient for a prosperous commercial system. This was first brought to the world's attention by the Greeks two thousand years before Elizabeth.

Of all her fiscal achievements, ending the debasement of the coinage may have been the most important, with lasting consequences. These measures provided a basis for long-term economic stability, the expansion of industry, trade, and commerce—the development of natural resources, foreign trade and colonies in the New World—and thus marked the prosperity of her reign, the Elizabethan Age. In all these positive measures, like her tax and spending policies, Elizabeth took a strong personal interest. She was as wise as her father was stupid. Her policy of maintaining a stable currency lasted for four hundred years, until British leaders in this century decided to emulate her father, as have all other countries including the United States. Today we even do one better than Henry VIII. We don't debase the coinage by 40 percent base metal—we make it all base metals with no silver, just pot metal, giving the world junk money and paper money, both with no intrinsic value. Only time will tell if this stack of cards can hold up. If history is any guide, worthless money, debased money, will eventually bring fiscal disasters to those nations who undertook such a folly.

25

Taxes Caused the British Civil War

The liberties, franchises, privileges and jurisdiction of Parliament are the ancient birthright and inheritance of the subjects of England.
—Edward Coke, 1620

When Elizabeth died the English throne passed to the Stuarts, a line of Scottish kings, beginning with James I. This new monarchy united England and Scotland and thereby gave birth to Great Britain. There was no love for the Scots by the English, and this became clear from the start when Parliament turned down James's initial request for more money to maintain his luxurious lifestyle. The Tudor monarchs, of which Elizabeth and her father were the most prominent, had accepted Parliament's authority and lived on whatever revenues were provided. Under the established Common Law of England, Parliament controlled the purse.

James admired the monarchies of France and Spain, which had effectively destroyed the power of taxpayer assemblies. By 1600 the Cortes in Spain approved everything the Crown requested; and in France, the Estates General destroyed itself by granting the king of France permanent taxing powers. James wanted to pull England in line with French and Spanish political evolution. Parliamentary government was out-of-step with the times. The trend in all countries was toward tax dictatorship by the monarchy. Taxation by assemblies was an antiquated medieval practice that was no longer practical in a modern, war-torn world.

It has been suggested that James never understood English parliamentary government. But it is quite possible he understood it well enough, but simply did not like it. When Parliament turned down James's request for funds, he immediately increased customs by 200 percent. A special customs office was established called "New Impositions." Goods coming into England had to go through two separate customs examinations.

251

The new customs tax was tested in the famous *Bates* case before the Court of the Exchequer, the king's special tax court. John Bates had ordered his driver to speed by the New Impositions office at the dock where he had just taken delivery of currants from Venice. Bates was arrested, tried, and convicted. The judges made a distinction between the Common Law of England, which could not be changed without the consent of the king *in* Parliament, and royal prerogatives such as foreign affairs which were outside Parliament's jurisdiction. The ports of England were the "gates of the king" and could be regulated as the king saw fit. The lawyers for Bates unearthed an old act of Parliament, from the reign of Edward III, which prohibited customs without Parliament's approval. The court ruled that this statute only applied to Edward, not his successors.

The House of Commons appointed a special commission to study the *Bates* case. The commission decided the Exchequer Court was wrong. The king's power to tax imports at will was limited to non-tax matters, such as customs to protect English merchants or against the king's enemies. Customs taxes for revenue must have the approval of Parliament. This distinction was extremely important, not only at this time, but in 1776 when the Americans revolted, as we shall soon see. James's New Impositions were pure revenue measures; England and Venice had excellent relations, and currants were not grown in England. The *Bates* case became a dangerous precedent in the Common Law of England.

The leading English scholar of that day was Lord Edward Coke (pronounced "cook"). He led the attack on the *Bates* case. The king decided to muzzle this great lawyer by appointing him Chief Justice. A judge who valued his rank and income had to render decisions consistent with the king's wishes, or otherwise he would be dismissed.

Lord Coke is still looked upon as one of the greatest judges of all time. In his day he was a great dissenter; his rulings became the forerunner of future legislation. He was admired during his lifetime in England as much as he is today. His decisions found support in ancient rulings; he began to revive the ancient writs, such as habeas corpus. Coke argued masterfully that the Common Law was the true sovereign of England and even the king had to obey it. As Lord Chief Justice, Coke became an even greater threat to James. His dismissal was inevitable.

Revenue from New Impositions proved inadequate so James revived the old ship-money writ that Elizabeth had used to raise a navy to resist the Armada. Only this time there was no threat of invasion or wartime emergency. This ancient writ still exists today in the power of the government to press citizens into emergency service. The writ was used in an informal fashion when a small armada of private boats was sent to rescue British troops trapped at Dunkirk in 1940.

James caught the English people by surprise. No one was prepared to resist the improper use of this ancient writ, which can be traced back to before William the Conqueror when the Vikings threatened England's coasts. A year later Parliament finally reacted and issued a document (written by Coke) entitled "Protestations from the House of Commons," stating that "from the time of Magna Carta the liberties, franchises, privileges and jurisdiction of Parliament are the ancient and undoubted birthright and inheritance of the subjects of England." James was so enraged he had the document destroyed. He appeared before the loyal House of Lords and said:

> For though Sir Edward Coke be very busy and be called the father of the law. . . . Yet all is not law that (he) say. . . . I hope in his vouching precedents to compare my actions to usurpers' or tyrants' times you will punish him, for the Star Chamber which is an inferior court to this will punish pro falso clamore (for false statements).

James died shortly after his appearance before the House of Lords. His son Charles faced an angry Parliament that refused to grant him the right to collect customs, a routine grant for all new monarchs. Charles needed additional funds for a new war against Spain, but nothing was given. He raised an army anyway and quartered his troops in private homes. He issued decrees ordering loans from people with wealth.

Charles tried to collect ship-money as his father had done, except he extended the writ to all of England, not just seaports. The City of London and other inland counties refused to pay. Charles was now learning that public opinion could not be ignored and legal chicanery and biased judges were not enough. Charles had to withdraw the writ and call on Parliament for money.

Parliament offered the Crown five "fifteenths" and "tenths," just what the king desperately needed, but on one condition. The king must sign a new document called the Petition of Rights, which would curtail his powers: (1) no taxation without the consent of Parliament; (2) no imprisonment without specific charges being laid so the accused could avail themselves of the normal processes of the courts; (3) no troops quartered in private homes; and (4) no martial law in time of peace. Charles disliked the imprisonment restriction most of all, for it would curtail his power to lock up uncooperative lenders and taxpayers, but his desperate need for funds compelled him to sign the petition.

To irritate Charles even more, Parliament delayed passage of his request to collect customs for his life. An exasperated Charles collected them anyway, which brought condemnation from Parliament. Merchants and importers resisted the levy. One defiant merchant on trial before the Star Chamber was held in contempt for stating in open court that the tax laws of England were more "screwed up" than the laws of Turkey. Another merchant tried to recover his goods seized by customs officers, but the Exchequer Court held that neither recovery nor an injunction could be issued to interfere with the king's tax men. Incidentally, this is currently the law in the United States (see IRC Section 7421) and in Canada.

When Charles's demand for the right to collect customs was referred by the Commons to a committee for "study," he promptly dissolved Parliament. For the next eleven years Charles raised revenue outside the law. He collected customs and instituted a number of revenue devices; fines were increased, alien taxes were doubled, there were heavy fines for trespassing on Crown lands and for defective titles. Lawyers searched for title defects and became seventeenth-century "ambulance chasers."

In 1634 Charles cautiously reintroduced ship-money. He succeeded and thereafter each year he used this writ to raise the revenue he needed. Eventually, a wealthy landowner named Hampden obtained a hearing before all the judges of the Exchequer Court. Seven judges upheld the tax, reasoning that ship-money was an emergency tax, but the king, not the courts, was the best judge of its need. Five judges ruled for Hampden. This shocked Charles. Lord Coke had died the year before, but his zeal for judicial independence lived on.

The judges who supported Charles should not be judged too harshly. The preamble to his ship-money writs recited that there were dangers to England from pirates and enemies. The use of sham preambles to stretch government powers is common. The United States Congress frequently circumvents its constitutional limitations by the use of fraudulent preambles. The Supreme Court has held (just as Charles's judges held) that Congress is the best judge of what it is doing and of its powers. With a correctly worded preamble, almost anything can be done.

Reliance on ship-money broke down when Charles was defeated by Scottish Presbyterians and forced to pay them £850 a day while they were on English soil. Charles had to ask Parliament for money. An angry and radical Parliament demanded concessions: no more ship-money; no more heavy fines and imprisonments; the abolition of the Star Chamber; and no adjournment of Parliament without its consent. Charles agreed, but he was as angry as Parliament. He ordered the arrest of Hampden and five others and personally appeared in the Commons with troops. Before these men could be found Charles left London and went north to raise an army to go to war against Parliament. In this vacuum of power Parliament took over the government, collected its own taxes, raised an army, and started England's terrible Civil War.

The new government was directed by the Puritan Oliver Cromwell, an extremely able leader and military commander. His Long Parliament, as it was called, adopted a number of new taxes. The "fifteenths" and "tenths" and subsidies were too slow to collect, so the hated European excise was adopted. There was a new wealth tax and even a weekly fast tax, based on the value of one meal a week.

The king could not compete with Parliament over taxes. He was defeated at Oxford and fled north to Scotland. With substantial revenues from new taxation, Parliament purchased the king from the Scots, and brought him to London for trial and execution.

The Civil War in England followed a course not unlike most modern revolutions. The control of the revolutionary Parliament shifted to the radicals and to the army. The moderates were even expelled from Parliament and a small clique of extremists seized control and ruled for a decade as the "Rump Parliament." Free elections were not held because this radical Parliament knew it did not have public support. Oliver Cromwell led the Rump Parliament for over a decade, but when he died the generals called for a restoration of the monarchy, providing it disclaimed any power to tax on its own. For what was to be the last time, the issue of parliamentary control over taxation was settled by the final tribunal of civilization—war. With that issue behind the British people, they could now honestly cry, "God save the King."

The English should not be ashamed of Cromwell. The events of his era are of major importance for the history of the world. Here, for the first time, a monarchy was overthrown and replaced with a representative government. In time, most of the monarchies of the world would follow the English experience. Even the restored monarchy after Charles's execution set the pattern for those few kingdoms that have survived to our day.

With Parliament firmly in control of the purse, the English tax story shifted from the issue of taxation by consent to the problem of the best and most equitable way to tax. In the course of the next two hundred years the English were to give more attention to that problem than any other people. Eventually their search would bear fruit, and their discoveries and inventions would be copied by almost every country in the world.

26

Parliament Searches for a Better Tax

Whoever hopes a faultless tax to see, hopes what ne'er was, is not, and ne'er shall be.

—Alexander Pope

If the purpose of the English civil war and the destruction of the monarchy was to check oppressive taxation—and I suspect it was—then the war misfired. But this is not unusual for tax wars.

The tax rebels of this period believed that if the sovereign had to obtain their consent to tax, taxes would not be excessive (no one consents to excessive taxation). This seems logical enough, but history does not behave logically. Post-revolutionary taxes, whether in Britain, Holland, or America, were much heavier than before. The alcabala of the Duke of Alba was not as burdensome as the excises the United Netherlands were forced to adopt after Dutch independence. Even the tax rebels in America discovered that taxation with representation was heavier than taxation without representation. As events turned out, when the rebels won, the taxpayers lost. This is one of the strange ironies of tax history.

History shows that taxpayers' consent, when expressed through representatives, is seldom an effective check on taxation. This first became apparent in sixteenth-century Spain when taxpayers' deputies usually sided with the Crown against the wishes of their constituents. If anything, taxation through representatives provides government with the opportunity for greater taxation, probably because the threat of rebellion is reduced. As a general rule, representatives open the purses of their taxpayers; they seldom close them.

Most visitors to the Tower of London will notice that the gold crowns and sceptres of the British monarchy are post-1660, i.e., after Cromwell. Cromwell was not planning to be an interim caretaker between kings. One of the first things he did was to melt down the treasures of the monarchy. When Charles II returned to claim the throne, goldsmiths were kept busy restoring the necessary crowns and sceptres for the new king. Unlike the goldsmiths, Parliament did not restore the old tax system. To make certain there would be no future misunderstandings, in 1689 the English Bill of Rights was adopted, which emphasized that there would be no taxation without Parliament. For people living in the British Isles the issue of taxation and consent was finally settled after a five-hundred-year struggle. Attention now turned to the problem of finding the best form of taxation.

New forms of taxation were found in the taxes of the civil war. The Long Parliament was forced to adopt a number of taxes repugnant to the British people—excises, poll taxes, and wealth taxes. These offensive revenue devices were to form the bases of the taxes for the future. The subsidy and the "fifteenths" and "tenths" disappeared forever.

When Charles II was restored to the throne in 1660, Parliament adopted a hearth tax, which had been in use in Europe for some time. Two shillings were assessed for each hearth (fireplace) in every house. A tax inspector had to go through a home, room by room, because a visual inspection from the outside was not accurate.

Assessment and collections were farmed out to private collectors, French-style. These collectors were called "chimney-men." It was not uncommon for the lady of the house to conceal a hearth or barricade herself against the front door to prevent entry. There were a number of ballads which condemned the tax. Here is a verse from one of the popular ballads of that day:

> There is not one old dame in ten,
> And search the nation through.
> But, if you talk of chimney-men
> Will spare them a curse or two.[1]

The hearth tax was abolished in the "Glorious Revolution" that deposed the last Stuart, James II. A Commons report under the new monarchy, William and Mary, called the tax "a badge of slavery upon the whole people, exposing every man's house to be entered and searched at the pleasure of persons unknown to him."[2] With this report, the tax was repealed. In its place, however, Parliament adopted the even more despised graduated poll tax.

Parliament had experimented with poll taxation for hundreds of years, never with success and always with the danger of rebellion. The Long Parliament adopted a poll tax in 1641 which taxed dukes at £100 and graduated down through the ranks of the nobles to £10 for a squire, paid annually. Commoners were not so easy. After some debate, Parliament decided not to use occupational categories; instead a 5 percent income tax rate was used. A man with £100 of income per year paid £5. The result was a dual system: fixed rates for the nobility according to

William and Mary end the strife of the civil war by accepting the British "Bill of Rights" in 1689, which defined "the true, ancient and indubitable rights and liberties of the people of this kingdom." Specifically, Parliament had to approve all taxation.

their rank, and a 5 percent income tax for commoners. William and Mary replaced the hearth tax with this scheme. It did not last. In 1698 it was repealed as "unsuited for England."

The despised hearth and poll taxes were finally replaced with a window and house tax and a land tax. Each house was taxed at one shilling per window, providing the house had more than seven windows. This exempted the poor, consistent with English tradition. Since windows could be counted from the outside, the objectionable intrusion into the house by tax-farmers was eliminated. Taxpayers resorted to all kinds of avoidance devices, like boarding up windows until the assessors finished and then opening them up again. In Edinburgh, a whole row of houses was built without a single window in the bedrooms. This tax lasted well into the nineteenth century.

The English countryside accepted a land tax, probably because it was like the subsidy. The appraisals had little to do with reality. In the civil war the subsidy was replaced with a monthly assessment adopted from the subsidy rolls, but payable every month, not every two years. Cromwell wanted to make this monthly assessment realistic, with current and accurate appraisals. Parliament was not enthused or optimistic. A member of Parliament paraphrased the ancient principle of English liberty—that a man's castle was beyond the surveillance of the king—with these words that still have application today: "As to this plan of surveying and searching into men's estates, it is that which your ancestors would never endure. That the chief magistrates should know men's estates was always avoided."

Another M.P. said: "Instead of giving my Lord Protector (Cromwell) a substance, we shall be giving him a shadow."[3] And that is exactly what happened. The whole country, from assessors to taxpayers, engaged in a national conspiracy against accurate assessments. As was customary and traditional, there was fraud at all levels.

The monthly assessment finally settled into a fixed land tax. Inquiries into anything other than visible land were not permitted. Once again values were ridiculously low. Local land commissioners would not dare question the word of a gentleman on his land values. In the end, the landowners liked the tax; they were once again "master of their own assessments," as they had been under the subsidy.

When the civil war started, the Long Parliament adopted an excise, undoubtedly the most hated of all European taxes. In England, liberty was equated with the absence of an excise tax in the same way that the ancient Greeks equated liberty with the absence of poll taxes and land taxes. The Venetian ambassador in London said that the absence of an excise in England was "singular and wonderful."[4] England was the only major European country without extensive excise taxation.

The first wartime excise applied to liquor, and the law specifically stated that the tax must be abolished when the war ended. But the war went on and on, and as it expanded the excise expanded, too. Soon it covered the necessities of life—clothing, bread, meat, and other foods. There were riots and the excise houses in London were burned. Parliament responded with some relief and a plea to the English people to accept the excise for the duration of the war.

There was also a punitive excise against the royalists (those loyal to the king). This tax was referred to as "extortions" in the revenue records of that period:

> An edict was issued, commanding the exaction of the tenth penny from all the royal party: and this oppressive tax, known by the name decimation, Cromwell's military substitutes very rigorously enforced. The whole country was exposed to their extortions.[5]

"Extortions" appear again during the reign of Charles II, but we do not know what they refer to. His tax records show he collected £100,000 from "extortions" and £640,000 from "plunder."[6] Blackstone, in his *Commentaries* (I:136), calls exactions without real and genuine consent to be extortion.

Parliament did not keep its promise to end the excise with the war. When the monarchy was restored in 1660 there were still a number of excises—on beer, liquor, soap, salt, iron, lead, and some luxury items. Excise taxes have continued throughout English history since that time, but never on a large scale as in Europe. There was never a "tenth penny" like the alcabala. Excises became a traditional wartime tax, usually being reduced or abolished when there was peace.

The English hatred for the excise may first appear to border on insanity, for the tax does have many virtues. It can be limited to luxuries and thus avoid the poor; it is easy to collect since only the merchants need be audited. But the English taxpayer did not see these potential virtues. To him the tax was a great evil and no amount of argument could change his thinking. After all, look at Spain, the Netherlands, France, and other excise countries—the evils of the tax were beyond dispute. The few excises at home only confirmed this. Even though they were limited in scope, the administrative side of the tax was often brutal: "The severe penalities inflamed men's minds and fostered hatred against the excise."[7]

Walpole's Excise Dragon

Britain's excise experience begins to take its final shape with Sir Robert Walpole, often called Britain's first prime minister, an office that did not exist until his ministry in the first half of the eighteenth century. The king's favorite minister, as might be expected, was the member of the House of Commons with the greatest influence over revenue. Walpole became "prime minister" because he controlled the purse as First Lord of the Treasury and Chancellor of the Exchequer. He was a tax man through and through, as all early prime ministers were.

At that time the Commons, unlike today, had a free vote on all tax matters. Members voted how they believed rather than how the prime minister instructed them to vote. The struggles over revenue and taxation throughout the eighteenth century can best be understood by recognizing that peculiar practice of British parliamentary government. The current obligation to vote party line on taxes came later, and recently cost Lady Thatcher her prime ministership.

Walpole saw the excise as the future, primary tax for Britain. In 1723, he had Parliament expand the excise to include tea and coffee. One member of the opposition asked, "Are we to sacrifice the constitution to prevent a few frauds on the revenue?" A few frauds was an understatement. The finance ministry had the facts: Britons consumed an annual average of 4 million pounds of tea, while H.M. Customs reported imports of only 800,000 pounds, meaning 80 percent of all tea evaded tax.

A few years later when the government reported a surplus of revenue, the Commons took up the question of repealing some of the taxes. The debates finally settled on the excise on salt or the excise on candles. The issue was whether to repeal the excise on salt and benefit everyone; or repeal the excise on candles and benefit the well-to-do.[8] The poor could not afford candles. The Crown, under Walpole, wanted to repeal the tax on candles and used the old French argument about how taxes benefited the poor by causing them to work harder. In the final vote, the salt tax was cancelled. This showed amazing magnanimity for that day and age. It also showed the independence of the members of the Commons in standing up to a very powerful prime minister.[9]

No sooner had the salt tax been repealed, than in 1732, Walpole tried to expand the excise further. He would cancel the customs on wine and tobacco and replace that tax with an excise, at the same rate. In the same bill he would reintroduce the salt tax and grant his primary supporters, the landed gentry, a one-third reduction in land taxes. Walpole expected little difficulty from the Commons. His position was logical enough ("no new taxes"), just a shift in assessment to check smuggling and assure the government of taxes, justly due.

Walpole was well prepared; he had a Commons committee, headed by John Cope, present a study on the operation of the custom laws and smuggling. The frauds committed in smuggling, especially wine and tobacco, were extensive, and he described scenes of dishonesty, perjury, informing, violence, and murder, "which appeared beyond belief."[10] The adoption of his tax reforms should have been, as the British say, "a piece of cake." Or was this just a more recent example of "the tradition of evasion in the realm" that Elizabeth I spoke about and accepted?

Smuggling was big business for many, and for the average Briton it meant lower prices for a great number of consumer articles. The excise was not so easily evaded. In the ensuing years, Walpole had greatly enlarged the powers of his excise officers by creating severe penalties for any evading the tax or even obstructing its enforcement. He was "in no way squeamish about the liberties of the individual or the privacy of a man's home." He had introduced "savage punishments, and the full authority of the Crown to make the public conform to his system [of taxes]."[11]

The British revolt against Walpole's attempt to introduce new excises showed itself not just in placards carried by mobs roaming through the streets of London, it even found itself on this tin-glazed earthenware bowl (ca. 1740–50): "Liberty & property without any new excise."

Newspapers attacked his proposal with a vengence. There were numerous caricatures condemning the tax and ridiculing Walpole in particular. The public got more and more enraged and responded with violence. Mobs roamed through the streets with placards in their hats which read, "Liberty, Property, and No Excise." Others sang ballads adding the words, "and No Jury," referring to the lack of the right to a jury trial over tax disputes.[12] This violence was, in the words of Walpole's leading biographer, "the expression of a profound and cumulative hatred of a system oppressive, tyrannical, and corrupt [with power]."[13]

The debates in the Commons were intense and continued for weeks. Finally, when Walpole looked around the House of Commons, which he had controlled for over twenty years, he saw dwindling support each day. In the face of mounting and growing opposition, he withdrew his tax bill and even offered his resignation to the king and queen. On the evening before his capitulation, some of his closest friends gathered at his house where he announced his decision to abandon his excise proposal:

> The dance will go no further, I meant well, but in the present inflamed temper of the people, the act could not be carried into execution without an armed force; and there will be an end to the liberty of England if supplies are to be raised by the sword. . . . I will not be minister to enforce taxes at the expense of blood.[14]

When news of Walpole's withdrwal of the tax bill reached the people, there were celebrations everywhere. The church bells rang out, bonfires lit up the sky, Walpole was burned in effigy, and in the cities you could hear people singing ballads, and there were shouts of "No excise, No wooden shoes."[15] The jubilation was not just for the financial benefits for the defeat of the tax, but for the defeat of an extension of Walpole's ruthless tax administration. The contest over the excise was like a war with the merchants and the lower classes against Walpole and the wealthy landed gentry.

Walpole's brutal tax system can best be understood by realizing how intense his hatred was for the merchant classes of Britain. All his new enforcement sledge-hammers fell on them, and it has been suggested that his brutal tax administration laws, for both customs and excises, were an act of revenge against a faction of society he hated and despised.[16] Thus a strange, personal vendetta by a powerful prime minister helps explain why and how the British Crown turned its back on long-established principles of British justice with regard to taxation. We saw this same situation occur in our times when Franklin D. Roosevelt

Excise in Triumph, 1733. England's first Prime Minister, Sir Robert Walpole, in caricature, with verse attacking the Excise Bill's tax on tobacco and showing a standing army in the background. The barrels contain tobacco. The verse raises the tax slave issue:

> "Dejected Trade hangs down its drooping Head,
> While Standing Armies daring Colours spread,
> By these encourag'd, on the Barrel strides,
> Excise in Triumph, and like Bacchus rides:
> Still to enslave and make us more distrest
> They clap French Shoes upon the British Beast,
> Ah! — cease such wicked Arts pursuing
> Or you your Self may be Excis'd for shooing."

turned the federal tax system, the rates as well as the criminal provisions, into a sword against wealthy classes of American society he didn't like.[17]

Walpole's "tyrannical" system produced a strong backlash from British taxpayers. In one period for which we have records, over 250 customs tax collectors were assaulted, six of which were murdered.[18] So even though the British taxpayer was getting it on the chin, he also got in his licks. This same pattern of rebellion against oppressive or even disliked taxation was exported to America and, as we shall see, when the colonists were taxed in a manner not "acceptable" to them they also resorted to violence.

For protection, British excisemen were armed. Not just for protection from taxpayers, but from highwaymen. One collector records carrying a blunderbuss with seventeen balls, which for that day was about as much armament an individual dare carry or could carry considering its weight. Even if robbed, an exciseman had to make up the loss.[19]

Taxpayers were not as violent as in France, but there are numerous accounts of excise tax collectors being attacked, beaten up, horsewhipped, and even murdered. We have the account of one man who was dragged from his bed and murdered in front of his family.[20] There is no doubt, however, that compared to the customs official, the excise tax collector had a much less dangerous job.

Long after Walpole's bone-crushing administration, his harsh methods lived on, but they were still not as severe as on the continent. In France and Germany the army acted as tax collectors in a pattern reminiscent of the ugly taxes of the late Roman Empire. We should also note that this same rough tax administration was imported to the North American colonies and has survived to infect the Internal Revenue laws which only now are being corrected. Bad tax laws, including bad administrative laws, which are productive of revenue, die hard if at all.

Decades later, William Blackstone, the great English jurist, remarked, "the rigour and arbitrary proceedings of excise-laws seem hardly compatible with the temper of a free nation."[21] These were gentle words compared to what others said. When the American colonists were complaining about being denied the rights of Englishmen, the English at home had the same complaint.

Here is how the excise system worked. The great majority of cases were tried summarily without a jury or even an independent judge, often before the very tax commissioners who collected the tax. This was not British justice at all, but the kind of justice (or injustice) one receives from a bureaucratic autocracy in a totalitarian state. The British tax system then, as now, was somewhat outside the constitution—one of the strange anomalies of British justice bequeathed to America. Here is a modern scholar's cogent analysis of the system:

> Yet the trader had little chance of escaping this excise juggernaut. Most excise statutes included a clause specifically denying the right of the accused to use a writ of certiorari to move his case to a higher court. Once before the commissioners, the defendant had the cards stacked against him. He was guilty unless he could prove himself innocent. . . . Even the traditional English stratagem of countersuing officials was rendered more

hazardous by the statutory provision of double or triple costs. . . . In these circumstances it is not surprising that the conviction rate in excise cases was so high: 79% in London and 85% in the country in 1789–90.[22]

Actually, if the above scholar had practiced at all in today's Tax Court, he wouldn't find the statistics any different, nor the due process much better. He also points out that the draconian system was mitigated by modest enforcement, most of the time, just the way we deal with most instances of evasion.

Surveillance was also on a modern scale. Candlemakers, who were subject to excise taxation, were rigorously watched. No one could make candles without informing the tax people of the time, place, and hours. Failure to report the exact number of candlemaking utensils resulted in a £100 fine. Every month a complete record of all candles made had to be reported, and cracked or broken candles had to be destroyed in the excise officer's presence.[23] Excise tax surveillance reminds one of the computer and income tax surveillance today. Brewers, liquor, and tea and coffee shops had similar regulations. You can understand, with this type of enforcement, why in Walpole's day there were riots, and excise houses were burnt to the ground.

What is most unique about the British experience with the excise is that the government could never obtain the consent of Parliament for a general excise, as was in operation throughout Europe. That state of affairs has continued into the twentieth century, not only in Britain, but with the federal government in the United States. Excises have been selective. When wars and revenue demands increased in the latter half of the eighteenth century, and there was some talk about a general excise, Chesterfield (who had lead the opposition to the extension of excises during Walpole's rule) in his later years (1767) wrote a letter to a friend about the British contempt for the mere word "excise."

> As for a general excise, it must change its name by act of parliament before it will go down with the people, who know names better than things. . . . For aught I know, if an Act for a general excise were to be entitled "An Act for the better securing the liberty and property of his majesty's subjects, by repealing some of the most burdensome custom-house laws," it might be gladly received.[24]

In the eighteenth century, British parliamentary government stands out above and beyond the other governments of that day. In many ways, except for matters of enforcement, the British approach to taxation was a model for our day. It was, primarily, the people's business, and they let their will be known through the Commons, and when that didn't work, they let the Crown know of their desires through rebellion. They were anything but compliant to taxes they didn't like, and in that they did the government a favor. Indeed, the main reason Britain achieved great power status at this time may have been because of the rebellions of the British taxpayer and the threat of more rebellions. The government was forced, probably against its will, to function on moderate taxation, thereby avoiding the economic drag that was so destructive to the Netherlands.

The British never found a tax that would be just for all and acceptable to the people. The people rejected extensive excises, the hearth tax, the graduated poll tax, and an accurate land tax. The most objectionable aspect of all these taxes was the invasion of privacy. Liberty meant privacy.

Privacy meant a man's home was beyond the surveillance of the king's tax men. All these forms of taxation, while theoretically equitable, required a sacrifice of liberty which the British were not willing to tolerate.

In the end the British accepted a system of many taxes which, as a whole, were reasonably fair. No one was oppressed. Everyone shouldered some of the burdens of the state. Landowners paid land taxes but they were protected by a tradition of ridiculously low assessments. Merchants paid customs and some excises, but their burdens were lightened by smuggling and evasion. Homeowners paid a house and window tax which exempted the poor. The most remarkable aspect of the system was the absence of tax immunity for the rich.

English tax makers were progressively oriented in a world that was decidedly regressive everywhere else. Parliament was moved by the principle of the greater the wealth, the greater the taxes. This philosophy of low or no taxes for workers and the poor was not the result of humanitarianism; it was based on more solid ground—economic common sense. If workers paid high taxes, British capitalists would have to pay high wages, as in the Netherlands. This would increase the price of British goods on foreign markets and hurt trade. By keeping workers free from taxation English traders could outsell their competitors from the Continent. That is what happened, and Britain became the leading commercial nation of the world for two hundred years.

Government spending was restricted by a tight purse. This resulted more from uncooperative taxpayers and downright evasion than the wishes of an enlightened Parliament and Crown. The British government was well aware that there was more to taxation by consent than lobbying a tax bill through Parliament. Walpole's successor, Henry Fox, summed up the problem facing tax makers with these words on the floor of the House of Commons:

All governments must have a regard not only for what the people are *able* to bear, but what they are *willing* to pay, and the *manner* in which they are willing to pay, without being provoked to a rebellion.[25]

The next generation of British rulers lost sight of that principle when they set a determined course to tax the British colonists in North America.

27

The Decline of the Super-Dutch and the Rise of the Super-British

> *War meant expense. Expense meant taxation. Taxation meant the strangling of trade.*
>
> —Charles Wilson, *The Dutch Republic*

The English-speaking people copied heavily from Dutch culture, politics, and commercial practices, yet they knew little about the history of these remarkable people. The American War of Independence was not the first modern revolution against colonialism, nor did the Americans establish the first modern republic. The United Provinces of the Netherlands came into being two hundred years before the United States of America, also as the result of a revolt against taxation without consent.

The British Empire was built with commercial practices of Dutch origin. The East Indies Company, the Bank of Amsterdam, textiles and china manufacturing, insurance, a merchant marine, plantations, and other such practices were reproduced with few modifications. Dutch taxation was the only major commercial practice that was not copied, and for good reason. The decline of the Netherlands after the collapse of Spain seemed to fortify the tax philosophy of the English people—but not their government—that excise taxes were a form of commercial cancer that would consume and emaciate the economy of even the greatest empire.

After the Dutch secured their independence from Spain, they rose to the top of the world leadership and became the super-power of the seventeenth century. North America saw the founding of New Amsterdam (New York), and adventurous Dutch colonizers controlled much of Africa, Asia, and the New World. The Japanese closed their ports to all

European ships except two Dutch merchant vessels that were allowed to visit Nagasaki once a year for trade.

When Peter the Great visited western Europe to see the advances in European culture, the highlight of his trip was a visit to Amsterdam to inspect Dutch shipbuilding. For every English ship on the North Sea, the Dutch had a dozen. The superiority of the Dutch aroused the jealousy of the English and French. At one time these two traditional enemies joined forces to fight the Dutch in one of the many small wars of this period.

The English used high customs duties to try to keep Dutch goods off English markets, and they also prohibited the export of English wool which was being smuggled to Holland, manufactured into woollen goods, and then smuggled back into England. English consumers sought the superior Dutch products, or low-priced, smuggled tobacco, brandy, rum, wine, tea, and a great variety of other consumer goods. Most smugglers found it easy to avoid H.M. Customs because of the numerous bays and coves along England's shores. Smuggling was so extensive that English farmers found it difficult to find workers to harvest crops grown along the seacoasts. Young men found smuggling more profitable than farming. It has been estimated that over 50 percent of all imports escaped taxation, which must have caused enormous losses for the Crown. Walpole's attempt to introduce excises was primarily a device to frustrate customs tax evasion.

Rotterdam and the small seaport of Campvere (now Veere) were the main shopping centers of the smugglers, not only for Britain, but the rest of Europe. Most Dutch traders were caught up in the business of smuggling. It was big business and the major enterprise at Campvere. There were special Scottish houses to accommodate rich Scots who had come to live and trade beyond the arm of British Customs. Scottish wool came to Campvere and on the return voyage Scottish vessels were filled with a wide variety of goods to be smuggled into Britain.

The intensity of the economic struggle between Britain and the Netherlands touched off at least three Anglo-Dutch wars. The biggest blunder the Dutch made was to swap New York for a piece of jungle in South America, but at the time the bargain looked good to the shrewd Dutch; after all, they had only recently purchased New York from the Indians for sixty guilders.

Dutch superiority was not limited to commerce. This was the age of the great Dutch masters in painting. The Dutch also led the world in new scientific and medical discoveries. In philosophy there was Spinoza, while the great English philosopher, John Locke, did most of his writing in Holland because he had been forced into exile by the British government.

In their economic struggle with Holland, the English banned the export of wool, which was being smuggled back as manufactured goods. To enforce this ban, the transportation of wool at night was made a criminal offense. This etching shows British smugglers—known as "owlers" because they worked at night—loading wool onto a small vessel by the light of a lantern. The boat would rendezvous with a larger, seagoing vessel offshore.

The Netherlands was a relatively free and open society. European Jews were tolerated and there were many prosperous Jewish communities throughout the provinces. In 1650 Jews were still personna non grata in Britain. During Cromwell's era the wisdom of England's anti-Jewish immigration laws was questioned. The leading argument for opening Britain to Jewish settlers was the example of Dutch superiority and prosperity. Were the Jewish-Dutch communities a factor in Dutch supremacy? This argument has considerable support, even today.[1] It prevailed in 1655, and Britain opened its doors to Jewish immigrants, but not without seriously considering, and then rejecting, a special *fiscus judaicus* as a tax on all Jewish residents.

Dutch supremacy over the Spanish was highlighted by a kind of commercial vassal-lord relationship. With industry in Castile wrecked by taxation and the flight of taxpayers, the goods Spain needed came from Amsterdam. To pay for these goods Spanish silver fleets, under convoy, sailed through the English Channel to Amsterdam. With this silver and gold the Dutch jeweler was born, and he still dominates world commerce in precious stones and jewelry making.

By the end of the seventeenth century, the golden age of the Netherlands was passing. The Dutch Republic did not collapse; it declined, much like the British Empire, from the burdens of too much taxation, too much debt, and military expenditures beyond her capabilities. The Dutch had to maintain costly military and naval forces to protect their commercial life-lines. Constant warfare put a drain on the economy; taxes increased, prices soared, and Dutch goods priced themselves out of foreign markets. Goods in Amsterdam cost twice as much as in London; taxes were many times higher, and wages had to increase to enable Dutch workers to pay the high cost of living, especially the taxes on food and clothing. The high taxes built into the cost of Dutch products brought inflation which wrecked Dutch commerce and, in turn, started a declining spiral in revenues for the Dutch government. With less revenue the Dutch had to withdraw from the competitive struggle for world colonies in which England and France now competed fiercely. The Dutch made an orderly retreat and retained some of their colonial empire.

The Dutch republic was a confederation of United Provinces. The central government was not strong and the power to tax was left to the individual provinces which used poll taxes, hearth taxes, stamp taxes, land taxes, and worst of all, the excise, the very tax they revolted against in the first place, except that this time the excise was by consent. These excises baffled the British; in 1659 an English economic agent in The Hague wrote home to London about Dutch taxes:

It is strange to see what readyness this people doe consent to extraordinary taxes be yett as great as they were duringe the warr with Spaine. . . . I have reckoned a man cannot eate a dishe of meate in an inn but that one way or another he shall pay 19 excises out of it. This is not more strange than true.[2]

Apparently things worsened. Some years later Sir William Temple, an English diplomat in Holland, said: "When in a tavern, a certain dish of fish is eaten with the usual sauce, about 30 several excises are paid."[3] The English were amazed at the heavy excises paid by their Dutch rivals. Even Dutch fishermen paid excises on the fish they put on their own tables.

The heavy taxation which infected Dutch society also brought with it the usual corruption. The ruling families perpetuated themselves into an aristocracy and administered the tax laws for themselves. As time went on, it became virtually impossible, except by marriage, to penetrate from the outside the privileged ranks of various urban oligarchical families. Moreover, these people voted the taxes, collected them by means of agreements with their clients, might well have their returns audited by their nephews, and disputes adjusted by their sons-in-law.

The situation was so bad that foreigners who wanted to enjoy freedom from burdensome taxes were put to the expense and uncertainty of employing a resident officer for the special purpose of bribery, not unlike doing business in many countries today. Modern international businessmen generally operate in one of two systems: the bribery system for corrupt nations and the tax loophole system for nations that are less corrupt but more sophisticated. The end results are similar. The modern businessman soon learns which countries require payments under-the-table and which countries play above-board.

High prices at home and trade barriers abroad forced Holland into an economic decline. In time even the great painters disappeared. There was an eighteenth-century "brain drain" in the Netherlands as the more enterprising and talented Dutch people moved abroad. In 1747 there was a tax revolt at home. Mobs rose up in the leading cities to plunder and destroy the houses of Dutch tax-farmers. After compensating the tax-farmers for their losses from these riots, the government abolished the two-hundred-year-old system of tax-farming.

Excise taxes, not tax-farmers, were responsible for Holland's financial troubles. These taxes depressed trade and injured Dutch commerce, and while the tax-farmers were corrupt, that corruption was not the root of the problem. By contrast, Britain had limited excise taxation. When mobs rose up in London in 1732 to protest against excise taxation, they carried placards which read: "No slavery, no excise, and no wooden

In the eighteenth century, the Dutch learned from the British taxpayer and finally rebelled against the taxation that had crippled Dutch commerce. Here, in 1747, Dutch tax rebels are wrecking the house of a rich tax-farmer. Unfortunately, the rebellion came too late to save the superpower status of the Netherlands in world affairs and commerce.

shoes." The Dutch had become synonymous with extensive excise taxation and, of course, wooden shoes. The British people wanted neither.

The excise tax was the dominant tax on the continent of Europe during this period. The Dutch used it before Alba; the Germans and French used it along with Spain. Even today, Europe has an affinity for excise taxation with the value-added tax required for all members of the European Economic Community. This tax is simply an excise based on the value added to goods at each stage of manufacture, rather than the value of the goods as a whole. Tax credits transfer up and down the manufacturing process, greatly reducing evasion and making the system self-administering. This rather ingenious and sophisticated excise reduces the importance of income taxation.

Looking backwards from the eighteenth to the sixteenth century, the Dutch revolt against the Duke of Alba hardly appears to have been worth the trouble. If the American revolutionists in 1776 had studied their Dutch history they would have realized that taxation with representation does not necessarily lessen the tax burden—something else is required.

Britain: The New Superpower

If the Dutch declined because their tax system overburdened commerce and trade, then the British rose to become a superpower because they learned how to master their tax system. Scholars are now beginning to realize that Britain's rise from a mediocre European state in the seventeenth century to a super power in the eighteenth, nineteenth and twentieth centuries was a triumph of good tax management.[4] Even the sharp decline of Britain at mid-twentieth century can be explained as the consequence of Britain's venture into socialism, 95 percent tax rates, and welfare state-ism. Capital fled from England to evade confiscation as it did from Cuba more recently, and the labor government's takeover of industries compounded the problem. British cars which were once admired worldwide, ended up being as unreliable and as defective as Soviet washing machines.

The British tax system started to improve after Cromwell. The first most notable change was the abolition of all tax-farming during the period from 1660 to 1690. In place of the farmers, a professional tax bureaucracy began to function with efficiency. It was based on merit. The tax officers had to take exams to qualify, and they were made accountable for everything they did. They were frequently moved from one tax district to another to prevent them from becoming too friendly to the local businessmen. Full remittance was made on a regular basis to London as were full accountings made to their supervisors.

From 1721 to 1724, Walpole made some of the most positive steps of his administration toward economic growth. He cancelled export taxes on manufactured goods and greatly reduced or eliminated many tariff items, thus stimulating trade and the competitive position of British goods on world markets. One early biographer wrote in 1798, "He found our tariff the worst in the world, and left it the best."[5]

The excise tax, which was such a scourge on the continent, grew in Britain to become the major tax in the mid-eighteenth century, but it was never as burdensome or as all pervasive as it was in France, Germany, or the Netherlands. It was burdensome, but the burdens were limited to a few articles. There was no *general* excise as on the continent on everything in sight. Consumers paid more, but never the horrendous rates as elsewhere in Europe. The British experience demonstrates the truism, that most any tax can be administered with good economic sense. The problem is that good taxes tend to go bad because governments demand too much of them. The British, unlike the rest of the world at that time, had the wisdom to keep the excise down in rates and limited in its application. This may have been more the consequence of the hostility the British people had for the tax than for the wisdom of the government. In 1691, William Carr, an English writer, gave the English definition of an excise as "an infamous tax levied by scoundrels," undoubtedly referring to the tax-farmers that were so popular in Europe. He also commented on the hostility to the excise by the people:

> Should we in England be obliged to pay the taxes that are here [Netherlands] imposed, there would be rebellion upon rebellion. And yet after all that is here paid, no man may bake his own bread, nor grind his own corn, or brew his beer, nor dare any man keep in his house a hand-mill, although it be but to grind mustard or coffee.[6]

We do not find in Dutch literature any of the caricatures condemning the excise as we find in Britain in the century that followed. When Britain embarked on increased excise taxation, it was done on a cautious, limited, basis. In the Netherlands, the excise covered everything in sight, even servants, street lights, and a graduated tax for coaches, carriages, and sleighs. Some of these taxes were in the nature of poll taxes and property taxes, but they were part of the total excise package. There were tolls for crossing any bridge or canal, even for leaving a town at night. "Milk first pays as milk, and again if it be made butter; yea the buttermilk and whey pays a tax likewise, for all which a man would think that a people that stand so much upon maintaining their liberty should mutiny and refuse payment."[7]

The great tragedy of this monstrous scheme of taxation was not just the loss of liberty, which was so obvious, but the economic decline caused by the high price of Dutch goods in world trade. The final check on British taxation was economics and the rebellious nature of the British people. Perhaps if the Dutch people had been a bit less submissive and compliant, their economic decline may have not been so dramatic. There were, as we noted, Dutch tax revolts, but they did not bear much fruit. The high tax habit was too well ingrained and accepted by the Dutch people.

There is little doubt but that Britain's rise to be the most dominant and powerful nation in the world in the eighteenth century was only possible because of her superior revenue system. Much has been written about the importance of the public borrowing by British governments to finance the many wars the Crown engaged in and won. But this public finance was only possible because the British tax system guaranteed payment of the government's debts. The tax system was centuries ahead of any other country, and when you look back at the British system, the basics are still sound and are copied today by all modern states. The British also had the good sense not to provoke a major revolt. That they operated with a kind of "brinkmanship" for their day cannot be refuted, but they had the intelligence not to go too far most of the time. Only in North America did they crack down hard on tax discontent, and they lost the jewel in their crown for doing so.

Jean Luzac, a champion of American Independence and a Dutch writer in the eighteenth century, lamented the decline of the once-miracle Dutch economy. The heavy burden of taxation, he said, resulted in the flight of skilled artisans—an eighteenth-century brain drain. Parents refused to put children into jobs where there was no money. Parishes were unhappy if there were too many marriages because this increased the poor tax rates. Men even preferred prostitutes to wives. The many wars in Holland's backyard required, or seemed to require, heavy military preparations, which were a great expense. "Expense meant taxation. Taxation meant the strangling of trade."[8] Holland, not unlike America today, was no longer developing new patterns of trade or introducing new products and technologies to the degree it once did. A nation of ambitious Hollanders who once threw off the yoke of the Spanish and built the superpower of the seventeenth century, now a century later was exhausted.

The increasing burden of heavy taxation, compared to its rivals, was reflected in the decline of Holland's once great centers of industry. Leyden was a desolate town, its once flourishing cloth industry in a depression. The linen industry of Harlem had similarly shrunk. The products these centers once produced and exported could now be purchased abroad, in Britain, at much lower prices. Perhaps the irony of it all is that a Dutch businessman and writer, Matthew Decker, left Holland for England. His writings greatly influenced Adam Smith by expounding laissez-faire: freedom of trade, fewer and simpler taxes, no tariffs, and no monopolies.

The relation of Britain to Holland in the eighteenth century may have some shadows in the late twentieth century with Japan and the United

States. Holland invented and flourished with commercial and even tax practices that were later copied by Britain when it was anything but a superpower. By copying what the Dutch had invented and initially developed, the British simply developed them much better and as a result quickly eclipsed Holland on the Northern European scene. Holland, overburdened with the expense of military and naval demands, overtaxed itself into decline. Britain used Holland's taxes, especially the excise, but the British had the wisdom to not overburden commerce and to tax modestly at rates the traffic would bear, without impeding the traffic. The same challenge faces America today in the global economy.

28

The Enlightenment Had the Word on Taxation

No one got the word.

—An old navy expression

The philosophy of the eighteenth century, which is referred to as the Enlightenment, cut loose from the superstition of the past and attempted to establish reason as the foundation of all belief and rules of political conduct. The United States and its Constitution were founded upon the principles of the Enlightenment. In matters of taxation, this marked a high-water mark for tax wisdom, ethics, jurisprudence, and just plain common sense. The great legal and political thinkers of that age, even the common man, *had the word on taxation.*

The wisdom of this age of reason grew out of the violence and strife of the seventeenth century. In England the monarchy was overthrown, a king beheaded, and the nation suffered through a terrible civil war, all brought about by taxation. Under the stress of six major tax revolts the great Spanish Empire collapsed. The Netherlands went into a sharp decline because of too much taxation. In France, tax revolts were everywhere. They were bloody and cruel, as we observed. Perhaps France was the worst of all with its paramilitary tax police to enforce collection and punish dissidents.

No doubt the havoc bad taxation brought to civilization stimulated the men of that age to ponder over the wreckage. They searched through history for taxes in the past that had worked, or had not worked. They frequently spoke about the relation of taxes and despotism. They spoke often of the relation of taxes to prosperity. It was, as now, no easy task to find a just and prudent tax. These thinkers used the past as a guide in their philosophy. They knew their history well, something our tax makers have ignored—all too well.

Baron de Montesquieu, the great sage of the Enlightenment. His ideas about government inspired the Americans and Europeans, especially in the form of government, the concept of moderate (limited) government, and those kinds of taxes that led to slavery.

At first, it may seem to be a great mystery why an intelligent society like ours, with so much knowledge of the past at our fingertips, should embark down a road leading to ever increasing taxes, to unbelievably high taxes, without examining the past to learn what excessive taxation has done to other nations. The reason we have been so foolish can be found in our immediate past—the nineteenth century. Our ignorance is born from bliss. If our past century had been filled with bloodshed and economic collapse over bad taxes, with wars and violence over taxes, and with the destruction of liberty over taxes, we would probably have given the matter of taxation more serious concern. The tax peace and low taxes of the nineteenth century dulled our senses to the evils our tax system would ultimately produce.

The men of the Enlightenment had an advantage we did not have and this may account, in part, for their good judgment. Looking at the tax catastrophes of their immediate past, they drew lessons from the harm bad taxation had produced. They used the raw materials of history, of man's past experiences with taxation, and from that data they used their best thinking and reason. They were the world's first practicing tax historians.

It is difficult to fault any of their views, many of which we hold with reverence. They propounded the political concept of the separation of powers, of checks and balances, of representative democracy, and limited government. Their wisdom with regard to taxation dominated the thinking of the Western world. Throughout the nineteenth century in the debates in Congress, in the British Parliament, with the French government, you read and feel the ideas of Locke, Montesquieu, Adam Smith, and the other great thinkers of the Enlightenment. Somewhere along the way in the early twentieth century, these views got lost in our zeal for big government, big wars, and big spending. They speak to our century like Isaiah and Jeremiah spoke to their people during the troubles and wars of 800 B.C. to 600 B.C. Like prophets of old they have foretold of the troubles that would come upon us if we espoused big government and taxed too much.

The words of wisdom these men gave to us are many; I have summarized the ten most important points in this chapter. Most of these ideas have disappeared from the world of ideas we now live in. Modern experts in the field of tax and government seem to be unaware of what these men left to posterity. Search as much as you like, but you won't find strong support for their thinking in the writings of the "experts" of our day. Even when they might be touched upon, they are lightly passed over. Perhaps this is an example of the simple truth about life—what comes easy is taken lightly. Our liberty and freedoms were handed down to us by generations past that had to fight for the liberty we now enjoy. Liberty to us is an inheritance, not something we earned or achieved on our own. We take liberty lightly, and we don't seem to realize how hard it is to get it back once lost.

Here is the priceless legacy the men of the Enlightenment pass on to us:

1. Government is at best a necessary evil.

The men of the Enlightenment had no illusions about government. "Government," said Thomas Paine on the first page of his famous pamphlet called *Common Sense* (1776), "even in its best state is but a necessary evil, in its worst state an intolerable one." Washington had Paine's pamphlets distributed to his troops in winter quarters during the early years of the Revolutionary War. Jefferson, Franklin, and Madison all praised Paine for his contribution to the cause of the Revolution. John Adams went so far as to say that "Without the pen of Paine, the sword of Washington would have been wielded in vain."[1] Paine's dominant theme was that taxation produced tyranny. The root of the problem lay in the foolish, naive attitude of the people towards their governments by believing "that government is some wonderful mysterious thing." And when they believe that illusion, "excessive revenues are obtained."[2]

Paine described himself as a champion of "the cause of the poor, of the manufacturer, of the tradesmen, of the farmer, and of all those on whom the real burdens of taxes fall."[3] The turmoil of the revolutionary period of the late eighteenth century in both Europe and America, was, in fact, produced by angry taxpayers who had had enough. In 1792 he wrote while living in London: "There are two distinct classes of men in the Nation [England], those who pay taxes and those who receive and live upon taxes. . . . When taxation is carried to excess it cannot fail to disunite those two."[4]

Revolution was necessary primarily to bring about a government that was "less expensive, and more productive" bringing about a reign of "peace, civilization, and commerce." In short, when a government is just, "taxes are few." What drove men to revolution was primarily and simply a taxing and overblown government. "The enormous expense of government has provoked men to think," and ultimately to revolution.[5]

When governments tax too much, they steal from their citizens by taking the fruits of their industry and property. Instead of providing protection for the people's liberty and property—which is the state's sole justification for existence—the state turns out to be a real enemy of the people, just as villainous as a foreign invader:

> When we survey the wretched condition of man under [bad] systems of government, dragged from his home by one power, or driven by another, and impoverished by taxes *more than by enemies*, it becomes evident that

those systems are bad, and that a general revolution in the principle and construction of Governments is necessary.[6] (emphasis added)

Paine had specific reference to the monarchial and aristocratic systems of Europe, which were the high-tax countries of that age. No doubt, however, that his same sharp criticism will apply today to our bureaucratized societies with the economic drag and penal laws heavy taxation has produced. When Paine said that taxation was tyranny, he was really pointing out that all taxation requires some degree of tyranny, some degree of destruction of liberty. Heavy taxation is simply a great destroyer of liberty as well as property and industry, and in the end impoverishes the people more than foreign enemies. Paine's arguments had great popularity among the people for he was simply focusing their attention on what was easily self-evident. He saw America as the great land of liberty because it was a land of low taxes.

2. *The imaginary wants of the state.*

Baron de Montesquieu in his *The Spirit of Laws* (1751), a book which greatly influenced the Framers of the Constitution, explained this problem:

> The *revenues of the state* are a portion of that each subject gives of his property in order to secure or to have the agreeable enjoyment of the remainder.
>
> To fix these revenues in a proper manner, regard should be had both to the necessities of the state and those of the subject. The real wants of the people ought never to give way to the imaginary wants of the state.
>
> Imaginary wants are those which flow from the passions, and from the weakness of the governors, from the charms of an extraordinary project, from the distempered desire of vain glory and from a certain impotency of mind incapable of withstanding the attacks of fancy. Often has it happened that ministers of a restless disposition, have imagined that the wants of the state were those of their own little and ignoble souls.[7]

There were centuries of waste and follies by governments to back Montesquieu in his observation. If governments were on short rations, the amount of imaginary wants could be curtailed. The Swiss have the only nation today with a constitutional structure to attack the problem Montesquieu raised. Government spending in Switzerland and tax increases go to the people. The government can only propose; the people have the final say.

The Vietnam disaster is a remarkable example of what Montesquieu had in mind. President Johnson was elected as a peace candidate ("the real wants of the people"). The voters turned down Goldwater's supposed hawkish attitude. Once in office, Johnson replaced the wants of the people with his "imaginary wants of the state," which we now realize were the product of a mentally unbalanced mind.[8] It took years of suffering and expenditures of life and wealth for the nation to extricate itself from that senseless war. National self-respect was lost.

The Vietnam War fits Montesquieu's caveat: "The charms of an extraordinary project" (American hegemony over Southeast Asia); the "distemper of vain glory" (what we might call Manifest Destiny over the Orient); and "attacks of fancy" (America's ability to succeed where France had failed). It is all there, except, of course, the real wants of the people, which were to stay out of colonial wars half way around the world, to have a sound currency, and not to slaughter tens of thousands of the nation's young men for a military adventure based upon a paranoid fear of communism, which, if left alone, would in time prove its worthlessness as a sound economic system.

3. Governments should stay out of business.

The best modern example of the folly of government bureaucratic business management is found in the socialist and communist states—even the capitalist states that have ventured into government ownership of businesses have been burned. Today, Russia is paying the price of absolute government control and planning. The washing machines don't work; everything the state businesses produce is grossly inferior to the products in private economies. Adam Smith explains the problem about as well as any writer since:

> Princes, however, have frequently engaged in many other mercantile projects, and have been willing, like private persons, to mend their fortunes by becoming adventurers in the common branches of trade. They have scarce ever succeeded. The profusion with which the affairs of princes are always managed, renders it almost impossible that they should. The agents of the prince regard the wealth of their master as inexhaustible; are careless in what price they buy, are careless in what price they sell; are careless at what expense.[9]

4. Liberty carries the seeds of its own destruction.

This is the most startling conclusion to come out of this period. Montesquieu has a chapter on the "Abuse of Liberty" (Book XIII, ch. 15); he notes that men living in a state of liberty tend to let their guard down and tolerate great taxes, but once granted they discover they cannot take a backward step:

> To these great advantages of liberty it is owing, that liberty itself has been abused. Because a moderate government has been productive of admirable effects, this moderation has been laid aside: because great taxes have been raised, they wanted to raise them to excess: and ungrateful to the hand of

liberty of whom they received this present, they addressed themselves to slavery who never grants the least favour.

Liberty produces excessive taxes; the effect of excessive taxes is slavery.[10]

The logic of this is simple according to Montesquieu. Once excessive taxation is granted in a liberty-oriented society, the tax man must be "invested with extraordinary means of oppression, and then the country is ruined."[11] To recapitulate, men in a state of liberty foolishly grant their governments the right to levy heavy taxes, this in turn fosters evasion, and this in turn requires great punitive measures. It is the consequence of these punitive measures that ruined the country.

5. *Direct taxes are the badge of slavery; indirect taxes the badge of liberty.*

This belief, as we noted, came from the Greeks and early Romans. Montesquieu expressed it this way: "Capitation [direct taxes on the individual] is more natural to slavery; a duty on merchandise is more natural to liberty, *because it has not so direct a relation to the person* (emphasis added)."[12]

Montesquieu's view that excessive taxation leads to slavery, and also that direct taxes are "more natural to slavery," does not mean the kind of chattel slavery we had in the economy of the South before the Civil War. He is talking about an entirely different kind of slavery—tax slavery. It means a Big Brother tax bureau that enforces taxes on the individual with savage punishments, spying, and confiscations.

6. *Tax evasion is not a criminal act.*

This was an era when the great legal thinkers looked upon the criminal law with a degree of respect and reverence lacking today. Governments had no right to make "criminal" what did not conform to the laws of Nature, or what we might call today "common crimes." The principle of jurisprudence in issue was expressed by John Locke, in his *Second Treatise on Civil Government*:

> Thus the law of Nature stands as an eternal rule to all men, legislators as well as others. The rules that they make for all men's actions must, as well as their own and other men's actions, be conformable to the law of Nature.[13]

When the Declaration of Independence spoke about the right of the colonists to separate from Great Britain and set up their own government, they justified this revolt by referring to Locke's philosophy, "to assume among the powers of the earth, the separate and equal station to which the Laws of Nature and Nature's God entitle them." Their revolt was, in a word, in accordance with the laws of Nature, as "all men's actions must" be.

Locke's views, while a powerful influence and basis for the United States, were not very popular in monarchial Europe where the divine right of kings predominated. Kings had the power to create crimes, and the laws of Nature be damned. Henry VIII manufactured almost two hundred petty regulations which he enforced as felonies, with hanging. One was a law against begging. But Locke's philosophy rose above governmental power to criminalize regulations at will. Governments could not do so, because laws had to conform to the laws of Nature. On the matter of disobedience, the followers of Locke had strong views, condemning the criminalization of tax evasion. In 1751, Montesquieu set the stage for the thinkers that followed. Tax evasion is the consequence of excessive taxation which entices men to evade because of the "extreme lucrative benefits" high tax rates provide to the evader.[14] (Hamilton also noted this in *The Federalist*, No. 35.) Said Montesquieu:

> Recourse must be therefore had to extravagant punishments, such as those inflicted for capital crimes. All proportion then of punishments ceases. People that cannot really be considered as bad men, are punished as villains, which of all things in the world, is the most contrary to the spirit of a moderate government.[15]

Fifteen years later, Blackstone wrote his great *Commentaries on the Laws of England*, with a number of sections on the liberties of Englishmen. He emphasized that these liberties apply to everyone who sets foot on English soil. Even the black slave, notes Blackstone in 1766, becomes instantly a free man. I have often wondered how the Americans in the South evaded that great principle of British law. On tax evasion, Blackstone adds weight to both Locke and Montesquieu:

> Recourse must therefore be had to extraordinary punishments to prevent it; perhaps even capital [felony] ones: which destroys all proportion of punishment, and puts murderers upon equal footing with such as are really guilty of no natural, but merely a positive offence.[16]

A "positive offense" was one manufactured by the state, not worthy of being called a true crime. The reference to "capital" punishment probably refers to some of Walpole's brutal laws against tax offenders.

We don't end with these two giants of the law. Ten years later in 1776, Adam Smith's great classic, *The Wealth of Nations*, was published. He also categorized tax evasion as a synthetic or unnatural offence. To make this offence a "crime" was contrary to the laws of Nature. The tax evader, said Smith, was often a person not capable of violating the criminal law, and is

> in every respect, an excellent citizen, had not the laws of his country made that a crime which nature never meant to be so. In those corrupted governments where there is at least a general suspicion of much unnecessary expense, and great misapplication of the public revenue, the laws which guard it are little respected.[17]

Albert Jay Nock, in his remarkable book *Our Enemy the State*, is a modern disciple of natural rights:

> The theory of freedom rests on the doctrine of natural rights, and I have always held with the Declaration of Independence that this doctrine is a sound one, that mankind is endowed by its Creator with certain inalienable rights, and that one of them is liberty. But the world is fast going away from old-fashioned people of my kind, and I am told that this doctrine is debatable and now quite out of style; that nowadays almost no one believes that mankind has any natural rights at all, but that all the rights it enjoys are legal and conventional, and therefore properly subject to abridgement or suppression by the authority that confers them.[18]

7. Liberty's most dangerous foe: arbitrary taxation.

"But the most pernicious of all taxes are the arbitrary. They are commonly converted, by their management, into punishments on industry. . . . It is surprising, therefore, to see them have place among any civilized people."[19]

If you were astounded at the idea of the thinkers of the Enlightenment that men in a state of liberty were inclined to tax themselves into slavery, even more upsetting may be their belief that taxation which was *arbitrary* justifies evasion, defiance, violence, treason, armed revolt, and the overthrow of the government by force. Unfortunately, the term appears to have been self-evident to them for they didn't define it. The full meaning of the term *arbitrary taxation* is not entirely clear to us. It has never been the object of intensive research in our day, and until that happens, we will remain somewhat in the dark about its full significance, and why it was held up as liberty's archenemy, above all other foes. It seems clear it didn't apply to just one kind of taxation or one type of defect a faulty tax may incur. It was a danger that appeared to apply to any type of taxation, not properly enacted or administered. To be arbitrary, a tax would have to lack principles, but what principles? From the writings of the Enlightenment, three principles stand out as most important, and when taxation violated these principles, it would be *arbitrary*.

Adam Smith, whose great classic, *The Wealth of Nations*, focused on taxation and the four signs of a bad tax system.

The first principle is that taxation must be with consent. To them the right to be taxed with their consent—and only their consent—was the first and most basic of all human rights. All other rights were subordinate to it.

A taxpayer wrote in the *Maryland Gazette* in 1748 that the right to be taxed only with your consent, "is the great Hinge upon which Liberty hangs, and whenever it is weakened or thrown down, Liberty must be proportionably weakened or fall with it." Taxation by consent, said this writer, was

> one of the most distinguishing Marks of British Liberty, nay the very Soul and Essence of it, for the People, or (which is the same Thing) the Representatives of the People, to be possess'd of the Power of keeping their Purse in their own Hands, to be the sole Judges how much is necessary to be raised upon them and to direct the Disposal of it.[20]

So sensitive were these people to the importance of real, bona fide consent, that New England assemblies would refrain from taxing towns that had not sent delegates to the assembly; and in 1769, when the governor of Georgia refused to permit representation to four new parishes, the legislature would not tax them.[21]

Locke emphasized the principle of consent, which we could relegate to the seventeenth century and the British civil war. The matter of consent was, for the British people living at home, settled with the Bill of Rights, as we noted in Chapter 23. But this did not settle the matter for the English living in the colonies in North America, as we shall soon discover. The concept, however, underwent considerable refinement in the eighteenth century, and the most astute and clear thinkers were in Great Britain, not in the colonies. The concept of "consent" put taxation outside the realm of normal law making and legislation. A government may make all kinds of laws and regulations for the good of a society, but when it came to tax, tax laws had to have the consent of the taxpayer; other laws did not. Lord William Pitt, who tried hard to prevent the Revolution in the colonies, explained the concept with these words: "taxation is no part of the governing or legislative power. The taxes are a voluntary gift and grant of the Commons alone."[22]

He was supported by a large number of leading British statesmen, one none other than the Chancellor of the Exchequer, Lord Camden, who served from 1766 to 1770, and helped in the repeal of the Stamp Act. Said Camden:

> My position is this—I repeat it—I will maintain it to my last hour,— taxation and representation are inseparable—this position is founded on

the laws of nature; it is more, it is itself an eternal law of nature, for whatever is a man's own, is absolutely his own; no man hath a right to take it from him without his consent, either expressed by himself or representative; whoever attempts to do it, attempts an injury; whoever does it, commits a robbery; he throws down and destroys the distinction between liberty and slavery. Taxation and representation are coeval with and essential to this constitution.[23]

Another leading British political leader, Lord Shelburne, who presided over the Board of Trade and was secretary of state for colonial affairs after the Stamp Act was repealed, said the principle of consent to taxation was the first and most basic liberty of the British people—the primary liberty upon which all other liberties exist and depend. "It is the only privilege we can depend upon," said Shelburne, "for the preservation of all the privileges and immunities we have a right to."[24]

The American Revolution arose out of a dispute as to what "consent to taxation" amounted to. Was it a facade? A matter of form? The British government believed in consent just like the Americans, but they needed the revenue, and "consent" just like liberty has to yield to the tax man. So they created a fictional consent. Parliament "consented" for everyone—those at home or abroad, voters and non-voters, men and women, Christian or Jew. Having a bona fide representative was not at all necessary. But the best legal thinkers did not agree. Blackstone, in his *Commentaries*, set forth the many liberties of the English people, and spelled out the principle of taxation by consent, in which the taxpayer had "*his* representative," and that consent had been lacking at times in British history when taxes were "extorted without a real and voluntary consent."[25] Edmund Burke argued that an Englishman would not be a good citizen, "If, with any effectual means of prevention in our hands, we were to submit to taxes to which we did not consent."[26]

The second principle is that taxes had to be apportioned among the people by a definite standard or rule. Lacking a rule of apportionment, taxation was ipso facto arbitrary. Hamilton explained the concept in a speech on July 4, 1782, in Fishkill, New York:

Wherever a discretionary power is lodged in any set of men over the property of their neighbors, they will abuse it. Their passions, prejudices, partialities, dislikes, will have the principal lead in measuring the abilities of those over whom their power extends. . . . The genius of liberty reprobates everything arbitrary or discretionary in taxation. It exacts that every man by a definite and general rule should know what proportion of his property the state demands. Whatever liberty we may boast in theory, it cannot exist in fact while [arbitrary] assessments continue.[27]

A hundred years later the concept was still alive, and had been very much alive in the nineteenth century. Thomas Cooley, the leading constitutional law scholar of that age, explained the meaning of arbitrary taxation:

> Taxes are distinguished from arbitrary levies in that they are laid according to some rule which apportions the burden between the subjects thereof. An exaction which is made without regard to any rule of apportionment is therefore not a tax.[28]

If it is not a tax, what is it? Justice Cooley, like so many in the nineteenth century, was probably a disciple of Adam Smith, or at least a scholar who respected the founder of modern economics. Smith had said when you abandon the principle of apportionment, you enter the realm of extortion.

The third principle is equality, which is necessary to counter the inclination of everyone to push their taxes off on to someone else. Said David Hume: "Every man, to be sure, is desirous of pushing off from himself the burden of any tax, which is imposed, and of laying it upon others."[29]

Along with consent, the maxim of equality was a guiding principle of a just tax system. The state was like a large estate of real property with many owners, and since the primary duty of the state is to protect the national wealth, just as with a large estate of land, the costs of maintenance should be paid in proportion to one's ownership. You should, in short, pay for what you get. A man who owns five times as much of the estate as another, should pay five times as much. That is a principle. Adam Smith explained it this way:

> The expense of government to the individuals of a great nation, is like the expense of management to the joint tenants of a great estate, who are all obliged to contribute in proportion to their respective interests in the estate. In the observation or neglect of this maxim consists, what is called the equality or inequality of taxation.[30]

In 1690 John Locke, who lived through the great British civil war, may have fathered this principle with these words:

> Thirdly, the supreme power cannot take from any man any part of his property without his own consent. For the preservation of property being the end of government, and that for which men enter into society. . . . It is true governments cannot be supported without great charge, and it is fit everyone who enjoys his share of the protection should pay out of his estate his proportion for the maintenance of it. But still it must be with his

own consent. . . . For what property have I in that which another may by right take when he pleases himself?[31]

By the nineteenth century, the principle of apportionment became axiomatic, beyond the realm of argument: "For as every man is bound to contribute to the public revenue in *proportion* to the benefits he receives from the public protection (emphasis added)."[32] Taxes developed from this concept are not burdens, just payment for benefits received.

A tax, then, to these men, must be based on a principle of apportionment, and a tax which was not, was arbitrary and was simply confiscation under the guise of taxation.

Apologists for our system of "progressive taxation" argue that our guiding principle is the "ability to pay," rather than any apportionment or equality in taxation. But ability to pay is no principle at all. It is a takeoff from Karl Marx's dogma of "from each according to his ability." Friedrich Hayek, in his *The Constitution of Liberty*, pointed out the fallacy of this thinking:

> Unlike proportionality, progression provides no principle which tells us what the relative burden of different persons ought to be. . . . the argument based on the presumed justice of progression provides no limitation, as has often been admitted by its supporters, before all incomes above a certain figure are confiscated, and those below left untaxed.[33]

For example, the legislators in the 1950s thought that 91 percent was a fair top bracket. The wealthy were able to pay that much. In 1986, a new legislature thought 28 percent was an appropriate "ability to pay" top bracket. Progressive taxation has evolved into arbitrary taxation in its most pernicious form, but more on that later.

8. *Common sense economics: the supply-siders.*

Supply-side economics, with its apparently absurd theory that a reduction of tax rates increases revenue, is not a new theory at all, and, as we shall see, goes back into antiquity. It also found favor in the Enlightenment. One treatise in 1788 from an unknown author put it about as succinctly as possible: "We may add, that if revenue is here the only object, taxes that are moderate are confessedly the most productive."[34] The supply-siders believe that low rates encourage more earnings, savings, and investment, thereby expanding economic activity and the total taxable national income or wealth. Montesquieu expressed it in simple terms:

> Nature is just to all mankind; she rewards them for their industry; whilst she renders them industrious by annexing rewards in proportion to the greatness of their labor. But if an arbitrary power deprives people of the

recompenses of nature, they fall into a disrelish of industry, and then indolence and inaction seem to be their only happiness.[35]

The reader should understand that, by our standards, the term "moderate" as applied to taxation in the Enlightenment, would be very low. When the 10 percent income tax came at the end of the eighteenth century, it was considered an outrage. Today, such a rate would be like manna from heaven.

The Enlightenment thinkers were not just supply-siders, they were what we could call super-supply-siders. They believed that the right kind of moderate taxation actually benefited commerce:

> Taxes, in their own nature, if they are properly and judiciously laid on, are so far from causing commerce to stagnate, that they quicken and enliven it: And therefore may be compared to the *pruning* of a tree by a *skilful* hand, by which the tree is preserved in health, and lasts longer.[36]

9. The marks of a bad tax system: Adam Smith's four points.

In Adam Smith's first chapter on taxes, he sets forth a number of maxims about taxes—about good taxes and bad taxes. He was not so much interested in matters of liberty as he was interested in taxes that were smart, that worked well for all concerned. Here are Smith's four points:

1. A tax was bad that required a large bureaucracy for administration.
2. A tax was bad which "may obstruct the industry of the people, and discouraged them from applying to certain branches of business which might give maintenance and employment to great multitudes. While it obliges the people to pay, it may thus diminish, or perhaps destroy, some of the funds which might enable them more easily to do so."
3. A tax was bad that encouraged evasion. "The law, contrary to all the ordinary principles of justice, first creates the temptation, and then punishes those who yield to it." Evasion is also bad, says Smith, because it tends to "put an end to the benefits which the community might have received from the employment of their capitals."
4. A tax is bad that puts the people through "odious examinations of the tax-gatherers, and expose them to much unnecessary trouble, vexation, and oppression. . . . It is in some one or other of these four different ways that taxes are frequently so much more burdensome to the people than they are beneficial to the sovereign."[37]

10. What a good tax system should be: Lord Kames' six rules.

Our scholars in the fields of history, political science, philosophy and ethics, spend little time, if any, on tax issues. But in the eighteenth century, scholars considered taxation an essential subject in those and other related fields. In philosophy, for example, William Paley's *The Principles of Moral and Political Philosophy* contains substantial material and philosophizing about tax issues.[38] Lord Henry Home Kames, a remarkable scholar of that era, published his *Sketches on the History of Man* (1769), which contained long discussions and analyses of tax isues. His book greatly influenced Adam Smith who copied extensively from Kames. Here are Kames' "Rules to be observed in Taxing":

1. When the opportunity for evasion exists, taxes must be moderate. It is unjust for a legislature "first to tempt and then to punish" for yielding to temptation.
2. Taxes that are expensive to levy should be avoided.
3. Arbitrary taxes are "disgustful to all." The amount paid is determined by the "vague and conjectured opinion of others."
4. To remedy the "inequity of riches," the poor should be relieved of any significant tax burdens.
5. Taxes which sap the strength of a nation should be avoided. Such taxes "contradict the very nature of government, which is to protect not oppress."
6. Taxes which require an oath are to be avoided.

Said Kames:

Perjury has dwindled into a venial transgression and scarcely held an imputation to any man's character. . . . Lamentable indeed has been the conduct of our legislature: instead of laws for reforming and improving morals, the imprudent multiplication of oaths [for tax enforcement] has not only spread corruption through every rank, but by annihilating the authority of the oath over conscience, has rendered it ineffectual.[39]

Condemning the use of oaths for tax administration was common in the Enlightenment period and, as noted, goes back to Queen Elizabeth. Twenty-five years before Kames, the great poet Alexander Pope said that while it may be permissible for government to impose "heavy and ruinous Taxes," to command an oath for taxes was a "shameful and dishonest thing."[40] An oath was a sacred act. In a God-fearing society, when a person swore an oath he was renouncing the mercy of God and calling upon God for vengeance against himself if he breached the oath. To use such a device for collecting taxes was as corrupting as it was blasphemous.

The ideas of the Enlightenment about taxes and government lived on through the next century. Henry David Thoreau gave renewed vigor to Paine's concept of limited government, and that government is best which governs least, or "not at all." When government was out of line, Thoreau advocated civil disobedience, and in his own life he put that into practice by going to jail for not paying his taxes.[41] Adam Smith and his tax principles continued to dominate economic and tax philosophy and practice everywhere. David Ricardo carried on where Smith left off, and he in turn was followed by John Stuart Mill.[42] The condemnation of oaths for tax administration was propounded by J. R. McCulloch, a leading mid-nineteenth-century economist, who preached that the decline of morals among the people was a consequence of this evil practice.[43] Even the Supreme Court condemned the use of oaths for tax administration as late as 1885.[44]

As the nineteenth century came to a close, political philosophy shifted from the idea of limited government to paternalism in government. Wolves began to appear in sheep's clothing. Words that once stood for the noblest ideals of Western civilization took on alien meanings. The state could take away anyone's property under the guise of taxation and this was "social justice," or "revenue sharing." Communist dictatorships called themselves "Democratic Republics." Even the term "equality" was bastardized in tax philosophy, as we shall see.

In the twentieth century, Western man was seduced by the philosophy of socialism and welfare state-ism, and with that seduction the thinking of the men of the Enlightenment passed away. In its more brutal forms, paternalism found expression in Italian Fascism, National Socialism (Germany), and Japan's Greater East Asia policy. Marxism was more a kind of rape than seduction, since it never came by popular consent. The Italian dictator Mussolini expressed the basic tenant of all paternalism, the brutal and the benign, with this comment: "We were the first to assert that the more complicated the forms of civilization, the more restrictive the freedoms of the individual must become."[45]

Even though we pay lip service to the ideas of the Enlightenment, in reality we have neither moderate government nor moderate taxation (the two go hand in hand). If we review the many teachings of this chapter, we have rejected just about everything they stand for. Adam Smith's four aspects of a bad tax system are all functioning with full force in our system. If that isn't bad enough, we have even picked up the additional evils other wise men gave us. In short, when examining the tax wisdom of the Enlightenment, it is obvious, as the old navy expression goes, "No one got the *word*," at least, not our tax makers.

Part VII

The Rocky Road of Early American Taxation

No modern revolution was deeper rooted in taxation than the revolt of the Thirteen Colonies in British North America. British taxation not only caused the revolution, but perhaps most important, it acted as a unifying force in the colonies. The once-disorganized and squabbling colonies rallied around the cause of taxation-without-consent, took up arms against the British, and finally formed the United States of America. The American independence movement was not deep-rooted; it began in 1766 when colonial leaders met to protest British taxes under the Stamp Act. The Stamp Act Congress, as it was called, was the real birthplace of the United States.

The rallying cause against taxation by the Crown was at first a confused concept in the minds of most Americans. The colonists first argued that internal taxes, like stamp taxes, were bad, but external taxes, like import taxes, would be acceptable. The British Chancellor of the Exchequer, Charles Townshend, quite properly called this position by the Americans as "perfect nonsense." This nonsensical reasoning made it difficult for the Crown to know what to do. In the end the Americans revolted when Parliament adopted the kind of taxation the colonists said they were willing to pay. You could justifiably say that the American Revolution occurred, not because we objected to taxes without representation, but because we objected to taxes, period.

And the American attitude didn't change much after the war. What were the people doing in 1765? They were tarring and feathering British tax agents. What were they doing in 1794? They were tarring and feathering American tax agents.

Once the War of Independence had been won, there was little thought of creating a national government with taxing power. Everyone agreed that Congress should not be able to tax—that would defeat the very purpose of the revolution—but within a few years it became apparent that their common problems could not be solved unless Congress could

The British North Americans were more rebellious than their cousins in Britain, primarily because they had no voice in tax laws handed down by Parliament. This etching shows an English tax collector being beaten off by a colonial housewife. Until recently, tax collectors engaged in one of the most dangerous of occupations. Because of the risks, most tax collectors received a percentage of their collections as an inducement for the hazardous occupation.

tax. As much as everyone disliked the idea, there was no alternative. The feeble government under the Articles of Confederation failed because it could not tax; all other considerations were secondary. In 1789 the Americans tried again with a new Congress that could tax. Without taxing powers the first Congress of the United States barely lasted seven years; the second Congress, with taxing powers, is still going strong after two hundred years.

Sectionalism between the rich planters of the South and the rich industrialists of the North highlighted the struggles within the new nation for seventy-five years. Finally, in 1861, after Lincoln's election, the Southerners walked out of Congress and formed the Confederate States of America with a new constitution to check the power of their new government to tax. Secession by the South was in part a reaction against Northern high-tax policy. In 1861 the slave issue was not critical. Lincoln and the Congress gave unequivocal assurance that slavery in the South would be respected, yet the South would not budge from its secessionist plans. The leaders of the South believed secession would attract world trade to Charleston, Savannah, and New Orleans, replacing Boston, New York, and Philadelphia as the chief trading ports of America, primarily because of low taxes. This was the pot of gold behind secessionist dreams.

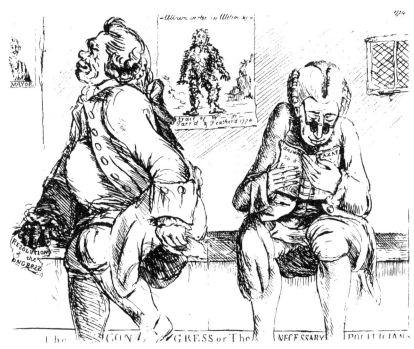

This English caricature shows two politicians in a "necessary house" (outhouse). One rips up a resolution of the Continental Congress protesting taxation by Parliament (1774), the other is reading Samuel Johnson's *Taxation No Tyranny*, which asserts that Americans should bear some of the costs of their defense. A tarred and feathered tax man is shown in the picture on the wall.

29

Tax Revolt in the Colonies

From the fullest conviction, I disclaim every idea both of policy and the right internally to tax America. I disavow the whole system. It is commenced in iniquity; it is pursued with resentment; and it can terminate in nothing but blood.

— Marquis of Grandby, Speech in House of Commons, 5 April 1775

It is not difficult to argue that the founding fathers of America revolted over taxes that were neither unfair nor oppressive. The Americans were among the most blessed and fortunate people on earth; they had the protection of the British nation and their land was rich and choice. Business was good and there were jobs for everyone. Europe's social castes did not enchain them and their sons were not conscripted to fight wars in far away places. If revolution is the consequence of oppression then the American Revolution should never have occurred.

The taxes the British tried to collect were modest; the money was to be spent entirely in the colonies for their benefit and protection. It was not going to be sent back to the mother country. Why all the ruckus and cry of "tyranny"? Did the mother country have a bunch of spoiled brats who did not realize just how well off they were? Why shouldn't they pay their share of the costs of maintaining the military forces that secured their borders? The Americans were the beneficiaries of recent military victories that removed the threat of French imperialism and opened up the western frontier. Did not the Americans have a moral obligation to pay for some of the costs incurred in securing these benefits?

The American Revolution had its roots in the attitudes of the first settlers who came to the New World in the seventeenth century. Most of them were embroiled in the English Civil War and carried with them the ideals of Lord Coke and the Petition of Rights. Their colonial charters from Parliament guaranteed them "all the rights, privileges, and immunities of Englishmen." This meant that they would have the right to trial by jury; they would be governed by the Common Law; they could not be arbitrarily imprisoned; and they could not be taxed without their consent. In theory the Crown was just as restricted in dealing with them as with Englishmen at home. Their attitude is illustrated in a letter written home by one British civil servant who said that if you approached a colonist about providing funds for British armies fighting in America, he responded by giving a "lengthy lecture on his rights." [1] The chances are this lecture was not very logical.

An Englishman living in the colonies had no member of Parliament to represent him. Under those circumstances it was not possible for him to "consent" to laws and taxation. His rights as an Englishman were illusory, especially when he found himself in the clutches of arrogant bureaucrats sent out from the mother country to interfere in his way of life.

This unfortunate situation was no one's fault. Political forms and practices that guaranteed his rights had not been invented. Local courts helped somewhat; jury trials were provided and the Common Law governed—but much was missing, especially some means by which he could debate and consent to taxation. Local assemblies could be overruled by the Crown. It may be that the real cause of the American Revolution was this lack of political machinery to protect the colonists' rights. The British Parliament was not designed to work for Englishmen living in faraway places. As events turned out, the American Revolution was a radical solution to that problem. In the years that followed, other colonial areas such as Canada, Australia, and even twentieth-century Commonwealth countries, were to find more moderate solutions. The basic problem in eighteenth-century North America was that British colonial practices were incompatible with the "rights of Englishmen," and the American Revolution was an expression of that incompatibility.

British colonialism in the eighteenth century was based on mercantilism, an economic practice which tied colonies to their mother country. Colonies shipped raw materials to Britain where they were either consumed or used for manufacturing and trade. Most important, the colonies had to buy their imports from the mother country. Mercantilism gave British merchants a monopoly on colonial trade. Smuggling hurt them more than it injured the revenue, since trade regulations and high customs were designed to prevent foreign competition, not to collect taxes. One mercantile law, the Molasses Act of 1733, placed a high tax on molasses from the French West Indies. The law was never effective because of the ease with which cheap French molasses could be smuggled into the colonies. British sugar merchants complained bitterly.

"The American," they said, "derived his right of cheating the Revenue, and of perjuring himself, from the example of his fathers and the rights of nature"; and would continue to "complain and smuggle, and smuggle and complain, till all Restraints are removed, and till he can both buy and sell, whenever, and wheresoever, he pleases. Any thing short of this, is still a Grievance, a Badge of Slavery." Actually, British merchants had no right to accuse Yankee traders of smuggling—which was much more extensive along the coasts of England than in North America.

During Cromwell's era, customs officers were authorized to search for smuggled goods in Britain by a Writ of Assistance issued by the Exchequer Court. To obtain this unique writ, the customs officer would swear under oath before a judge that smuggled property was in a particular place; if probable cause was shown, the writ would be signed and the customs officer would conduct the search with the assistance of a local peace officer.

This writ came to the colonies in 1755 in a novel form which attracted no attention at first. But in 1761, in Boston, James Otis resigned as attorney general to represent the merchants of Boston in a law suit to prevent the renewal of the writ (the king had died and a new authorization was required by the courts). Otis charged nothing for his services: "In such a case, I despise all fees." A young lawyer named John Adams (later to become president) sat in the courtroom and took notes of the proceeding. Otis argued for five hours and charged that the writ

> was the worst instrument of arbitrary power, the most destructive of English Liberty and the fundamental principles of law that ever was found in an English law-book. . . . Not more than one instance can be found of it in all our law-books and that was in the zenith of arbitrary power, namely, the reign of Charles I, when the Star Chamber powers were pushed to extremity.[2]

Otis didn't object to the use of the writ for the search of a specific place when authorized by a court upon an oath and affidavit of the customs officer; what he did object to was the power this peculiar writ gave to any officer to search without a court order. Not even Parliament could authorize such a monstrosity. Said Otis: "An act against the Constitution is void."[3] The judges of the court ruled against Otis and issued the writ to the customs officers in Boston. But, even though Otis lost, the case attracted attention and thereafter judges and lawyers worked together to frustrate customs officers trying to obtain the writ. Contrary to popular belief the colonists were never oppressed with the use of the Writ of Assistance. It was on the books and it irritated the Americans, but thanks to the guts and ingenuity of a courageous bar and bench, most writs gathered dust waiting to be signed in the chambers of colonial judges.

The Writ of Assistance is important in American history because the threat of its use caused the founding fathers to place the Fourth Amendment in the Bill of Rights. While that great amendment is not now used to restrain revenue agents, it was initially adopted to do just that. The amendment prohibits "unreasonable searches and seizures," which meant, most of all, that tax agents cannot snoop without a court order based on an affidavit establishing probable cause.

For more than fifty years before the American Revolution the British government considered taxing the colonies. Sir Robert Walpole was told by the retiring governor of Virginia that colonial taxation was feasible. Years later, in 1732, when the excise crisis developed over wine and tobacco, one minister suggested extending the new excise to the colonies. "No," said Walpole, "I have old England against me, do you think I will have New England do likewise?"

By mid-century the peace of Walpole's era ended. Britain was at war with France. The revenue demands of the war became increasingly severe. By 1764, British armies had pushed the French out of North America and it was not unfair for the American to shoulder some of the financial burdens that benefited them. If they did, the land tax in Britain could be reduced to peacetime levels and some of the excises could be withdrawn. Furthermore, stories abounded in Britain about the profiteering of American merchants from free-spending British soldiers, war contracts, and smuggling. To many Britons, America was a land of milk and honey, lace and linen, silver and silk, paid for by British taxpayers.

Parliament responded in 1764 with the Sugar Act, which was the Crown's first and only successful tax law in the colonies. Yankee traders in New England protested vehemently, but the rest of the colonies showed little interest in their plight. Smuggling was open in New England and most colonists believed the New Englanders were probably getting what they deserved. Years later, after the revolution, President John Adams of Massachusetts fame said the Sugar Act imposed "enormous taxes, burdensome taxes, oppressive, ruinous, intolerable taxes."[4] But at the time, outside of New England, no one felt that way. Taxes under the Sugar Act covered a wide range of non-British goods. The rates were really quite modest.

Protests against the Sugar Act were really directed against administrative provisions designed to check evasion. The act was a typical sledgehammer revenue measure which treated every trader as a cheat. A maze of regulations entangled all importers, even little coastal vessels, and any breach justified seizure of the vessel as well as the entire cargo.

Even the personal chests of ordinary seamen were seized if the contents were not listed on customs declarations. The Sugar Act trapped the innocent more than the guilty.

Besides the presumption of guilt which the law made, tax litigation was moved from local courts and juries to Halifax, Nova Scotia, for trial before pro-government Admiralty Courts. Acquittals were common in trials in New England because under the Common Law, unlike today, a jury would acquit if the members believed the law or the punishment was unjust.[5] An acquittal paved the way for a civil action for damages against the Crown's tax agents and informers for false charges. Under the Sugar Act such civil actions were prohibited. Informers were encouraged by rewards of a third of any confiscated property.

Revenue from the Sugar Act did not bring much relief to British taxpayers at home. In 1765 there were serious riots in Britain. After excise tax collectors were mobbed, cider excises were repealed. In the search for new revenue, the rich and undertaxed colonies attracted the attention of the British government. The prime minister asked Parliament if any members questioned the right of the Crown to tax the colonists. There were no dissenters. He then asked if the colonies would refuse "to contribute their mite to relieve us from the heavy burdens which we lie under?" (Approximately ten thousand British troops were stationed in America for its defense.) He even suggested that the colonists could use any form of taxation they desired—but for the present, the government would introduce stamp taxes.

The Stamp Act was no mere mite to the colonist. Colonial legislatures held emergency sessions. There were town meetings, speeches, and pamphlets condemning the tax. Mob violence erupted; property was destroyed. Governors wrote home to Britain advising the government that the rebellion could not be curbed. Even the strongest opponents of the tax spent their time trying to cool the mobs and restore order. Most important, the Stamp Act united the colonies—something that had been impossible up to 1765. Massachusetts called for a congress of the colonies, and delegates appeared from almost all colonial governments.

Stamp taxes were popular throughout Europe at this time. By 1750 they were in use in the colonies by colonial governments. The British Act of 1765 followed the established practice of taxing newspapers, legal documents, business licenses, diplomas, and a few other items. The funds from these taxes were to be used exclusively to pay for British troops stationed in North America. To make the tax more tolerable, local citizens were granted the exclusive right to sell or issue the stamps. No arrogant bureaucrats would be sent out from the mother country, as had been the case with customs. Even Ben Franklin applied for the job of stamp salesman.

British soldiers roughly clearing the road for the transport of the stamps.

The Stamp Act Congress petitioned Parliament for repeal, arguing that taxes were internal and thus required the consent of the colonists. Parliament could not speak for them, as it lacked a natural bond to the colonists. When the congress adjourned a few prominent citizens were sent to London to lobby for repeal.

Benjamin Franklin was one of those sent to argue for repeal. He was the agent for New Jersey, Georgia, and above all, Massachusetts—the seedbed of the rebels. He was invited to speak to the House of Commons.

Here are some of the questions put to him by the Commons, with his answers:

> Question: "What was the temper of America towards Great Britain before the year 1763?"
> Answer: "The best in the world. They submitted willingly to the government of the Crown and paid, in their courts, obedience to acts of Parliament. . . ."
> Question: "And what is their temper now?"
> Answer: "O, very much altered."
> Question: "Did you ever hear the authority of Parliament to make laws for America questioned till lately?"

Answer: "The authority of Parliament was allowed to be valid in all laws, except such as should lay internal taxes. It was never disputed in laying duties to regulate commerce."[6]

At the time of this testimony (January 1766) Franklin spoke with the moderates. When he spoke of internal taxes he was talking about the Stamp Act. He certainly made it clear that customs (external taxes) were not objectionable.

The Stamp Act was repealed and there was jubilation throughout the colonies. British merchants in England opposed the Stamp Act as much as the colonists. Repeal meant victory for everyone but the Exchequer and the cabinet.

There was an addendum to the repeal act that was to irritate the colonists in the years to come. In effect, the addendum said Parliament had the power to tax if it wanted to. Parliament wanted to make it clear they were not abdicating their power over the colonies in any way, especially the power to tax. At the time, Franklin said this provision would not have any adverse consequences as long as Parliament did not try to assert it. Years later, on the eve of the revolution, Franklin felt otherwise, saying with bitter derision:

But remember to make your arbitrary tax more grievous to your provinces, by public declarations importing that your power of taxing them without their consent has no limits; so that when you take from them without their *consent* one shilling in a pound, you have a clear right to the other 19.[7]

When the furor over the Stamp Act subsided, Parliament followed Franklin's suggestion and adopted a number of new customs duties on goods imported from Britain. If the Americans foolishly believed there was a difference between external and internal taxation, the Crown was willing to give the Americans the kind of taxation they asked for, however absurd and ridiculous their thinking might be. These new duties, said a member of the British Cabinet, were "perfectly consistent with Doctor Franklin's own arguments, while he was soliciting the repeal of the Stamp Act."

These new customs, called the Townshend duties, ran into some opposition in the Commons (the vote was 180 to 98). Edmund Burke, an extraordinary thinker in his day, argued that the Townshend duties did not differ from the Stamp Act and he predicted that the Americans would see the folly of their own thinking. The Crown would not receive a shilling from the Americans, regardless of whether the taxes were internal or external. Burke knew the Americans better than they knew themselves, and certainly better than Franklin knew his own people.

Under the Townshend Act, customs were charged on a few items from Britain—paper, dyes, glass, and tea. There was a quartering provision requiring the colonists to support British troops in America, which would indirectly accomplish what the Stamp Act had failed to do.

Rebellion to this act came from the colonial merchants, who boycotted British goods. In Britain business slumped, many shipping firms went broke, and there was unemployment. The Crown had no alternative but to repeal the duties, except for a small tax on tea, reduced from 12 pence to 3 pence for a pound of tea.

The Quartering Act, which was a disguised tax, was tolerated except in New York, which had the largest number of British soldiers. The act was decidedly unfair and placed an undue burden on New Yorkers, who refused to provide for the full needs of the troops. An enraged Parliament suspended the New York legislature and annulled its future acts. A hawkish mood developed. Dr. Samuel Johnson, a leading scholar of letters, said: "They are a race of convicts and ought to be thankful for anything we allow them short of a hanging."[8]

The worst aspect of the Townshend Act was the establishment of a new Board of Commissioners of Customs. Writs of Assistance were given to the board and the arrogance of three leading agents in Boston played no small part in the eventual revolution. Said a prominent American historian:

> Had it not been for the unfortunate personalities of Robinson, Paxton, and Hulton there might have been no revolution. From 1768 to 1772 almost open warfare existed between the agents of the commissioners and (the colonists).[9]

Canada may have stayed out of the conflict because of its superb governor who refused to tolerate any corruption and misconduct by customs agents in that region. As things finally turned out, the revolution was probably more the consequence of the oppressive administration of taxes than the taxes themselves, despite all the talk about taxation and consent.

The best record we have of the tyranny of British tax agents is in a small article written by Benjamin Franklin in 1773, which has no resemblance to his remarks to Parliament in 1766. His later article was called, "Rules by which a Great Empire may be Reduced to a Small One." He did not name Great Britain specifically, but he listed 20 grievances the colonies had against the British. This document is probably the best summary of the sins of the mother country toward her colonies. It deals with human, rather than legal issues, and it was written at a time when Franklin still had considerable rank and prestige among the British. Regarding British revenue agents, he said:

> XI. To make your taxes more odious, and more likely to procure resistance, send from the capital a board of officers to superintend the collection, composed of the most indiscreet, ill-bred, and insolent you can find. . . . If any revenue officers are suspected of the least tenderness for the people, discard them. If others are justly complained of, protect and reward them. If any of the under officers behave so as to provoke the people to drub them, promote those to better office.

Franklin said about the navy:

> V. Convert the brave, honest officers of your *navy* into pimping tide-waiters and colony officers of the *customs*. . . . Let them learn to be corrupted by great and real smugglers; (to show their diligence) scour with armed boats every bay, harbour, river, creek, cove, and nook throughout the coast of your colonies; stop and detain every coaster, every wood-boat, every fisherman, tumble their cargoes and even ballast inside out and upside down; and if a penny worth of pins is found un-entered, let the whole be seized and confiscated.[10]

Franklin's complaints about the British navy were true. British naval personnel received a handsome share of the cargo and proceeds from the sale of confiscated ships they seized. British warships along the American coasts were in effect given a license for piracy. Improper documentation was all that was needed to permit seizure; smuggling was not required.

The Townshend duties helped the colonists clarify their thinking about taxation and consent. The Americans were not to leave the door open again. Distinctions between external and internal taxes were abandoned. Any tax required consent. American thought began moving toward a political arrangement that gave limited sovereignty to Parliament. Unfortunately, war broke out and this novel political idea did not take root. To the very end, Parliament demanded the right of absolute power over the colonies. It is doubtful if they ever would have surrendered their supreme authority. Into modern times the British Parliament held supreme constitutional power over the Canadian people, though it did not dare to interfere with their wishes for many years. Not until 1981 did Canadian politicians agree on the terms for the repatriation of Canada's Constitution, enacted by Parliament as the British North America Act in 1867.

Many British leaders agreed with the colonies. The former prime minister, Pitt the Elder, opposed taxing the colonies. But the best thinking came from Edmund Burke, who opposed military action when war clouds started to appear, saying: "People must be governed in a manner agreeable to their temper and dispositions."[11]

The Americans finally realized that any taxation without their consent was against their disposition. Perhaps if they had taken that view in 1766 when they opposed the Stamp Act, an acceptable solution may have been discovered, short of war. Unfortunately, the issue was resolved by following the example of the sixteenth-century Dutch—war against a mother country that insisted on taxing them in a manner they did not like.

The Boston Tea Party was a turning point in colonial reaction to British rule. By 1773 the tax issue was becoming obscure. Both parties were moving toward war.

Recently American postage stamps have depicted the Boston Tea Party as a glorious act of defying British colonialism. Most people believe it was a protest against British taxes on tea, but this is not true. American tea merchants had been boycotting British tea for five years. Smuggled Dutch tea was used throughout the colonies. In response, the British government decided to remove the duties on East Indies tea when it arrived in Britain so it could be sold in America at a price cheaper than smuggled Dutch tea. In addition, a monopoly on this

The Boston Tea Party. In this etching, tea crates are hoisted from the hold and pried open and their contents dumped into the sea. Franklin believed the owners of the tea deserved compensation for this wanton destruction of private property.

cheap tea was given to loyal British merchants in the colonies. American tea smugglers would be put out of business. The Crown's plan was based on the assumption that American consumers would not boycott low-priced English tea, but would purchase it rather than the higher-priced, smuggled Dutch product.

The implication of this to American merchants was frightening. If a monopoly could be granted for tea, it could be granted for other products as well. Economic sanctions of this kind could destroy American merchants. In protest, Bostonian merchants disguised themselves as Indians, boarded merchant ships loaded with tea, and threw the tea into the harbor. This was a wanton destruction of private property in an age when private property was held in great esteem. The first obligation of any government is to protect the lives and property of its citizens.

The Boston Tea Party is a sobering event that raises difficult legal and moral issues. It is anything but the cause célèbre American historians have made of it. This wanton destruction of property was not well received in the colonies. Massachusetts was a known seedbed of hotheads and warmongers. Franklin was shocked and acknowledged that full restitution should be paid at once to the owners of the tea. Most Americans believed this way, but unfortunately the majority of Americans were to feel the heel of the British boot. A number of "Intolerable Acts" were adopted by the Crown and started the Revolutionary War. British warships and troops literally invaded the colonies. Oppressive revenue agents, no matter how bad, were to look kindly compared to fleets of warships and battalions of redcoats in battle array. Cannon, muskets, and bayonets replaced Writs of Assistance, seizures, and tax levies.

The Americans won the war after six years because the British found the logistics of supporting troops three thousand miles away in a hostile country too burdensome. The American army was ill-fed and seldom paid. This ragged bunch returned home to bankrupt farms and state governments. The burdens of taxation under the British were a pittance compared to the financial obligations they now faced. The war had to be paid for and taxes, even with representation, were going to be enormous.

Loyalists suffered most. Their property was seized, and tarring and feathering was common. A long stream of refugees moved north to Canada. Benjamin Franklin made a personal visit to Canada to persuade loyalists to join the United States, but the scars of war were deep and would not heal. Franklin had spent the war in Europe. If he had been home and witnessed the suffering of the loyalists he would have known that the last thing these people wanted was further association with the Americans. There was bitterness on both sides, but no atrocities. The loyalists, for all their suffering, were fortunate. In other times and places they would have been slaughtered.

The Americans conducted the war through the Continental Congress, which had become a joke by the end of the war, especially in the press. It could not even pay the back-pay of combat veterans or interest on the war debt, yet it went forward and adopted a number of costly programs to rebuild the nation. Naturally, nothing was accomplished without money, but money required taxes, which was one of the powers the Congress did not have.

The British learned from the war. In 1778, two years after the Revolution began, Parliament enacted a law, approved by King George III, which declared "that the King and Parliament of Great Britain will not impose any duty, tax, or assessment for the purpose of raising a revenue in any of the colonies, provinces or plantations." This wise enactment, unfortunately, came too late. In the next 150 years Parliament continued to assert absolute sovereignty over its colonies, but when taxation was to be levied, local assemblies, in one form or another, had to give their consent.[12] Even in Canada, where colonial governments were weak and dominated by British governors and civil servants, taxation was submitted to assemblies. The Americans won the war not only for themselves but for the whole British Empire until its final demise after World War II.

A loyalist newspaper depicts fiendish Sons of Liberty tarring and feathering a British tax agent while tea is being dumped into the harbor. Twenty years later the Sons of Liberty re-emerged and were tarring and feathering American tax agents. As it turned out, they were not just against taxation without representation—they were against taxation, period.

30

The Tax Struggle for "a More Perfect Union"

In June 1776, one month before the signing of the Declaration of Independence, the Continental Congress appointed a committee to draft Articles of Confederation for the colonies. The first draft permitted the federal government to do just about anything but levy "any Taxes or Duties." This broad endowment of political power without taxing power was understandable because the revolution was against taxation by an external political agency above and beyond the states. All taxation must be at the state level. This thinking followed the practice of the United Provinces of the Netherlands, which produced the first modern republic with an Estates-General (congress) that could not tax.

The final draft of Articles was ratified by the states in 1781. The national government, called the "United States in Congress assembled," was limited. Many of its powers required a three-fourths vote, especially on matters of finance and war. As expected, the Congress could not tax—everyone agreed to that—but when money was needed, a requisition was made upon the states based on the value of privately owned real property. Requisitions based on population or personal property were ruled out because of difficulties with slaves. Slaves were "property" to Southerners, but "population" to Northerners. Revenue based on real estate avoided that difficult issue.

The Confederation gave America a number of things: First, its name, the United States of America; second, its currency, the Spanish dollar; but most important, its experience in self-government at the federal level.

The requisition system of finance was copied from the Dutch Republic along with a number of federal-state relations, but what worked in the Netherlands would not work in North America. Most of the new states were in desperate financial shape and simply did not have the money required of them by the Congress. Without money, the Congress became the laughing stock of the new nation.

Within two years the Congress was debating the tax issue all over again. Every known method of taxation was discussed: poll taxes, excise taxes, hearth taxes, salt monopolies, and import duties. Import duties had long been a favorite revenue device of British people, in the colonies as well as at home, and as much as everyone disliked the idea, resort to import taxation by the federal government appeared imperative. But there were opponents, especially the fire-eaters from Massachusetts represented by Sam Adams, who led the revolt against British customs in the War for Independence. He argued that if the Congress had the power to levy a tax on imports, every seaport, from Maine to Georgia, would be filled with an army of overpaid excisemen, tide-waiters, and cellar rats. And what would happen to the funds raised from the sweat of the people? Would Congress guard it with utmost vigilance? Would they dole it out with a frugal hand? No. They would squander it with a reckless profusion, he said. With heated emotional appeals of this temper by some of the leading American patriots, it is no surprise that the Confederation could not agree to tax. An amendment to the Articles would require unanimous consent; a Massachusetts veto was a certainty. For the next four years the Congress accomplished absolutely nothing. Robert Morris, the chief financial officer of the Congress, summed up the situation in these words: "The Congress had the privilege of asking for everything," but the states were given "the prerogative of granting nothing." What money the states would grant and when they would do so was "known only to Him who knoweth all things."[1]

Eventually the Congress called for a convention in Philadelphia to revise the Articles. Initially only a few states appointed delegates and it looked as if the convention would fold from inadequate attendance, but fortunately for the struggling nation a rebellion erupted in Massachusetts, the hotbed of resistance to national taxing power. This so-called Shays' Rebellion was not much more than a riot, but it frightened the people of Massachusetts and emphasized to the rest of the country the need for a stronger national government.

Shays' Rebellion was the first of three tax revolts to plague the new nation in the first fifteen years of its existence. The rebels were havenots, overburdened with taxes and debts from the war. They demanded a state constitutional amendment (like Proposition 13 in California in 1978) to curb the spending and taxing powers of Massachusetts. Old war veterans formed a number of regiments and there was talk of rebellion. When one of these regiments tried to seize a federal arsenal, two volleys of cannon were fired, the rebels dispersed, and the rebellion was over. Newspapers exaggerated the story and this acted as a spur to the states to form a stronger national government. One newspaper said the city of Genoa could defeat the military forces of the United States. In haste, delegates were sent to Philadelphia. Like the Stamp Act of 1765, Shays' Rebellion brought the squabbling states together again, this time to form "a more perfect Union."

The delegates in Philadelphia in 1787 quickly abandoned the idea of revising the Articles. Life under the Confederation had been intolerable. With no money the government could do nothing but talk. By 1787 there were no voices clamoring for a continuation of the tax anemia of the Confederation; everyone now agreed the federal government must be able to tax, but what limitations should there be on that power? The Congress must not be a Parliament; there must be definite limitations and controls on its taxing power. Everyone agreed to that as well.

Constitutional restrictions on taxing power were not new. Taxation by consent through tax representatives was common throughout Europe, but in addition, many European peoples enjoyed protection from certain kinds of taxation as well. Many medieval charters provided that tailles and poll taxes could not be collected. The Framers of the Constitution decided to define and control the taxing powers of the Congress. Controls were needed besides the "consent" of the taxpayers through their representatives. It would be easy for one class of citizen to gain control of the tax-making machinery and adopt taxes that oppressed some minority group. Whatever taxes were adopted, they should fall equally upon the majority and the minority. In other words, if farmers should control tax-making, they must not be able to burden urban people with taxes that they themselves did not actually bear. The need for standards to assure fairness was too obvious to need much discussion. The men at the Constitutional Convention were not blind to the evils inherent in democratic tax-making without constitutional standards to prevent injustices.

In 1787 no citizen could vote who was not a taxpayer; consequently, the delegates decided to have a legislative body of taxpayers' representatives where all taxation would originate. The requirement that all voters be taxpayers was not in the new constitution; it was a matter of custom not only in the colonies but in Europe as well. The primary economic function of a legislature is to tax and raise money for the executive branch of government to spend. It follows that no one should have a voice in how the government's money is spent who is not a contributor. Conversely, if a taxpayer is not a voter, the process of "consent" is undermined. Voters, therefore, must be taxpayers.

The very first power granted to the new Congress was "to lay and collect Taxes" which are "uniform throughout the United States." The most significant word is "uniform." It evolved in the convention from the word "common to all," which was proposed on July 23, 1787. Later in the draft approved on September 12, 1787, the words were "uniform and equal." This draft went to the Committee on Style which, for some reason, dropped the clause completely. Madison penciled in the clause as it now reads, omitting the word "equal."[2] Were either of these omissions intentional? Is that significant? Probably not. Constitutional law in the early days of the American republic considered the terms "uniform and equal" to be redundant verbage. Thomas Cooley, the leading authority on constitutional law in the nineteenth century, explains the principle in 1868 in his treatise on *Constitutional Limitations*:

> State constitutions have been very specific, but in providing for equality and uniformity they have done little more than to state in concise language a principle of constitutional law which is inherent in the power to tax.[3]

Since "uniform" was to be the standard for all taxation throughout the United States, to understand what they meant, the writings of this period clarify what really doesn't need clarification. The word "uniform" is basic English with a common meaning. When the Constitution was up for ratification in the states, the strongest proponents—the federalists as they were called—all proclaimed that taxing powers were limited and restrained. No one then wanted Congress to be able to tax at will. Noah Webster, one of the strongest federalists, wrote a pamphlet on October 10, 1787 (shortly after the Convention), addressed "To his Excellency, Benjamin Franklin, President of the Commonwealth of Pennsylvania," in which he emphasized, "But the idea that congress can levy taxes at pleasure is false, and the suggestion wholly unsupported."[4]

In the debates before the New York legislature for ratification, Alexander Hamilton (also a strong federalist) said: "It is infinitely more eligible to lay a tax originally which will have uniform effects throughout the Union, which will operate equally and silently."[5] Again we see the word equality applied to uniformity.

A remarkable book published in 1832 by Benjamin Oliver, a man in love with his country and anxious to tell the world about its virtues, had this to say about Congress's power to tax:

> This right [property] is not infringed by equal taxes for public purposes, imposed by adequate legitimate authority. A misapplication or misappropriation of funds in the public treasury, however, must be considered as a violation of this right [property]. . . . As it would be unconstitutional,

therefore, to lay an unequal tax, as well as an act of oppression upon those who were compelled to pay the larger proportion of it.[6]

In *The Federalist*, No. 36, Hamilton concluded a series of seven essays discussing taxing powers and the controls to prevent "partiality and oppression." The possible abuse of the power of taxation had been adequately guarded against, with the final protection that taxes "shall be UNIFORM throughout the United States." Hamilton capitalized the word UNIFORM, which is the same as the modern style of italicizing, i.e. emphasizing to imply the full and the most basic meaning of the term. And what did the word "uniform" mean?

The nineteenth-century Oxford English Dictionary is a multi-volume work that took decades to complete. It traces the meaning and usages of words back to the late Middle Ages. It defined uniform as: "that is or remains the same in different places, at different times, or *under varying circumstances*; exhibiting no difference, diversity, or variation (emphasis added)."

In the mid-nineteenth century the Supreme Court seemed to have no trouble with the meaning when they reviewed a tax on distilleries:

> The law is not in our judgment subject to any constitutional objection. The tax imposed upon the distiller is in the nature of an excise, and the only limitation upon the power of Congress in the imposition of taxes of this character is that they shall be "uniform" throughout the United States. The tax here is uniform in its operation; that is it is assessed equally upon all manufacturers of spirits, wherever they are. The law does not establish one rule for one distiller and a different rule for another, but the same rule for all alike.[7]

This view was also found in the state courts, which had constitutions that required uniformity. But as we noted, even without a constitutional command, uniform and equal were essential requirements for any "tax" in a democratic society, even if not expressed. An early Ohio Supreme Court ruled that one rule cannot apply to one owner, and a different rule to another owner. One could not be assessed 10 percent, another 5 percent, another 3, and another left altogether unassessed.[8]

Professor Cooley's monumental work on Constitutional Law, summarized the rule as having both social and geographical application: The rule of uniformity was designed to provide equality of burdens by preventing the legislature from taxing some region or class of citizens different from or in excess of some other region or class of citizens.[9] In effect, no "loopholes" in taxation.

As we shall see, the rule of uniformity passed away in the twentieth century. You could tax one person's income at 90 percent, another at 70 percent, another at 20 percent, and another left altogether unassessed. The Supreme Court re-interpreted the rule of uniformity to only be a "uniformity clause," which might as well have been deleted from the Constitution.[10] Noah Webster was wrong, Congress can tax at its pleasure.

In Britain, in 1871, the question of uniformity came up in the House of Commons, not as a constitutional question, but as a matter of policy and graduated income tax rates. The Chancellor of the Exchequer opposed graduated income tax rates with these words, "If an Income Tax must be maintained, it must be a uniform tax. That is, the same tax rates for all—what uniform means."[11]

After demanding uniformity for all taxes, the Framers wanted to further restrict Congress's taxing powers with respect to direct taxation. Such taxes, said Madison, would only be adopted in an extraordinary emergency, like Cicero said almost two thousand years before. They would have to be apportioned among the states by population. In *The Federalist*, No. 10, Madison gave this astute explanation:

> Yet there is, perhaps, no legislative act in which greater opportunity and temptation are given to a predominant party to trample on the rules of justice. Every shilling with which they overburden the inferior number is a shilling saved to their own pockets.

Madison went at length to emphasize the point that in a democratic society tax laws favor those in control of the government and overburden those on the outside. This was all too common in Europe at that time and over the past hundreds of years. Protestants taxed Catholics and Jews at double rates and even quadruple rates. Governments dominated by aristocratic classes, as in France, usually taxed themselves at low or even no rates. Direct taxes were, as always, looked upon with disfavor.

In the debates, Rufus King of Massachusetts asked, "What was the precise meaning of *direct* taxation?" Madison comments in his notes, "No one answered." This was not a dumb question. These classifications were historical, not legal, and precise meanings were unknown. In 1798 the question came before the Supreme Court on the legality of a carriage tax. The Court concluded that direct taxes were poll and land taxes. A hundred years later the question was raised in the famous income tax case of 1894, and as we shall see the court struggled for over a year and reached a very confusing definition.

The distinction between direct and indirect taxation was picked up by the Canadians in their constitution, the British North America Act, which restricts the taxing powers of Canada's provinces. In the late

1970s, a special oil tax in Saskatchewan was declared illegal because the tax offended the Canadian constitution's classifications and restrictions. Incidentally, the Canadian and British define "direct taxes" quite differently than do the American courts.[12] Income taxes are direct taxes and are frequently referred to as such. Most American legal authorities consider them to be excises on the receipt of income and hence indirect.

The primary control over runaway taxation was to be in the restrictions on the Congress's spending power. There is no question but that bad taxes are the product of too much spending. Control spending and taxes will automatically be controlled. The recent Balanced Budget Amendment to the Constitution is designed to do what the Framers tried to do with Article I, Section 8: Congress had the power to levy taxes "to pay the Debts and provide for the common Defence and general Welfare of the United States." The key words are Debts, Defence, and general Welfare. Once again, in the debates for ratification and in *The Federalist*, these terms were held up to be the final cap or restriction on the federal government. Expenditures outside of those terms would be illegal and unconstitutional. Thus by controlling expenditures you control taxes and prevent the federal government from becoming an all-powerful national government. Of course, that's all history. Like the rule of uniformity, the expenditure restrictions have no meaning whatsoever. But let us take a moment to see what the Framers had in mind.

Did the term "common Defence" mean that military expenditures could only be made for defense? That is, no funds for aggressive wars? That is exactly what the Framers were talking about. In *The Federalist*, No. 34, Hamilton said they were embarking on a "novel . . . experiment in politics, of tying up the hands of government from offensive war, founded on reasons of state; yet certainly we ought not to disable it from guarding the community against the ambition or enmity of other nations."

The reason for limiting Congress's power to spend for the military was because of the high costs and taxes that are required. As Hamilton said, the costs of nonmilitary expenses of government "are insignificant in comparison with those which relate to national defence."

As we noted, the concept of limiting tax moneys for defense found strong support in England and the Spanish provinces. It also came to the New World and found expression in the early American constitutions. In *The Laws and Liberties of Massachusetts* (1648), conscription for military service (which is a tax in the form of labor) was limited to defensive wars, within the Commonwealth.

Looking back over the past two hundred years of American history it is obvious there were a number of wars that were not defensive, but were in Hamilton's category of "offensive war, founded on reasons of state."

The "general Welfare" clause was also held up to be a restriction on government spending. It did not mean anything in general, quite to the contrary. It meant benefiting the whole nation. General meant no expenditures for some "special Welfare." You couldn't build a project to just benefit New Yorkers; the project must benefit the nation as a whole. That's history too. "Pork barrelling" is simply a political science term for expenditures that are for a politician who was able to lobby a "special Welfare" spending bill through Congress. Enforce the "general Welfare" provision of the Constitution and most corruption by misappropriating taxpayers' money would disappear.

The Framers of the Constitution were all realists about government, with no illusions about the dangers of political power, even in the best of hands with the wisest of men. Government had to be kept under control, and in keeping with the spirit of the Enlightenment, government must be limited and this could only be accomplished by tough controls on taxing and spending powers. They all believed that the Constitution they had produced would do just that; and in the beginning—it did. Nevertheless, when they finally finished their work and the time came to sign the document, there was no euphoria over their work product. The philosophic Dr. Franklin signed the instrument "with tears, and apologized for doing it at all, from the doubts and apprehensions he felt." He then observed and predicted, "that its complexion was doubtful; that it might last for ages, involve one-quarter of the globe, and probably terminate in despotism."[13] The fear of despotism appears again and again in speeches and writings, even among strong supporters like Franklin. This negative view subsided with the Bill of Rights and with the strong arguments put forth at the ratification debates pointing out that taxing and spending powers were greatly restricted. So long as these controls were in place said the supporters, despotism would be curtailed. But, we may ask, if the controls fail, will Franklin's prophecy come to pass?

The Whiskey Boys

Wherever the ends of government are perverted, and public liberty manifestly endangered, and all other means of redress are ineffectual, the doctrine of nonresistance against arbitrary power, and oppression, is absurd, slavish, and destructive of the good and happiness of mankind.[14]

A federal whiskey tax collector, tarred and feathered, being driven out of town by Pennsylvanians protesting against the whiskey tax enacted under the recommendations of Alexander Hamilton.

Alexander Hamilton became Washington's secretary of the treasury. His appointment has been called "the right man, at the right time, in the right place," but it's doubtful that farmers on the western frontier in 1794 agreed. Hamilton, following Adam Smith's *Wealth of Nations*, persuaded Congress to adopt an excise tax on whiskey to supplement revenues from customs, which were inadequate to pay the war debts of the states. The whiskey tax was, in Hamilton's words, a luxury tax. Furthermore, the nation drank too much of it, so the tax would be a health measure as well. Also, there had been taxes on whiskey before the war, and those experiences had not been bad. Congress eventually followed Hamilton's request and placed a tax on whiskey, some luxury items, auction sales, and negotiable instruments.

The tax on whiskey was an excise. Rumors soon spread that the government was about to tax food and clothing and introduce the hated European excise in America. The excise may have ranked first among grievances that drove immigrants to America. An eighteenth-century English dictionary defines an excise as: "a hateful tax levied upon commodities, and adjudged not by common judges of property, but by wretches hired by those to whom the excise is paid."[15] This fascinating definition, obviously prejudiced against the excise, expresses English sentiments about the tax. To many in America, Hamilton's excise was a betrayal of the revolution.

The whiskey excise ran into trouble immediately. On the western frontier, whiskey was not a luxury item, but rather the basic medium of exchange. Money was almost nonexistent. Farmers would grow rye, distill it into whiskey, and transport the whiskey across the mountains to Philadelphia where it could be sold or used as barter for trade. Grain was too bulky to be transported, so the tax hit the western farmer hard. The 25-percent excise in hard cash was outrageous; it was in reality a tax on money. By 1794 the entire region was in open revolt. Excisemen were tarred and feathered, their houses were burned, and it was fortunate they were not lynched. Even those who were willing to pay the tax could not do so. As one moderate of the Whiskey Rebellion expressed it: "A breath in favor of the tax was sufficient to ruin any man."[16]

The forerunner of the Internal Revenue Service was created to enforce the tax. The country was divided into fourteen districts with as many district directors. Each director received 1 percent of the taxes collected in his district; each agent received 4 percent of the taxes he collected. This left 95 percent for the Treasury. The commission system turned the excise into a type of tax-farming—it pitted the revenue agent against the taxpayer. The more tax collected, the more personal profit for the tax man.

In 1792, when the tax was adopted, the frontier region protested peacefully. There were speeches, meetings, and petitions. At a meeting in Pittsburgh, Albert Gallatin, who became a famous senator and Secretary of the Treasury under Jefferson, said that the tax was unjust and outrageous. Excises were the scourge of the earth. Said Gallatin: "All taxes upon the articles of consumption, because of the power that must necessarily be vested in the officers who collect them, will in the end destroy the liberty of any people that permits them to be introduced."[17]

Gallatin's reasoning was supported by the long-standing hatred of excises by British subjects, plus three hundred years of European experience. When the government did not take any steps to repeal the tax, reasoned arguments soon turned into demands for secession. Liberty polls were erected as they had been in Boston to protest the Stamp Act. Revenue agents were called "outlaws" and an oath was administered among the rebels, who called themselves the Whiskey Boys, to give no comfort or aid to excisemen. Sheriffs who accompanied excise collectors were seized, stripped naked, shaved bald, and covered with tar and feathers. The whiskey stills of farmers who paid their excises were shot full of holes by a kind of Robin Hood who called himself "Tommy Tinker."[18]

The hostility of the Whiskey Boys is illustrated in the story of a local village idiot who playfully pretended to be gathering information for the excisemen. Rational men would have ignored this unfortunate soul, but angry taxpayers are not rational. The idiot was snatched from his bed, taken to a blacksmith shop, stripped naked, seared with a hot iron, and tarred and feathered.

When civil order collapsed by 1794, a judge of the Supreme Court certified the existence of a state of insurrection in Western Pennsylvania. Hamilton persuaded Congress to authorize President Washington to call out the militia from four adjacent states to make a show of force. Washington led these troops. This was the first and only time a U.S. president has assumed his position as commander-in-chief and led troops in the field, in full dress uniform. Fortunately, military confrontation was averted; the rebels surrendered and accepted an agreement of amnesty offered by the federal government. No rebel ever went to jail.

The final outcome of the rebellion favored the rebels. Jefferson repealed the entire excise tax law, which these farmers considered to be unconstitutional. This excise was not uniform. Southern planters paid no excise on their basic farm production (cotton and tobacco); the produce of New England farmers was not taxed; other farmers, merchants, and artisans throughout the nation were not taxed. In order for taxation to be uniform to all, under varying circumstances, should not these other people have borne a similar burden? This argument was never answered.

Textbooks have always praised the strong military action against the whiskey rebels as an important victory for the new federation. But just recently, historians have discovered they were wrong. Justice was on the side of the rebels, and the whole military operation was a political charade instigated by Hamilton to show to the nation the muscle of the federal government.[19] The rebels had already capitulated before the army took to the field. Of the twenty rebels who were brought back to Philadelphia to face treason charges, only two were convicted, and they were pardoned by Washington. Not only are the rebels now vindicated, the revolt is looked upon as having an important political message for our times. Said one recent scholar: "In 1991, as in 1791, tax resistance sends signals of popular beliefs about how democracy should work, signals that deserve reasoned attention."[20]

In addition, the Whiskey Rebellion has an important historical message as well. Here on the frontier of America a courageous group of citizens stood up for their rights against what was clearly an unjust tax under their peculiar circumstances. They capitulated in the face of a prospective invincible military force, but in the end when Jefferson became president, the tax was repealed, and they accomplished through democratic means what they were first unable to achieve by violence. The question remains, however, without the violence would the tax have been repealed? And, was the revolt therefore "necessary medicine" for the sound health of government as Jefferson believed?

Fries Rebellion

Soon after the Whiskey Rebellion was crushed, another tax revolt erupted on the eastern seaboard, this one by German settlers. In 1798 Congress levied its first direct tax of two million dollars on land, houses, and slaves. The tax was allocated among the states as the Constitution required. Pennsylvania's quota was $237,000, which fell largely on land and houses. Houses presented a valuation problem. Assessments were determined by the number and size of windows on each dwelling.

When assessors arrived to count and measure windows, the German settlers thought the government was about to levy the hated European hearth tax. They organized into small bands, armed themselves, and scoured the countryside for assessors, who were then seized, assaulted, and driven from these counties. When some of the rebels were arrested, an auctioneer named John Fries marched on the courthouse and freed them. President John Adams called out the militia. Fries was arrested, tried, and convicted of treason and sentenced to death. Soon thereafter he was pardoned by President Adams, against the advice of his entire cabinet.[21]

President Adams, like Hamilton, was a federalist. His direct federal land tax, like Hamilton's excise, was hated throughout the country. When Jefferson ran for president in 1800, his anti-federalist tax platform endeared him to the hearts of the people and assured his victory. Discontent against the tax policy of the federalists was everywhere. Thereafter the Federalist party faded from national leadership and, with its policies, soon disappeared from history. Historians emphasize the sound money policies of the federalists and their beneficial effect on the new nation, but they fail to point out that the tax laws supporting these fiscal policies were loathed by the people. Many Americans openly questioned the wisdom of the revolution. Because of the federalists, taxation with representation had turned out to be much worse than taxation without representation. Hamilton, as secretary of the treasury, may have been the right man in the right job at the right time, but his taxes were the wrong kind for his cause. And while these taxes may have benefitted the new federal government, they destroyed the Federalist party in the process.

We can now put in historical context Jefferson's comment that it was good medicine for government to have a rebellion every twenty years or so. In the course of his lifetime there had been almost a dozen rebellions he was acutely aware of. Six were in the United States, starting with the Stamp Act Rebellion and ending with Fries Rebellion. All of these rebellions, including the American Revolution, were tax revolts of varying degrees of intensity. In Europe, there were a number of tax revolts in the seventeenth century, from the excise revolts in Britain, to the tax-farmer revolts in the Netherlands, to the innumerable revolts and the revolution in France. Again, all were tax revolts. So when Jefferson tells us rebellions are good tonic for government, in his frame of reference he was talking about tax rebellions. For a nation that believes in checks and balances in government, no doubt the most effective check on a bad tax system is what Jefferson had in mind. He even felt governments should not discourage rebellions or be too punitive against unsuccessful rebels:

> An observation of this truth should render honest republican governors so mild in their punishments as not to discourage them too much. It is a medicine necessary for the sound health of government.[22]

Jefferson justified tolerance for civic disorder and rebellion by referring to a Latin maxim, no longer espoused much today: "Malo periculosam libertatem quam quietam servitutem" ("Rather a dangerous liberty than a peaceful servitude").

31

Was It Taxes, Rather than Slavery, that Caused the Civil War?

The pretence that the "abolition of slavery" was either a motive or justification for the war is a fraud of the same character with that of "maintaining the national honor."

　　　　　　　　　　　—Lysander Spooner, *No Treason*, 1870

The tariff, then nearly synonymous with federal taxes, was a prime cause of the Civil War.

　　　　　　　　　　　—*American Heritage*, June 1996

One of the most popular myths in American history is that the Civil War was started over slavery, and that Lincoln, as the Great Emancipator, drove the nation into a bloody war to break the chains of bondage that shackled over three and a half million black Americans. This popular childhood history story is fable.

At the eleventh hour before the Civil War began, the Southern slave owners had no need to go to war. They had already won all the battles without firing a shot. With the Supreme Court in their back pocket, with Lincoln and the Congress approving a Constitutional amendment protecting slavery forever, they were undoubtedly the victors in their struggle to preserve the slave system of America. There had to be something else that caused them to fire the first shot.

During his campaign for the presidency in 1860, Lincoln repeated time and again that he would not interfere with slavery in the South. His first inaugural address said it all. He emphasized the anti-abolitionist policy of his administration, which can be found "in nearly all the published speeches of him who now addresses you. I do but quote from one of those speeches when I declare that 'I have no purpose, directly or indirectly, to interfere with the institution of slavery in the states where it exists. I believe I have no lawful right to do so, and I have no inclination to do so.' "

Lincoln continued in his inaugural address to assure Southern slave owners that fugitive slaves would be returned. To provide even further assurance, the Congress, with Lincoln's approval, proposed and passed a new Constitutional amendment which declared that the federal government could never interfere with slavery in any state. Even the Supreme Court gave its blessing to slavery in the famous Dred Scott case (1857). All three branches of the federal government had bent over backwards to appease the South over slavery. They could hardly have done much more.

When the Civil War started, the moral cause of the South was strong—they wanted self-government; there was nothing wrong with that. Why should half the states in the Union be denied the right of self-determination? Is not that a fundamental human and social right?

The Civil War was two years old when Lincoln issued the Emancipation Proclamation, and then only after repeated military defeats, and as a last resort to rally the North behind a worthwhile cause. Here are Lincoln's words on the subject:

> Things had gone from bad to worse, until I felt we had reached the end of our rope on the plan we were pursuing; that we had about played our last card, and must change our tactics or lose the game. I now determined upon the adoption of the emancipation policy.[1]

The American Civil War has been given many names. It has been called the War between the States, the War of the Rebellion (the official name), the War of Northern Aggression (as it was known in the South), and most accurately—"the Rich Man's War and the Poor Man's Fight." The conflict had been brewing for decades. There had been a prolonged struggle between the rich planters of the South and the rich industrialists of the North—and it was not over slavery.

By 1860 this struggle was turning against the South. New territories were becoming states and the majority of them were tied to the North. The center of the economic life and population of the country was shifting strongly to the North and the commercial interests that dominated Northern politics. The Southerners believed it was only a matter of time before they would become vassals to their Northern business rivals. They were probably right. Their defeat in the Civil War only hastened the day of inevitable Northern domination.

Most people do not realize that before 1860 Southerners dominated federal offices in the United States. More key figures in the national government came from the South than any other place. The following chart demonstrates the strength of Southern leadership in the federal government up to the time of the Civil War:

	From the South	*From the North*	*Total*
Presidents	11	5	16
Attorney Generals	14	5	19
Supreme Court Justices	17	11	28
Speakers of the House	21	12	33

The above list represents the situation as it was in 1860.[2] If the same offices are analyzed in the hundred years from 1860 to 1960, the number of Southerners is almost nil. President Nixon finally gave up trying to put a Southerner on the Supreme Court, which had not had a Southerner for a hundred years. We have had four Southern presidents in the past century and two of them came to office from the vice-presidency when the president died in office. Lincoln's presidency marked a new era in national politics which was highlighted by the exclusion of Southerners from all major positions in the national government. This was the permanent price of the defeat that the South suffered in the Civil War. Until Jimmy Carter became president, "Southerner" was still a bad word in national affairs to most of the nation.

What were the causes of the Southern independence movement in 1860? In what ways did the North dominate the South to drive them to secession? Since the emancipation of the slaves was not a part of Lincoln's platform in 1861 when the war started, what was it that drove the South to secession and rebellion when Lincoln was elected?

The answer to these questions is found in the writings of the period, especially the speeches of the leaders of the South. The most outstanding spokesman for the South was John C. Calhoun. He was not a rebel and he did not espouse the cause of secession. In 1850 he was dying. Daniel Webster had delivered a great speech in the Senate on preserving the Union. Calhoun was too sick to appear and answer Webster. He sent his reply to the Senate chamber to be read by one of his colleagues. It listed three grievances of the South which could lead to secession from the Union.

The first two complaints were mainly fears of what could happen. They were not a bill of particulars for which redress was sought. The first was the fact that the South had been excluded from most of the new territories. It was feared these new states would side with the North against the South and upset the balance of power between them. The second fear was of the growth of federal government powers, despite the limits set by the Constitution. Calhoun could see on the horizon the coming of an all-powerful national government that would obliterate state sovereignty. He had remarkable vision, and his fears have come to pass. The federal government no longer has any significant limitations but in 1850 an all-powerful national state was a long way in the future.

The one concrete complaint Calhoun expressed involved taxation. It was a complaint that had dominated the struggle between the North and South for thirty years. Northern commercial and manufacturing interests had forced through Congress taxes that oppressed Southern planters and made Northern manufacturers rich. That is why the Civil War is sometimes called "the Rich Man's War and the Poor Man's Fight." Here are Calhoun's words:

> The North has adopted a system of revenue and disbursements, in which an undue proportion of the burden of taxation has been imposed on the South, and an undue proportion of its proceeds appropriated to the North. . . . The South as the great exporting portion of the Union has in reality paid vastly more than her due proportion of the revenue.[3]

Federal import tax laws were, in Calhoun's view, class legislation against the South. Heavy taxation on the South raised funds which were spent in the North. This was unfair. Calhoun argued further that high import taxes forced Southerners to pay either excessive prices for Northern goods or excessive taxes. Competition from Europe was crushed, thereby giving Northerners a monopoly over Southern markets. Federal taxation had the economic effect of shifting wealth from the South to the North—not unlike what the OPEC nations have been doing to the oil consuming nations since 1973.

The first rebellion in the South over high import taxes came in 1832. A convention was called in South Carolina to nullify the new federal import duties. They were declared unconstitutional and the governor was authorized to resist any attempt at enforcement by the national government. Andrew Jackson reacted strongly and it looked as if a civil war was in the making. Cool heads prevailed and a compromise was worked out. The tariff (import taxes) was to be reduced over the next few years to levels South Carolina would tolerate. This was the great Compromise of 1833.

The doctrine that a state could nullify a federal law it believed was unconstitutional had a respectable history. Jefferson and Madison first suggested the doctrine in 1798. It had been used to nullify federal laws in Pennsylvania, the New England states, Georgia, and Alabama. It was a peaceful alternative to civil war and secession. The federal government received its power from the states, so the states had the right to withdraw what was given if the federal government abused its authority. Today in Canada a similar doctrine has been proposed by Alberta and other anti-federalist provinces.

The tariff of 1828 was called "the tariff of abomination," a biblical term meaning the greatest evil. Prior to that time the tariff was needed to repay the national debt from the wars of 1812 and the revolution itself. By 1832 the national debt was paid and there was no justification for the import taxes at high rates, except to promote a monopoly in the hands of Northern industrialists to raise prices for Southern consumers. The South exported about three-quarters of its goods and in turn used the money to buy European goods which carried the high import tax. This means that the South paid about three-quarters of all federal taxes, most of which were spent in the North. If they didn't buy foreign goods and pay high taxes the alternative was to buy Northern manufactured products at excessively high prices. Either way Southern money ended up in the North. The injustice of this arrangement dominated Southern hostilities toward the North. Said one historian: "Indignation against the tariff as an unfair tax injurious to their economy was general throughout the South." A Southerner, a year after the Civil War ended, expressed that indignation in a book appropriately called *The Lost Cause*:

> In every measure that the ingenuity of avarice could devise the North exacted from the South a tribute, which it could only pay at the expense and in the character of an inferiour [sic] in the Union.[4]

The Civil War started in 1861 when Southern Carolinians fired on the federal garrison at Fort Sumter, an island in the harbor of Charleston, South Carolina. The man who directed the firing of the first shot was Edmund Ruffin. He later committed suicide on hearing of Lee's surrender in 1865. On the eve of the Civil War (1865), he wrote an article that was popular throughout the South, urging secession and predicting a great future for the Southern States: "The Northern states would not have attained half of their present greatness and wealth, which have been built upon the tribute exacted from the South by legislative policy [high import taxes]."[5]

The South, said Ruffin, would be twice as rich and powerful if it were not for Northern tax policies. Southerners saw themselves as tribute-paying vassals of the North every time they bought Northern goods or paid import taxes.

With respect to the slave issue, most Northerners did not care much about black men in bondage, any more than they cared about the Indian in the West or poor illiterate workers in factories. By and large many black slaves received better treatment and more compassion than their counterpart in the North.[6]

Lincoln was the most powerful president the United States has ever known. He was often brutal. Civilians were tried by military courts so they could be denied a jury trial and other proper judicial procedures. People who disapproved of his policies were locked up without a trial. One shocking example involved a Northern democrat from Ohio named Clement Vallandigham. He was a "dove." He opposed the war and advocated peace. In March 1863, before a political meeting in Ohio when he was a candidate for governor, he denounced the war as "wicked and cruel," and charged that it was undertaken to "enthrone Republican despotism on America." He called Lincoln a dictator and denounced his income tax policy in these words: "Through a tax law, the like of which has never been imposed upon any but a conquered people, they [the Republicans] have possession . . . of the entire property of the people of the country."[7]

Lincoln reacted with a fury. Mind you, this was a political rally for the Democratic Party. It wasn't the first time a U.S. president had been called a tyrant by the opposition. There was nothing in Vallandigham's sharp remarks that was not part of the rough and tumble of American politics. But Vallandigham was arrested and charged before a military court in Ohio, even though civilian courts were open and Ohio was not a war zone. The military court found him guilty of expressing "treasonable sentiments." Rather than have Vallandigham locked up or shot, Lincoln had him forcibly exiled to the South. He wasn't a Southerner, so Vallandigham fled to Canada and from there he was able to get the Democratic Convention in 1864 to brand the war a failure.

His conviction by a military court for expressing "treasonable sentiments" is akin to past practices of the former Soviet Union. Aleksandr Solzhenitsyn was thrown out of the Soviet Union for the same reason that Lincoln threw Vallandigham out of the United States. Just imagine, the Soviets could have used Abraham Lincoln as an authority for deporting Solzhenitsyn and other Russian dissidents!

Lincoln did not stand alone in his harsh policies or stern tax measures. The president of the Southern Confederacy, Jefferson Davis, was attacked by Southerners with the same vehemence:

> The Richmond government nevertheless grew speedily into despotism, and for four years wielded absolute power over an obedient and uncomplaining people. It tolerated no questioning, brooked no resistance, listened to no remonstrances. It levied taxes of an extraordinary kind upon a people already impoverished almost to the point of starvation.[8]

One contemporary newspaper artist attacked the presidential treatment of Vallandigham and other Civil War "doves." The caption to the "Little Bell" cartoon quoted a letter from Secretary of State William H. Seward to Lord Lyons, a British minister, in these terms: "My Lord, I can touch a bell on my right hand, and order the arrest of a citizen of Ohio; I can touch a bell again, and order the imprisonment of a citizen of New York; and no power on earth, except that of the President, can release them. Can the Queen of England do so much?"

The "extraordinary" tax law was an income tax, which many Southerners regarded as proof of Confederate despotism. There was a 10 percent profits tax and a 10 percent tax on the yield of all crops. This was a kind of "gross income tax." There were apparently no deductions for costs and expenses. Davis was as unpopular to some of his fellow Southerners as he was in the North.

The rebellion in South Carolina in 1832 was a prelude to greater and more violent things. It was the South's first try at rebellion; 1861 was its last try. Lincoln was supported in his bid for the presidency by the rich industrialists of the North. He was their man and he had long been their lawyer. At the heart of his platform was a return to high import taxes, reminiscent of the "tariff of abomination" of 1828. No sooner had Congress assembled in 1861 than the high tariff was passed into law and signed by President Buchanan before Lincoln was inaugurated. The Morrill Tariff, as it was called, was the highest tariff in history, doubling the rates of the 1857 tariff to an average of 47 percent of the value of imports. Iron products were taxed over 50 percent. This was the Republicans' big victory, and their supporters were jubilant. They had fulfilled their IOUs to the industrialists and commercial men of the North. But by this outrageous tariff for the South, the doors of reconciliation were closed. In Lincoln's inaugural address he had committed himself to collect customs in the South even if there was a secession. With slavery, he was conciliatory; with the import taxes, he was threatening. Fort Sumter was at the entrance to the Charleston Harbor, filled with federal troops to support U.S. Customs officers. It wasn't too difficult for angry South Carolinians to fire the first shot.

At the time the Republicans were pushing a high tariff through the Congress, the Southerners were doing just the opposite. Their new constitution was adopted, patterned after the U.S. Constitution, with a unique provision banning high import taxation. The Confederate Congress couldn't create a high tariff even if it wanted to. Jefferson Davis, the first president of the Confederacy, justified secession in his inaugural address by making reference to the Declaration of Independence, then emphasizing the import tax issue. Duties and customs and trade restrictions would be held to an absolute minimum, he said. With low duties the trade of North America would shift from New York, Boston, and Philadelphia to Savannah, Charleston, and New Orleans. This would compel the North to set up a chain of customs stations and border patrols from the Atlantic Ocean to the Missouri River, and then some. Northerners would clamor to buy duty-free goods from the South. This would spell disaster for Northern industrialists. Secession offered the South not only freedom from Northern tax bondage, but an opportunity

THE SITUATION.

OFFICER LINCOLN. "I guess I've got you now, JEFF."
JEFF DAVIS. "Guess you have—well now, let us Compromise."

This early Civil War cartoon promotes peace through negotiation. Northern military power is depicted by Lincoln as a policeman seizing Jefferson Davis on Queer Street (a place for people in trouble). Davis has a hold on the U.S. Treasury, symbolizing Southern wealth and taxes. Unfortunately, this peace view did not prevail.

to turn from the oppressed into the oppressor. The Yankees were going to squirm now!

In the British House of Commons in 1862, William Forster said he believed it was generally recognized that slavery was the cause of the U.S. Civil War. He was answered from the House with cries, "No, No!" and "The tariff!"[9] It is quite probable that British commercial interests, which dominated the House of Commons, were more in tune with the economics of the Civil War than were the intellectuals and writers. The view that slavery caused the Civil War was popularized by John Stuart Mill, the leading English writer on political economy at that time. He forcefully expressed his view in the popular British periodical *Frazer's Magazine* in February 1862. This article was later reprinted in America in *Harper's* magazine. It was a rebuttal of the articles written by his old enemy of the pen, Charles Dickens, who wrote that taxes were the cause of the conflict, not slavery. Mill's thesis that slavery caused the conflict has dominated Civil War thinking in America (except in the South, of course) to this day.[10] It gave a noble purpose to the Northern onslaught on the Confederacy to gloss over the real economic issues at stake.

The causes of the Civil War have been discussed for over a hundred years. The most common reasons given are slavery and great cultural conflicts. The differences in culture were great, but cultural differences do not ordinarily produce a rebellion. The slave issue was emotional on both sides, especially the South, except that Lincoln and the Congress bent over backwards to guarantee slavery in all places where it existed, and the *Dred Scott* decision even appeased the slave owners more: Congress's power to prohibit slavery in the territories was curtailed, and citizenship did not apply to persons of African descent. The institution of slavery was never more legally secure than it was in 1860.

In 1832 the Southern defense against the high tariff was the power of "nullification." By 1850, Southern constitutional thinkers had shifted to secession. Calhoun was one of the great proponents of nullification in 1832; by 1850 he was answering Webster with threats of secession.

The generation of leaders in the North and South in the 1850s have been called "the blundering generation." The Websters, Clays, and Calhouns, who had held the Union together through compromise, were gone. It takes great leadership and ability to settle differences through peaceful means. Any idiot can start a war. This was a generation of idiots.

After the war ended the slave did not do so well. When the chips were down in a tight presidential race, the Republicans sold the black man down the river for a couple of electoral votes. The Supreme Court followed suit and gave full support for segregation. "Separate and equal" was the ruling of the high court, though even any village idiot knew public facilities provided for blacks were anything but equal. Armed with the power to segregate, Southern legislators pushed the black man back into economic servitude, educational illiteracy, and social "Uncle Tomism." If slavery was such an important issue in the Civil War, in which over a third of a million Northern men died, why was the black man's struggle for freedom nipped in the bud a decade later?

Wars are not really fought to free some unfortunate minority not directly involved in the conflict. People who want freedom have to fight for it themselves. Outsiders who come to their aid normally have ulterior motives, especially if the outsider happens to be a nation. The concern of the North for the enslaved black man was more facade than substance.[11] There were economic concerns that were far more compelling. This editorial in a Boston newspaper on the eve of the Civil War is very revealing:

> It does not require extraordinary sagacity to perceive that trade is perhaps the controlling motive operating to prevent the return of the seceding states to the Union which they have abandoned. Alleged grievances in regard to slavery were originally the causes for the separation of the cotton states; but the mask has been thrown off, and it is apparent that the people of the principal seceding states are now for commercial independence. They *dream* that the centres of traffic can be changed from Northern to Southern ports. The merchants of New Orleans, Charleston and Savannah are possessed with the idea that New York, Boston, and Philadelphia may be shorn, in the future, of their mercantile greatness, *by a revenue system verging on free trade*. If the Southern Confederation is allowed to carry out a policy by which only a nominal duty is laid upon imports, no doubt the business of the chief Northern cities will be seriously injured thereby.
>
> The difference is so great between the tariff of the Union and that of the Confederate States that the entire Northwest must find it to their advantage to purchase their imported goods at New Orleans rather than New York. In addition to this, the manufacturing interests of the country will suffer from the increased importation resulting from low duties. . . . The [government] would be false to its obligations if this state of things were not provided against.[12]

It is difficult to see the foregoing editorial as anything other than a call to arms against the South. The North and South struggled over trade, with all Northern businessmen threatened by extremely low import taxation in the South that could bring economic ruin to trade and commerce in the North. The South was going to do to the North what Rome did to Rhodes. (See Chapter 8.)

The tax issue in the Civil War was not a glamorous cause like slavery. It involved no high purpose on either side. The noble issues which both sides held up as the cause for their struggle remind one of the lofty purposes superpowers often profess to cover their imperialism. The point here is that the North did not go to war to free the slaves and the South did not secede because of a trigger-happy anti-slavery crusader in the White House.

For all Southerners in all walks of life, the Republican tariff in 1861 meant higher prices, a higher cost of living, fat profits for the Yankees up North, and Southern money in the national coffers for Lincoln to spend for the Republican Party and its supporters. Secession offered a release from Republican bondage. In addition, it opened up opportunities for the South to replace the North in New World trade.

In Lincoln's supposedly conciliatory inaugural address there was one remark which is bound to have caught Southern attention. Lincoln promised that there would be "no bloodshed or violence," and "no use of force" against the seceding states; even the mails would be abandoned if they were not wanted. But taxes were another matter. Lincoln would "collect the duties and imposts, but beyond what may be necessary for these objects, there will be no invasion, no using of force against or among the people anywhere." In other words, the South could secede as long as they paid their taxes to the North! No wonder they fired on Fort Sumter. Lincoln had given them an ultimatum of taxes or war.

Lincoln's address also caught the attention of British writers. In the popular *Fraser's Magazine* (like our *Time* and *Newsweek*) Lincoln is pictured as a respectable leader, not anxious to go to war. Except for collecting taxes at Southern ports, for retaining federal forts on Southern soil to collect taxes, and using force to retake any forts Southerners had seized, he would not invade the South.[13] It was this policy that started the Civil War, and there was not the slightest suggestion that slavery was any kind of an issue whatsoever. In fact, it was the one issue that most Southerners and Northerners saw eye to eye on.[14] Abolitionists were an extremely small and unpopular minority that had been repudiated in the elections of that era.

The collection of taxes and the recovery of federal forts were intimately related. As early as January 15, 1861, the *Philadelphia Press*, the leading newspaper in Pennsylvania, spelled out the relationship between the two, both of which would, in Lincoln's words, be an excuse for an invasion of the South. Said the *Press:*

> In the enforcement of the revenue laws, the forts are of primary importance. *Their guns cover just so much ground as is necessary to enable the United States to enforce their laws. . . .* Those forts the United States must maintain. It is not a question of coercing South Carolina, but of *enforcing*

This anti-tariff cartoon, "At the Bottom," appeared in a Northern newspaper on June 6, 1863, some months after the Emancipation Proclamation. The tariff is a heavy anchor, "The dead load that keeps down American commerce." In the background are merchant ships bearing foreign flags, showing vigorous activity in world trade. The Southerners weren't the only people who hated the high tariff. The maintenance of the high tariff in the face of substantial opposition indicates the hold that powerful industrialists in the North had over the Republican Party and its leader, Lincoln. If slavery caused the Civil War, then why are there no caricatures and cartoons on the matter, and why are the cartoons centered on tax and tariff issues? If cartoons are the "truest history of the times," what does that tell us?

the revenue laws. . . . The practical point, either way, is—whether the revenue laws of the United States shall or shall not be enforced at those three ports, Charleston, Beaufort, and Georgetown, or whether they shall or shall not be made free ports, open to the commerce of the world, with no other restriction upon it than South Carolina shall see proper to impose. . . .

Forts are to be held to *enforce the revenue laws*, not to conquer a State.

Five years after the Civil War, Lysander Spooner of Massachusetts, a free-spirited lawyer who had been a strong, vociferous abolitionist, wrote a pamphlet condemning the hypocrisy of those who professed that the Civil War was fought to free the slaves:

All these cries of having "abolished slavery," of having "saved the country," of having "preserved the union," of establishing "a government of consent," and of "maintaining the national honor," are all gross, shameless, transparent cheats—so transparent that they ought to deceive no one.[15]

In 1927, the great scholars Charles A. and Mary R. Beard came forth with what may have been the first in-depth study of American history. It captivated scholars and laymen alike. After carefully examining the facts concerning slavery and the Civil War, they concluded:

Since, therefore, the abolition of slavery never appeared in the platform of any great political party, since the only appeal ever made to the electorate on that issue was scornfully repulsed, since the spokesman of the Republicans [Lincoln] emphatically declared that his party never intended to interfere with slavery in any shape or form, it seems reasonable to assume that the institution of slavery was not a fundamental issue during the epoch preceding the bombardment of Fort Sumter.[16]

Finally, the question of what "caused" the Civil War depends on what you mean by cause. Montesquieu, in his work on Rome's fall, said there were general causes and special causes at work in any state, and when a nation fell because it lost a battle, there were always general causes at work which made that possible.

There is no doubt the societies of the North and South had many conflicts which, up until 1860, had been resolved by peaceful means, or simply tolerated without any resolution. But in 1860 the South changed its tactics and saw secession as a better solution to these conflicts and as a road to greater prosperity. You could say the act of secession came about from a yearning for independence, like the Soviet republics today. If Northern tax policy had appeased the South, would they have left the Union? Unlike the slave issue, the tax conflict was non-negotiable on both sides. Appeasement was Northern policy toward slavery; toward avoidance of heavy taxation, enforcement with military power was policy.

Secession was unquestionably the cause of the Civil War. It is the thesis of this chapter that taxation was the most significant factor on both sides. Southern slavery was to be tolerated by the North; Southern free ports were not. The war was caused when Southern hotheads bombarded a federal fort in Charleston harbor. The war was also caused when Lincoln decided to put down this rebellion with military force. But behind these acts of violence and secession itself was a tax issue neither side would compromise. Freedom from oppressive taxation caused the American Revolution, the French Revolution, and revolts and rebellions throughout history too numerous to mention. The War of the Rebellion, as it was officially called, had at its core what has been at the core of most rebellions from our earliest historical records, taxes.

Part VIII

The Monster that Laid the Golden Egg

Governments have been taxing income in a roundabout way since the beginning of history. Indeed, most if not all taxes are paid out of income, although they are not measured by it. When the Romans and Egyptians took a percentage of the harvest, they were taxing income, except they taxed the estimated gross production; there were no deductions for costs and expenses and no allowances for a bad harvest. A 10 percent production tax could easily have been a 20–50 percent income tax by modern accounting methods. The early English subsidy was related to income as were some poll taxes, especially the graduated ones. The first income tax came in the late medieval period in 1404. Unfortunately, we know very little about this tax. An early English historian, Thomas Walsingham (1372–1422), writing shortly after this tax and its records were obliterated, said the tax was to be kept concealed from posterity because it was such an evil. No evidence of it was to be preserved at the Treasury or the Exchequer and, by order of Parliament, every written record of the tax was to be burned. Another British historian, as late as 1803, called it a "hideous monster without precedent."[1] This poem did survive:

> A monstrous birth shewn to the world to let it know what could be done, and concealed by historians, that the world might not know what may not or ought not to be done.[2]

The income tax came to Britain again as a war tax measure to meet the terrible fiscal demands of the wars with Napoleon. It proved to be far more productive of revenue than imagined. Soon, the tax spread throughout the world—a tax that laid a golden egg had been found. The spread of the income tax throughout the world added further proof to Adam Smith's observation, "There is no art which one government sooner learns from another than that of draining money from the pockets of the people."[3] The evolution of the income tax into the practices developed in the twentieth century illustrates another historical theme that recurs too often—i.e., a good tax becomes bad. The income tax, which seemed in the nineteenth century in Britain to be a good tax, with low costs, high production, a tolerable amount of intrusions into personal liberty, plus a reasonable sense of equity, evolved into a vehicle that, if not restrained, was easily capable of transforming a liberty-oriented society into a totalitarian state in which rebellion, flight, and fraud would run rampant. The espionage against all citizens by government, which so characterized the internal security bureaucracies of totalitarian states, found a counterpart in Western democracies in their tax spies. The spy agencies of the totalitarian states are concerned with internal security, the tax police in the West are concerned with revenue security. The ends differ, but the scope of the espionage does not.

The income tax as it has evolved presents civilization with a great many problems and difficulties. The future of our liberties and even our civilization itself will probably depend more on how we solve those difficulties than anything else. This is not a unique observation, nor is ours a unique condition. It has occurred throughout history so often as to not need much comment. The alcabala wrecked imperial Spain, and when the government finally got around to correcting the evils in its tax system, it was too late. The habit of fraud had become too ingrained in the social order. Most governments can't recognize the wisdom of these simple truths: you cannot legislate against culture and human nature. When you tax too much, the inevitable consequence will be rebellion (the Spanish Empire was plagued with revolts), flight to avoid tax (the best brains of Spain fled the mother country to avoid tax), and fraud (evasion was everywhere in a myriad of forms). Adding greater punitive measures to enforce bad taxes only aggravates the situation. The income tax is following the pattern of the alcabala with a modern twist. The alcabala initially provided the revenues to make Spain the superpower of the early modern period; the income tax has permitted the United States to become the superpower of our age.

The income tax has had its positive points. It provided the revenue to permit America to take part in a number of wars in the twentieth century, some good and some not so good. Perhaps its greatest benefit has been its alteration of capitalism. Governments were able to command a large portion of the national wealth and use it to correct social injustices and improve the social order without revolution.

In most industrial countries poverty has been greatly reduced and in some countries it is non-existent. Marxist claims that capitalism would increasingly oppress workers—that child labor, starvation wages, longer working hours, and unsafe working conditions would get worse—have not come to pass. Today, such predictions are so much nonsense. Workers in industrial capitalist states have living standards far in excess of the best of the former communist states, as the Eastern Europeans realized. Capitalist nations have corrected the defects in their nineteenth-century system without the necessity of remaking the social order. Taxation has curbed the accumulation of too much wealth in the hands of the few. The wealth of the super-rich has been broken up. New laws protect workers, and guarantee good wages and working conditions. Child labor does not exist. The Marxists have been outflanked by the ingenuity of taxation and labor laws. It is ironic that Marx was the author of high progressive taxes, which in themselves have revolutionized society. Little else has been needed, certainly not revolution and all the suffering and chaos it brings to humanity. Marxism's most glaring defect has been its zeal for overkill. Similarly, the income tax's most glaring defect has been its zeal to overtax.

32

The Tax that Beat Napoleon

Modern income tax laws come from the British Income Tax Laws of the Napoleonic era, beginning in 1799. The tax returns of this first income tax show a remarkable similarity to the returns we file every April. Even the schedules are similar. You could attach them to your modern return and they would probably pass audit. This income tax law has been called "The tax that beat Napoleon." It was undoubtedly Britain's most significant contribution to the fiscal systems of the modern world.

The French Revolution was a sad event for those leaders of the Enlightenment who had high hopes in the ability of man to govern himself with reason and justice. We have learned much since the French Revolution, and most of all we have learned that revolutions tend to get out of hand, more often than not substituting one tyrant for another.

The government of revolutionary France fell on the National Assembly, which had no experience in running a nation. It had no money and little common sense—idea men were everywhere, but taxes and tax men were nowhere. The Assembly condemned the salt tax and then turned around and asked everyone to pay it until something else could be devised. After this voluntary salt tax was ignored, the Assembly asked all Frenchmen to donate one-fourth of their income to the Assembly. With no tax bureaucracy this extremely sophisticated revenue device was ignored as well, along with a land tax which was adopted. Finally, the Assembly decided to steal the church, Henry VIII-style. Paper money was issued, backed by church lands, but once these lands were sold, the government refused to redeem the paper money. Soon it became valueless.

Fiscal chaos was followed by danger from abroad. Europe's aristocratic states joined together to oust the new republic. With the country in danger, the Assembly turned the government over to a daring, aggressive general, Napoleon. But as with Castro in modern Cuba, the future of the revolution was determined by Napoleon's personality more than ideals and principles.

Once in power Napoleon ignored the constitution, which prohibited aggressive wars, and tried to fulfill his dreams of conquering Europe. Taxation was to be his Achilles' heel. French peasants naively believed they were fighting to end taxation. As the emperor rode through the streets of Paris on his white horse, he was cheered with these words: "Plus d'impôts, a bas des riches, a bas la république, vive l'Empereur!" ("No more taxes, down with the rich, down with the republic, long live the Emperor!").

Napoleon could not, of course, end taxation, but any increases or new burdens were out of the question. In the end, he was compelled to pursue his grandiose military ventures without the revenues to sustain them.

Poll taxes were not acceptable under any circumstances. They were the yoke of despotism. Income taxes were simply another form of poll

"Down with taxes": This battle-cry of the French Revolution proved to be Napoleon's most indomitable foe, and eventually contributed more to his defeat than the Russian winter or Waterloo. The many-headed dragon of taxation is again portrayed.

taxation. Taxes on consumption (excises) were associated with tax-farmers, who had been liquidated in the revolution. Finally, the government fell back on the Physiocrats' land tax. The Physiocrats believed all wealth ultimately came from land, hence only land should be taxed. This meant that commerce should be free from tax or burdensome regulations—what we could call the ultimate laissez-faire.

Some commercial taxes were adopted in addition to the land tax. Shopkeepers and businessmen paid a license tax assessed at 10 percent of their annual rent. There was a tax on "movables." Rich people paid a tax on carriages, hearths, and even domestic servants. Workers and peasants were hard to assess so the government took three days' wages per year. The most successful tax was a house and window tax, British-style, which lasted until 1925.

Napoleon introduced more unsuccessful taxes than successful ones. The octroi, or city toll, was tried, but the peasants once again burned down the tollgates and customshouses. Salt taxes were introduced and quickly repealed. "Kill the gabeleurs" was still in the hearts of the people.

Finally, borrowing was ruled out because Napoleon believed that the hand that lent was above the hand that borrowed, and he was not about to stoop to anyone, especially bankers.

The basic taxes Napoleon did develop were sensible and equitable as a whole, but they could not sustain his military adventures. In the end, Napoleon tried to run his armies on plunder, which meant he could not sustain defeats. Without a solid revenue base, Waterloo at some place was inevitable. In short, Napoleon's downfall was brought about by Britain's newly invented income tax and by his determination to carry on costly military ventures without an adequate tax system. Almost any solid tax system would have beaten Napoleon.

At first, the British tried to support the war with traditional revenues—excises, imposts, inheritance taxes, land taxes, and customs. But these taxes were not enough, even though expanded to the limit. The brains at the Exchequer searched for a new revenue device.

Excises were not the answer because they taxed commerce at the wrong place—at consumption. The bulk of Britain's commercial wealth was with the producer, not the consumer. A tax should fall on the producer, but not his capital. An income tax was, therefore, the only alternative.

We could say that the income tax came in through the side door. Pitt introduced a large package of petty taxes called the Triple Assessment, which taxed everything from hair powder to coats of arms. One British writer called this assessment, "a fiscal fiasco unequalled in the history of our taxation." This so-called fiasco was coupled with a unique proviso which gave taxpayers the option of paying income tax graduated up to 10 percent in lieu of the assessments. To adopt an income tax the government simply dropped the assessments and left the income tax provision. Pitt could not know that the income tax option he originally attached to his assessments would become the most important tax invention in the modern world; within a hundred years it would be adopted by every major nation in the world.

Pitt's income tax was supposed to be replaced six months after the war ended. But by 1816, the tax had been in operation over fifteen years, many bugs had been worked out of the system, and many revenue men in the government wanted it to continue. But most Britons hated the tax, more than the government imagined. The leader of the opposition to the tax summarized, on the floor of the Commons, the feelings of the British people:

> It injured in a higher degree than it produced revenue and he was willing
> to admit that it was a most productive tax. He hoped that the country would

WE ARE THE ASSESSED TAXES.

"We are the assessed taxes." December 1797. Unwelcome guests introducing themselves to John Bull in bodily form. He asks in surprise, as well as alarm, "What do you want, you little devils? Ain't I plagued with enough of you already? More pickpocket's work, I suppose?" The devils courteously reply, "Please, your honor, we are the assessed taxes." The real devil, as the British were soon to discover, was the income tax alternative contained in this tax legislation.

rise up as one man against it. . . . This extension of bureaucratic power into everyday life might be the herald of an all-embracing tyranny.[1]

The tax was repealed by a large vote which provided for the total destruction of every government record pertaining to the tax, as with the income tax of 1404. Burned tax records, like dead men, tell no tales.

There was a strange, and still unexplained, historical twist to the burning of Britain's first income tax system. The income tax minister retained a duplicate set of all tax records at the Exchequer Court, which was not destroyed, though it was reported that the minister actually stoked the fires of the burning tax records. Why he intentionally held back a complete set of everything is not known. Why did he risk his job for a matter that did not concern him? Was it by secret order of the prime minister? We will never know.

The generation of Britons who lived under Pitt's income tax had to pass away before the tax was reintroduced. In the interim a myriad of petty taxes burdened society. British tax theory had moved from the search for the just tax to a policy of taxing everything in sight: "To bear lightly on an infinite number of points but heavy on none. In other words, simplicity in taxation . . . ought to be most sedulously avoided."

One of the unusual taxes of this period was a "tax on knowledge," which was a newspaper tax designed to curb the press. Newspapers had freely criticized the government since Walpole's time, and the government could not directly curb the press, but it could tax opposition newspapers into silence. A stamp tax closed the door of most anti-establishment newspapers. Upper-class newspapers were also taxed, but they stayed in business because their readers could afford to pay. Thus through taxation the government could accomplish indirectly what it could not do directly—muzzle reformist and critical newspapers.

This practice is common today, and has been so for over a century. For years the poll tax in the South prohibited black people from voting. Topless waitresses, auction houses, or any other business pursuit can be put out of business by a heavy tax. The U.S. Congress adopted a marijuana tax to stamp out pot smoking. One day in San Francisco a young man went to IRS headquarters to pay this tax. After waiting for some time an irate IRS official told him to leave. The IRS was not geared to collect this tax, only to prosecute for non-payment.

In time British commercial interests began to complain about the depressing effect these innumerable taxes had on commerce. A new tax philosophy started to develop, which was that no tax should be collected that did not produce a substantial amount of revenue. Since all taxation injured someone, or some business activity, it followed that no tax was justified unless it was productive, in other words, the country

This cartoon on the newspaper tax shows a single page about ten feet long as a way to reduce the tax, which was levied by the page. The world's newspapers today continue large pages, which were initiated for tax avoidance.

should have the smallest number of taxes that produced the greatest amount of revenue. In 1842, this philosophy finally prevailed when Sir Robert Peel adopted a modest, fixed 3 percent income tax to be withheld at the source in most instances. Tax records would be private and special commissioners were set up to assure the maintenance of privacy. Said Peel:

> You must either resort to direct or indirect taxation, it is but a comparison of evils. I have never denied that a good deal of inconvenience arises from enquiries . . . from the imposition of an income tax. . . . A certain degree of inquisitorial scrutiny is, therefore, inseparable from an income tax.[2]

The 1842 income tax was to be repealed in three years, when government revenues were expected to be in balance. Unfortunately (or fortunately), the income tax produced 50 percent more revenue than was anticipated. Peel had unearthed a pot of gold; there was little chance it would ever be repealed; and in fact, it never was. Businessmen liked it because it removed the shackles of the innumerable petty taxes that hurt trade and produced little revenue.

William Gladstone followed Peel in setting a determined course to abolish income taxation, but like Peel he could not find a suitable alternative. Gladstone believed the tax could never be justified as a permanent revenue device, regardless of its revenue potential:

> The public feeling of its inequality is a fact most important in itself. The inquisition it entails is a most serious disadvantage, and the frauds to which it leads are an evil such as it is not possible to characterize in terms too strong.[3]

Gladstone also saw taxation as the Almighty's check on war. Man was a war-prone animal, but man hated taxation, and war meant taxation. As long as taxation came down hard on people, wars would be avoidable.

By 1875, contrary to Gladstone's intentions, the income tax had become permanent in British life. The culprit for this, said Gladstone, was the "public expenditure" and the abandonment of the spirit of thrift in government. Members of Parliament were more interested in spending money than in developing a modest, equitable tax system.

Liberty also suffered from heavy taxation, for the collection of great revenues requires an army of tax officials with great power. In such a situation, the delights of spending cause the politician to lean toward the tax official who butters his bread rather than toward the taxpayer who produces the butter. Gladstone's bread-and-butter analogy pinpoints the problem facing the reformers in our age.

DARING ROBBERY OF AN OLD GENTLEMAN NAMED "BULL,"
By the Aid of Chloroform.

John Bull, "chloroformed" by repeal of the window tax, has his pocket picked by Peel's income tax, which replaced it.

The income tax has become a great compromise tax, even though it was not initially adopted in an atmosphere of compromise. Politicians and philosophers in the eighteenth century struggled to find the most just modes of taxation. In the seventeenth and eighteenth centuries the big issue had been "consent." But consent did not guarantee fairness— that was the painful lesson of the eighteenth century when class warfare raged in Parliament over tax privileges. In France, where the monarchy was supreme, this same class warfare raged in the king's court. Both systems produced taxes that overburdened some and underburdened others.

By the end of the eighteenth century, philosophers of the Enlightenment reverted to the ancient Greek concept that a just tax must fall proportionately upon the revenues and wealth of a nation, except for the poor who should be tax-exempt or pay very little. There should be no other exemptions. This theory was sound enough, but administrative problems were insurmountable. The invasions of privacy necessary to properly assess a wealth tax were unacceptable to a society romantically in love with liberty. A modest hearth tax was called slavery, and it almost drove Britain to revolution when a tax inspector was only required to enter a building and count the number of fireplaces. A restricted inspection of income under careful limitations was unquestionably as far as any politician dare go in Britain. In France, no politician would dare go that far. The guillotine was still well greased for unpopular tax men. The search for the just tax stopped. Tax makers became practical. Would a tax hurt trade? Would it be accepted by the people? These issues, rather than philosophical ideals, would dominate tax-making right up to the present day.

The income tax was not only a compromise form of wealth taxation, but it was an alternative to the Physiocrats' land tax. The wealth of a nation can best be measured by its income, not its land. Land ignores commerce, money, personal property, and income from labor and services. The income tax only misses non-income-producing property. But this is not a serious problem; no one would intentionally acquire property to avoid a 10 percent income tax. In other words, no one would give up 90 cents to save 10 cents; so argued the proponents of the income tax.

There were commercial benefits. The income tax was an alternative to increases in customs, excises, and stamps—the natural burdens of trade. For all its imperfections the income tax was the best form of taxation yet devised. Finally, as the years passed, the fears of the early critics proved groundless. The leading economic scholar of 1911, Professor Seligman, pointed out in his classic study of income taxation that after a hundred years the income tax never exceeded 6 percent, and the "early complaints against the inquisitorial character of the tax have long since well-nigh completely disappeared."[4] That observation, of course, looks ludicrous today. But in 1911, how could one have predicted otherwise?

During the nineteenth century the German states were also experimenting with income taxation. Unlike the British, the Prussian system summoned taxpayers before revenue authorities for examination. All taxpayers were required to declare and pay their tax. Prussian surveillance was so extensive that one German legislator declared, "The country is covered with a perfect system of espionage." But Prussian oppression was of no concern to the democratic West. Seligman dismissed the Prussian system as an aberration. Such an inquisitorial system "would be impracticable almost anywhere else . . . nowhere else are the people so meek in the face of officialdom. In no other country in the world would it be possible to enforce so inquisitional a procedure as we have learned to be customary in Prussia."[5]

In a few short years this observation by the leading tax expert in America would be contrary to the course of development of almost every income tax system in the world. The very worst fears of the alarmist in the Napoleonic era would come to pass. The spirit of Britain's modest income tax law would become outmoded and unworkable;

The Germans like cartoons depicting taxpayers being crushed in one form or another. This cartoon dealing with the income tax in Germany in the nineteenth century involved a tax rate of 8 percent maximum. The burdens were the result more of the way the tax was administered than of the rates.

A hundred years later (1967), a German taxpayer is again crushed by a huge press. German readers should recognize Chancellor Kiesinger with the bucket and the Ministers of Finance (Strauss) and Economics (Schiller) turning the screw. The caption reads: "Wait, and you will have a second economic miracle."

while the spirit of the Prussian income tax system would soon infect every high tax nation on earth. In short, the British invented the form of our modern income tax laws, but the Prussians gave us the muscle by which they now operate.

The French income tax story followed a course unlike that in Britain. Even though the income tax was the tax that beat Napoleon, it wasn't until the middle of World War I that the French got around to adopting the British income tax system. The main reason can be traced back to the French Revolution, which was a revolution rooted in a rotten tax system. As bad as the Revolution was with its overtime operation of the head slicer and the psychopaths who for a time directed that homicidal monster, it did produce a revulsion to bad taxes that lasted a hundred years. The French debated, proposed, discussed, and cussed the income tax throughout the nineteenth century. The progressive rate idea was an outrage of injustice and they would have no part of it; the inquisition the tax required was no less outrageous and they wanted no part of that either. So no matter how productive the tax may be, they would be defeating the very purpose of the Revolution if such a monster were instituted.

Since the Revolution and after Napoleon, the French did have an income tax of sorts, but most of all they had principles of taxation that had to be followed. The income tax would have to comply with those principles:

1. A tax must be on a thing, not a person.
2. It was, so far as possible, an estimated income tax. The taxable income was not the exact or true income, but a mean income, the average income of a given estate or a given business over a span of years.
3. The taxable income was ascertained from without, by means of external signs (how prosperous one looked), in other words, your presumed income. The idea of a declaration setting forth your income, with punitive provisions, was to the Frenchmen, intolerable, an interference with the liberty of the citizen.

In short, the tax system bore a strong sense of individualism that was founded on the ideas of the Revolution. It was a system of taxation made for a nation of small proprietors, of manufacturers and traders on a small or moderate scale, each one firmly entrenched in his farm, shop, or business, and very jealous of his rights and looking on the State as an enemy. It involved, most of all, the minimum of contact between the tax man and the taxpayer, with a maximum of freedom for the latter. For a century, until the harsh demands of World War I, France actually did what is usually the impossible—they made the tax system subordinate to liberty. The Great War ended all that. By the War's end, the Frenchman had his income tax form with the usual array of "schedules" that British style income taxation requires.

It was during this anti-income tax period that the French gave to America the Statue of Liberty. At that time both the Americans and the French looked upon inquisitional income taxation as anathema to liberty. One wonders, would the nineteenth-century Frenchman have made such a gift if America had had an inquisitional tax in operation then, as it does today?

33

Scaffolding for Plunder

If the graduated system of 1 per cent to 80 per cent is not a "scaffolding for plunder" I should like to know what it is.
　　　—James Coffield, *A Popular History of Taxation* (London, 1970)

The year 1894 may have been civilization's most important tax year. Britain adopted new death duties with progressive rates, and the United States adopted an income tax. The progressive rates in Britain soon applied to income taxation everywhere. The taxing habits of civilization would never be the same again. In the United States the income tax and the estate tax would soon revolutionize society. The connection between the real 1894 and Orwell's fictitious 1984 may turn out to be more than a transposition of numbers. If Orwell's society, with its all-seeing Big Brother, comes to Western civilization, the roots of that monster may be traced to the tax laws of 1894.

We have two distinct forms of death taxation—inheritance taxes and estate taxes or death duties. An estate tax or duty is levied against the estate of a deceased person, with little regard for the beneficiaries. In contrast, an inheritance tax looks at the beneficiaries and taxes them at varying rates depending on their kinship to the deceased.

Modern inheritance taxes came from the Dutch, who patterned their taxes after the Romans. Children and wives were exempt; brothers were taxed at 5 percent; and the rates increased for more distant relatives. Strangers paid 30 percent. Dutch style inheritance taxes were copied by the British to finance the war against American independence. The British prime minister, Lord North, was a disciple of Adam Smith, who espoused inheritance taxation. Parliament fixed the tax rates at 2 percent for legacies to brothers and 6 percent for gifts to strangers. This tax only applied to bequests of personal property, not real property, thus it is sometimes called a legacy tax. Later, children were taxed at 1 percent as the rates increased for everyone else with a 10 percent tax for strangers at the top of the scale. It is remarkable that this format has been copied almost word for word in the inheritance laws in most of the states in the United States. Outside the United States, inheritance taxes have been of mixed importance. Many countries, such as Canada and Australia, have abandoned them.

Estate taxes were popular in the Middle Ages. A 25 percent estate tax was not uncommon against a wealthy Jew. Peasants gave their lords the best cow of a deceased member of their household. As we observed, the cow was usually given back to the peasants as a gesture of good will and common sense. In the higher reaches of medieval society, the heirs of a nobleman paid the king a year's income from their inherited lands. In return, the king bestowed aristocratic status on the heirs.

Modern estate taxation is of British origin. The tax can be traced to the Stamp Act of 1694. Legal documents required stamp taxes and this included the "Letters" of an executor. "Letters Testamentary" were issued to every executor by a probate court, pursuant to a directive in a will. Executors were required to affix a revenue stamp on their letters of appointment. In 1853, Gladstone tried to rid the nation of income taxation by making the stamp tax for executors more productive and equitable. By 1881, the executor's stamp tax became an estate duty. A tax of 3 percent of the value of an estate became the rate for the new tax. Real property was valued at its rental value rather than its true value. The scope of the tax was expanded to cover trusts, joint tenancy estates, and life estates. With these changes the modern estate tax was just a step away.

In 1894, Sir William Harcourt finished what Gladstone started. All property was valued for what it was worth at progressive rates ranging from 1 to 8 percent. The basic format for Harcourt's Estate Duty has remained unchanged and has been copied in the United States. The top rates are now 55 percent in the United States and even higher in Britain. This direct wealth tax is a Grim Reaper for the super-rich. The only way great wealth can survive is through careful estate tax planning. In Europe, rich Englishmen take up residence in a tax haven, such as Jersey or Monaco. In the United States, private foundations were a favorite. The foundation permitted the heirs of a wealthy estate to manage the holdings of the estate for charitable purposes, but with a considerable amount of latitude and discretion in managing these funds and properties. In 1969 Congress required private foundations to act like public charities. Detailed regulations and tax penalties were enacted to prohibit the foundation from becoming a family show. The super-rich in America who established private foundations discovered that they had walked into a trap. Wealthy Europeans in tax havens had absolute ownership over all their family wealth, while rich American families had lost everything by trusting in the benevolence of the Congress.

The income tax in Britain in the Napoleonic era had progressive rates. When Peel and Gladstone restored income taxation they used a single rate for everyone; otherwise, the law would never have passed. They sweetened the administration of the tax by providing for withholding at the source whenever possible. When Harcourt asked for progressive rates on estate duties, the question asked in Parliament was: Did the honorable Chancellor intend to introduce progressive rates for the income tax as well? Harcourt said no—emphatically no! Withholding at the source accounted for 75 percent of all income taxes, which eliminated much of the evil inherent in income tax administration. If rates were progressive, the benefits of withholding would be lost:

> There is no inquisitional prying into the ways and means of each individual. You do not demand the sight of his cash book or his pass book but the tax is deducted in the majority of cases from the income before it reaches him . . . measures of penal discovery and irritating inquisition which requires the determination of every man's income from all sources would render the collection of the Income Tax so odious as to imperil its existence and in all probability make it impossible to maintain the tax.

Harcourt's reply to the Commons allayed their fears that progressive rates might be applied to income taxation. For an estate tax, progressive rates involved no additional investigation or "inquisitional prying." There was still stiff opposition to progressive rates from a former Chancellor of the Exchequer, who condemned the idea with these words:

> But where are you going to find a standard of what it is right to take? . . . I think the standard will vary from Parliament to Parliament and from majority to majority; and the principle of taxation will depend on the wave of public opinion, and not on equality of taxation which has been insisted upon in our finances. . . . I am anxious that this graduation should not become a kind of *scaffolding for plunder*. . . . there is the possibility of inflicting injustice after injustice because you will have no standard to guide you—no landmarks to place along this road of taxation.[1]

The resistance to progressive rates finally succumbed in 1910 when Lloyd George pursuaded Parliament to introduce a "super-tax." This surtax, as we would call it today, had special commissioners and was assessed on incomes over £5000. The rates were very modest, just a few percent. George argued to the Commons that the rich wouldn't mind, and there was "no real resentment against this proposal. . . . We have not made it oppressive. We have made it perfectly fair. The graduations are quite gentle."[2]

Thus by 1910 British income taxes evolved in form to where they are today, and that same form has spread throughout the world with little real change except for greater and greater complexity, and greater and greater progression, until the "quite gentle" graduations have become brutally severe, and consent has evolved into extortion. In short, Dr. Jekyll has become Mr. Hyde.

Congress adopted an income tax in 1894, the year of Harcourt's Estate Duty. The Americans who fought this peacetime income tax had a super-weapon the British did not have—they had the Constitution on their side.

America's first income tax was adopted in the Civil War, and as we noted, it was repealed after the war ended. In the 1880s a populist movement developed among farmers and workers who objected to high customs taxes that increased prices and injured the consumer. An alternative to high customs was an income tax, British-style. Opposition to the income tax was emotional. The famous John Stuart Mill, who was as popular in America as he was in Britain, said that the tax was a "mild form of robbery." Two congressmen charged that the tax was "a punishment for the rich man for being rich," and that it was "defensible on the same ground the highwayman defends his acts." Another said it was devised by "the professors with their books, socialists with their schemes and anarchists with their bombs." These harsh words were not without some foundation. Karl Marx was a strong advocate for high progressive income taxes.

The 1894 income tax law taxed all income in excess of $4,000 at 2 percent, and $4,000 in 1894 was like $80,000 today. As a result, 98 percent of the people were tax-exempt. The law was immediately attacked and challenged in the courts. Within a year it was before the United States Supreme Court under the title *Pollock v. Farmers Loan and Trust Co.* The reports of the hearings and rehearings almost fill a full volume of the Supreme Court reports. It was the most talked-about and celebrated case of the period. In the closing arguments before the court, a lawyer summed up the importance of the case in these words:

> No member of this court will live long enough to hear a case which will involve a question more important than this, the preservation of the fundamental rights of property and equality before the law, and the ability of the people of the United States to rely upon the guarantees of the Constitution. . . . There is protection now or never.[3]

This charge to the court was not unreasonable even though the tax was only 2 percent. The issue at stake was whether or not a special tax

A *Harper's* magazine cartoon in 1878 bitterly attacks the income tax law proposed after the Civil War. The cartoonist shows Liberty with a millstone around her neck and the badge of "slavery," borrowing from the ideas of Montesquieu's *The Spirit of Laws.*

could be directed against a small minority within the country. The long-range consequences were significant. As one lawyer argued, if the rate was 2 percent today, it could be 20 percent tomorrow. No one suggested it might be 91 percent tomorrow; that would have been laughed out of court as an appeal to the absurd. But tax laws which are productive of revenue have a tendency to become absurd. Another lawyer argued that "the fundamental principle at stake was whether or not the United States would be a land of equality in taxation." For, once you decided that the many could tax the few, it would be impossible to take a backward step.

The majority of the court decided the case on the technical question of whether or not the income tax was a "direct tax" and therefore had to be apportioned among the states by population. A tax on real property was a direct tax; consequently, a tax on the income from real property was also direct, and this rendered the whole tax law unconstitutional.

The equality issue was discussed, but not ruled upon. The majority opinion said that taxation which is wanting in uniformity and equality would be a taking of property without due process of law. Justice Field decided the case upon the equality issue. The immunity from tax of 98 percent of the population was arbitrary, without justification, he said,

> Such favoritism could make no pretense to equality; it would lack the semblance of legitimate tax legislation. . . . Under wise and constitutional legislation, every citizen should contribute his proportion, however small the sum, to the support of government, and it is no kindness to urge any of our citizens to escape this obligation.[4]

The great Justice John Harlan wrote a dissenting opinion upholding the tax; it was not a direct tax at all. He felt the $4,000 exemption was not unreasonable, but he cautioned that if it got out of hand and became legislative plunder "under the guise of taxation," it could not stand.[5] Exemptions from tax were "dangerous" and "most liable to objection," said Harlan. There is no question but that the entire Court took its constitutional duty to scrutinize taxation very seriously. Today, that is ancient history. Justice Field's above comment that tax laws should come from "wise and constitutional legislation" has been replaced with President Carter's self-evident comment that the Internal Revenue Code is "a disgrace to the human race."

The advocates for income taxation pushed the Sixteenth Amendment through the state legislatures which gave Congress the power to tax income without apportionment. This new amendment succeeded because of assurances the rates would never exceed a few percentage points.

The income tax law of 1894 was not only attacked in the courts, it was evaded by the rich. This 1895 cartoon shows three of America's richest citizens brought before the Internal Revenue Bureau with evasion money stuffed in their pockets. Hetty Green was reputed to be the richest woman in the world; she held a seat on the New York Stock Exchange. Russell Sage and George Gould (son of Jay Gould) were great railroad tycoons as well as stock wheeler-dealers.

Shortly thereafter, Oliver Wendell Holmes made his famous statement that he liked to pay taxes because "with them I buy civilization." The question that first comes to mind is, what kind of a civilization did he buy and for what price? The tax rate at that time was in the 1 percent to 10 percent range. For this Holmes bought a very stable civilization and a government without a vast spy network to collect taxes. The income tax of that day was very much of an honor system with rates that were fair and reasonable for all. The America of his day wasn't trying to police the world, fight offensive wars, nor was it trying to tax and spend itself to death. Holmes got a bargain for his tax dollar—no wonder he liked to pay.

Holmes wasn't the only person who liked to pay taxes. When the first income tax law was enacted, some paid the tax even if they didn't owe anything. They wanted to pay something towards the costs of the government they enjoyed. Of course, we are talking about a 1 percent bottom rate.[6] The cartoon below appeared in *Life* magazine on the first filing date.

The rich were not so enthusiastic. They were the targets, and like an animal in a slaughter house, they may have sensed that, without any controls, progressive rates would easily produce legalized extortion. In 1894, *The Times*, commenting on Adam Smith's *The Wealth of Nations*, wrote: "When the rule of arithmatical proportion is broken the door is open to extortion." The cartoon on the next page from an Iowa newspaper says it all.

Odious Arbitrariness

> The moment you abandon the cardinal principle of exacting from all individuals the same proportion of their income or of their profits you are at a sea without a rudder or compass and there is no amount of injustice and folly you may not commit.[7]

When Madison predicted in *The Federalist*, No. 10 that in a democracy the majority would over-tax the minority, the Framers thought they had provided against that truism by the constitutional provisions of apportionment and uniformity. Madison's conclusion, which scholars have never quoted, was "The majority . . . must be rendered . . . unable to concert and carry into effect schemes of oppression." There is proba-

The income tax law was the "Law," as this *Life* magazine cartoon reveals.

Initially, the income tax was class legislation against the rich, as this 1914 Des Moines, Iowa, cartoon clearly depicts. In time, it has proven the truth of the old adage that when you dig a ditch for your neighbor to fall into, you will likely fall in yourself.

bly no scheme of oppression in taxation more effective than runaway progressive rates. Our original 7 percent income tax rate in 1916 ran to over 90 percent within the next thirty years, and if there ever was legislative plunder "under the guise of taxation," as was Justice Harlan's concern, this was it. It happened simply because the tax makers were unrestrained by constitutional standards—they became like a ship without a rudder, and there has been no limit to the injustice and folly they have committed. The early critics of progressive rates have been prophets.

Louis Thiers, one of France's leading political leaders of the nineteenth century, said, "In this I perceive a principle. Proportionality is a principle, progression is simply an odious arbitrariness."[8] Another critic of this period put the matter in simple terms: "What would you say of a baker or a grocer or any merchant who would demand for the same commodity a price varying with the wealth of the purchaser."[9]

To bring that analysis down to even more earthy terms, a congressman during the Civil War era made this comment in a debate on taxes: "The tax is very much like a boil that a man had on his nose. He complained of its being there very much, and his friend asked, 'Where else would you want to have it?' He thought for a while, and then answered: 'Well, I believe I would rather have it on some other man's back.' "[10]

The history of tax making for the past five thousand years can be summarized in simple terms: How much of my taxes can I shift off on someone else? To prevent this, political thinking in the early modern period found support in the concept of taxation by consent. Frankly, there is nothing wrong with 90 percent tax rates upon any class of taxpayers, as long as they, as a class, consented, for there is a maxim of the law that they who consent cannot be injured. There was nothing wrong a few centuries ago with taxing Jews at four times the rate of the Christians—providing the Jews themselves consented (they didn't). In point of fact, it was the Christians who consented for and on behalf of the Jews. One of the rationales for representative democracy is that the representatives must accept for themselves whatever burdens they put upon their people. I wonder how the tax rates would have faired if every congressman had to pay the highest rates they put on the backs of a few of their constituents?

How then, did the Supreme Court come to approve progressive tax rates? They did it in the case of *Knowlton v. Moore*, and they handled the problem of legislative plunder, or the "scaffolding for plunder" with this comment:

The grave consequences which it is asserted must arise in the future if the right to levy a progressive tax be recognized involves in its ultimate aspect the mere assertion that free and representative government is a failure, and that the grossest abuses of power are foreshadowed.[11]

This oft-quoted remark has no foundation in history. It represents a childish view of the democratic process. Compare this view with that of Judge James Kent, the leading legal scholar in the United States in the early nineteenth century, who spoke to the delegates at the New York Constitutional Convention in 1821, warning them of the inherent dangers of the democractic process with respect to taxation. In a democracy, he said, there is a tendency to

> jeopardize the rights of property and the principles of liberty. . . . Liberty rightly understood, is an inestimable blessing, but liberty without wisdom, with injustice is no better than wild and savage licentiousness. . . . We have to apprehend the oppression of minorities, and a disposition to encroach on private rights . . . and to weaken, degrade, and overawe the administration of justice; we have to apprehend the establishment of unequal and consequently, unjust systems of taxation and all the mischiefs of a crude and mutable legislation.[12]

Did not all these fears come to pass with the progressive tax rates of the twentieth century? Is not the view of the Supreme Court oblivious to five thousand years of recorded history? To the reality of class politics in tax making? Of Madison's assertion that in tax making there is an inherent "temptation" on the part of the "predominant party to trample on the rules of justice"?[13]

Not all the justices were so naive. Justice David Brewer was a great champion for uniformity and he felt it applied to tax rates and percentages. He dissented. His position a year before in an inheritance tax case was stated a year before: "The tax must be uniform on a particular article, and it is uniform within the meaning of the constitutional requirement, if it is made to bear the same percentage over all the United States." Progressive rates were a vice, he said, because it creates "a tax unequal because not proportioned to the amount of the estate; unequal because based upon a classification purely arbitrary, to wit, that of wealth—a tax directly and intentionally made unequal." Justice Brewer makes the further—and most intriguing—observation that the majority of the Court "conceded that if this were a tax upon property such increase in the rates of taxation could not stand."[14] Thus, in 1898, the Supreme Court would have ruled against progressive rates outside of inheritance taxes.

The first income tax law after the Sixteenth Amendment started out with low progressive rates, with a 7 percent maximum. As was expected the question of constitutionality was promptly taken to the Supreme

Supreme Court Justice David Brewer, the last of the surviving justices who believed progressive tax rates violated the Constitutional commands of uniformity and equality.

Court. The Court disposed of the question with not much more than a "one-liner." The assertion that progressive rates were unconstitutional in income taxation was without merit, having an "absolute want of foundation in reason."[15] As soon as the Court's decision was handed down, legal scholars started hammering away at the Court's position. They were almost dumbfounded at the ease with which the Court side-stepped what they believed should have been the most important tax case in the history of the nation—"a question of very grave importance," said the prestigious *Yale Law Review.* "In the opinion of a great many lawyers this feature of the income tax violates that principle of equality which requires that all taxable income, so far as amount is concerned, be treated alike."[16]

Defenders of the Court came forth with logic reminiscent of the specious logic used a few years before by the supporters of segregation. The bastardized concept of "separate but equal" would make segregation compatible with equality, and now a bastardized concept of "equality of burdens" would make progressive rates equal. If, by a progressive tax rate, the state confiscated everything a man earned above bare subsistence, this would make him equal with the man who only earned enough to subsist on and paid no tax. In the end, everyone would be equal by being reduced to the poverty level.

The Supreme Court decision became very conspicuous, not just because of its refusal to really face the issue of equality and uniformity demanded by constitutional principles, but because a host of state court decisions had rejected progressive rates, as was pointed out by the *Yale Law Journal* and other legal scholars.[17] Forty years later, in the 1950s, constitutional experts were still castigating the Court for its 1916 decision. The scholarly treatise, *The Uneasy Case for Progressive Income Taxation*, published by the University of Chicago in 1953, started the debate all over again. The *Yale Law Journal* put the issue of equality in easy to understand, common sense logic:

> The principle of equality in taxation is in itself so just and so reasonable, and so generally has it been acquiesced in, that no argument is needed to sustain the position that the legislature in deliberately violating this principle does nothing else than convert what purports to be a statute law into an exercise of arbitrary power, which in reality is no law at all. When the question is put, does a graduated tax conform to the rule of equality, but one answer can be returned.[18]

Supreme Court Justice Stephen J. Field, in the *Pollock Case*, twenty years earlier, put the principle in issue in more ominous terms: "If the Court sanctions the power of discriminating taxation and nullifies the uniformity mandate of the Constitution . . . It will mark the hour when the sure decadence of our government will commence."[19]

Finally, *Knowlton v. Moore* and the decisions of that time, which approved graduated tax rates based on wealth, were really political decisions in keeping with the temper of the times. Enormous wealth had been accumulated by the Rockefellers, the Vanderbilts, the Astors, railroad tycoons, and "robber barons," as the super-rich were sometimes called. They were an extremely unpopular and despised minority whose great wealth gave them aristocratic status and power. It was believed that heavy taxes on this wealth were necessary for the health of the country. Edward Bellamy's book, *Looking Backward* (1888) was popular everywhere. There were "Bellamy Clubs" which extolled the virtues of socialism and his vision of a new utopian-socialist society. *Looking Backward* even found its way into one Supreme Court opinion.[20] It is interesting to note that sixty years later, an infinitely wiser world saw the socialist state more like Orwell's *1984*, not Bellamy's *Looking Backward*. At that time socialism seemed to be the song of the future, and the Supreme Court got the message and danced to its tune. A few years before, the Court had no trouble reconciling racial discrimination with equality, so reconciling wealth discrimination with uniformity was achieved with ease. Still, there may have been a little tinge of guilt, for it took the Court seventy pages to rip the guts out of the uniformity clause.

34

How a Good Tax Goes Bad

There is a large measure of totalitarianism even in the freest of free societies.

—Eric Hoffer, *The Passionate State of Mind*, 1955

The income tax as it has evolved can be likened to a dirty industrial smelter that does an efficient job of refining an ore that is essential for society, but which pollutes the air, poisons the streams, and kills the forests. These direct side effects will be tolerated if the refined ore is essential and if no cleaner method is available. Like the dirty smelter, we pollute the social order with our income tax system. We seek a society in which equality, integrity, and liberty abound, but the income tax pulls us in the opposite direction. Instead of equality we have inequality, intentionally and deliberately fostered upon us. Instead of integrity we have fraud. Instead of liberty we have totalitarian surveillance and inquisitions. In short, the income tax is a dirty tax and the more we have demanded of it the dirtier it has become. We are stuck with it because we have not taken the time to either clean it up or develop something better. We are living in a time when we need heroic leadership in matters of taxation and expenditure; otherwise, our descendants in the year A.D. 2200 may be looking back at us trying to figure out what went wrong, just as we look back at imperial Spain and the Netherlands to see what caused their decline. In looking for clues, like wise historians, our descendants will take a hard look at our cartoons and caricatures. It was Ralph Waldo Emerson who astutely observed: "Caricatures are often the truest history of the times."

Our descendants will discover that every March and April our newspapers and magazines carry articles admonishing taxpayers to pay their coming income taxes with a heart that is pure. At the same time, these historians will note, cartoons appear which express what no writer would dare say. I have shown in this chapter some common types of

'Just tell him it's about a matter that's something like pulling teeth!'

With the income tax came a new style of cartoons, which to some degree replaced the more sober caricatures of the seventeenth to nineteenth centuries. The IRS agent becomes the center of attention with his off-the-cuff humor about Mr. Average Taxpayer, as this old Bureau cartoon shows. More of interest, however, are those cartoons that say in pictures what many publishers would not say in words.

cartoons. In the cartoons that follow, Type I makes light of petty tax fraud. The taxpayer has been called in for questioning. He has been caught straining the law in what are petty tax frauds. The agent is a kind of nice guy and the whole episode is treated lightly.

In Type II the IRS is portrayed as an American Gestapo. These cartoons contrast with the previous ones. When called for an audit, the taxpayer is scared out of his wits by an agent who is anything but a nice guy. Even on the street when casually meeting a tax agent, our taxpayer tries to hide by climbing a tree. In this class of cartoons, petty evasions produce terror. Our current capacity for humor about abusive tax administration is a peculiar phenomenon of our age. When Benjamin Franklin attacked British tax men as "indiscreet" and "insolent" he was calling for rebellion, while we make a joke of such matters. Contrast Franklin's remarks with this spoof from the *Washington Post Magazine*:

"You say you made all these charitable deductions directly to God?"

"We've asked you down for a few words about your return, Mr. Cargill. The words are: Nice try."

Type I: The IRS nice guy with petty evasions.

In a sweeping post-coup reform move, Gorbachev abolishes the Communist Party and fires thousands of entrenched hard-line Kremlin bureaucrats, all of whom are immediately hired by the Internal Revenue Service.[1]

Type III, the oldest types of tax caricatures, still popular today, show taxpayers being crushed in a press. This simple cartoon (Type IV) is not a very dominant theme of cartoonists, but for just about every class of taxpayer it has an appeal. It indicates what taxes really are—confiscation of property. And unless a system is meticulously fair and equal for all, it will easily degenerate into the minds of many as legalized robbery. Historians looking back to Rome or many other heavily taxed societies have often used a term like robbery, or legalized theft, to describe the system. Will historians of two hundred years from now use that same term for us? If they look hard enough at the innumerable

Type II: IRS Gestapo.

cartoons, they will find support from our times. Furthermore, if they have affection for Adam Smith and John Locke, or many of the other writers of the Enlightenment, they will find philosophical support for the view that any tax lacking bona fide consent is extortion.

The political cartoonists of every age perform an invaluable function for the historian. In tax affairs, they let historians of the future know exactly what the people felt. In short, we make light of tax sins and make the tax bureau look mean and ugly. Our cartoonists reveal in a

Type III: The huge press and the lowly taxpayer.

Good Tax Goes Bad

Type IV: How we really feel.

simple way the national contempt and rebelliousness of the people for the income tax system we now have. The government is going in one direction, the people in another. A few years ago Commissioner Gibbs hired the Advertising Council (who gave us Smokey the Bear) to try to improve the image of IRS agents. It bombed. In the 1970s commercial television tried to show tax agents as police-type heroes. The series *O'Hare, U.S. Treasury* also bombed.

Type V: How we see the tax man—the man to fear.

Type V: Agents take the heat, but are they the villains?

Unfortunately, the workers in the tax bureaucracy bear the brunt of the people's anger as the cartoon of Type V reveals. After looking at the cartoons, the historians of the future will then look deeper to find the root causes of this contempt and decline. First, they will discover that:

1. Taxpayers were in revolt. The system lost consent.

Historians in the future will discover a great number of books, innumerable articles, and many organizations, all calling for a tax revolt in one form or another. This is unquestionably the most serious and visible indictment against our tax system. The tax reform movement of the 1970s in California left a trail of books and articles and a new state constitutional amendment. This movement was highlighted by Howard Jarvis's book, *Mad as Hell*, a title which expresses the way the majority of Californians felt. At the other extreme are the resisters who are active on the federal level. Unlike the Californians, they have no real ability to initiate constitutional changes, so they buck the system head-on by not filing returns, or if they do file returns, they fill them will all sorts of weird constitutional objections to the tax. Karl Hess is the most notorious and admirable of the resisters. In his book, *Dear America*, he explains:

> I became a tax resister, not simply because of the [Vietnam] war, not simply because of corruption. . . . I became a tax resister, at that particular moment, because I got mad and because somewhere in everybody's life there probably is a line in the real world which you will not or cannot cross and which, often with the sort of sudden anger I felt, you balk at, stand on, and fight on.[2]

The life and struggles of the indomitable Karl Hess were the basis for a motion picture, *Toward Liberty*, which won an Oscar as the Best Documentary in 1981. Hess withdrew from the political life of Washington, moved to the back hills of West Virginia, and proceeded to earn his living as a welder, exchanging his services for the necessities of life, almost Thoreau style. He kept speaking and writing against the IRS with a sharp and penetrating wit. The IRS took up the challenge and sent two carloads of agents to his remote cottage to snoop into his affairs. He has left posterity a remarkable collection of books and articles that put the tax system on trial, which, as he explains, is a fascist organization: "If the fascists ever want to make a real run at this country, they already have formidable cadres in every major town."[3]

The IRS organized a full-scale attack on the resisters, starting with red flags on their tax files and ending with the full weight of arm agents from the Criminal Division. A number have been convicted and sent to prison.[4] Unlike judges in colonial America, the current federal judiciary has not been sympathetic to their cause. Perhaps if they had based their resistance on more solid constitutional grounds, which, unquestionably, are available and rationally sound, they might have received a better hearing. As it is, their "Mickey Mouse" tax returns and constitutional nonsense have probably done the tax reform movement more harm than good. A few judges have given these resisters an option to either accept the system or go to prison. Many went to prison. Whether or not the resisters are true patriots or simply screwballs is hotly debated among the middle-of-the-road reformers.

The tax revolt movement of our age will be clearly visible to historians in the future. They can't help but note the weakness of the movement, somewhat like the tax revolt in France under the ancien régime. It has no center, no strong national leadership; it is, at best, a hodgepodge of disorganized groups that are divided and easily conquered.

On the positive side, the revolt is grass roots and is pervasive among the populace as a whole—it is a mood. It is among the rich, and many of them leave the country and take up residency and citizenship elsewhere. No studies have been made that indicate how many people leave the United States to avoid the tax system, but considering the millions who live abroad and who, according to the General Accounting Office of the Congress, don't file tax returns, the tax motive could be a major factor in their emigration.[5]

With the poorer classes, the cash economy offers defiance as well as relief. With those in the middle, it is axiomatic that most citizens, however law-abiding in other respects, will yield to the temptation and evade taxes when it is easy to do so. In short, the tax revolt stems from public opinion that you are getting a raw deal from the tax system and government expenditures. This is the underlying message in the writings of the tax reformers and resisters, the one common denominator of an otherwise badly divided movement.

You might believe that tax resistance to the income tax has always been with us, and that the current state of affairs is not new. Actually, it is new, and that is the reason for alarm. In the 1940s, Justice Jackson of the Supreme Court, former chief counsel for the IRS, boasted about how law-abiding the Americans were in reporting their income taxes— and that was at a time when there were very few information returns. It was an honor system and was held out to be such; tax resisters didn't exist and the underground economy was of little significance. Said Justice Jackson:

> The United States has a system of taxation by confession. That a people so numerous, scattered and individualistic annually assess itself with a tax

liability often in highly burdensome amounts, is a reassuring sign of the stability and vitality of our system of government.[6]

What impressed Justice Jackson was the rare instances of recalcitrance, self-serving mistakes, and outright evasion. That, of course, is not the way it is today. Fifteen years later, in 1962, Commissioner Caplin assessed his generation in the same glowing terms:

No other nation in the world has ever equalled this record [of voluntary compliance]. It is a tribute to our people, their tradition of honesty, and their high sense of responsibility in supporting our . . . government.[7]

Compare these observations with that of Chief Justice Neely in 1982 that tax cheating is everywhere:

Cheating on federal and state income tax is all pervasive in all classes of society, except among the compulsively honest, cheating usually occurs in direct proportion to opportunity.[8]

More recently (1996) one of America's most respected journalists, David Brinkley, agreed with Justice Neely:

The American people as taxpayers have begun in wholesale numbers to cheat, out of resentment of a tax system they think is unfair, too complicated and wasteful of their money. The so-called underground economy is growing rapidly—people working for cash only, reporting nothing, paying nothing.

What went wrong? Historically, it takes a few decades, perhaps a generation, for a backlash against bad taxation to bear fruit. The U.S. tax makers are now reaping what they have been sowing for a long time.

Some years ago when talking with my grandfathers about the income tax, I learned it was a hotly debated issue when it was up for ratification. There was an assurance by the proponents that the rates would never be high—that rates would never reach double digits. The first income tax law had a 7 percent maximum, which was changed to 15 percent in 1916. In 1917 it jumped to 67 percent, then 77 percent. When these ultra high rates hit, high incomes quickly began to disappear, "as if by magic." The Treasury reported 206 million-dollar incomes in 1916 when the tax rate was 7 percent. In 1921, when the tax rate was 77 percent, only 21 million-dollar incomes were reported. This means that 9 out of every 10 million-dollar earners had vanished.

These statistics on the disappearance of the million-dollar incomes vividly illustrate the rebellion of the rich. They may have left the country. Most likely, they arranged their financial affairs so they reduced the amount of their taxable income. The 77 percent tax rate was, to be blunt,

nothing short of extortion—at least that was the label the British government would have used in the seventeenth century. The British Treasury had the integrity to label taxation that was lacking consent, extortion.[9] Certainly no one consents to a 77 percent tax—even the village
idiot knows that. We are using "consent" in a real sense. The 90 percent
of million-dollar earners who disappeared simply expressed their non-
consent by voting with their shoes or their wits. Not just million-dollar
earners disappeared. In 1916, there were 1,090 incomes in the $300,000
to $1 million range. By 1921, these were down about 80 percent to only
225.[10]

The broad revolt against the income tax—the emigration of the rich,
the underground economy, the inclination to evade whenever and wherever possible—all these rebellious acts against the system have historical roots at other times and places. The meaning is clear—the income
tax is no longer levied with the consent of the taxpayer. We have learned
that the consent of a Congress, a Parliament, a house of deputies or
assemblies, is not necessarily the consent of the taxpayer. When English
kings tried to levy (with the consent of Parliament) a poll tax in the
fifteenth century, the people rebelled, and after lengthy and repeated
efforts to enforce this type of taxation, the chancellor of the Exchequer
recommended that the tax be abandoned in favor of a tax the people of
England were "most easy, ready and prone" to pay.

A century later, Henry VIII tried the poll tax. He also had to abandon
it. After the British civil war in the late seventeenth century, Parliament
introduced the hearth tax, which was hated by the British housewife.
The "chimney men," as the tax collectors were called, met strong resistance. When this tax was repealed, Parliament tried the poll tax for a
third time. Once again the British people rebelled. In a short time, it
was repealed as "unsuited for England." Three hundred years later,
again with the consent of Parliament, Britain's dynamic Margaret
Thatcher tried to reintroduce poll taxes and was driven from office by
her own party after riots erupted throughout Britain. Her successor,
John Major, announced he would abandon the tax. It is still "unsuited
for England." Perhaps if the Iron Lady had studied, or been advised on,
England's tax history, she would have stayed in office, for otherwise
her popularity was unchallenged.

The excise in the eighteenth century was adopted, with the consent
of Parliament, with little resistance until the Crown tried to expand the
tax under Walpole. There were riots and the Crown had to cancel the
tax. A few years later, with the consent of Parliament, taxes were introduced in the American colonies. Again there were riots and strong resistance to taxes without the approval of the colonists. This time the British government decided not to back down (as it had done so often in the
past) and the American Revolution was the consequence.

Consent, then, must ultimately come from the people. Taxation is, after all, the people's business, and when a government is out of tune with the people's wishes, resistance will follow. In a democracy, resistance will take the form of evasion, emigration, and riots. Sometimes a new government will be elected. In California the people took things in their own hands and adopted a constitutional amendment forcing the government to yield to their wishes. When that avenue is not available, as with the federal government, a long cold war of smoldering evasion spreads throughout the land.

A bad tax, then, is any tax that the people don't want and won't support. It is not up to the experts to decide the issue. What the people want should be the final arbiter of tax policy. When evasion is rampant, the government should get the message. A society bent on evasion, as was imperial Spain, will in time go into decline. Sometimes compulsion can stabilize a rebellious society, as with Rome under Diocletian, who solved the evasion problem by force and slavery. In a democracy, that is not an easy course, but governments seem to think it is good policy. Next we consider the second factor that future historians will discover.

2. *Our tax system was a pocket of tyranny in an otherwise free society.*

This is a new phenomenon. The income tax system Justice Jackson spoke about, the system the people supported with relatively little evasion in the 1950s, was voluntary, indeed an honor system. By contrast, the honor system has been replaced with a system in which all taxpayers are under surveillance because of the strong inclination to evasion. There is a cold-war tax rebellion, and without force, compulsion, and spying the revenue system would probably collapse. In Justice Jackson's day the system had consent and was successful as an honor system. Today, with consent gone, compulsion is in force.

Historians in the future will discover that in the tax system of the 1950s no bank informed the IRS about customers' affairs. Interest was not reported, withdrawals of cash were not reported, and nothing that went through your account was photographed and held in storage for Big Brother to see. Real estate transactions were not reported to the tax man, stock transactions and dividends were not reported, income from other sources, as with independent work or services (Form 1099), was not reported. Only wages were reported, and that was for the taxpayer's benefit so he could claim a refund. U.S. Customs did not require a declaration of the amount of cash you carried with you, nor did they confiscate any amount in excess of the limits permitted without informing on yourself. It was an honor system, through and through, and it worked.

The erosion of the honor system began over twenty-five years ago and has continued, year in and year out, until today practically everything of any fiscal significance is reported to the tax man. Before this avalanche of tax surveillance legislation, in the 1950s it was routine for a tax auditor to begin an audit with the comment that ours was an honor system, which is required in a free society. Taxpayers usually responded positively to this. Today, that is not the case, the honor part is gone. Does that also mean the free society is in jeopardy as well?

In a way, yes. Liberty does not exist in any abstract form. It attaches itself to some object. With the Swiss, it is privacy. With the founders of America, it was taxes. What it is today with us, is something different. Consider these words of Edmund Burke, on March 22, 1775, in a speech to the British House of Commons, trying to heal the breach between the colonies and Great Britain:

> This fierce spirit of Liberty is stronger in the English Colonies probably than in any other people on earth. . . . They are therefore not only devoted to Liberty, but to Liberty according to English ideas, and on English principles. Abstract liberty, like other mere abstractions, is not to be found. Liberty inheres in some sensible object. . . . It happened, you know, Sir, that the great contests for freedom in this country were from the earliest times chiefly upon the question of Taxing. Most of the contests in the ancient commonwealths turned primarily on the right of election of magistrates. . . . The question of money was not with them so immediate. But in England it was otherwise. . . .
>
> The Colonies draw from you, as with their life-blood, these ideas and principles. Their love of liberty, as with you, fixed and attached on this specific point of taxing. Liberty might be safe, or might be endangered, in twenty other particulars, without their being much pleased or alarmed. Here they felt its pulse, and as they found that beat, they thought themselves sick or sound.[11]

3. We terrorized taxpayers with brutal punishment.

At the time Edmund Burke spoke, it was a felony, punishable by death, to consort with gypsies. In 1726, the British Parliament passed the Waltham Black Act, as a means of checking evasion of taxes. Death was the punishment for anyone found at night with a blackened face or disguise (the common dress of smugglers). Defacing Westminster Abbey was also a felony, punishable by death. In early America, our most celebrated Massachusetts Bay Colony, in its *Laws and Liberties of Massachusetts* (1648), states, "a WITCH, that is, hath or consulted with a familiar Spirit, shall be put to death." We know all too well about the execution of the witches of Salem, which was no isolated event. "Blasphemie" was also punished by death. We have the record of a case of a woman put to death for saying, "Jesus was a bastard and I can prove it by the Bible." Obviously, the term "liberty" did not include the liberty of religious expression or practice. As might be expected, adultery was also punished by death. Homosexuals were likewise put to death. The tax system, on the other hand, which included wealth and poll taxes, had no criminal sanctions.

With Common Law, a sharp distinction was made between real crime and offenses (not crimes) which were manufactured by the state. These "positive" offenses, as they were called, were deemed to be "artificial" and not part of the natural order of things. It was Blackstone who pointed out that the use of criminal sanctions against tax evaders was wrong, as the offender was "guilty of no natural, but merely a positive offense." [12]

In the former Soviet state, totalitarianism for most citizens did not come from the KGB. The major tool for control over all citizens, like in America, came from fiscal crimes. If a person needed a life-saving drug, the doctors directed the family to the black market where the drug could be bought. The hospital will administer it. Not all fiscal crimes are so noble. Most Russians had to live on the dark side of the law to obtain the products and goods missing from state stores. As a result, just about anyone could be arrested at any time. While the probability of arrest was low because everyone was breaking laws, the sense of criminality was strong, casting a shadow of fear and paranoia over the land.

David Shipler, bureau chief for the *New York Times* in Moscow for a number of years, made this observation:

> From the viewpoint of political control, it must be convenient for the authorities to have most Soviet citizens in a constant state of illegality, always arrestable on apolitical grounds. Tangled in webs of indebtedness, the individual feels frail against the massive righteousness of the state. . . .
>
> Because so much of ordinary life is enveloped in vast areas of illegality . . . vilified in the official press . . . crime . . . becomes both serious and light, grave and ubiquitous. It stirs revulsion and a sly, winking envy. And the concept of crime becomes blurred, disorienting, until synthetic crime and regular crime fade in and out of one another, melting into a vague mash of disreputable acceptability. [13]

Consider this in the light of our innumerable criminal tax statutes which make almost any disobedience to a tax law potentially a felony. Our criminal tax laws are no different than Soviet fiscal laws, with "citizens in a constant state of illegality." As an IRS agent said in the delightful book, *The April Game*:

> I nodded, then made a production of pulling a small black notebook and pen out of my inside breast pocket. "May I have your name sir?" That got him. It almost always does. There is hardly an American citizen above the poverty level whose tax conscience is so completely clear that he isn't scared of being audited. [14]

This interesting episode is not at all unusual because it is part of a tax agent's training. It does show that our tax bureaucracy is, indeed, like a miniature Soviet state with the power to intimidate just about everyone, and this because of the synthetic crimes Congress has manufactured to make these tax police, especially the IRS criminal division, masters of the art of intimidation.

There are millions of people every year who receive income that is not reported, which is the reason for what is called backup withholding for interest; there are vast numbers who get caught now that part-time service income produces the Form 1099. No one gets punished, although most of the time the omission is willful. Not even harsh civil penalties are assessed. A letter goes out from the IRS with a tax bill and most taxpayers wisely pay the tax. The punitive provisions are not applied. If they were, especially the criminal provisions, what would happen?

In the first place, we would have to build more courthouses, hire more judges and probation officers, and build more jails. The criminal arm of the IRS would require an increase in personnel tenfold.

The tragedy of this state of affairs cannot be over-emphasized, especially in a nation that condemns other totalitarian states for secret police, domestic spies, and even fiscal police-type bureaucracies that have the power to punish just about anyone, at will. Throughout most of Western civilization where tax evasion is a crime, fines are almost always levied. In Canada, for example, where tax evasion convictions are about ten times as high as in the United States in relation to population, less than three out of a thousand convictions ever see a jail, and then for short terms. In Germany one of the cabinet ministers, Otto Lamsdorff (economic minister), was indicted and convicted for evading 1.5 million DM (about a million dollars). He was fined 180,000 DM, and immediately thereafter was re-elected to the Bundestag. He called the trial an "inconvenience." Two others were convicted with him, one man was the chairman of the Dresdner Bank. For evading 1.6 million DM, the bank chairman, Hans Friderichs, was fined 61,500 DM. The trial was lengthy, involving over eighty witnesses.[15]

By contrast, tax evasion convictions in the United States, though rare, occasionally produce barbaric punishments. In December 1988 the Associated Press reported that a Kansas judge named Dean Whipple handed down a thirty-year prison term to a lady named Trula Walker for evading a million dollars in taxes. Her husband got twenty-five years. Trula would have fared better if she had robbed a federal bank (a savings and loan?) at gunpoint and stolen a few million in cash. Compare Trula's thirty years, and Leona Helmsley's four years in a penitentiary, with Sophia Loren's thirty days in a private home for a similar-sized tax offense. The Kansas judge is not a rare exception. Recently a

Portland, Oregon, high school coach who masterminded a team of tax planners whose "team" exceeded the bounds permitted by law, got twenty-five years from Judge Robert Maloney. When the coach's lawyers tried to obtain a reduced sentence the judge held fast.[16] The coach too would have been better off having robbed a bank at gun point.

The former Soviet Union and its communist cohorts were the only countries in the world that have a record of similar brutal punishments for fiscal crimes. What these psychopathic sentences show is what Blackstone and Montesquieu warned us about what happens when we make tax evasion a crime: "People that cannot really be considered as bad men, are punished as villains, which . . . is most contrary to the spirit of moderate government."[17] When historians in the future look back at our brutal tax punishments, they may not judge America too kindly, especially in view of the recently enacted income tax law in the now defunct Soviet Union. The penalties for evasion are only monetary.[18] No one goes to prison for tax sins, so citizens who evade their taxes won't have to worry about spending the rest of their lives rotting in a fiscal *gulag*, American style.

Looking at the IRS from the inside, the stories reported by Mike Klein, an IRS agent on sick leave, shed light on the bureaucratic problem. Mr. Klein became an agent when he was about fifty years old, and began butting heads with his superiors in the West Palm Beach office. His managers were "enraptured with case statistics, promotions won based on how many tax summonses were issued, delinquent businesses seized, taxes collected." At home he lost all his friends. "My brother stopped calling. He said, 'You've joined the enemy.' "

Many of the agents loved to "bust chops . . . Some were vicious—they'd brag back at the office, 'Boy did I make that guy jump,' or 'I had that woman crying when I told her I'd put her on the street with her kids.' One agent bragged about padlocking a man's business, and when the man asked how he could possibly make payment now, the agent said, 'Go get your wife to peddle [herself].' "

The most upsetting tale Mr. Klein tells is of the man who came in for an audit and died of a heart attack in the IRS office. "They put the body in a vacant office and threw a blanket over it . . . then snuck him out the back so other taxpayers waiting in the lobby wouldn't see him. Imagine their reactions: You come in for an audit and go out in a box."[19]

Recent hearings in the United States Senate (1997–98) have produced a number of witnesses, especially IRS employees who have told of outrageous abuse of taxpayers by the IRS against small taxpayers who do not have the means to stand up to the big bully tax man. There are even accounts of some harrassed taxpayers being driven to suicide.[20] America, of course, is not alone. Our friendly neighbor to the north, Canada, had the misdeed of its revenue officials brought home when a Parliamentary commission traveled through the country and invited taxpayers to come to local hearings and tell of their woes. Canada's top revenue minister was soon to comment that each day they were to hear new "horror stories," worse than the day before.

4. *Taxes were administered through a massive system of surveillance.*

Historians in the future will have no trouble discovering that our financial privacy had been destroyed by laws that enforce the tax system. Spying by tax bureaus is rampant throughout most of the Western world. One Swiss apologist noted: "Even in the non-Communist world there are many countries where hardly anything private is left free of state intrusions, hardly anything intimate that it does not wish to know, scarcely any remaining bounds to its intrusiveness."[21]

In looking at our laws, our historians of the future are bound to discover the Bank Secrecy Act, which is no bank secrecy law at all. It should really have been called a Bank No Secrecy Act. The whole purpose being to make sure everything that goes through anyone's bank account is recorded and made available for the government to examine. This is something no other country in the free world does. The present Chief Justice, William Rehnquist, justified the law at the time because it would be useful in criminal and tax investigations. Three justices dissented. Justice William O. Douglas attacked Rehnquist's "useful" logic:

> It would be highly useful to governmental espionage to have like reports from all our bookstores, all our hardware and retail stores, all our drugstores. These records too might be "useful" in criminal investigations. . . . A mandatory recording of all telephone conversations would be better than the recording of checks under the Bank Secrecy Act, if Big Brother is to have his way.[22]

This case, which is called the *California Bankers' Association* case, had to deal with these words from a case in 1885 (*Boyd v. United States*), which struck down a tax law that required taxpayers to bring in their records for examination:

> And any compulsory discovery by extorting the party's oath, or compelling the production of his private books and papers, to convict him of a crime, or to forfeit his property, is contrary to the principles of a free government. It is abhorrent to the instincts of an Englishman; it is abhorrent to the instincts of an American. It may suit the purposes of despotic power; but it cannot abide the pure atmosphere of political liberty and personal freedom.[23]

Louis Brandeis, who's on almost every list of the greatest Supreme Court Justices, and whose brilliant dissents usually became the law, in time, said in one of his famous dissents, that the *Boyd* case "will be remembered as long as civil liberties live in the United States."[24] Our future historian will discover that the *Boyd* case was cited over three thousand times in state and federal courts in the first century following that decision. If our historian studies these cases it will be discovered that they were mainly dissents or opinions sidestepping, distinguishing, or overruling *Boyd*. It took a woman justice of the Supreme Court to acknowledge that the Court had "sounded the death knell for *Boyd*."[25] In doing so, so often, the Court was really sounding the death knell for a large bundle of our civil liberties.

The Court has become basically anti-*Boyd*, and Rehnquist has been a leader in that assault. On June 20, 1986, the *New York Times* prophetically observed that with his appointment as Chief Justice, "we could have a different country, one in which our freedoms are less secure, official power less restrained." Polite words to describe judicial tolerance for fascism.[26]

Our future historian will frequently come across references to the federal tax bureau as a Gestapo. Are these comments from tax cranks, a few vociferous tax resisters? Or are these frequent extremist expressions the popular view of the general public? In 1975, when surveillance was much less than in the 1990s, an IRS agent wrote a best-seller, *The April Game*, with a chapter entitled, "An American Gestapo":

> Of all the information-gathering agencies in all the world's governments, past or present, the very cleverest must surely be the United States Internal Revenue Service. That monster organization gathers more information about more people, does it more quietly and raises less public outcry in the process than any other government outfit I know anything about.
>
> It may be that the Soviet Union and Red China can boast of agencies that beat IRS on all these counts. I strongly doubt it. . . . The Gestapo? Not a contender either.[27]

Relative to Sweden, the United States doesn't appear to be the worst offender, but America stands out because of its vociferous love of liberty. Consider what the Swedes have to put up with. Sweden's tax men are permitted to use an anti-terrorist law to enforce tax administration. In 1976, they drove one of their most illustrious citizens into exile. Ingmar Bergman was arrested suddenly while directing a motion picture. He was taken to Swedish tax-investigation headquarters and interrogated for hours. Bergman was so upset he spent the next few days in a hospital. For the world's most famous director that was enough, even though no charges were ever brought against him. He packed his bags and left his homeland. Under Swedish law this Gestapo tactic can be used without restraint, even against those not under investigation.

The story did not end with Bergman's voluntary exile. The Swedish press investigated the incident and found others were treated in the same

Film star Bibi Anderson felt the Gestapo touch from Sweden's taxmen when they thought she could help their probe of director Ingmar Bergman's finances. She too was arrested and held for long hours of interrogation and was even denied one phone call. In her words, "They acted like Nazis."

brutal fashion.[28] A fluke in the system exposed the self-employed to a tax of 105 percent (85 percent income tax plus 20 percent employers' tax). As a result of this adverse publicity, the government that had ruled Sweden for thirty years was driven from office. Thereafter Bergman returned.

Flight and voluntary exile, like Ingmar Bergman's, has been repeated thousands of times in the modern world. The list of notables who have fled their homelands to avoid heavy taxation would read like an international Who's Who. Flight is the number one device used by wealthy people to avoid heavy taxation. It is not as dramatic as rebellion and violence, or as intriguing as fraud, but it is safe and seldom illegal. In the declining years of the great empires of Egypt, Rome, and imperial Spain, the flight of taxpayers reached epidemic proportions.

The income tax in the field of revenue can also be compared to atomic power in the field of energy. Both have enormous potential for good and evil, for prosperity and happiness. Both also have a great potential for destructiveness. Atomic energy for physical destruction; the income tax for social, ethical, and spiritual destruction. Gladstone saw the income tax as a gigantic engine for a great national purpose, to be used with caution.

A look back at what the income tax has done since its beginning reveals it has been both a blessing and a curse. It has financed wars; indeed it was initially a war tax in Britain, and it was the heavy revenue demands of war that drove the tax rates up into the confiscation sphere. A war tax has always done that since ancient times. It financed the war against Hitler, it financed the Marshall Plan, and it has financed many worthy programs to strengthen the social order, but it has two tragic wars to its credit that brought much suffering to the world. The worst was the American participation in World War I. Wilson thought that by entering the war and winning the war the world order could be restructured to be safe for democracy and to create a League of Nations to ensure peace. That war had no such purpose and the peace was no peace at all.

The Treaty of Versaille brought back to civilization an ancient and hated form of tax—tribute. The German people defeated in battle were defeated again at the peace conference by forced "reparation," which was a modern word for tribute in every sense of the word. This tax destroyed the fiscal economy of Germany, produced the worst inflation ever known, and paved the way for Hitler and an enraged German people willing to go to war again to recover their lost lands and empire. At the war crimes trials at Nuremberg after World War II, the defense tried to raise the issue of the injustices of the Treaty of Versaille as an excuse for Germany's aggression in World War II. Edward N. Luttwak, a leading scholar at the Center for Strategic and International Studies in Washington, D.C., makes this disturbing observation about World War I:

> The United States joined in the fight with their fresh vast energies, preventing the natural European outcome of a compromised peace, irremediably damaging the very structures of civilization on the Continent and leaving a wasteland in which both Hitler and Stalin could flourish.[29]

Many Americans saw this and opposed the war. The U.S. government brought sedition charges against people making unpatriotic verbal complaints about the war. There were over two thousand charged, seven hundred convicted, with prison terms as long as twenty years. Free speech in America was in a dark age at this time.[30]

Vietnam was another war made possible with this gigantic engine for national purpose, and this war, too, was a blight on American history.

Taxes, then, if they raise great revenues, enable a government to do many things, including foolish and destructive things. Perhaps the reason Montesquieu favored moderate government is because it lacked the revenue to try to police or dominate the world. The Framers of the Constitution did not envision a federal government that could do that. Were they wrong in that vision?

35

The Artful Dodger: Evasion and Avoidance

Notwithstanding that people in general may not today believe in tax plan-
ning or tax avoidance my prediction is that they will believe in it within
the next ten years. I don't think that the established pattern of government
intervention is going to endure for any great length of time. I don't think
we necessarily further ourselves or society in general by going along with
it to the extent of full cooperation. We have a duty to resist.

—Francis E. LaBrie, Professor of Law, University of Toronto, 1974

Rotterdam houses a unique museum, called the Professor Van der Poel Museum of Taxation, located at Parklaan 14–16. Admission is free and there is a library with extensive literature. It was originally founded in 1937, but was destroyed during the bombing of Rotterdam in 1940. At that time it was called the Netherlands Museum of Taxation. It took decades for Professor Van der Poel to rebuild the collection after the war. When he retired in 1967, the museum was named after him. The most fascinating part of the museum is the main exhibits concerning tax evasion practices of the past, showing all kinds of paraphernalia used to evade the tax man. It seems fitting for the Dutch to have such a museum. Tax avoidance and evasion has a long and even honorable history in Holland, as well as most of Europe. During the Napoleonic wars, Napoleon set aside special docks and wharfs at Dunkirk to accommodate those in the British smuggling trade.

Tax evasion is probably the oldest profession, despite the claims of the ladies of pleasure. There is no civilization that did not tax, and there are probably no taxes that haven't been evaded.

Before the income tax, evasion was centered around excises and customs. There probably was no such thing as tax avoidance or planning.

Reduction of taxes by evasion involved falsification of records, bribery, and concealment of some kind. Usually it involved skilled specialists. Smuggling along the coasts of Europe operated upon a grand scale for centuries. A number of fascinating old books are available which are filled with tales of smugglers and wonderful illustrations.[1]

Centuries of heavy abusive taxation in Europe may explain the lax attitude of Europeans over tax sins. To carry out military adventures, European governments have been plundering their citizens for so long under the guise of taxation that it is understandable why Europeans feel the way they do. Except for a small number of wealthy people caught-up in high progressive rates, North Americans have lived in a semi-tax-free climate. Modest and low taxes for the essentials of government breed respect, and America and Canada have a long history, until recently, of modest and down right light tax burdens. Evasion was justly the mark of a poor citizen. Unfortunately, that attitude is changing and being replaced by the European point of view. Corruption, waste, stupid wars, mind-boggling spending, outrageous rates, and exemptions have all combined to make every taxpayer's fair share often a fair share of government mismanagement and fiscal injustice and follies. Americans are thinking like Europeans because their government is acting like a European one.

It is not as difficult as it used to be to find a forthright discussion on

Tax evasion in the past: On the Cornish coast, hotbed of British smuggling, a cargo is landed out of sight of H.M. Customs men.

this side of the Atlantic about tax evasion. It was once in the same category as sex, something nice people didn't talk about. The press was not very talkative either, for fear of saying the wrong thing and encouraging people to shirk their fiscal duties. The tax bureau is pictured as a tough but fair agency. Those who pay their taxes with a heart that is pure (like Tennyson's Sir Galahad) need have no fear. The bad guys—the evaders—will be punished. This is like news reporting during wartime. Truth is said to be the first casualty of war, and it doesn't do too well in tax articles during March and April.

The income tax has always been associated with frauds, even in Britain when it was a very low 3 percent. Gladstone said fraud was an unavoidable part of income taxation. I am going to offer an explanation that has nothing to do with greed or evil mindedness. There is a naked confrontation between the citizen and the state in the income tax system that does not exist with indirect taxes. The demand for taxes on income is backed by an inquisition into the taxpayer's affairs—his personal life, how he runs his business, and how he spends his money. This is the power associated with despots, and every taxpayer knows the tax system is a pocket of totalitarianism in an otherwise free society. This makes him mad and rebellious. When the rates of tax become progressive to the point of confiscation, he knows he is being robbed, and any assertion that anyone would consent to this kind of robbery is perfect nonsense.

The standard argument that he is buying civilization in return for the tax paid begins to run thin as the so-called benefits of civilization are called into question. This is especially true when he realizes his tax moneys are spent for purposes he may not approve of, purposes the founders tried to prevent in the Constitution; or when, in fact, much of his tax money is being squandered or even lost. Adam Smith's observation that taxes will be evaded and tax laws shown little respect when there is "a general suspicion of much unnecessary expense, and great misapplication of the public revenue" is as true today as it was two hundred years ago, and it will be just as true two hundred years in the future.

The People's Republic of China newspaper *The People's Daily* reported in March 1989 that tax evasion in China is rampant ever since the state allowed capitalism with progressive income taxes. In the past two years, thirteen income tax agents have been murdered and over seven thousand have been injured by angry taxpayers. Now that's rebellion in the violent state. In addition, the underground economy is everywhere. Tax revenues have declined over one-third, even though private business has been on the rise.

"Why should I pay taxes?" said one actress who earned a large sum by Chinese standards. "All those forms to fill out. I'd rather spend my money on fun things like eating and clothes." The state newspaper tells the story about a group of pig farmers in Jiangxi province who stuffed four tax officials into a pig pen. "The masses," said the newspaper, "are attacking, surrounding, and beating" tax men.[2] America's tax bureaucracy should appreciate the fact the taxpayers on this side of the Pacific only cheat, which sure beats being stuffed into a pig pen.

The former Soviet Union is having its troubles too, but it is still on a peaceful level. The Supreme Soviet, which was like the American Congress, did the unthinkable when Gorbachev's new tax laws were introduced. To the government's shock, the delegates turned down increased tax rates.[3] Not only did that take courage, but it tells us something about human nature and taxes.

The Russian resistance to high taxes may be somewhat inborn. A few years back, on a talk show in the United States, two recent Russian immigrants who had become very successful and were making a lot of money, were asked about their new life in the West and the freedoms they now enjoyed. After expressing appreciation for all these aspects of Western living, they started in on the IRS, and stated that not even in Russia was there such an operation that could take over half of what you had earned. The talk show host was dumbfounded, didn't say a word, and changed the subject. In tsarist days, the Russian government always had a tough time with tax compliance.

As a general rule, widespread tax evasion is a sure sign a government's tax system is bad. People will pay taxes, even income taxes, if the rates are reasonable. A recent study reveals that most of the American people were delighted with the first income tax. It meant, so they thought, a reduction in tariffs and hence, lower taxes for goods. "Seventy-five years ago," said the author, "Americans paid their first income tax. And liked it."[4] I think Americans would still like the tax if the government had kept it simple, fair, and modest.

The belief that some people are more inclined to evade than others is questioned by Jude Wanniski: "Latin Americans or Italians or Asians are no more predisposed to evade taxes than are New Yorkers or Germans."[5] A German survey found tax morality to be rather low. A French study indicated that the majority of businessmen and professionals felt that tax evaders were justified. A study in Italy in 1962 indicated that there were about a million tax returns filed, when, in actuality, about 2.5 million should have been filed.

As a rule, tax lawyers and accountants look upon tax evasion with displeasure because the evader doesn't use their services. After all, they make their living doing legitimate tax avoidance, which is often complicated and time consuming. When their clients shift from avoidance to evasion, the tax professional loses business, and if too many people evaded, he would be looking for a new job. Tax evasion not only threatens the state's revenue, it threatens the tax professional even more.

The layman is not sanctimonious about tax sins. He does not see a great deal of difference between the businessman who cleverly manipulates his accounting methods to halve his income, and the businessman who buries half of his income in a can in the backyard. The effect is the same. The man who buries his income in the backyard is better off (if he doesn't get caught) because he did not have to pay a high-priced accountant for his scheme. All he had to do was punch "no sale" at his cash register and buy a watertight box, or engage in some other similar "off the books" technique.

Sophisticated and wealthy taxpayers in North America generally stick with avoidance. It may cost more, but it is safer in the long run. Tax evaders are foolish and lazy for operating "off the books." After all, there is no statute of limitation for tax evasion. Tax avoidance, even if poorly done and vulnerable to attack, cannot be attacked after the running of the statute of limitations, which takes three to six years.

How extensive is tax evasion in our society? Lie detector operators in North America often ask the subject if he cheats on his taxes. The reaction to this question is usually intense, and this gives the polygraph operator an insight into the emotional responses of his subject. Since most people have cheated on their taxes, a negative answer gives the operator an indication of how the subject reacts when he lies. European polygraph operators would not use this question because tax evasion is not a crime in many European countries, and even where it is, people do not consider it a moral wrong. "So what else is new?" is a typical European reaction.

The frequent use of the tax evasion query by polygraph operators indicates that evasion is widespread, but the amounts evaded by most people may be petty and insignificant. Until we have a tax evasion survey along the lines of the Kinsey Report we can only guess. Treasury and finance officials often state that evasion could be in the billions, that a substantial amount of the commerce of the West operates "off the books." These claims should be discounted for two reasons: first, they have no basis in fact, and the government officials who cite them are usually trying to entice the Congress to give them greater powers. An honest and candid answer must be that no one knows how much income moves in society "off the books." Second, most of the business and commerce of our day is centered in large corporations, both public and private. The very nature of this form of business enterprise makes tax evasion unlikely. Skillful accountants carefully audit all transactions. Tax fraud, when it does occur, is often an incident of embezzlement, not a primary pursuit. Furthermore, tax must be withheld by employers before pay checks are issued, and the withholding tax schedules are sufficiently high to exceed the amount of tax the worker actually owes. Our income tax system, for most taxpayers, is evasion-proof, contrary to what the tax bureau may say.

Tax evasion is not a "common crime" in Western civilization; in fact, in most of Europe it is more of an international sport. The European who does not practice a little evasion is often the laughing stock of his fellow businessmen. One honest importer was accused of trying to defraud customs in North America because his cost of goods was considerably less than the costs reported by other importers. Customs insisted (and eventually prevailed in its assertion) that his invoices were understating his costs. This honest importer was such a decent fellow that he wouldn't snitch on his competitors and tell customs that they were all marking-up their invoices so money could be diverted to a secret account somewhere.

One common bit of nonsense published by the tax bureau is that the evader forces the honest taxpayer to pay more. But tax burdens that are evaded or avoided are not assumed by others. If my neighbor operates "off the books," and pays no tax, my tax rates do not increase. That argument may have been true in ancient Egypt, when each villager was responsible for the taxes of the whole village, but there is no such rule today. The less tax paid, the less the government has to spend, and most people believe that the government has too much money to spend anyway. Over twenty years ago an Englishman named Parkinson formulated a couple of aphorisms about taxation and bureaucracy: "Expenditure rises to meet income," which means that a government will spend whatever it receives; and "Work expands so as to fill the time available for its completion." In other words, governments (and their employees) will waste time and money if given the opportunity. Conversely, governments will be thrifty if their purse is small. So that evasion could, in the long run, have some beneficial effect on public expenditure.

Gladstone spoke of the "public feeling" of the inequality of the income tax, which adds further excuse for the evader. The opportunities for tax avoidance within any income tax system also stimulate evasion. The evader is simply cutting out the middleman—the tax accountant, shelter planner, and tax lawyer.

Finally, there is the public dislike of what we could call legalized Robin Hoodism: revenue sharing. The robbery label has been applied to improper taxation since Roman times. Since Magna Carta, Englishmen have believed that taxes are bad and evasion is justified if governments pursue improper objectives. Excessive waste and expenditure is also an incentive to evasion. Many people went to prison in the United States for not paying their income taxes during the Vietnam War. They argued that the tax was illegal because the revenue expenditure was illegal. This point of view has sound historical support, but not legal backing. The philosophy behind this was expressed to the Canadian House of Commons in 1876 by Richard Cartwright, liberal finance minister and chief tax spokesman for the Canadian government for almost forty years:

> All taxation, however disguised, is a loss per se . . . it is the duty, and the sacred duty, of Government to take only from the people what is necessary to the proper discharge of the public service; and that taxation in any other mode is simply in one shape or another, *legalized robbery.*[6]

This was also the American view for 150 years, up until the time of the New Deal. It was best expressed by one of the chief spokesmen for Jacksonian Democracy in the nineteenth century, William Leggett, who said, our government "possess[es] no delegated right to tamper with individual industry a single hairs-breadth beyond what is essential to protect the rights of persons and property."[7]

Seventy-five years later, Justice Brewer, the late-nineteenth-century champion of the uniformity tax provision said, "The paternal theory of government is to me odious. The utmost possible liberty to the individual and the fullest protection of his property is both the limitation and duty of government."[8]

Civil disobedience to unpopular laws encourages the evader. Western society has a long and deep-rooted tradition of disobedience to bad laws, especially bad tax laws. The evader is simply measuring up to the highest ideals of the English tax rebels of the last four hundred years on both sides of the Atlantic. If bad tax laws justify rebellion—and history amply supports this viewpoint—then the modern tax evader could be the most justified tax rebel of all time.

For most people today, the moral issue is clouded, and in the end, fear and compulsion sustain our tax laws. The issue will remain clouded as long as our tax laws are the product of class politics and are not bound to constitutional standards of fairness and equality. There is little doubt that evasion will be tried when the opportunity presents itself. The barber has as many opportunities as the diamond merchant and he will yield to the temptation just as often, even though the amounts are smaller. When the Supreme Court in the United States recently upheld a new law for government surveillance of bank accounts, ailing Justice William O. Douglas dissented because he was not yet willing to believe that everyone in the country was a crook. Apparently, the majority felt otherwise, and I suspect they were probably more realistic than was Douglas, even though they were silent on the issue. In general, sophisticated and educated tax commentators remain silent on the evasion issue, so the frankness of Douglas, in a formal judicial opinion, is especially unusual. It is reminiscent of comments made by the very down-to-earth humorist, Will Rogers.

Will Rogers was not formally educated, yet he won respect and admiration around the world. People not only laughed at what he said, they believed what he said, probably more so than any other man in American history. Rogers said that "the income tax has made more liars out of the American people than golf has." He was not just talking about his fellow taxpayers; he was talking about himself. In 1924, he claimed a phony $26,000 deduction for payments to his wife as his secretary. About all she did was open the mail. Rogers was simply expressing in the language of the common man what the Eton- and Oxford-educated Gladstone had said fifty years before when he spoke of the frauds inescapable from an income tax.

In the 1920s, when the income tax was simple by today's standards, Rogers found it easy to ridicule the complexities of the law. When he paid his income taxes "on the level," he was not sure if he "was a crook or a martyr"—the law was too uncertain to know which.

On the subject of taxes in general, and tax justice, Rogers was a common man's Aristides. He said, "People want *just* taxes more than they want *lower* taxes. They want to know that every man is paying his proportionate share according to his wealth."[9] In other words, tax justice is to be measured by wealth. In the eyes of Rogers, like most people, it is immaterial how wealth is acquired, whether by working, operating a business, gift, investments, or by inheritance. The duty to pay should be measured by what a person owns or possesses. How it was acquired is immaterial.

The most famous comment on tax avoidance was made in the 1920s by a British judge: "No man in this country is under the smallest obligation, moral or otherwise, so to arrange his legal relations to his business or his property as to enable Inland Revenue to put the largest shovel into his stores."[10]

Tax avoidance, like evasion, is an inherent aspect of income taxation. Opportunities for tax avoidance have given birth to a new industry. The brightest lawyers and accountants often move into the business of tax-planning, along with a few promoters. Most high-bracket taxpayers soon learn that a tax dollar saved is much larger than an ordinary dollar earned. A few hours of skillful planning can often save tens of thousands of dollars for the rich. In what other pursuit can a lawyer make so much for his clients with such a small expenditure of time? Skillful tax planning, however, is not an easy endeavor; it often takes years to become a grand master or "tax alchemist."

In the Middle Ages an alchemist was a crackpot metallurgist who tried to transmute ordinary metals into gold. Today, a tax alchemist

Will Rogers, America's most beloved humorist, who said the income tax made more liars out of the Americans than golf had. He must have been excusing himself for phoney income tax deductions on his return. When he made his tax return "on the level," he didn't know if he was a crook or a martyr.

transmutes ordinary taxable income into low-tax or tax-free income. Unlike the alchemist of old, the tax alchemist is no crackpot; he is a highly successful, skilled technician. A brilliant tax lawyer in the San Francisco area, of considerable notoriety, and whose methods are as unorthodox as they are ingenious, boasted that he could reduce the taxes of any taxpayer to zero. There was one drawback, however; the legal fees would often be higher than the tax avoided.

Howard Hughes, whose wealth turned out to be less than the billions reputed to him, was still one of the richest men on earth. He paid no income taxes. An annual wealth tax would obviously have eliminated this absurd result. Mr. Hughes had a large income, but his tax lawyers generated enough deductions to reduce his taxable income to zero. Of course in the end, with no will and no estate tax planning, the lion's share of Mr. Hughes's wealth went to Uncle Sam. The tax return of President Nixon, which made the cover of *Time* magazine, and which almost put Nixon in jail, showed him owing no taxes. The theory supporting the tax planning was sound enough, and if someone had not been lazy in the Nixon camp, the tax return would have cleared audit. Nixon's tax planners backdated a document to come under the benefit of a tax loophole that had been closed but which could have been utilized if Nixon had acted promptly.

Unfortunately, the richer a taxpayer, the easier the avoidance. Howard Hughes's planning was so simple any junior accountant could have done it. The most fascinating entry was an annual $50,000 (plus expenses) payment to Jane Russell for twenty years for doing nothing.[11]

Suppose Taxpayer T has ten million dollars. At the bank this money will earn about one million in interest, fully taxable in the top brackets at about one-third of a million dollars. If T puts his money into growth stocks, tax deferral items, raw land, gold, diamonds, art works, or other similar investments, he pays no tax because he has no income. T now has privacy, security, and a hedge against inflation. If T needs $100,000 cash to live on each year, he will select and sell assets to produce what cash he needs. Most of the $100,000 will be a return of cost—no tax. Gains are often taxed at reduced capital gains rates. Loss items can be sold to offset gains. Ten thousand dollars a year in taxes is about all T should ever plan on paying. Compare this to the heavy taxes from $350,000 to $600,000 he would pay with his money earning interest. Is not this alchemy at its best?

Governments frequently publicize information on large income earners to show that they are paying a substantial amount of tax. From these statistics the situation for the super-rich appears to be under control. What these statistics fail to reveal is the number of multimillionaires who have little taxable income, pay low taxes, and who could, if they had the nerve, apply for welfare!

Nixon's tax return made the cover of *Time* magazine, by claiming he owed only $878.03. It turned out to be tax planning at its worst—back-dating documents to come under repealed sections of the tax code.

36

Flight to the Havens: The Offshore World

The in-flight magazine of British Airways a few years ago said that the Cayman Islands was discovered as a tax haven by "a British lawyer named Charles Adams." These islands had previously been "discovered" three times. First, by Columbus in 1503; then by the pirates who used them as a base to plunder Spanish shipping; and later by deserters from Cromwell's forces who seized Jamaica from the Spanish. The previous discoveries never registered much with the world, but the tax

"Tax havens? Certainly. Do you plan to go, or will you just be sending your money?"

haven discovery could be likened somewhat to the discovery of gold in the Klondike. People flooded to the place to make their fortune in a new land of gold. With Cayman, it was a land of sun and sand with no taxes, which for many was just as good as gold. Most people didn't go there, they just sent their money.

Grand Cayman is only one small facet of a much larger offshore world on which the sun never sets. Indeed, the day begins at the international date-line in the Pacific and there are tax havens there to receive the first rays of the sun heralding the new day. By the time the new day reaches the Cayman Islands, the banks in the Pacific will have closed and everyone will have gone to bed. But the repercussions of what has been done in the Pacific will penetrate Grand Cayman when the sun rises in the Caribbean.

The offshore world then, is a complex geographical mosaic spread across the face of the globe. It is also a complex financial and legal mosaic, with a vast amount of services to meet the needs of all kinds of people seeking to avoid, in either legal or illegal ways, the fiscal and often political authorities of their native lands. Most uninformed writers don't appreciate this and see the offshore as an array of fiscal and legal institutions engaged in a very common pursuit—not altogether straight.

You'd be amazed at the variety of services that are available in the tax haven world. Like a good smorgasbord, you can find just about anything if you take the time and are willing to seek out what you are looking for. Besides services you never dreamed existed, you will find a full range of competency and incompetency. On the darker side, these financial centers, as they like to be called, are a no-man's land, teaming with soldiers of finance, crooks and con-men, fools and hustlers of every kind imaginable. *Caveat emptor*, or buyer beware, was never more appropriate than when dealing in the offshore world. W. C. Fields's remark about never giving a sucker an even break also has considerable application. Consumer or investor protections we have all learned to rely upon are nonexistant.

Tax havens are inevitable whenever taxes are too high. In the later Roman period, hordes of Roman taxpayers went over to the barbarians to avoid Rome's ugly tax enslavement. Nothing very sophisticated, just raw flight to avoid tax. Islam was a tax haven to Christians in the seventh and eighth centuries. The first tax haven in the post-medieval world was America. Historians readily acknowledge that more people fled from Europe to the new world to avoid Europe's hated taxes than for religious or political freedom. The flight to the havens in the twentieth century is a pattern mankind has been undertaking from time to time since history was first recorded.

The term haven is derived from heaven and is not just an analogy.

The overtaxed peasants in Europe of a few centuries ago had religious hymns just as we do, and many of the verses are similar to what we sing in our churches. There was one remarkable distinction, however. The religious hymns of these peasants referred to heaven as a place of peace and rest, which had the added feature of being free from tax collectors—a tax haven no less.

The rise of tax havens in this century was foretold in an editorial in *The Times*, on May 17, 1894, when progressive rates were introduced in Britain:

> Single out the big and moderately big properties for attack, and very soon, as if by magic, they will begin to evade you and disappear, as all things in the world very reasonably do when they are singled out for attack. Even the half-starved crow will not wait to be continuously shot at.

Shortly after America adopted high progressive rates, President Coolidge learned first hand from the Treasury that high progressive rates lead us to "the point of getting nothing at all."[1] Where did the income go? Ten years later when Roosevelt increased Coolidge's income tax by 170 percent, a wealthy American financier told a friend of Roosevelt while in a bar in Paris: "My fortune is in the Bahama islands and is going to stay there as long as that bastard is in the White House."[2] Today, those same high incomes and fortunes would probably end up in the Cayman Islands. There are over two dozen other tax havens around the world, but Cayman's success story surpasses all the rest. With good government, a stable, safe society, and no income and estate taxes, a great amount of the money of the world has been directed into its banking system.

The Cayman Islands began as a tax haven in the 1960s. There were no paved roads. The only communications with the outside world were through the mails. There was a telephone cable through Jamaica, but it was so garbled it could not be depended upon. The airport was a wooden shack with windows of chicken wire. The hotels, if you could call them that, were anything but first class. There were a handful of banks in primitive offices. The Royal Bank of Canada had its trust offices in an old warehouse on the harbor front. The harbor was very small and could only handle little steamers. Today, there are paved streets and a multitude of new office buildings. Over one hundred banks have their own offices and staffs; hundreds more have licenses and are registered there. Corporations based there number in the thousands. The hotels and condominiums are luxurious, even the mosquitos have all but disappeared. In Cayman's early days it was not uncommon for someone to yell "fresh meat" as new visitors arrived at the airport. Within minutes swarms of noxious insects would start stinging visitors and buzzing in their ears. It is understandable why the *National Geographic* in the 1920s called Cayman "The Land Time Forgot." In the early tax haven years of the 1960s, it was still that way, but then something happened.

Cayman was basically an island suburb of Kingston, Jamaica, which was under British rule. When Jamaica became independent, the Caymanians had the wisdom to break away from Jamaica, and become a Crown Colony of Great Britain. Except for sport diving and one lovely beach, Cayman was probably the most unattractive island in the entire Caribbean. Most of the island was underwater swamp lands. They had one world's record. Not far from George Town, the center of what civilization the islands could boast, a mosquito trap caught over 300,000 mosquitos in thirty minutes. Cattle sometimes suffocated when their nostrils filled with mosquitos.

The founding fathers decided to establish streamlined banking and trust laws, modelled after Nassau in the Bahamas, hoping to improve the economy with some tax haven business. For centuries the Caymanians went to sea and could be found on many of the merchant ships of the world. This meant that the men were often away from their families for six to nine months out of the year. With tax haven facilities, this undesirable aspect of Cayman's economic life might be reversed. The men could stay home with their families. In the beginning, few Caymanians could have even imagined what prosperity the tax haven business would produce. Good government, a stable society, and low taxes—an unbeatable recipe for success.

We should compare Cayman to another tax haven which was growing in the Middle East, and in the 1960s had a much more promising future than little obscure Grand Cayman. It was Lebanon, which referred to itself as the "Switzerland of the Middle East." Its great banking center was Beirut. Lebanon appeared to be so safe and promising that even the Russians established a bank there—The Moscow Norodny Bank. It's not there anymore, nor are any of the other banks that went there in the 1960s. No need to elaborate on what happened. Lebanon's chances of ever becoming an international financial center are gone forever. Switzerland's great success has been her political and social stability—her ability to stay out of Europe's many wars, her wisdom in maintaining a stable currency tied to gold, and her banking privacy, which is simply another aspect of safety. In their own peculiar way, the Caymans emulated the Swiss. In some ways, the Caymans are much better. The Swiss charge a 35 percent tax on interest earned on deposits with Swiss banks; the Caymans are tax free.

By definition, any place is a tax haven where money or income is secure, private, and tax free or low tax. Many foreigners consider the

VRYHEDEN

By de Uergaderinghe van de Negenthiene vande Geoctroyeerde West-Indische Compagnie vergunt aen allen den ghenen / die eenighe Colonien in Nieu-Nederlandt sullen planten.

In het licht ghegheven,

Om bekent te maken wat Profijten ende Voordeelen aldaer in Nieu-Nederlandt , voor de Coloniers ende der selver Patroonen ende Meesters , midtsgaders de Participanten , die de Colonien aldaer planten, zijn becomen,

Westindsen Kan syn Nederlands groot gewin .
Verkleynt sijyands Macht brengt silver-platen in .

T'AMSTELREDAM,

Voor Marten Iansz Brandt Boeckverkooper / woonende by de nieuwe Kerck / in de Gereformeerde Catechismus, Anno 1630,

Today we could utilize this 1630 pamphlet entitled "Freedom" as an advertisement for the benefits of a tax haven, like the Cayman Islands. The pamphlet summarizes the advantages and liberties in New York, especially the absence of taxes. North America was the first tax haven of the modern era, as more people immigrated to the New World to avoid taxes than for any other reason.

United States a tax haven. In some ways it is. Interest paid by U.S. banks to foreigners is tax free. Capital gains from securities are tax free, as are other types of personal property gains. When the IRS tried to tax gains from trading stocks, Congress responded with a law exempting such gains even when traded through a resident broker with discretionary authority. Most other countries do the same. High tax countries wanting to attract some of the world's money, especially dollars, have had to get into the tax haven act. The old adage, "If you can't beat 'em, join 'em," has application. Money has no allegiance except to safety and profitability. Tax havens, like Cayman, keep growing and getting richer because they outclass the competition. That is just good business. There is a lot of money out in the world's no-man's land—the Euro-dollars and the petro-dollars—and it goes to the highest bidder and safest bidder. For a time, the U.S. government made a move to try to attract much of that money by repealing income taxes on interest earned on bank accounts and government bonds. Unfortunately, they were outclassed by the competition and fell far short of what could have been done. They refused to give blanket approval to bearer instruments because they might be used to evade U.S. taxes. Evaders have a great market out there and hardly need U.S. securities. Canadian governments and literally hundreds of the world's biggest and most secure corporations issue bearer bonds in the offshore world.

Money in tax havens, as well as securities, are not physically in the haven. Tax haven banks transmit the money to New York, London, Zurich, Luxembourg, Paris, or other financial centers. If U.S. dollars are involved, sooner or later they come home. The tax haven simply brings them home in a manner that protects the privacy of the depositor, provides interest tax free, and does so from a stable base country; the more stability the better, which is why the Cayman Islands have been so attractive. Tax havens aren't going to go away; the economics makes that a certainty, and history confirms it. In short, the high progressive rates created tax havens, and now the many high-tax governments of the world are having to reap what they sowed. Flight to avoid tax is still, as it has been for thousands of years, the inevitable response to governments that tax too much.

Capital flight to avoid tax or exchange controls is only one of the uses for tax havens. Major corporations around the world have discovered these financial centers. International finance, banking, sales, royalties, licenses, insurance—just about every kind of taxable transaction imaginable can be developed in a tax haven to legitimately reduce taxes. One senior IRS attorney acknowledged that there were "millions of dollars in taxes that could be saved quite legitimately utilizing the Cayman Islands,"[3] and then he confided in me that after thirty years with the IRS he wanted to retire and go into the tax haven, tax planning business.

Most people who flee to tax havens do so because they are fed-up with the fiscal or tax laws of their homelands. The multimillionaire industrialist E. P. Taylor moved to the Bahamas to "avoid Canada's harsh winters." Everyone really knows he left to avoid Canada's harsh taxes. The tennis champion from Sweden, Bjorn Borg, and his fellow countryman, Ingemar Stenmark, the great skier, both left Sweden for Monaco for obvious reasons.

Tax haven refugees report that they are tired of fighting the tax man (a point Adam Smith emphasized). They have had enough of audits, year in and year out, of having their banking and accounting records picked over and questioned. They are tired of having their privacy totally destroyed by inquisitional tax agents. They are tired of appeals, big fees for tax professionals, and endless tax litigation. Many complain that the soak-the-rich philosophy of their homelands was not as intolerable as the harassment and scorn they receive from revenue bureaucrats. This was the complaint of Sweden's great director, Ingmar Bergman. He was willing to live with Sweden's high taxes, but not with the Gestapo tactics of Sweden's tax men.

The Rolling Stones on the Laffer Curve

In 1971 the Rolling Stones left England. In 1988 they explained why to a *Washington Post* writer:

> In 1971 we were forced to make a decision courtesy of the British government—live in England and [because of high taxes] not be able to afford another set of guitar strings, or move and keep the band together, Hence "Exile on Main Street."[4]

This exodus, or "Exile on Main Street" has been repeated by wealthy musicians, athletes, businessmen, investors, actors, writers, inventors— just about anyone in any field who has risen to the top. The loss their countries suffer by driving out this wealth and talent is considerable and is an aspect of the famous Laffer curve in full operation. The Laffer curve is a graphic illustration of what happens when a government taxes excessively. It shows that government will increasingly reap less and less, until it receives nothing when rates reach 100 percent.[5]

The Laffer curve only illustrates part of the revenue loss, and a small part at that, when wealthy income earners like the Rolling Stones leave the country. The many workers and businesses that serviced the Rolling

"Losses at home, profits abroad" is an old term used by tax planners depicted here. Business transactions are arranged between related companies for tax avoidance. Intercompany pricing can shift income from high tax areas, like the United States, to low or no tax areas. The Japanese are masters at this, and they have retained the former top brass of the IRS to represent them. The *Wall Street Journal*, on October 18, 1991, reported that ex-commissioner Gibbs is among the professionals looking out for the Japanese.

Stones lost a valuable customer. The income they would have earned from the Stones is lost to them and to the British tax man. In the end, the policy of Britain's socialist governments of "soaking the rich" didn't work at all. It backfired, and in the end was an economic and even cultural disaster on all fronts.

Tax havens are not all bad even for the U.S. government. In fact, they may be like a rose with a small thorn. The thorn being the tax loss. The rose part more than offsets the thorn. Let me explain.

A large portion of the investment capital and banking entering the United States comes from countries, not only with exchange controls,

— Drawing by Allan Bunce

While the income tax began as a modest form of class tax legislation against the rich, with the introduction of graduated rates it soon became a grim reaper for the rich as this cartoon illustrates rather dramatically. The rich are seen running from the tax man, and over the century they made a good run at it—secreting their wealth or changing their abode to places where the grim reaper has been kept at bay.

but in violation of those controls. And how does this hot exchange control cash get here? Via the hundreds of banks in Grand Cayman, Nassau, Hong Kong, and a score of other tax haven banking centers scattered around the world. This is what most of these banks are doing, and why the U.S. Fed permits American banks to have offshore branches—the country needs the money.

Even with harsh criminal penalties, there is no indication that the flow of this hot, flight capital is abating, and the U.S. Treasury would be the first to admit that this all-important recycling is made easier by the existence of tax haven banks and secrecy laws. You never hear a word about the U.S. government cracking down on exchange control evaders.

Exchange controls are a well-known device for governments to cover up their fiscal follies—too much government expenditure, and monetary carelessness. Most of the Third World countries in heavy debt to the West have exchange controls. The American government should not, and does not, have any qualms about aiding exchange control violators, since those controls too often are used for purposes which run counter to the vital interest of the United States and the West.

Major U.S. periodicals have all described in detail the recycling back of U.S. dollars to counteract our imbalance of payments abroad, and keep interest rates from going out of sight and our currency healthy. What these periodicals have been silent about is that exchange controls exist in most countries and would block recycling were it not for the tax haven world.

Exchange controls do more than restrict the conversion of local money into foreign currency, like the exchange of shekels into dollars. Exchange control authorities are powerful dictators who regulate all commerce with aliens. A resident often cannot enter into any commercial transactions with foreigners without exchange control permission; even money for travel abroad is restricted. This dictatorship decides if it is in the best interest of the country for you to buy Swiss cheese, Dutch cheese, or Goodyear tires. There is no appeal if they say no.

Not only are these controls arbitrary and at times oppressive, the penalties for disobedience can be vicious. Many American travelers are not aware of this. When they exchange their money for a higher rate with the bellhop, they may end up in jail. The horror stories that follow arrests are filled with tales of bribery, fines, and dirty jails. On occasion an unsuspecting American may be set up by the bellhop, who shares in the bribery funds paid for his freedom.

People living in exchange control countries usually have governments that grossly mismanage their currency; otherwise they wouldn't need exchange controls. These controls are designed to prevent people from taking steps to protect themselves from their government's misfeasance.

All local residents can do is watch their money decline in value, month after month. In such a hopeless situation, the best solution is self-help by smuggling or otherwise transferring your money to a tax haven where your privacy is assured and the money can be converted into dollars or hard currencies.

Anytime you find a wealthy family living in a country with exchange controls, where the currency is in chronic decline because the government mismanages its financial affairs, with severe inflation, you can be certain that family will have substantial wealth socked-away in a tax-haven country. Dangerous? Of course, but that is a fact of life they have to live with, and have probably done so for generations. And if you add heavy taxation to this scenario, or political instability with its inherent danger of confiscation, it is a certainty there will be a secret account somewhere, overseas. Indeed, the bulk of Swiss accounts, as elsewhere, are maintained by people trying to protect their wealth from exchange controls more than confiscatory taxes. Tax benefits are often secondary.

Consider the plight of a Peruvian family whose lands were about to be confiscated. Exchange controls prohibited them from taking their money and valuable personal property out of the country. What can they do? Legally—nothing. So they take all their money and personal wealth and hide it in their car and cross the border with nothing more than their lunch for a picnic on a Sunday afternoon outing. They are let through, but they keep going, abandoning everything, never to return. They only have the clothes on their backs, because suitcases with clothing would have blown their cover. They continue on to Panama and deposit their funds in Panama's tax-haven banks. The government took their lands, so what was there to return to? There are rich Cubans whose lands were taken by Castro, but whose moneys made it to tax havens, even banks in Miami and New York. As often happens, the Cubans came to Florida, and made a new home in Miami. But this is not always the case; more often than not, a family with a secret account continues to live in their homeland, and accepts what risks there are of discovery and punishment as an inevitable fact of life they cannot avoid, unless they are willing to let their government destroy their wealth in one way or another. These family holdings in tax havens are guarded with the utmost care and are not even shared with one's closest friends who have similar arrangements.

Fortunately, most unstable governments do not try and track down foreign accounts. They don't get any cooperation from foreign governments. Often the rulers have their own secret accounts they do not want exposed. Too intensive an effort to uncover this wealth may uncover the "presidente's" wealth, or that of his friends and relatives. Secret accounts are often a matter of self-preservation. When the next revolt comes, as it will sooner or later, the present rulers will have to flee in the night, often for their life. They will need to have a nest egg somewhere abroad, although too often the nest egg is a large chunk of the national wealth.

Businessmen living under harsh exchange controls divert some of their dollars into tax haven banks, using schemes as old as ancient history, as well as modern fiscal hocus pocus. Here are a few of the more interesting schemes of recent years:

The Jamaica Shuttle. This scheme is named after the method used during the Manley era (early 1970s), when Michael Manley surprised the Jamaicans one morning with new, tough exchange controls. He had been grossly mismanaging the economy and playing footsie with Castro. Within a matter of hours small light planes loaded with currency took off from small fields in Jamaica and flew 250 miles to the west to Grand Cayman where the funds were deposited in the banks in George Town. This method works for all kinds of wealth—art, jewels, money, small valuable articles, and gold.

When this shuttle was in full swing, the banks in Jamaica ran out of currency and made desperate calls to their sister banks in Grand Cayman to please hurry and send their Jamaican cash back to Jamaica as the island had run out of bills, and businessmen couldn't run their stores. Unlike traffic in drugs, traffic in movable wealth, which is the property of the owner, is legal most everywhere and often involves property that has no customs duty. Jamaica shuttles are routinely in full operation throughout most of the world, most of the time.

The Leaky Scow. You obtain exchange control permission to buy a small merchant vessel. You buy a leaky scow instead for a large sum, which soon sinks. The very accommodating seller deposits the majority of your funds into a tax haven bank. Besides leaky scows, there have been old airplanes (that crashed), obsolete machinery, equipment, or any other item that fits the bill and suffers misfortune and loss.

The Stamp Collector. A favorite device used by the British before the Thatcher government got rid of exchange controls. Buy a valuable stamp in London and take it or send it to a foreign country where it is sold for hard currency for the Englishman's tax haven account. Since stamps are so small, and early British colonial stamps are among the most valuable in the world, there was a ready supply available. What made this practice so apparent is that the prices of these stamps at the auctions in London were running much higher than world prices elsewhere. Englishmen, wanting to move their money out of British exchange controls, were obviously competing with one another. When exchange controls were repealed, London prices reverted to world prices.

The Soviet Caviar-Mackerel Switch (Kleptocracy).[6] The USSR was a state with one gigantic capitalist and 250 million non-capitalists. The capitalist was the government. Out among the mass of non-capitalists there have been a few daring entrepreneurs. One amazing group who structured the caviar-mackerel switch deserve some publicity. In the pre-perestroika Soviet state the government owned just about everything except your socks. They also owned the caviar and mackerel as well—all of it. In keeping with the French proverb that "no one can steal from the state," a few enterprising Russians operated the following "fishy" business.

The plan involved caviar that was shipped to the West in cans with mackerel labels and invoices. Caviar is in high demand by the connoisseurs of the West. A very small can sells for about $100. Mackerel is more often used for cat food than human consumption. In the process of this switch, the Russian government was paid for mackerel by the buyers in the West, who then opened the cans and marketed caviar. They then transferred the difference to Swiss accounts for the enterprising Russians who concocted this scheme.

Everything was going well until some dumb clerk shipped the "mackerel" to the food markets in Moscow. There, to the delight of most shoppers, they were able to indulge for a pittance in one of Russia's great gifts to the world. As might be expected, one Moscow shopper informed the Fisheries Ministry, and after an investigation the jails in Moscow were soon filled with personnel from the Fisheries Ministry all the way down to the shipping clerk. I understand the head man was executed. These enterprising Russians could be labelled do-it-for-yourself Robin Hoods and should be a boon to perestroika.

The concept, however, is not new and has been used in a myriad of forms by enterprising capitalists in Eastern block countries. Now that Eastern Europe has thrown off the shackles of communism, traffic on the fiscal underground railroad may become congested as more and more funds move to Western tax havens.

37

The Rise and Fall of the Miracle Economies

It wasn't very long ago that the Western world was wondering if the Japanese weren't the super-race they said they were when, in the Pacific War, they brought the United States, France, Britain, and the Netherlands to their knees. Even though the Japanese were eventually defeated, the fighting ferocity of their warriors was awesome. There were no cowards in the Japanese military and naval forces, as they often fought to the death to the last man. This super-patriotism for the Emperor was identified with the samurai warriors, past and present. What most people don't know is that the samurai were, for centuries, tax collectors. The step from tax collector to indomitable warrior is mystifying. Yet we saw a similar evolution in Russia when Ivan the Terrible's tax thugs, the *oprichniki*, eventually became the secret police of the Tsarists and Communists.

When the Pacific War ended, the Japanese superiority seemed to emerge once again—this time in trade, commerce, and superior products. Although Japan was once a land of shoddy goods, "Made in Japan" became a mark of exceptional quality. And this gave rise to a new label for the Japanese—they had developed a miracle economy that became a threat to any field they entered. Once again the world looked with awe at the super-energetic Japanese. The list of explanations began to grow. No one seemed to know for sure what the answer was to their phenomenal success. Perhaps the Shinto-militarists who directed the Pacific War were right. The Japanese certainly appeared to be a superior race, if not in war, then certainly in commerce.[1]

Yet again the Japanese have proven to be a very human society, whose invincibility lasted only a short season. Their whole fiscal structure began to crack in 1989. First, they instituted a few Western-style

Japanese caricature of a fierce samurai warrior; originally they were fierce tax collectors. How would you like to have one of these fellows as your tax auditor or collector?

tax reforms. Interest, which had once been tax free, was charged a hefty 20 percent tax rate, withheld at the source. An American-style capital gains tax was introduced, and shortly thereafter money fled from the Japanese stock market, demand faded, and the market collapsed. Where did the money go? And with it, Japan's robust stock market?

The real culprit may not have been the new taxes, although the flight of money to tax havens in order to avoid the Japanese tax bureau was all too obvious. The Japanese tax bureau, known as the *Okurasho*, is reputed to be the most feared in the modern world. Many rich Japanese, seeing the rising intrusions of this tax bureau into their lives, found the tax havens, even far away Cayman Islands, the refuge for their money. But the real culprit was the Central Bank. Unlike most cautious central bankers who learned the lessons of over-stimulating business into a boom-bust scenario, the Japanese, in accordance with their peculiar wisdom of copying from the West and then trying to make their copies better, seemed to have decided that they could play the game of central banking better than the West, and make it produce even greater economic miracles for Japan. In the 1980s, Japan's Central Bank geniuses set the nation on a boom-bust course. With Central Bank credits, Japanese banks were able to lend funds beyond what was available from the remarkable savings wealth in the Japanese private sector. The Central Bank then artificially pushed interest rates down below market levels. There was money galore for everyone. These rates pushed up demand for just about everything by easy borrowing by all sections of the economy. Prices soared. Some economists claimed Tokyo land was worth more than all the land in the United States.[2] A bust was inevitable, which hit in the early 1990s, soon after the stock market collapsed by 60 percent; then 80 percent. Thanks to the folly of Japan's Central Bank geniuses, Japan has had to say good-bye to her miracle economy. History may regard her fiscal planners to be the same as her military planners in the 1940s. Damn fools.

Despite the blunders of Japan's current central bankers—a blunder that is all too common throughout the Pacific Rim today—their tax system during their rise to super-economic status has been the admiration of tax men almost everywhere. At the height of the Japanese economic miracle, some of our best tax thinkers were suggesting that America get rid of its Internal Revenue Code and adopt the Japanese code as a replacement—lock, stock, and barrel, as merchants would say. What, then, was so appealing about the Japanese tax code?

First, it was business friendly, what was called "Japan Inc.," a close working relationship between private business and government bureaucracy. Japan's tax code after the war mirrored the U.S. Internal Revenue Code because the American occupation government forced America's tax laws on the conquered Japanese. But as soon as they could, the Japanese started to riddle the code with loopholes to indirectly lower and eliminate the heavy taxes that the American tax law demanded. The tax changes initiated by the Japanese permitted all kinds of go-go depreciation and write-offs, reserves were allowed against just about anything. Interest was made tax free, capital gains tax free, tax rebates and little tax on exports. The whole system provided exemptions and tax immunities for everyone. In the end, the American-style high progressive taxes existed only on paper. And under this tax code the Japanese economy flourished; its capital formation, which fueled Japan's economic miracle, exceeded anything known in history.

One of the strangest checks on excessive taxation—a built-in safety valve for evasion—was Japan's postal savings system, copied, as is usual for the Japanese, from others. This time it was from the United States. Years ago you could go to your local U.S. Post Office and purchase Postal Savings Certificates, which paid interest slightly above bank savings accounts. You would turn them in at the post office for redemption with the earned interest. The certificate was in bearer form, and no report of your interest income was made to the tax man, nor any record of who the interest was paid to. This American invention found great favor with the Japanese people. Today, there are more postal savings certificates in Japan than there are people living in Japan.[3] In 1982, when the Japanese government wanted to use identity cards for these accounts, there was a loud public outcry, and the law was withdrawn. The accounts remain anonymous because the postal service only requires a seal, not a signature, and depositors can use fictitious names if they want. But the tax man didn't give up, and in 1988, a flat 20 percent was automatically withheld for all interest, which seems to have quieted the tax man for now,[4] but also to have fostered a vast exodus of savings from Japan to no-tax countries, which means just about everywhere, including the United States. Foreigners with deposits in U.S. banks receive their interest tax free.

What attracted the world's tax gurus to Japan was the people's high propensity to save. However, there is a reason for that, and it isn't cultural. Many studies have noted, to our surprise, that in pre-war Japan the savings rate was the same as in the United States, so that isn't the reason.[5] The high savings rate can be explained by the tax-free and low-tax nature of interest income rather than any inclination to save. There is an economic truism at work here: "Whatever you subsidize, you get more of." Thus if a nation wants its people to save more, it should just exempt interest income and see what will happen. Japan's high propensity to save can be duplicated by almost any country that makes interest income tax free or low taxed.

The same kind of incentives were used to encourage business expansion and upgrading plants that soon surpassed the industrial plants in competitor nations. (Japan now accounts for 10 percent of the world's aggregate gross national product.) Dividends are rarely large as earnings are plowed back into growth and expansion. In America, if earnings are not paid out as dividends, a company runs the risk of a horrible penal tax, but that is not so in Japan. Thus the U.S. tax laws often are framed to create tax liabilities; while in Japan they are designed to promote enterprise. The Japanese and many of its Asian neighbors learned what Adam Smith told us over two centuries ago—heavy taxation cripples business, creates unemployment, and fosters evasion. Could anything be worse?

There is an old maxim, often used by your automotive repairman, but applicable almost everywhere, "If it ain't broke, why fix it?" The Japanese government could have learned from that and perhaps have saved the Japanese economic miracle. They could have refrained from playing central banking gamesmanship, thus avoiding the boom-bust scenario that wrecked the Japanese economy and fiscal affairs. They could have avoided introducing Western taxes on savings and enterprise. While the tax experts of the West were suggesting we adopt the Japanese tax system, the Japanese were busy tearing it down, in more ways than one. Apparently the Japanese leaders of Japan Inc. did not learn from the British (and Canadians especially) that you can't stimulate an economy in the long term by taxing or borrowing money away from productive segments of the economy and spending it on unproductive projects. The other fiscal factor they did not learn is that enforcement of high taxes is dangerous to a country's fiscal health. Japan went from a low tax country in the 1970s to a high tax country by 1990, which is when its troubles began. During that later period, deficits and debts rose to the point where Japan is now one of the world's most heavily indebted countries. Where did the wisdom of the Japanese go? In the passion to copy from the West, did they finally copy the wrong things? In the 1960s they were actually cutting taxes against the strong advice of the United States. In the 1980s, they had turned around and were now increasing taxes, this time following the advice of the United States.

The increased taxation of the 1980s did more than stimulate flight from the Japanese fiscal markets; it also stimulated the flight of business to overseas production, especially the United States, creating almost two-thirds of a million new jobs in the United States alone. And we must add to that all the employment created in the support or ancillary industries to the new Japanese companies. In short, Japanese companies have played a key role in recent U.S. industrial development. The recently observed bumper sticker on auto workers' cars—"OUT OF

WORK, HUNGRY? EAT YOUR IMPORT!"—no longer makes sense. The Japanese import is no longer an import, and is being exported back to Japan.

Perhaps it is time for the Japanese people to assert themselves as they did in centuries past, long before Japan was opened to the world by Admiral Perry. The long period of Japan's isolation from the world, the Tokugawa period (1600–1867), was highlighted by innumerable tax revolts. "Ikki, ikki, ikki" ("Revolt, revolt, revolt") was a common cry whenever tax increases were instituted.[6] Since the most recent Japanese fiscal leadership seems to have no brains, an angry populous could lead them back to their recent and ancient roots of tax wisdom.

The Pacific Meltdown

In late 1997, the world woke up to the shock of a massive chain reaction meltdown of many of the currencies along the Pacific Rim.[7] Japan's loan-happy banking infected the countries on the Pacific Rim. A huge borrowing binge available from ridiculously low interest rates (around 1–2 percent) helped bring on the pan-Asian meltdown. Only Hong Kong was able to protect its currency at that moment. To understand this shocking situation, let us digress for a moment back into history, French history no less.

During the French Revolution, when the guillotine was in full operation beheading tax men among others, one of France's most brilliant fiscal and scientific advisors, Antoine Lavoisier, had spent some time advising the tax ministry and even had a short stint as a tax farmer-general, as a reward for his service. His name was discovered by the revolutionaries on the records of the tax ministry. This aroused suspicion, and he was arrested by the Revolutionary Tribunal and condemned to the guillotine. His plea for sparing his life was that he was a genius who could serve the new government. The tribunal answered this plea by declaring, "The Republic has no need of geniuses." Except for its lack of civility, a good case can be made for dealing with today's fiscal geniuses in most governments. We have no need of them—certainly not the central fiscal and economic planners that so often lead a nation with good businessmen and workers down a primrose path to disaster.

The French story does not end at the guillotine. A century before, the French finance minister Colbert asked a group of businessmen what the government could do for them. One of them replied, *"Laissez-nous faire"* ("Leave us alone"). The meltdown in Asia, in large part, came from governments sticking their noses into economic and fiscal affairs—promoting excessive borrowing and spending, getting these nations "out on a limb," which the markets simply "cut off." The International Monetary Fund comes to the rescue, saves the bankers by providing the funds to cover a myriad of bad loans for projects that had little economic value in the business world. Loans that, on a different and larger scale, remind one of the Savings and Loan debacle in the United States when loans were made, guaranteed by the American taxpayer, on security not much better than a bottle cap collection.

To the south of Japan along the Pacific Rim, the small nations of Chinese descent have had economic miracles of their own—which are not mirages. The recent fiscal meltdowns should not distract from the phenomenal growth of these new countries over the past decades. The sound tax policies of these Asian tigers should help restore their economies once more, after the fiscal geniuses in the government have been removed—those who have played disastrous currency gamesmanship and fiscal stimulation to lend-happy banking. Only Hong Kong has been able to weather much of the economic typhoons that have wreaked havoc with her neighbors. Hong Kong should survive, even with the Chinese take-over, primarily because, out of all the Asian Tigers as they are called, they alone had enough sense to keep the government's economic "geniuses" from ruining a good thing.

Despite the current clouds that hang over the Pacific Rim, one of the lessons to be learned is their tax story, and Hong Kong provides the most wisdom.

Britain acquired Hong Kong 150 years ago. Viscount Palmerston, one of Britain's best but least remembered prime ministers, was not very impressed with the acquisition, which he called "a barren island with hardly a house on it." The British, with a few enterprising Chinese, set up a free port for oriental trade. In a short span of time, Hong Kong soon became a thriving trading center for Far Eastern commerce. In World War II, Japan quickly occupied Hong Kong. There was a fast exodus of the British and Chinese traders. When the war ended there were only 600,000 inhabitants, down from 900,000. The place was dead; the businessmen were gone; and the colony was a shambles. Even water had to be imported along with all the food for the impoverished colony. For a while it looked as if Hong Kong would be an international charity case, supported primarily by the British taxpayer.

The government, like most tax havens that were former British colonies, consisted of a governor sent out from London, and a local legislative assembly and executive council that took charge of local affairs. Even though Britain was experimenting extensively with socialism, the Hong Kong government wanted none of it. With the revolution in China creating economic chaos, hordes of Chinese fled to Hong Kong. These were not the rich, but were mostly small shopkeepers and entrepreneurs who knew what was in store for them under communism. Many were from Canton and Shanghai. There were a few textile manufacturers who had the foresight to send their manufacturing machinery to Hong Kong. Not only did these petite capitalists set up shop in Hong Kong, they also dominated the local government. The population soon swelled to 2.5 million. (Today it exceeds 6 million, a tenfold increase in just forty years.)

Rather than become an international charity case, the Hong Kong leaders put everyone to work. The government adopted a true capitalistic posture: Let the marketplace control; let the businessmen have a free rein; in short, non-intervention in economic matters. In an age in which laissez-faire was considered outdated, this was a very remarkable venture for a country that had nothing but too many people and no natural resources other than their brains and enterprising spirits. They adhered to the philosophy of Thomas Paine who said, "That government is best, which governs least." From the 1950s to the 1970s, no one believed that anymore. Instead, the idea was that government must get involved; it must promote the right kind of businesses, create jobs, give the economy direction, own a few businesses—plan the economy more or less, but *more* preferred. Total state planning like the Marxists demand was too much, but a healthy dose of socialism and government intervention was the new economic policy and theory of the age. It dominates Canadian economic philosophy to this day. There are three political parties in Canada, but all are socialist to varying degrees. Canada prospers most of all because its economy piggy-backs on America's laissez-faire.

In poverty-stricken and overpopulated Hong Kong, the government had faith in the businessmen, in their judgment and willingness to struggle in the marketplace. Are not the businessmen, the risk takers, better judges of how to invest their money? Can bureaucrats with taxpayers' money make better judgments? The Hong Kong government of business-oriented leaders believed the government was least qualified to direct the economy. Thus there was no promotion of the export business, no need for planning, no need for industrial projects or job creation projects. It was laissez-faire at its best, coupled with low taxes to increase profits. The profits in turn increased investments in new businesses which create jobs. It was not a vicious circle, but a wonderful one.

Profits are what make the world go around economically. They are the source of wages, of new businesses, of capital, even taxes for the government. Profits are also the primary flags and signals in the market place. The businessman is tuned in to profits, that is what motivates him. As we have now learned, and as the communists and socialist experiments have learned painfully, bureaucrats are ignoramuses with no feeling for profits. It is a world they don't even understand, let alone have talent in. Planning often distorts the market place for a while. Planned economies tend to be too large in some areas, too deficient in others. To be blunt, they tend to screw things up. The governments of Japan and Korea thought shipbuilding was a desirable pursuit for government support. They misjudged. They wrecked shipbuilding worldwide, including their own idle shipyards where billions have been invested. Thanks to government support, the billions have been lost.

If these eager governments had stayed out of subsidizing their shipbuilding businesses, the world's shipping needs would have been met with no overproduction and no wrecking of the shipyards elsewhere around the world. This is just one example. There are dozens more. Today, there is considerable downgrading of state intervention in both Korea and Japan. Canada may also have learned its lesson in its many state-owned aircraft plants. Most of them have been sold off to American aircraft manufacturers, or Canadian entrepreneurs, at horrendous losses for Canadian taxpayers. When government planners turn out to be right, we forget the costs to the taxpayers and that, with the right profit and tax incentives, private business would have been active anyway. Businessmen are drawn to profits just as the 49ers were drawn to California's gold. Wherever there is great profit potential, there will be a mad rush of investors and developers. When the bureaucrats misjudge, taxpayers are the inevitable losers as well as the businessmen who get sucked into the fly-trap.

The Hong Kong miracle has had a strong impact on other Asian "miracles." The leaders of Singapore, Taiwan, Japan, and Korea have all withdrawn considerably from government intrusions into business. The wisdom of Adam Smith and laissez-faire has more than proven itself over socialism and state ownership and intervention in the market place. I suspect that a hundred years from now our wise descendants will look back upon the twentieth century as an age which experimented with socialism in its many democratic and totalitarian forms. They should be able to easily note that socialism failed to solve the world's economic ills; it usually made them worse. The hybrid tax haven of Hong Kong, with its low taxes and non-intervention in business, may stand out as one of the many places that rejected socialism in toto, and reaped enormous prosperity out of what should have been a hopeless situation. Most Third World countries that tried socialism were a mess.

Three other Asian tiger countries have made miraculous progress using moderation in taxation, and all of them came out of the Pacific

War with little more to go on than a strong incentive to succeed. Singapore was once a Marxist country when it withdrew from the British colonial system. Having no capital and no natural resources, similar to Hong Kong, they offered foreign businessmen five to ten years of tax freedom if they would come and set up export manufacturing businesses. The tax immunity would continue if the company would continue to export and to plow earnings back into manufacturing. The government built industrial parks, and when labor became militant and strike threatening, the government regulated wages, hours, overtime, even pensions.[8]

As a rule with all of these pro-business efforts and a skilled work force, annual investment increased from $40 million to $500 million in twelve years. Exports, which these manufacturers were drawn to, increased from $2 million in 1960 to $35 *billion* in 1985.

Taiwan, like Singapore, also experimented with socialism—China Steel, China Shipbuilding, China Petroleum—government ownership of basic industries, the dogma of socialism. But in time socialism was abandoned, foreign investment enhanced, first the Japanese, then the Americans, then the whole world came. The motto of the government was: "People will produce if they are allowed to keep the fruits of their labor."[9] If you look back in our history, that motto was a Jeffersonian idea. But that motto is also a simple way of saying keep taxes low, what has made another miracle economy in the Pacific Rim.

The Asian tigers with their fiscal woes today have learned that there is more to maintaining prosperity than a moderate tax system. Big mega-buck projects are impressive to the visitor, but are they impressive on a balance sheet? A profit and loss? What will the marketplace do when excessive loans cannot be repaid, when the local currencies fall into disfavor. When governments and banks lose touch with astute business horse sense, what is left but a free-fall for the local currency, the local stock market, and local prosperity.[10]

On the positive side, the Asian economies are living proof of the virtue of moderation in taxation, and of the follies of central banking and excessive and imprudent borrowing on the negative side. But their belief in the wisdom of moderate taxation, in promoting prosperity through the private sector instead of government central planning, may at first appearance be simply copying from the wisdom of the West before we, in this century, got seduced by the philosophy of socialism. There was once a time when the economic maxim of America was: "The business of America, is business." Is this where the modern Asian tigers got their wisdom? From Adam Smith two centuries ago? Not entirely.

The economic philosophy of laissez-faire was popularized by the Chinese long before Adam Smith, as we noted with the Chinese emperor Ching-ti in the second century B.C. and his political and economic philosophy of "Governing by Doing-Nothing." His reign was noted by Chinese historians as one of peace and prosperity, and with imperial coffers and granaries filled to the brim.

Israel's Economic Drag

Israel came into being about the same time as the Asian tigers, but had much more going for it. With the spirit of devotion of the Jewish people throughout the world as well as in Israel, with huge sums of financial support including American aid, the state of Israel should be the most prosperous country on earth. No new country ever had such strong moral and fiscal support from abroad as did Israel. In addition, energetic human capital flowed into the country—people willing to accept whatever burdens the state placed upon them, and make whatever sacrifices were necessary to make the land flow with milk and honey. For a while, with all this support, Israel prospered, and her socialism appeared to be workable. But that is now past; except for Jews from the former Soviet Union, Jewish people are no longer immigrating to their Promised Land. The lure of their ancient homeland—the land of Abraham, Isaac, and Jacob, of Moses and the Tribes of Israel—has been overshadowed by the economic drag of the socialist policies espoused by all political parties. For the past decade, the net immigration of Jews to Israel is a minus. More Jews are leaving Israel than are entering.

Israel's decline begins with excessive, dumb taxes, which are too high for companies as well as individuals. As can be expected, these tax rates create large disincentives to economic growth and enterprise and yield little revenue. In short, Israel's tax code distorts prices and discourages work, savings, and investment. It also encourages the more enterprising Jews to emigrate to more gentler tax climes.

The state-owned enterprises and kibbutzim, which form the backbone of Israel's industrial and agrarian economies, are inefficient and act as a drag on the economy.[11] For nationalized companies taxes per employee are lower than in private firms, sales per dollar of investment are lower, profits per dollar of assets are lower, sales are lower per dollar of assets, and wages and operating costs are higher. Notwithstanding all the spirit and energy of the Jewish people, the economy is, and has been, going downhill relative to the rest of the world. Israel is a mess.

As two prominent Jewish scholars observe: "Israel has repeatedly broken every major economic rule in the book. In consequence, its socialist economy is suffering slow growth. This socialist drag is not only destroying Zionism but is also impinging on the nation's national security."[12]

How did this happen? How did the Jewish people, who claim to be among the most intelligent and creative people on earth, be so fiscally and economically stupid? When the more productive nations of the West are lowering taxes, abandoning exchange controls, privatizing government business follies, relying on market forces, getting the bureaucrats and politicians out of making business decisions, why are the Israeli's not getting the message?

We cannot answer that. Perhaps the bureaucrats who consider themselves to have the "know" are too entrenched, just as in Russia. But we can understand how socialism got such a hold on Israel. The founding fathers of Israel emigrated from Eastern Europe when the religion of socialism was strong. Capitalism was viewed as an enemy to progress, social justice, and economic well-being. The Great Depression was believed to be the consequence of the capitalistic systems. Socialism would be insurance against any such economic disaster. A nation's prosperity would be assured if its economy was directed by wise bureaucrats. Capitalism was, as Marx pointed out so well, the exploiter of the masses, leading to a society of innumerable poor, exploited by the few super-rich. Socialism would end all that. There is no doubt also, that both communism and socialism have had strong Jewish supporters and thinkers. Marx, Trotsky, and a host of other fanatics came from the ranks of Jewish thinkers. That thinking found its way into the thinking of all the founders of Israel's many political parties and leaders. As one writer states, "To this day, the Zionist-socialist matrimonial bonds remain strong."[13] And, we should add, as a consequence the economic system will remain weak.

The Laffer Curve: What a Tax System Should Be

Arthur Laffer, an economist at the University of Southern California, observed that there are always two rates of tax that produce the same amount of revenue, a high rate (the negative) and a low rate (the positive). The U.S. Treasury learned this early when progressive income tax rates escalated from 1916 to 1921. The surtax (progressive rates for income) which increased from 7 percent in 1916 to 77 percent in 1921, produced almost the same amount of revenue.[14]

Incomes over $300,000

Year	Rate	Taxes paid at progressive rate	Returns filed
1916	7%	$81,404,194	1,296
1921	77%	$84,797,344	246

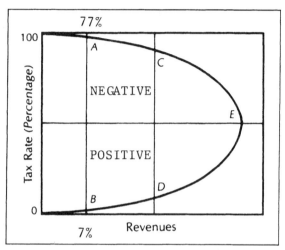

The Laffer Curve. In the 1920s, the treasury discovered that a 77 percent tax rate produced about the same revenue as a 7 percent tax rate. This truism was lost for about fifty years and still hasn't been rediscovered by most of our tax makers.

Putting these data on the Laffer curve, the negative side, point A, would be 77 percent; the positive side, point B, would be 7 percent. Both rates produce the same amount of tax. The low rate is the "positive" side, the high rate the "negative" side.

But you may wonder where all the rich taxpayers went in 1921? The 80 percent who vanished from the tax rolls? Isn't this the same problem the Romans had, when Diocletian was forced to enslave the once free Romans when they disappeared in wholesale numbers off Roman tax rolls? While many today have rebelled (like the Romans) with their shoes and left the United States, the main flight was via the tax planner, what I have called "Yankee Ingenuity." Taxable income simply found its way into non-taxable income or investment gains not subject to tax, or through some other fascinating loophole in the tax code. Unlike the

loopholes the Japanese government built into their tax code, the loopholes in the American tax code, most of the time, came from the tax
planner.

The tax man in America embarked on a plan to make the tax law
increasingly complex, partly to curb tax avoidance, but the tax planners
took this complexity and turned it back on the tax makers. The game
went on and on until we have a tax law so complex, so massive in detail,
that there is no one person today capable of becoming knowledgeable
about the whole code—it is, at times, beyond human comprehension,
and keeps becoming increasingly incomprehensible, even unintelligible. One thing is for certain, you can't accuse the government's tax
makers of being smart.

Will Good Taxes Make a Miracle Economy?

Bad taxes certainly are an impediment to creating a miracle economy,
and good taxes are an ingredient that will help a great deal, although it
is doubtful if we believe that as much today as did our ancestors of the
last century. In 1862, an editorial in the *Atlantic* magazine said:

> Introduce a wise and efficient system of taxation and life and energy will
> pervade the country. Without such a system, it will sink into general and
> fatal paralysis.

Europeans saw this as well at that time. When the American Civil
War was raging, Europeans who believed in America's democracy were
saddened that this great promise of democratic government had failed.
It was hoped that the American democracy would bring in an era of
peace, commerce and prosperity, when it had erupted with internal warfare on a level of devastation and slaughter unknown in the recent past.
But it did produce three important achievements, wrote the editor of
The Quarterly Review in October 1861. It produced a government that
was cheap and free from debt, low taxes, and a horde of immigrants
from Europe willing to work. And that produced the greatest prosperity
ever known in history. Unfortunately, peace and goodwill among the
citizenry did not happen. Democracy could not guarantee that.

Cheap government and low taxes were a remarkable achievement to
Europeans. Immigrants were a boon to prosperity as well, but does this
explain America's unparalleled prosperity and economic greatness? Is
there a hidden catalyst not apparent to the observer?

The hidden factor the European observer did not note was the enterprising spirit of the Americans, a spirit that was also at work in Europe,

but which was stifled to some extent by big, intrusive, taxing and regulating governments. That same spirit makes America great today, notwithstanding a government that is not cheap, not free from debt, and taxes that are not low. This spirit, which Franklin called the principles of honesty, frugality, industry, and good money management, was totally lacking in the Spanish colonization of the New World. Theirs was a lust for gold, exploitation, and indulgence. A Spanish novelist at that time acknowledged that one would die of hunger before taking up a trade and working.

Today, in the Third World nations in Africa, the Middle East, and Latin America, money and low taxes won't help and cannot provide the motivation and enterprising spirit necessary to produce riches. American foreign aid and oil wealth seem like money going down a black hole. Yet in Asia we have witnessed the adoption of the spirit of work and enterprise that came from the Western world. We saw a miracle economy rise in modern Japan when the Japanese a century ago threw off the samurai society and started copying Western ways. We saw this happen recently with the Asian tigers in the Pacific Rim, and while they have been badly burned by their bureaucratic follies and fiscal foolishness, they should reemerge as the amazingly vibrant and growing economies they have been. While no man is above the market, including the Asian fiscal fools, no man is wiser than the market either. And this is a lesson the Japanese have to learn if Japan is to get back on track.

David Landes, in his remarkable study *The Wealth and Poverty of Nations* (1998), predicted that the rich nations will get richer and the poor nations will get poorer, and there is nothing we can do about it because of the lack of the entrepreneurial spirit that is needed to acquire riches, no matter what. No amount of foreign aid, oil riches, natural resources, low taxes or even cheap government, can make up for this spirit.

38

What Constitutions Are Supposed to Do

Constitutions are formed to deter . . . the governors from tyranny.
—James Madison, *The Federalist*

When Madison called attention to the dangers in a democracy of the majority overburdening a minoriy with greater taxes, he further accentuated the problem by noting that "It is vain to say that enlightened statesmen will be able to adjust these clashing [tax] interests, and render them all subservient to the public good. Enlightened statesmen will not always be at the helm."[1] At the North Carolina convention for ratification, a wise delegate named Caldwell concurred with Madison: "It is remarkable—that gentlemen, as an answer to every improper part of it [the Constitution], tell us that every thing is to be done by our own representatives, who are to be good men. There is no security that they will be so, or continue to be so."[2]

We do not have to look back very far in time to realize just how wise these men were. The concept of checks and balances in government had its origin, most of all, in checks on the tax gatherers. The final check was to be the Constitution. Unfortunately, on the federal level, we live in a period devoid of protection, but throughout Western history, going back to the Edict of Paris in A.D. 614, and later through Magna Carta to the modern era, we see a continuing drama of checks on taxation through fundamental charters, treaties, and constitutions. America, however, only in this century has been without constitutional protection.

On the state level, many constitutions are alive and actively protecting taxpayers. On the federal level, constitutional tax controls evolved from the nineteenth-century position that taxes had to be equal,[3] to the twentieth-century position that they can be just as unequal as Congress desires—grotesque, abusive, destructive, brutal, just as ugly and bad as the legislature can devise. If the people don't like it, they have the ballot box. As early as the 1950s, legal scholars were resigned to acknowledge that federal tax legislation was no longer subject to any constitutional challenges.[4] There was one remaining restriction, and that was thought to be geography. Taxes had to be the same everywhere, but by the end of the 1980s, that too had become an "empty shell."[5] The Supreme Court has in effect engaged in a kind of strange "nullification" of expressed, constitutional commands, what legal scholars have called the "empty shell" technique, which could be more forcefully expressed as ripping the guts out of the Constitution.

This empty shell process began with this century, at the same time that many provisions of the Bill of Rights were "boldly thrown overboard," as the recently appreciated journalist H. L. Mencken observed in the 1920s. "How caused, I don't know," said Mencken, but "Holes began to be punched in the Bill of Rights, and new laws of strange and often fantastic shape began to slip through."[6]

The Court has developed a badly fragmented personality, almost schizoid. Segregation, which was legal for a century, was now unconstitutional because it was, in the words of the chief justice, "inherently unequal," even violating due process. By comparison, tax laws which are not just inherently unequal, but intentionally and deliberately so, are constitutional. In the matter of segregation, the Court strained the language of the Constitution to order equality among races. With taxation, it also had to strain the language of the Constitution, but this time in the opposite direction, recognizing and approving inequality, and nullifying the command of uniformity. The reason for this is partly historical, partly the consequence of specious scholarship and logic, and partly the consequence of a changing perception of liberty. We noted, perhaps with some surprise, how the Founders placed taxing at the very top of their list of what liberty stands for.[7] Today, taxation is no longer on the list, not even at the bottom. Perhaps this is what is behind the Court's flip-flop.

Constitutions thus have a long history of protecting taxpayers. There have been three primary devices in the constitutional sphere. The first deals with the matter of separating the power to tax from the power to spend. As we noted, this was at the heart of the British and English constitutional system before Parliament became all-powerful. Once the British Parliament started to spend taxpayers' money at will, the spending power soon overrode the interests of taxpayers and the long historical practice of moderation in taxation. The British government quickly moved from frugality to extravagance, to unlimited military adventures as opposed to defense of the realm, to unlimited governmental intrusions into the lives of the people. Liberty has given way and been compromised to increase Parliament's spending pot.

Neither kings nor the best democratic institutions can be relied upon to control their spending appetites when the power to spend and tax resides in the same political body. The concept of separation of powers, which is so fundamental to American constitutional thought, should, first and foremost, operate in the taxing and spending spheres of government.

Gorbachev's perestroika and his short-lived but dramatic Soviet government provides unexpected support and proof of the value and ease with which the separation of powers works in taxation. The Supreme Soviet had been a rubberstamp congress for over fifty years since it was created by Stalin in 1936. It approved whatever the communist government put before it. That ended with Gorbachev's reforms. Capitalism was legalized, and, as is to be expected, income taxation followed. However, for the first time in the Supreme Soviet's life of fifty-plus years, these deputies rejected the government's plan for high income tax rates. It shocked and shook-up the Soviet government; it surprised the political experts in the West, but it shouldn't really have surprised anyone. Having no real power to spend, and looking after the interest of the Soviet taxpayer of tomorrow, the deputies believed income tax rates should be modest. The rates the government sought were rates our Congress would have had no trouble with. Indeed, the highest rate (55 percent) the Soviet government sought was considerably lower than the highest rate we labored under from Franklin Roosevelt up to the time of Reagan.

If the rejection of high income taxes wasn't enough, in early October 1989 the Soviet legislature turned down another tax proposal for new taxes on beer, cigarettes, caviar, and a few other luxury food items. The legislature felt the price of these popular items was high enough, already too high for most consumers.

Now if these rejections had been done before Gorbachev, God knows what would have happened to the disapproving deputies. With perestroika and glasnost, the deputies had the liberty of voting how they believed rather than how they were told. This new Supreme Soviet, like the British Parliament of old, had not the real power to spend. And, like the English Parliament of the past, they looked out for the taxpayer first, and the government second.

The second constitutional method I will call the Swiss system, although it has been operating in the United States on the state and local level since the founding of the nation. Voters have to approve taxing and spending. Local school bond and road bond issues are examples.

The Swiss attack the problem on a national level. More often than not, the Swiss taxpayers turn down requests for increased taxes and spending and the government has to adjust itself to the food on the table, which is why the Swiss president rides to work on the streetcar. In theory, this is taxation by *real* consent rather than *vicarious* consent. In a democracy there are some decisions that should be left to the people alone, and to the Swiss, taxation and spending is such a decision.

Our present system is similar to a master-servant relation where the master permits his chauffeur to decide what kind of a car to purchase. The chauffeur, who does the driving, will naturally want the best for his pleasure and enjoyment—but the master may not want a Rolls Royce. Likewise, taxpayers may not want all the expensive services and activities that their legislators desire. Our problem is that we have let the chauffeur make a decision that should be left to the master, the taxpayer.

The third constitutional device was what the Framers of the United States Constitution had in mind. The concept was simple—set up constitutional controls over both taxing and spending. When fears of runaway taxation were expressed during the debates for ratification, both of these controls were held up as effective means of preventing abusive taxation and spending. Even the strongest advocates for the federal constitution readily admitted, as we have noted, that tax makers, without constitutional controls on taxing and spending, would not adopt wise taxation, but rather, abusive taxation. The temptation, said Madison, was too great, and minorities would be trampled upon. Without the proper apportionment, uniformity, and equality in taxation, governments would spend too much, tax too much, and overburden some and underburden others. This, of course, is the system we now live under.

When the delegates went to Philadelphia in 1787, they had no illusions about the dangers in granting a federal government taxing powers. They all agreed—standards, limits, and controls were absolutely necessary. No one then, or during the debates, ever suggested Congress should have the power to tax at will. No one wanted the big fish to eat the little fish (taxpayers). Two hundred years have passed and we are right back to square one, for the controls they thought were built into the system have failed. The importance of constitutional controls were frequently expressed in the nineteenth century by the Court. In one of the earliest cases, Justice Samuel Chase said the Framers of the Constitution cannot be supposed to have "contemplated taxation by a rule that would evidently create great inequality and injustice." Another Supreme Court justice (Paterson) said, it would be "absurd" to think the Framers would have allowed an inequitable tax. Again, Justice Iredell spoke of the "dangerous consequences" bad taxation would bring, which would be "altogether destructive to the nation of the common interpretation [on] which the very principles of the Constitution are founded."[8]

We don't find expressions like this in the twentieth century. One federal judge who foolishly thought the uniformity clause still had some force (he was slapped down by a unanimous Supreme Court decision) commented that a tax could be arbitrary, destructive, confiscatory—you name the evil—and it would still not be unconstitutional.[9] One wonders, if the Framers had said this in 1787 when the Constitution was up for ratification, would even one state out of the thirteen have voted for the Constitution? Indeed, would even one delegate from one of the state legislatures have voted in favor? To be blunt, without strict and clear constitutional standards for tax making, ratification wouldn't have had a prayer.

Constitutional controls have a long and successful history of keeping the big fish down to size. The most recent example, which captured the attention of the whole world, was Proposition 13 in California in 1978. The tax revolt in California that produced Proposition 13 was not anticipated by governments or even the press. Its leader, Howard Jarvis, was dismissed as a crackpot and his supporters were a small, but loud, minority. The landslide victory for California's taxpayers had repercussions all over the world. Newspapers in Sydney, Australia, carried bold headlines the size of wartime extras. There are more angry taxpayers in the world than most governments want to admit, and these angry people want better taxation and prudence on the part of governments. Changes in tax rates or even periodic modifications within the system are not enough. We desperately need new tax inventions. Proposition 13 was such an invention, and that is why it captured the imagination of the whole world. Most California taxpayers were not greedy, as the Canadian press had depicted them; they were desperate homeowners fighting to keep their homes. Property taxes in California had escalated far beyond the growth in earnings of the average householder. Something had to be done.

Proposition 13 was a constitutional amendment that set limits on real property tax rates. The idea that taxes should conform to constitutional standards is not new. Modern constitutions derived from the "charters" of the Middle Ages. Magna Carta, which was the most famous, was but one of many charters that limited the taxing powers of kings and nobles. Limits on tax rates and taxing powers were common. You could say that Proposition 13 was the resurrection of a very ancient technique of restraining the tax man.

If we are to resurrect the principles of constitutional control over taxation as the Framers intended, we wouldn't have to do much more than breathe life back into the provisions they handed down to us, especially

Proposition 13 was ridiculed by the press and by both political parties in California, but it not only changed the California constitution for taxpayers—it became a format for change for many other states.

the UNIFORMITY clause. There should be, as they intended, no more discrimination in taxation. No more "odious arbitrariness." No more tax immunities for some, or confiscatory rates for others. Whatever the rates, whatever the tax, it should be the same for all.

There are a fascinating number of words to describe the different kinds of tax immunities that exist. Illegal schemes are called evasion, or more recently, improper self-help; tax gamesmanship is called avoidance, or tax planning; exemptions are loopholes expressed in the tax code. Taxpayers who pay the most tax are those who sit back and do nothing. While tax planning was once an exclusive game for the rich, it is now the pursuit of everybody except the foolish.

Personally, I think we should describe all tax immunity as evasion, because all wealth (labor included) should pay its fair share of the cost of maintaining society. Wealth that does not do so evades its responsibility to the society that protects and sustains it. Tax morality should apply to governments as well as individuals. It is just as immoral for governments to grant exemptions as it is for citizens to hide their income. This, of course, is a new concept of tax morality, but we are in need of new thinking from which new tax inventions can be developed.

We would be shocked if any citizen were granted immunity from the criminal law, yet we tolerate immunity from the tax law on a grand scale. All kinds of pressure groups are demanding and receiving tax favors from the government, like the many classes of commoners who demanded and received noble status in the kingdom of France. Modern constitutions deprive governments of the power to grant aristocratic status. Should they not also be denied the power to grant tax immunity status, which is what noble status was all about in the kingdom of France? The most serious defect in our tax system is its conflict with the foundation of democracy, which is that a law, to be just, must mete out equal treatment to all.

Class politics would not dominate tax-making if our legislators were prohibited from granting tax immunity and exemptions. When that happens, the last bastion of aristocracy within our society will disappear. A constitutional mandate requiring equality in taxation would be welcomed by the people, like a cleansing of the temple of money-changers. Naturally, our legislators wouldn't like this because they are the money-changers of the modern world.

In the 1950s the Warren Court reversed the decisions which gave constitutional support to segregation. The Court breathed life back into the equal protection clause. Unfortunately, the Supreme Court should not be counted upon to breathe life back into the uniformity clause, at least not today's Court, even though the constitutional command for uniformity in taxation is much stronger than that for school busing or even segregation. There is ample precedent in the opinions of the Court in the nineteenth century to support a judgment that the Internal Revenue Code is so lacking in uniformity in so many ways as to be blatantly unconstitutional. To avoid fiscal chaos from such a decision, the Court could stay the execution of the judgment for five years to enable Congress to clean up the mess they have created and adopt wise and uniform tax legislation. Unlike the desegregation decision which enraged the ruling establishment in the southern states, a renewal of uniformity in taxation would produce a tax renaissance for all Americans, which is certainly better than another Boston Tea Party.[10]

Next, Congress's spending powers should be curbed, just as the Constitution provided. There is no doubt the Framers believed this was an important key to keeping the big fish down to size. They thought they had achieved this by providing that tax moneys could only be spent for military purposes for the "common Defence" of the nation, and for the general welfare. Most of all, these provisions were tax control devices, to keep taxes moderate. We have gone so far away from these commands we could hardly return to them.

But the intention was clear and unequivocal—tax expenditures only for defense. You wonder how our government could have trampled over this remarkable restriction and the wisdom it tried to give to future generations. We have paid a heavy price in human life and taxes by rejecting their wisdom. The Spanish-American War, even World War I, and certainly Vietnam, were wars that had nothing to do with the defense of the country. It is not at all inconceivable that if America had stayed out of those wars, the world, and America's stature, would have been much better than it is today.

Alexander Hamilton acknowledged in *The Federalist*, No. 34, that under the Constitution we have "tied the hands of government" from engaging in "offensive wars founded on reasons of state." This may not have been as "novel" as he said it was, at least, not a few centuries before. Feudal aids sought by kings throughout Europe were routinely rejected if the military action was not for the defense of the taxpayers' lands. In the early modern period the tax revolts that wrecked imperial Spain were caused by taxation which was to be used to protect the "vital interests" of the empire overseas, and not the lands of the taxpayers. War taxes could only be justified for defense. This was not a novel idea at all and had its roots in Christian morality. As one European historian writes:

> they [the Netherlands] were constantly on the alert to ensure that the Spanish king did not use Dutch tax revenues for [offensive] wars. . . . This strategy was in line with the prevailing Dutch and Spanish view that tax revenues were only to be spent on wars in the defense of one's own country.[11]

The key issue in Hamilton's comment is the term "Reasons of State," which was well understood in Hamilton's day and throughout most of history all the way back to the Greeks. Sparta went to war against Athens in a preventive war to check the growing power and threat of the

Athenian empire. The domino theory for the Vietnam War was a similar excuse for a preventive war against communist expansion. When the Athenians made brutal attacks on neutral cities, Thucydides tells us they justified their action by a plea of necessity. Germany made the same excuse in 1914 when it violated Belgian neutrality. "Reasons of State" is the universal principle that permits every nation to do militarily whatever it feels is necessary "to preserve the health and strength of a state." [12] It has been said to be "The just cause, necessity, or evident utility of making law, doing justice, of fighting a war for the public and common utility, the *status*, of the kingdom." [13]

The Soviet invasion of Afghanistan was fully justified by the principle of the Reasons of State. Unfortunately, this principle takes morality out of war. Senator J. William Fulbright in 1959 said, "To infuse moral concepts into a political discussion is simply to confuse the issue. . . . Morality is not involved in achieving policy." [14] In short, the state is amoral, even immoral. It can do things that, if done by a private citizen or group of citizens, would be a heinous crime.

In the past few years American military actions in Panama, Grenada, Vietnam, and the Persian Gulf were founded on and justified by Reasons of State. But were they justified by the Constitution, a higher law than the law of nations? The Constitution does not prohibit offensive military action for Reasons of State. The U.S. government can engage in all the wars it wants to with congressional permission. What it can't do is use tax moneys for such purposes. That is why Hamilton used the term "tying up the hands of government," i.e., prohibiting the use of tax moneys for such purposes.

The fact that no American government has seriously wrestled with this issue would suggest that no American government has been aware such a prohibition exists. The military expenditures for the Nicaraguan rebels, for which President Reagan's aides were prosecuted, were actually forbidden by the Constitution. Congressional prohibitions against military expenditures were not only unnecessary, they were illegal, since Congress did not have the power in the first place to spend tax moneys for this civil war. In the Persian Gulf War against Iraq, Japan and Germany refused to send military forces because their Constitutions prohibited this; actually, so does the U.S. Constitution. In Washington's Farewell Address, he said: "The Constitution which at any time exists, until changed by an explicit and authentic act of the whole people, is sacredly obligatory upon all of us." [15]

Finally, the general welfare clause was designed to prevent spending tax moneys for the welfare of some special groups, areas or persons, that is, to prevent Pork Barrelling. Unless an appropriation benefits the nation as a whole, it would be unconstitutional.

Constitutional changes don't come easy as those who have worked for the adoption of the balanced budget amendment have learned. That Amendment was designed to prevent the huge budget deficits that until recently had plagued the nation. We now pass our huge debts on to our children and grandchildren. It would be infinitely better to curb spending by preventing uncontrolled and unlimited expenditures for whatever may suit the Congress's fancy. Unfortunately the desire of the Framers to control spending by specifically stating what tax moneys could be used for, has not worked.

The basic concept of federalism was set forth in the Tenth Amendment, which provided that the federal government could only do what it was expressly authorized to do in the Constitution. All other political powers were reserved to the states and to the people. The recent history of constitutional law is a history of how to circumvent the limitations against unlimited federal power as set forth in the federal Constitution and its Amendments. We have arrived at the sorry state of affairs where there is nothing the federal government cannot do in matters of taxation or anything else as long as it wants to and follows the appropriate loophole in the Constitution—loopholes, incidentally, which were never intended, but were discovered and tolerated with the Supreme Court's blessing.

The constitutional history of the United States could be well illustrated by a story concerning W. C. Fields in his later years when someone found him propped up in bed reading the Bible. "Bill," said his friend, "What are you doing reading the Bible?" "Looking for loopholes," Fields replied.[16]

39

Learning from the Past

History makes men wise.

—Sir Francis Bacon

Polybius, considered the greatest historian of the ancient world, said that the best preparation for politics was the study of history in order to avoid the disasters of others.[1] A modern philosopher, the late George Santayana, echoed him in saying that those who cannot learn from history are condemned to relive it. As often as these axioms are repeated, we do not apply them to taxation—at least, not in the twentieth century. It should seem irrefutable from this study, however, that the wrong kind of taxation has brought terrible calamities to civilization. A government that taxes excessively is like a spouse that engages in adultery. Its destructiveness is usually not apparent until it is too late.

The famous football coach from Ohio State University, the late Woody Hayes, was once asked why his juggernaut football teams did not pass the football more often. Woody replied that when a team passes there are three things that can happen and two of them are bad. There is an analogy to heavy taxation in Woody's remarks. When a government taxes too much there are also four things that can happen, and three of them are bad: rebellion, flight to avoid tax, and evasion. There are even more things that go bad with society: chronic inflation, low productivity and slow economic growth, strangulation of freedom by state regulatory bureaucracies, a gradual erosion of individual freedom and self-determination by a paternalistic state, and a punitive and confiscatory tax system.

Most taxpayers do not look beyond their daily burdens, which are depressing enough. Until the 1980s, tax rates were out of control. Governments seemed to be unable to stop the ever-accelerating rates and ever-more-complex tax laws. We have finally started to rollback the rates, but the complexity has gotten worse. Taxation could be called a scourge of the entire twentieth century, along with world wars, pollution, and over-population. In our search for wisdom, tax history provides many startling conclusions.

We have attempted to bring to light the impact of taxation upon history and upon the lives of individuals. The suspicion of many writers and historians—that great empires tax themselves to death—finds support in history and has become a fashionable theme.[2] Many of the great events of history, certainly most revolutions, have been rooted in taxation. Taxes have often been the fuse that ignites the powder of human discontent, but once the explosion occurs, we seldom take notice of the fuse. Even with the civilizations lost from history, of which we know so little—if their silent temples and ruins could speak, what tax tales would they tell? The ancient Mayan civilization, according to one scholar, ended when taxpaying citizens simply disappeared into the jungle instead of paying taxes.[3]

By now it should be clear that taxation is a good barometer of a social order. Nothing reflects a nation more faithfully than its tax system. A society can best be evaluated by examining who is taxed, what is taxed, and how taxes are assessed, collected, and spent. Those in control of the political process invariably bear lighter tax burdens than those on the outside. Tax avoidance is thus a prerogative of those in control of the system; evasion is the alternative for those on the outside.

We have noted how, from the earliest records of civilization, the history of human liberty is intertwined with the history of taxation. Tax laws have taken away liberty more often than foreign invaders. This is a major blindspot in our historical vision. We kept a sharp eye on the Russians and the communists, even to the point of bankrupting our nation with military expenditures beyond our means, yet we ignore the villain at home that each year takes away more and more of our privacy and civil liberties in the interest of protecting the revenue.

We have also learned that patriotism is soluble in taxes—it dissolves easily. Flight to avoid tax has been a major force in the emigration of people from their homelands. To understand this phenomenon, we need to draw another analogy to the unfaithful spouse. In the marriage contract from early biblical times, "for better or worse" did not include adultery. Not only was divorce justified, at times the guilty wife was put to death. Like marriage, the political relation of man and state is also based on contract and there is also a "for better or worse" understanding in that relationship. Also, as in marriage, there are certain sins for which tolerance is neither expected nor required. Taxation is in that category. In the Declaration of Independence, the Americans justified treason and violence because Britain was "imposing taxes on us without our consent." This principle is ancient.

In the fifteenth century, following the death of Charles the Bold who ruled over much of France and the Low Countries, his daughter, Mary of Burgundy, was confronted with angry, overtaxed subjects on the verge of rebellion. To promote peace she moderated taxes and promulgated a famous charter, like Magna Carta, which was called the "Great Privilege." It expanded the principles of Magna Carta—if any ruler violated the tax rights and liberties of the people, the people would be relieved of their civic duties to the state.[4] In other words, they had the right of divorce, and that state had lost its right to rule, much like the Chinese Mandate of Heaven we observed in Chapter 5.

Infidelity in matters of taxation has had a long history of disasters and calamities. The American Revolution was not unique. Guilty governments, like guilty spouses, have been put to death. Most often the injured party divorces the unfaithful spouse and leaves his ancestral homeland with no remorse. When that is not feasible, violence is often the consequence when evasion is not available. Atrocities committed by our ancestors against tax men they didn't like reminds us of the violence that can erupt when a spouse is unfaithful. In a decade of law practice I had two clients commit murder and suicide; both cases involved marital infidelity. Human behavior in conflict with the tax man can be explosive. A man shackled with tax debts he abhors often reacts like a wild animal in a trap. We differ from our ancestors primarily in the way we handle the stress taxes generate within us. We take tranquilizers or, like the Swedes, drink excessively.[5] Our ancestors rid themselves of their frustrations by lynching the nearest tax man, even innocent ones.

Our federal Constitution, as we have seen, is no help even though it was designed to protect taxpayers. The Supreme Court today, when confronted with constitutional tax issues, is like Pontius Pilate who "took water, and washed his hands before the multitude." Taxpayers will find no friend in the high court,[6] and the procedures that deal with tax disputes are short on fair play. In the end, it is the press and public opinion that provide what little protection we have from runaway ruthless tax administration. The law doesn't provide it, and our congressional representatives are more concerned with pleasing the tax man who butters their bread than with the plight of taxpayers who produce the butter.

Unfortunately, we can't do as Nero proposed and make a beautiful gift to the human race by abolishing taxes. We can't survive without responsible government, and that requires taxes. Voluntary contributions for the support of government, like the Greek and Roman liturgy, are alien to our social order.

Taxes are forced exactions. The loss of money through taxation often

LASATE·OGNI·SPERANZA·OVOI·CHENTRATE

"ALL HOPE ABANDON, YE WHO ENTER HERE." These words appear over the gates of Hell as the Roman poet Virgil and Dante peer inside. Taxpayers appearing before the Supreme Court confront a similar, hopeless situation so far as the Constitution is concerned.

enrages people and drives them to revolt. Governments, therefore, must face their tax management with the utmost prudence and wisdom. Many laws will be tolerated even if they are disliked and clumsy in operation, but tax laws, when bad, will not be tolerated with ease. When citizens get mad about taxation there is a good chance something will happen, sooner or later. There may be violence, like the American Revolution, or simply evasion and flight to avoid tax. Angry taxpayers often do not limit their discontent to grumbles—they are prone to react in some direction for relief, using force and violence if necessary. This is, unquestionably, tax history's most important lesson.

In the final analysis the moral aspects of taxation should apply to the state as much as to the taxpayer. This has been ignored completely by governments everywhere. A government that shackles its people with grossly inequitable tax laws and despotic enforcement practices loses all moral persuasion with respect to compliance, and can hardly complain if its taxpayers resort to all kinds of schemes to protect themselves, including illegal ones. In fact, such a government under the principle of the "Great Privilege" or the Mandate of Heaven would lose its right to govern, and would be what we have called here, an unfaithful spouse.

The ethics, then, of society's tax policy should develop from two moral maxims: First, it is the duty—the first duty—of every government to develop a just and sound revenue system. *Just* in the way taxes are assessed and collected, and *sound* in the way public revenues are administered and spent. Second, it is the duty of every person to pay his (or her) fair share of the costs of maintaining the government that serves and protects them. This second moral maxim cannot operate if governments fail to fulfill their end of the political contract. A taxpayer cannot pay his fair share if the laws do not obligate him to do so.

Finally, there are other lessons and maxims this study has brought to light, not as all important as the foregoing, but nevertheless, valuable lessons that cannot be ignored. For the reader's benefit, here is a summary of the most important ones:

1. Many great nations taxed themselves to death; conversely, many nations became great because of the right kind of taxation, taxation which stimulated growth and enterprise.

2. Whatever is taxed must be surveyed; consequently, if a tax system is all encompassing, liberty must give way.

3. All-encompassing taxation vests enormous power in the tax bureau, which, in time, tends to overpower, not only the taxpayer, but the other branches of government. Even kings and emperors have had to yield to the power of their tax bureaus.

4. The ancient Greeks produced the first civilization without despotism and they achieved this by discovering that tyranny is the product of the wrong kind of taxation, especially direct taxation.

5. When wars or other great emergencies demand great revenues, then all citizens should be taxed according to what they are worth by equitable principles, not odious arbitrariness.

6. Nature will not bestow wealth equitably. A few citizens will inevitably acquire great wealth, which by natural justice they should share with the community. But this sharing should be enforced by moral persuasion and a strong public opinion, not force and confiscation.

7. All citizens, from recruits in the military to the chief leaders of society, should serve the state unselfishly, and if possible, without pay, motivated by a love for their country and an obligation to serve. Their primary reward should be the praise they receive from fellow countrymen for a job well done.

8. Taxpayer discontent threatens the peace and prosperity of the so-

cial order, more so than misbehaving taxpayers; consequently, the criminal arm of the tax system should be directed against oppressive tax agents rather than angry taxpayers.

9. Consent is required for all lawful taxation, either by long-standing custom, or by the common consent of the taxpayer. When a state taxes without bona fide consent, regardless of the equities or reasonableness of the tax, rebellion and civil disobedience are justified.

10. Tax exemptions are inherently unjust unless they actually apply to everyone. If the constitutional principle of equality before the law is ever applied to taxation, then those in control of tax making must bear the same taxes as those on the outside. This means that in an aristocracy or oligarchy, the few would have to bear the same taxes as the many; and in a democracy, the many should bear the same taxes as the few.

11. If liberty is to be defended with success against the dominance of the state, financial privacy must be preserved. Banking privacy is one of the cornerstones of liberty, having its roots in the principle of early English law that a man's castle (primarily his treasury) is beyond the surveillance of the king.

12. Taxes have been, more often than not, the cause of revolution. People seldom rise up and revolt if their tax burdens are reasonable.

13. A wise ruler does not change an effective tax system. Destroy the social order if you must, like Cortés in Mexico, but never destroy a tax system that works well.

14. Wars produce new taxes and high tax rates, but when the emergency ends governments will try to retain their newly enlarged taxing powers.

15. As taxes increase, evasion increases.

16. Once tax evasion becomes deeply rooted, it is almost impossible to root it out.

17. Tax evasion is not always an evil; it has often been a safety valve against violence and rebellion.

18. Great wealth, as if by magic, disappears when governments adopt taxation to "soak the rich." The rich have always had the means to escape heavy taxation.

19. The income tax is a bastardized form of wealth taxation because the more wealth a taxpayer possesses, the easier it is for him to avoid taxable income. A person's wealth and ability to pay does not necessarily bear any relation to his taxable income.

20. People tend to resist heavy taxation in the following ways: First, lawful avoidance; second, if avoidance fails, then either evasion

or flight to avoid tax; third, rebellion; and finally, when there is no other alternative, they have accepted serfdom when it offered the only relief from outrageous taxation.

21. Progressive tax rates have no principles or standards and have quickly evolved into odious arbitrariness when directed at minorities rich in money but poor in votes.

22. Patriotism is soluble in oppressive taxation, oppression in the rates of tax or in the manner in which taxes are assessed or collected.

23. Historically, the conscience of tax makers has often been like Swiss cheese—full of holes; when that happens, the conscience of taxpayers is also like Swiss cheese.

24. Taxes that are not apportioned among all taxpayers with impartiality and fairness lose all force of moral obligation.

25. "Taxes are what we pay for a civilized society," but how we tax and spend determines the extent to which our society is good or evil.

26. Liberty tends to carry the seeds of its own destruction, for free men will often grant extensive taxing powers to their governments, not realizing that these taxing powers will, if carried to excess, destroy the very liberty they sought to preserve.

27. War means heavy expenditures. Heavy expenditures means heavy taxation. Heavy taxation strangles commerce and fosters economic stagnation and decline.

As the 1990s come to a close, we have seen the tax reductions of the 1980s begin to disappear, and tax exemptions have disappeared as well. We have also seen the rise of tax reform movements to get rid of our insane income tax system: a uniform rate system called the flat tax, and more revolutionary, a national consumption tax of some form. While the polls show a vast majority of the people want to get rid of the income tax, their representatives in Congress and the federal tax bureaucracy like the system, "just the way it is," and unfortunately they hold the power to change. We are like Imperial Spain four hundred years ago, when many wise citizens wanted to change the tax system, but couldn't move the government. Is not our predicament the same? As expressed in 1600 by Gonzales de Cellorigo: "Those who can, will not; those who will, cannot." In tax matters representative government today seems no more responsive to the people's wishes than was Spain's absolute autocracy.

The most crucial problem, seldom addressed by any tax reformers, is not the question of rates—for you cannot judge a tax system by rates alone—but is the dangers created by the growing powers of spying and tough penal laws used to enforce tax compliance. This, and not tax rates, may be the most significant struggle of our age between government and citizen. The outcome will determine the kind of civil liberties our descendants will inherit from us in the next century. Unlike the Swiss, they may not be saying they "want to be as free as their fathers." They will probably want to be more free, much more free.

The course of our civilization could parallel the final era of the ancient world when tax compliance was enforced by the Roman state with bondage to the tax collector. This bondage was instituted to ensure compliance and to check the frauds, flight, and rebelliousness of Roman taxpayers. Gibbon described this period as a time of "perpetual struggle between the powers of oppression and the arts of fraud."[7] But Gibbon was wrong. For the average Roman taxpayer the struggle was not perpetual. Shortly after Diocletian's reforms, the contest was over for most Romans; they, their children, and their children's children, were shackled to the tax system. Roman citizenship, which was once the pride of every Roman and the envy of all others, was nothing more than slavery except for those few who obtained tax immunity. This bondage of the once-free Roman citizen was the tax man's final victory over the extensive frauds and flight that had endangered the emperor's revenue.

These conditions are present today and have not been abated. Except for the very few, most taxpayers cannot hope to win against the awesome powers vested in the tax bureaus of the modern state. If the tax bureau achieves its final victory over us, we may not be shackled to our jobs like the Romans, but all indications are that the earnings from our jobs and from all other sources will be shackled to the state. Even money may disappear as super-human computers record every commercial transaction with a tax identifying number. What is most likely to occur, and most frightening, is that our Social Security cards will become like our Visa cards and Mastercards. With every commercial transaction we undertake, the card will be zipped through the little computers they now use in most every store. Instantly, the computer tells if our credit card is good. With our plastic Social Security card, instantly everything we do could be recorded on our record at the tax bureau, a record which is no longer private as it once was. A paranoid president or FBI chief could instantly know just about everything about you—your beliefs, actions, probably what you are thinking and where you are at the moment.

The ubiquitous scribes of the pharaohs who were snooping, spying, and recording will have their counterpart in the modern world. Silently the tax identifying number and the computer will make a mockery of freedom and privacy. Even the former Soviets may have been under less surveillance. Today, they envy us; tomorrow, we may envy them. As in

Egypt nothing was beyond the surveillance of the scribes; so it could very easily be with us.

Will we end up as citizen-serf-taxpayers like the later Romans? The current direction of our tax system's penal laws and spying devices make that a possibility. We could find ourselves shackled to a kind of neo-serfdom to the modern *fiscus*. If that happens, then the struggle between democracies and dictatorships will enter a new phase in which the choice will be not liberty or bondage, but rather, which kind of bureaucratic bondage.

40

Taming the Monster

Rise Britannia! The Monster that so long oppressed and trampled on you is at last subdued.

—Cruikshank cartoon, on repeal of the income tax, 1816

Cruikshank's words expressed the sentiments of the British people when Parliament repealed the income tax which was adopted to finance the war against Napoleon. As we noted, this was no ordinary repeal. Parliament ordered the tax bureau to destroy all records of the hated tax. Burned tax records, like dead men, tell no tales. So hated was the tax that the generation of Britons who lived under the world's first income tax had to pass away before the tax was reintroduced, and then it was brought forth in a modest form supposedly on a short-term basis.

Unfortunately, we may not be in a position to do as the British did in 1815, even though it is time to subdue the monster we have unleashed on our people. Instead of developing new tax systems, we have been steadily increasing the vicious and avaricious propensities of the income tax monster. If we can't subdue the monster as the British did, we can at least *tame* the beast. Perhaps our descendants in the next century will have the motivation, wisdom, and inventiveness to get rid of this dangerous tax, a tax that if not controlled inflicts misery upon hundreds of thousands of taxpayers. It is very difficult for officials even with the best of intentions to administer an inquisitorial law with humanity.

Besides using the eighteenth-century monster analogy, in this age we are more attracted to the idea of a shark—a vicious, inhuman man-eater. Or the analogy that is used in most law schools to illustrate what happens in a corporate merger—a big fish eats a little fish. The big fish (tax makers and spenders) have been eating the little fish (taxpayers) ever since the income tax system was adopted. Any reform, any taming of the monster, must reverse this imbalance. If the fish were the same size,

457

Cruikshank cartoon, on the repeal of the income tax, 1816.

on equal footing, the system would work better. All we have to do is bring the big fish down to size. But, how did this imbalance come about in the first place?

The tax system established after Magna Carta was directed, when it worked, by frugal and incorruptible parliamentarians who checked the appetites of many of England's kings. In this remarkable system, as we noted, the power to tax was separated from the power to spend. The king could spend, but not tax; the Parliament could tax, but not spend. This was the key to the success of the system and to the moderate tax England lived under.

We still consider our system to be a copy of the earlier English system of taxation by consent, but is it? Our representatives have a conflict of interests the early English representative did not have—they have been corrupted by the power to spend. Our tax makers no longer check spending; in fact, they will consent to almost anything that increases their spending pot. When the power to tax and to spend reside in the same political entity, whether king or legislature, without controls, the spending power will override the taxpayers' interests—the big fish will eat the little fish. William Gladstone, British prime minister during the latter half of the nineteenth century, wanted to repeal Britain's second income tax but was unable to do so because of the "public expenditure," or what we have called the power to spend, overriding the interests of taxpayers.

While a rebirth of constitutional controls is by far the proper and most lasting way to protect the little fish, for the immediate future wise and prudent tax reforms could go a long way to curb the vicious aspects of our federal income tax system. The accounts of abusive behavior and misuse of the tax system have been publicized extensively. In the 1970s the conservative *Reader's Digest* ran a series on "The Tyranny of the IRS," and "60 Minutes" gives us numerous accounts with live witnesses and stimulating commentary to dramatize the problem. Art Harris's story of "The Tax Man and the Big Sting," in the *Washington Post* on April 16, 1989, the recent blockbuster book by David Barnham called *The Abuses of Power: Misuse of the I.R.S.*, and Shelley Davis's *Unbridled Power, Inside the Secret Culture of the IRS* (1997) are just tips of the iceberg. The IRS is a bureaucracy out of control because of the lack of checks and balances which are so fundamental to American political practice and to good government.

What follows are nine suggested reform items to tame the monster. These are not band-aid remedies like the recent anemic Taxpayer Bill of Rights. These reforms go to the root of the problem and would be a big step towards collecting taxes in a civilized manner. We will make reference to the historical roots and practices, some of which we previously presented.

1. Tear down the spy system.

Just as President Ronald Reagan said to Chairman Gorbachev about the Berlin Wall, "Tear down this Wall!" so we need to tear down the spy system we have erected against taxpayers.

The income tax system has evolved in the last thirty years from an honor system to a spy system. As late as the 1950s, paying your income tax was a matter of honor, the mark of a good citizen. IRS agents would often present themselves to taxpayers when initiating an audit with this comment: "You know, our tax system is an honor system, which is the only way it will work in a free society." But by the end of the 1970s, this presentation of honor was no longer appropriate, as the thrust of all compliance efforts was to spy on all taxpayers. Not only have we erected a "perfect system of espionage," to quote from a German legislator on the tax system of nineteenth-century Germany, we have gone much further with a vast array of "information returns" on all fiscal activities, even, as we will note, photographing everything going through your bank account for Big Brother to see.

But if, as the IRS used to say forty years ago, the income tax will only work in a free society as an honor system, does that not mean that our society is no longer free?

Taking the honor out of the tax system and replacing it with compliance by fear, moves that aspect of our government into the realm of totalitarianism. The most dreaded phone call today is one from the IRS, telling you that your affairs will be audited. One recent suggestion (in jest I hope) for wives to get back at their husbands, is to tell them, just as they are about to go to sleep, "By the way dear, the IRS called today. Said they will call back later." Sweet dreams? Hardly.

I suggest that the main culprit, which has tolerated the evolution of our tax system into a spy system, has been our mainstream media. Except for "60 Minutes," the IRS's growing awesome powers have been forbidden territory for NBC, ABC, and CBS. There is, by contrast, open season on the White House and the president on just about everything, any rumor, any dirt, but not so with the IRS. Finding fault with the tax bureau is dangerous territory. But there are tax stories they tell about taxpayers. Tom Brokaw complained on NBC that Americans who left the country to avoid being plundered by the IRS were bad guys, Benedict Arnolds. He called this flight to avoid tax "The Fleecing of America." It seems he got who was being fleeced all mixed up.

Senator Peter Deminici, an outspoken tax reformer, at the 1998 hearings, said that his polls showed that two-thirds of all taxpayers would rather be mugged by an armed criminal than face an IRS audit. Another senator said that taxpayers would rather face a dentist for a root canal than face an IRS agent. But is this new? It shouldn't be, if the media had been doing its job.

But in all fairness to the chicken media, it is well understood that the

First Amendment's right to criticize the government does not apply to the IRS—they are off limits, out-of-bounds. Consider a teenager in Buffalo whose only asset was a bicycle. He wrote a letter to the local newspaper finding fault with the IRS, probably from something he'd heard. The next thing that happened was that the criminal investigation division put him under twenty-four-hour surveillance. About the only matter of interest in their report was a few moments the boy spent in a drug store looking at girlie magazines. These armed "special agents" even followed his mother to work on a local bus. If the IRS will do this to a sixteen-year-old kid for expressing disapproval of the tax bureau, imagine what they could do to the mainstream press, to force them to silence.

Even more dangerous than what happened to our Buffalo teenager is the firing of the one and only IRS historian, Shelley Davis, who thought her job as a professional archivist was to preserve records, the good and the bad. She discovered records being destroyed, or which should have been destroyed. Records which showed the IRS's darker side. She soon got the boot as well as the "special agent" investigation into her activities. Scary stuff. There will be no more historians at the IRS. And for all this outrageous behavior, our mainstream media, like the Mafia, maintains its code of silence, and Congress does nothing. They, too, like the media, are fearful. The fact that millions of taxpayers are abused by the IRS is the price we pay for letting this agency get out of control. Perhaps our tax troubles are what Cicero had in mind when he lamented the troubles in Rome during his day: "Surely we are being punished for having let the crimes of so many go unpunished."

But you can point to a number of band-aid remedies passed into law to deal with the IRS's misdeeds as discovered in recent hearings before the Senate. Until Congress tears down the spy system, their remedies for this leviathan are about as significant as it would have been to rearrange the deck chairs on the *Titanic* on the evening of April 14, 1912.

2. Establish a crime for tax extortion as well as a civil action for damages.

Throughout the entire period of Roman history, until the very Fall of Rome, the Romans had tough, even brutal laws, which punished tax men who collected or tried to collect more than the law required. In the *Theodosian Code of Laws* under Constantine's direction in A.D. 313, this tax extortion criminal decree was enacted: "If any person shall complain in court that payment has been unduly exacted of him, or that he has sustained any arrogance and if he should be able to prove this fact, a severe sentence shall be pronounced against such tax collector."[1]

The Roman attack against misbehaving tax men went back to the Republic and the famous Extortions Court where Cicero prosecuted high ranking Roman tax administrators. The Romans were not alone. In ancient India a wise ruler "punished and dismissed those officers who realized from the subjects more taxes than were due."[2]

The great medieval theologian Thomas Aquinas put the matter into sharper focus in his *Summa Theologica*.[3] He asked the question: is it possible for robbery to take place without sin? He concluded: it is no robbery if princes exact from their subjects that which is justly due for safe-guarding the common good. But if they tax excessively, it is robbery even as burglary is. "Wherefore they are bound to restitution just as robbers are, and by so much do they sin more grievously than robbers, as their actions are fraught with greater and more universal danger to public justice whose wardens they are."

The Romans provided further protection to taxpayers with a cause of action for civil damages. According to the Roman historian Tacitus, Nero issued a decree in A.D. 58 which required all Roman governors and praetors to "give special priority to cases against tax collectors."[4] Are there any civil damages cases against tax collectors today? None, for they have immunity and cannot be sued for extorting more than the law demands. In Roman times, in civil suits against tax men the damages awarded were the exact amount of the unjustified tax.

Later, the Theodosian Code provided civil remedies against any judge who was derelict in his duty to protect taxpayers. If a judge refused to take action against a misbehaving tax man, a fine of thirty pounds of gold was assessed against the judge, with the fine going to the taxpayer.

A civil tax liability like the Romans used would eliminate a lot of arbitrary, groundless assessments used to intimidate taxpayers for bargaining purposes. In the "Outrage of the Month," in *Dollars and Sense* magazine, an agent is described who arbitrarily slapped a $35,000 assessment on a taxpayer whose CPA asked for a short postponement of a scheduled meeting. The CPA said: "Is it any wonder why most taxpayers (including myself) despise the IRS and the over-zealous power-mad people who use strong-arm tactics."[5] With a civil liability this kind of behavior would not occur, and tax assessments would be based on fact and law, and not for some abusive, tactical advantage.

Harsh punishments against excessive tax collections continued after the Fall of Rome into the Middle Ages. The only surviving painting by the Dutch Master Nicolas van Galen can be found in the town hall in Hasselt, Overijssel, in the Netherlands. It is entitled *The Administration of Justice by William the Good*. This magnificent work of art shows the king witnessing the beheading of a tax man who collected more than he should have. (See Chapter 13.) So remedies, both civil and criminal, for tax extortion have a long history in Western civilization as a protection for taxpayers. Today, we obviously need to revive such legal remedies.

3. Establish a civil action for damages for tortious tax administration including: malicious tax investigations, extortions, leaked information, and grand jury abuse.

It has now come to light that the executive branch of the government has used the IRS to harass, punish, and even destroy businesses, prominent individuals, unpopular political organizations, senators, congressmen—just about anybody. Presidents, including Roosevelt, Kennedy, Johnson, and Nixon are among the most conspicuous abusers.[6] Roosevelt went after Andrew Mellon, the Republican secretary of the treasury for so many years. Kennedy went after right-wing Christian ministers who criticized his Catholicism in the 1960 campaign. Johnson went after all the key men in Goldwater's organization. According to Karl Hess, one of the rights of the victors in a presidential election is to audit the losers.[7] Secret Nixon tapes reveal a dangerous conspiracy, led by Nixon, to use the IRS to purge the government of his enemies. If then Commissioner Johnny Walker would not cooperate with the purge, the White House was to replace him with a new Commissioner willing to do the dirty work. To cover up the real motives, a number of Nixon's friends would also be audited, but they would only receive a light touch.[8]

Even more threatening and dangerous to the nation is the abuse of power by the IRS itself against those people it doesn't like. This kind of a conspiracy is almost impossible to unearth. It is not just abusive "special" audits, but the leaking of "information" taken from a taxpayer's files that is most threatening. Senators Edward Long and Joseph Montoya were both toppled from power when they sought to have the Senate hold hearings on IRS misdeeds.[9] They were silenced not much differently than if they had been critics in a totalitarian regime where dissidents are exiled in one form or another.

Private citizens need protection from vindictive but groundless indictments by grand juries. Our tax law is so complex and so screwed up, and the definition of "evasion" so fuzzy and vague, that anyone with complicated financial affairs can be indicted easily. Consider the ordeal of an associate of the late Harry Margolis, an aggressive tax lawyer on the west coast who was a thorn in the IRS's side. His associate did not cooperate with the government's attack on Margolis, so he was indicted along with his boss. At the trial, after three months of testimony, the government completed its case. The judge promptly threw out the case against the associate. There never was a case against him in the first place. Like so many others, so often, he was indicted for being "unco-operative," a word of art that goes back to imperial Spain under Charles I. This indictment, again like so many others, was malicious and in bad faith. It occurred because there are no remedies to check this abuse—no civil action or criminal charges can be brought against those responsible. In another famous but phoney indictment case, *United States v. Kilpatrick*, a U.S. attorney threatened a tax law professor who was going to testify for the defense. He, too, said the U.S. attorney would be a "target," and that so far as the defendant was concerned, even if he wasn't guilty "the government would 'break him' with the cost of the defence."[10]

4. Have all federal tax districts coincide with congressional districts and provide for the recall of district directors.

Besides granting taxpayers the right to sue misbehaving tax agents, we also need to have the tax chiefs responsible to the people they tax. Congressional representatives are constantly receiving complaints from their constituents about harsh and abusive treatment. There really is nothing they can do, and most district directors send off a mild rebuff telling the congressman this is none of his business, which is what happened in the 13th Congressional District in California in the mid-1960s. IRS agents in California decided they could break the attorney-client privilege by seizing lawyers' trust accounts. In one case the U.S. congressman Charles League was contacted, he wrote a letter to District Director Schmidt complaining about the matter. Schmidt wrote back telling the congressman they had a job to do, and this was none of his business. The matter was then referred to the California State Bar, and when they threatened to haul the district director before a federal court to explain his conduct and position, the district director ate humble pie and apologized to the Board of Governors and promised not to continue the practice. Unfortunately, the IRS was able to kill legislation introduced to stop this abusive practice.[11]

Every IRS district should coincide with every congressional district. Members of the House are supposed to be the taxpayers' representatives, which is what the Framers envisioned. Every congressman should be able to act as a censor for his people vis-à-vis the tax system. In addition, in every congressional election there should be submitted to the voters a question like this: Should Joe Tax'em be retained as district director of the Internal Revenue Service for this congressional district?

Too many "no" notes would encourage the IRS to appoint a new director, and every director would know that every two years his job would be up for review by the voters. This would make the local IRS man responsible to the people, and this is what democracy is all about.

Today, with accountability only to the top bureaucrats in Washington, district directors are compelled to act like colonial bureaucrats out of the eighteenth century, not unlike the bureaucrats sent from London in the 1770s whose conduct inflamed the Americans and sparked the

American Revolution. You can have colonialism from within as well as from without, which is what the carpetbaggers were practicing in the South after the Civil War. The important point is that the arrogance and abuse now in the system is inherent in its structure. The problem will not go away as long as tax men cannot be called to judgment by taxpayers through civil suits and by the electoral process.

5. *Adjudicate tax disputes like any other debt.*

It is time to put an end to special laws giving extraordinary rights and powers to tax men. The tax man is usually a creditor claiming money. He should have the same rights and obligations as any other creditor, and taxpayers should have the same rights and duties as any other debtor. If the tax man claims you owe, then he should have to sue you just like everyone else. Similarly, if you have paid too much, you should be able to sue the tax man and have the same status as any other creditor.

The whole legal apparatus of the tax process has operated in a world of its own, separate and apart from the ordinary rules of law for settling money disputes. It has become a kind of American *oprichnina*, like the revenue agency of Ivan the Terrible in Russia that operated outside the regular judicial system and produced the NKVD and KGB. A British judge helped explain the problem this way:

> Taxation originally expressed only the will of a despot, enforceable by torture, slavery and death. Though it may be conceded that in modern times it is more often to further a benevolent social policy, and that the civil servant has usurped the position of the executioner as the agent to enforcement, yet in essence taxation is still arbitrary and depends for its effectiveness only on the executive power of the State.[12]

While we have abolished torture and have cancelled a few of the other barbaric enforcement devices carried over from the ancient world, there are still a number of abusive tax enforcement laws that put due process to shame.

People are often dumbfounded to learn that in a tax dispute, if they want to go to a regular court, they have to pay the tax debt and then sue to get their money back. Who ever would have imagined that in the twentieth century, a debtor, in order to have his day in court, would have to pay his disputed debt first, and then sue to get his payment back. The counterpart of this is that you can't enjoin the collection of an illegal tax. If you can't pay—if the tax might destroy your business, take away your home or livelihood—that is too bad. On top of all this there are over 150 penal provisions to trap and punish you for just about any error or slip up, however excusable, you may make in dealing with the vast jungle of rules and regulations every taxpayer is required to know but obviously doesn't know. Penalties often exceed the taxes owed. These penalties add a kind of audit-terrorism to the system. The GAO (General Accounting Office) reports that the IRS can't manage this vast web of entrapments, and that 44 percent of all penalties assessed by the IRS are wrong.[13] If this outrageously high percentage of penalties are wrongly assessed, how many are wrongly paid by taxpayers wanting to get the tax man off their backs?

The current stacked-deck arrangement is found frequently in history when equality under the law did not exist. Most people do not realize that throughout most of history few litigants had an equal footing in the courts. In a dispute between a master and a slave, or even a freeman and a slave, the presumption of truth went against the slave. In Europe, contests between commoners and aristocrats were governed by presumptions in favor of the more noble members of society. Why? Because the aristocrats had a bigger voice in law making just like the tax man today. The 150 penal provisions we now find in the tax code did not come from the urging of taxpayers.

In colonial America the Americans did quite well in tax disputes with the British government until 1764; in fact, they did too well so far as the British tax authorities were concerned. To stack the deck in favor of the British tax bureau, all tax cases were taken away from the local colonial courts and transferred to the British Admiralty courts in Halifax, Nova Scotia. The Americans seethed with anger over this maneuver and it helped spark the American Revolution some twelve years later.[14]

The presumptions and stacked-deck procedures in favor of the tax man go against the grain of a democratic society in which all litigants should be equal before the law. All I am proposing is that the tax man should be equal along with the rest of us, rather than more equal as he now is.

On the criminal side of tax enforcement, a tax fraud should be a genuine, honest-to-goodness fraud, with the same ingredients as a common law fraud. In California in 1987, a physician was convicted of felony tax evasion for simply not paying the tax he accurately declared on his tax return.[15] The concept is an outrage. If we applied this to ordinary civil debts, it would mean that if you deliberately didn't pay your American Express bill, you would have committed a felony.

6. Decriminalize the tax law.

The penalties Congress keeps piling up every year to trap taxpayers, innocent or guilty, along with the fuzzy criminal provisions, amounts to barbaric overkill. It reminds one of the twenty thousand nuclear warheads the military has in storage, or the queen in *Alice in Wonderland* who proclaimed, "Off with your head!" for anything she didn't like.

The number of criminal convictions is infinitesimal when compared to the reality of what taxpayers are doing. To be charged with evasion you usually are on the IRS blacklist, like the doctor in California. If ever there was a law that should not be enforced, and with the new civil penalties, need not be enforced, this is such a law.

We noted in history how Constantine decriminalized the Roman tax law. We noted how many of the wisest men in our own civilization have condemned making simple tax evasion a crime. In many of the enlightened nations of the world, only tax fraud is a crime; tax evasion is not. Our current practice puts America on a par with the former Soviet Union with its arbitrary use of synthetic economic crimes as a weapon against dissidents and as a device to put fear and terror into the hearts of everyone, because everyone is vulnerable. Hopefully, for the Russian peoples of the former USSR, that may now all pass away. Thomas Paine told us in *Common Sense*, "An avidity to punish is always dangerous to liberty." The French essayist Michel de Montaigne wrote in the sixteenth century, no man is so honest or upright that if he were carefully observed in his actions and thoughts, under the law, "ten times in his life he might not be lawfully hanged."[16] That certainly would apply to almost everyone under our criminal tax laws, and until recently, to almost everyone in the former Soviet Union.

This is the crux of the problem—everyone in a constant state of illegality, arrestable at any time for a "felony" manufactured by the state. The ultimate means of political control by all totalitarian states is to have most members of society under surveillance and in a state of illegality. Everyone is vulnerable to the bureaucracy that holds this power. In Nazi Germany and Soviet Russia it was the security police; in the high-tax West every country has a special branch of tax police: offices of "Special Investigations," the "Intelligence Division," and "Fiscal Police." In every tax audit the possibility of criminal prosecution is held over the head of every taxpayer. The intimidation and resulting fear give the government the power of easy extortion.

In tax matters the grand jury system was broken down as a protection from over-zealous, trumped-up tax charges. Our tax law is so complex, so incomprehensible, that in most complicated financial arrangements the line between avoidance (which is legal) and evasion (which is illegal) is too difficult even for the experts to determine, let alone laymen who have to do simply what the prosecutor tells them to do. Harry Margolis, the California planner we have mentioned, was indicted over a period of ten years for thirty-four different criminal tax felonies. After lengthy and costly trials, not one charge was ever sustained against him.[17] The corruption of a grand jury in Denver was so bad that the Justice Department tried to cover up the misconduct of the IRS and a U.S. attorney by muzzling the federal judge and preventing him from publishing the facts in his opinion. The Supreme Court, except for Justice Marshall, could find no fault with this. Marshall, in his dissent, understood what was at stake. The secrecy aspect of grand jury proceedings means that prosecutors can corrupt the proceedings "with impunity," said Marshall, against which there is no protection, no checks, no safeguards.[18]

If the vague and fuzzy tax crimes in the tax code were vigorously enforced, most taxpayers would be arrestable after a cursory audit. When news reports of tax charges come out every March and April, most taxpayers, if they were honest, would feel like John Bradford (1510–1555), who saw a man being led off to the gallows, and said, "There, but for the grace of God, goes John Bradford." Shortly thereafter, he too was executed. Tax fraud should be a crime; tax evasion should not. It would be wise to purge the tax law of its many synthetic crimes and let the civil penalties take care of tax sins.

7. Make congressional representatives and federal judges immune from the IRS.

It is essential in order to establish good tax laws and fair administration to have our federal tax lawmakers and judiciary immune from intimidation or undue influence from the tax bureau in the performance of their duties to the people. Recently, Senator David Pryor brought forth a bill called "The Taxpayer Bill of Rights."[19] It was a mild piece of legislation, but the IRS didn't like it; they don't like any curbs on their power. The senator was alone at first, because he had trouble finding a cosponsor. Why? Because congressmen are as intimidated by the IRS as their predecessors were intimidated twenty years ago by J. Edgar Hoover. Once you were on his blacklist, life could be intolerable, as Martin Luther King, Jr. learned.

Our Internal Revenue Service is a kind of institutionalized J. Edgar Hoover. Everyone is intimidated and no special files are necessary, as with Hoover. No congressman's tax conscience is so clear he isn't afraid of the IRS. Since there were no congressmen or even presidents with the courage to rid us of the Hoover pest, there are certainly few, if any, willing to rid us of the IRS's abuses and take a tough stand against the tax police. It is not possible as things now stand for the tax makers to do what they really think is for the best interest of the country. Ruffling the feathers of the IRS is dangerous to their political health. They all know what happened to congressmen in the past who simply sought to investigate IRS abuses. The IRS destroyed them. Representative George Hansen of Idaho courageously took on the IRS in the 1970s, publishing a book about their misdeeds. Many of the accounts he publicized were almost beyond belief.[20] He too felt the heat. There was a whispering campaign against him that he was a tax cheat, his popularity fell, and he was eventually defeated. When he and several other congressmen went to the powerful tax committee of the House (the Ways and Means Committee), they received a "deaf ear," because, as one writer explains, "They [the congressmen] were terrified of what the IRS might do to them individually."[21] The power of the IRS to intimidate Congress has to be completely eliminated and the way to make sure our congressmen are protected in that regard is to make sure the IRS is removed from their life—take them off the IRS tax rolls.

The judges are also vulnerable. Why are the judges audited? Is it for revenue, or is it to let the judges know Big Brother is watching and looking for "interesting" bits of information about their affairs that might be useful should the need arise? Justice William O'Douglas faced impeachment from information leaked about his financial affairs which, in all probability, came from his tax file. Douglas dissented without opinion against the IRS on innumerable cases.[22]

This nation was founded upon the sacred belief that the judiciary must be free and independent. The reason is found in British history. In England, a few centuries ago, a judge was dismissed if he displeased the king. The most famous case involved the greatest of British judges, Edward Coke, who was fired as chief justice by James I for ruling against the king's wishes. In the famous *Bates* and *Hampden* cases, which we discussed in Chapter 27, the justices in both of those cases ruled against the taxpayer and for the king, for obvious reasons. A minority ruled for the taxpayer, for courageous reasons.

The IRS can't fire judges, but it can leak information and intimidate them if they, like James I and Charles I, are displeased. If federal judges were immune from the IRS's power to hurt them with audit information, every taxpayer standing before a federal judge would know his case would be judged free of any possible pressure, influence, or intimidation from the tax bureau. We need that kind of air of freedom; judges should be like Caesar's wife.

One can't help but wonder if the pro-IRS Supreme Court isn't biased because of the potential power the IRS has over its members. In the 1960s, Commissioner Sheldon Cohen did a favor for the wife of Justice Abe Fortas concerning a tax problem. He commented, in writing no less, that the IRS may "need Abe's vote one day." Fortas must have done something wrong because he was forced to resign thereafter from information the IRS gave to a reporter from *Life* magazine.[23] So in the 1960s, two justices on the High Court felt the heel of the IRS boot—one forced to resign, the other put through the impeachment mill. Since then, have the justices "got the message"—especially the chief justice who goes out of his way to rule for the IRS? If the justices were removed from the IRS tax rolls, would the key cases the IRS won have been decided differently? If James I and Charles I had not the power to fire British justices, would the *Bates* and *Hampden* cases have been decided differently? The answer to both questions is probably yes.

How would we take them off the IRS tax rolls? There are two ways: either make them immune from federal income taxes, or seal their tax files and have their returns reviewed by independent auditors removed from the eyes of Big Brother.

8. Make our federal tax system indirect as much as possible.

One of the most repeated follies in tax history is the evolution of a good tax into a bad tax. Once a tax goes bad, seldom do tax makers have the wisdom to go back. The income tax in its better days was an indirect tax for almost everyone. I define indirect the way Montesquieu did—a tax that is not directly assessed against the individual. This would be an income tax like the British had before World War I. Because this tax worked so well and did not operate oppressively, the United States adopted the Sixteenth Amendment to the Constitution. As an indirect tax collected at the source, uniform tax rates are required. In this form it is like sales and customs taxes. Life would be intolerable if every year we had to calculate and pay our sales taxes instead of having the merchant collect, pay, and be responsible. The 1842–1914 British income tax was just such a tax. As we noted, in 1894 the British government was asked in the House of Commons about progressive tax rates for income taxes and the Chancellor of the Exchequer told the Commons that progressive tax rates were out of the question. Progressive rates would mean all taxpayers would be subject to audits and inquisitions. The British people would not tolerate this and consequently the system would collapse. Collection at the source was the key to the success of the income tax system, said the Chancellor.

Much of the evil in the income tax system comes from the direct confrontation between taxpayer and the all-mighty, self-righteous state. If we had a flat collection at the source of 10 percent for most people, there would be no April 15, no confrontation between citizen and state, no intimidation. Only payers or those in business would have to file a tax return. Ten percent is selected because this was the tax in the ancient world that operated for thousands of years, called the *decuma*. Not only was this the tax in the ancient world of Israel, Rome, and Greece, but it was also the rule for ancient China.

Recently, a former secretary of the treasury espoused this same ancient rule, although one wonders if he was really aware of the antiquity of the concept. He said things were getting out of hand in the tax field, and that something had to be done to bring some clarity to the vipers' tangle that passed for the "law" in this area. His basic suggestion was to scrap the current code and start over, substituting a flat 10 percent tax on all economic gross income, broadly defined and without "special" exemptions.[24] Thirty years before, another more famous secretary of the treasury, Andrew Mellon, espoused the same idea:

> It is not too much to hope that some day we may get back on a tax basis of 10 percent, the old Hebrew tithe, which was always considered a fairly heavy tax.[25]

The modern genesis of this idea came from two Stanford scholars whose article in the *Wall Street Journal* inspired the thinking that brought forth the Reagan reforms five years later.[26] They called their idea the *uniform* rate system; it was later called the flat rate system, which was an unfortunate misnomer directing attention away from the sound constitutional foundation of their idea.

The flat tax has received considerable support from the Congress (Congressman Dick Army of Texas) and presidential candidate Malcolm Forbes, Jr. A single tax rate with a minimum of deductions would permit a tax return the size of a post card for some. Not a bad idea, of course. But it had some political flaws, like exempting taxes on the receipt of interest dividends, capital gains, and death taxes. Hardly an attractive idea for the vast majority of taxpayer-workers, who have the votes. If the flat tax is ever to be viable, it is going to have to be truly uniform to all income receivers. The IRS would still continue much like it is today. If getting rid of an overpowering tax bully is an objective of tax reform, then the flat tax won't do the job.

The flat tax would still be a direct tax, repudiated by the Founders, by Montesquieu, and the ancient Greeks and Romans as an archenemy of liberty. Our ninety-year affair with the direct income tax has only proven that they were right. This is perhaps the greatest objection of all.

9. Another reform measure that may take the forefront in tax reform is a national consumption tax, like a sales tax.

The virtues are many, especially that of its being indirect. It was a form of tax Montesquieu said was consistent with liberty. Only a small segment of society, those providing goods and services, would be under tax scrutiny. Thus the IRS would cease to be the dreaded leviathan it now is to every citizen. Every worker would see a big increase in his or her paycheck, for income tax withholding would end.

When New Zealand adopted its consumption tax, the government wisely and dramatically reduced income taxes. Workers were ecstatic with the great increase in their paychecks, and in the next election the party that introduced this tax reform was returned to office. Canada, on the other hand, instituted its national consumption tax on top of an already heavy income tax. A tax rebellion followed that drove from office the political party that was responsible for the tax. The defeat was the worst ever known in the history of parliamentary government. From almost three hundred seats in the House of Commons, the PC party (responsible for the tax) ended up with only two seats. So the lessons to be learned by the wisdom of New Zealand and the folly of Canada are all too obvious.

There are other virtues of a national consumption tax. The insane complexity of our income tax would be gone, and the huge service industry for income taxes could be dismantled. The underground economy would be taxed. Foreign companies who import billions of dollars of goods annually for American consumers would no longer get a free ride on America's economy and taxpayers. American exports would be more competitive abroad with the elimination of an income tax expense on the price tag of American products.

The current effort to reform the income tax by a few band-aid remedies has been tried so often as to be nothing other than a joke. Congress and the Treasury have put on a big dog and pony show when they introduce all these "reforms," which taxpayers have heard and seen before. How dumb do they think the American people are? Fortunately, for serious and genuine reform, the Chairman of the House Ways and Means Committee, Bill Archer, is an advocate for the national sales tax. He visualizes the income tax and its numerous "reforms" of the past as hopeless. Like trimming back a noxious weed, he noted, it soon grows back and the only way to get rid of it is to tear it out by the roots.

Strangely enough, no reforms have ever been introduced to reduce the complexity of the tax code. The most recent reforms in 1997 added hundreds of new pages to the tax code and will add even more pages for the Regulations. So the insanity continues. We have a tax code that is beyond the capacity of the human mind to fathom. When the 1986 income tax reforms were passed into law, Boris Bittker, a leading tax scholar at Yale, had this to say:

> I submit, therefore, that to a fee-maximizing tax professional, the Internal Revenue Code of 1986, as amended, is merely a platform waiting for energetic entrepreneurs to construct a superstructure of previously unimaginable complexity.

So there are beneficiaries of our insane law and its complexity—the tax planners, tax preparers, tax seminars, tax schools, tax lobbyists, tax accountants, tax lawyers, etc., etc., etc. And then there is the tax bureaucracy, over 120,000 strong, using billions of taxpayer dollars to administer the tax. Add to that the billions paid by taxpayers into the private sector. The costs to administer the tax law have been estimated at somewhere between $300 billion and $600 billion.[27] No wonder H & R Block has done so well on the New York Stock Exchange. Obviously, investors are betting the income tax is here to stay in its noxious-weed form.

In the final days of the Roman Empire, ancient writers record that there were more people administering the tax system than there were taxpayers. Most likely we won't end up like that because of our modern computer technology. But if we translate into man hours the work of the computers, we may indeed already be like the Romans.

Many prominent writers and tax scholars have expressed themselves on the prospects of real tax reform and tax simplification.[28] They point out the numerous new tax laws over the past few decades with titles like "The Tax Simplification Act of . . ." And also titles like the "Tax Fairness Act" or "Tax Equity Act." You have to wonder, who do they think they are kidding? And how can you respect a government that continually lies to its people? Especially about taxes. Here are the words of one scholar:

> I find this blatant flouting of the truth both offensive and alarming. The United States is a democracy. When we allow our elected representatives to lie to us, then we're lying to ourselves. This is especially disturbing in the tax area, because nothing is more central to the relationship of the government to the governed than taxation.[29]

The hopelessness of the present endeavor to fix the income tax system was highlighted over 130 years ago in the first issues of a new periodical that was born in 1865, and which is still in print today. The September 1865 issue of *The Nation* praised the American people for their willingness to keep paying income taxes even after the Civil War had ended, which was necessary to help pay the huge war debt on the government's books. This was commendable because the income tax

> Is a tax that can be defended only by the necessity of the case, seeing that it bears hard upon men of moderate means, and that it is by its nature essentially inquisitorial and places everyone's business and mode of life at the mercy of tax gatherers, who in all ages have been regarded as *the most odious of mankind* [emphasis added].

The recent senatorial hearings that brought out the horror stories of IRS misdeeds produce nothing not known throughout the country, and not known throughout history. If history is to be our teacher, there is no fix, other than to develop an indirect system of taxation, where the tax man is far removed from the average citizen.

Polls show that about 75 percent of the American people want to get rid of the income tax as we know it, yet those who can change it will not. At 1996 congressional hearings about getting rid of the income tax, the Treasury sent one of their top officials, Lee Samuelson, who put a damper on the hearings by saying, "We like the income tax, just the way it is." The *Wall Street Journal* recently reported on current programs for real tax reform: "Treasury Secretary Robert Rubin has led the cabinet in snubbing the tax cutters as if they were a bunch of unseemly aberrants."[30] Worse still are the views of the ranking Democrat on the powerful House Ways and Means Committee, Charles Rangel: "I'm sick and tired of politicians beating up on the IRS. We have the best and fairest tax-collection system in the world." When we hear that from those who are in the position of power to reform the tax system, and who know better, one wonders what chance or hope there is of reforming the system. What we need is someone on the national level like the late Howard Jarvis in California, who aroused the people to force upon a reluctant government real tax reform, which the people wanted.

41

Half-Slave and Half-Free

I believe this government can not endure permanently half slave and half free.

—Abraham Lincoln, 1858

While the word slavery is a very powerful term—a very ugly and horrifying memory in our society—we assume that slavery has been abolished in the world, the one great social accomplishment of the nineteenth century. But for many centuries the philosophers and great minds of Western civilization pondered over the moral issue of slavery as well as the kinds of slavery. There was chattel slavery, in which a person was the property—a chattel of another person. But that was only one kind of slavery—the worst kind. Then there was land slavery, or *real* slavery as it was called, in which the person belonged to the land. Whoever owned the land got the slaves whether they were wanted or not, and sometimes they were not wanted. A study of land values in what was White Russia discloses that land free from landed serfs was worth more than land with serfs.

There were other kinds of slavery, such as what was called political slavery, where you were the property of the ruler, and you had no rights except those the rulers passed out. Today Cuba and Iraq would be such countries. While you are not "owned" like chattel slaves, your lives are greatly controlled, regulated, and restricted by an all-powerful government. Any type of totalitarianism would be political slavery, which, of course, still exists in the world.

Chattel slavery and real slavery were abolished in Europe primarily by the moral force of Christianity, but this abolition was limited to Western Europe and to European peoples. Russia retained its chattel and real slavery until the 1860s, the very same time the Americans were getting rid of chattel slavery in the South. Portugal and Spain were the last holdouts in their colonies in the New World, but by 1900, all vestiges of chattel slavery by European nations were gone.

We know that serfdom (land slavery), which dominated the world for a thousand years, came into being from tax practices of the later Roman Empire. At the time it seemed like the best way to keep tabs on Roman taxpayers. When the Roman emperor instituted serfdom he was merely protecting his revenue, what the IRS claims it is doing and why it needs Congress to give the agency all these awesome powers over taxpayers.

The reader should also recall the unsuccessful tax rebellion by Boadicea in the first century A.D. to rid Briton of Roman rule, especially Roman taxes. Her exhortation to her troops is a classic expression of what tax slavery is all about. In five thousand years of recorded history, no one said it better than Boadicea:

> Do we not pay yearly tribute for our very bodies? How much better it would be to have been sold to masters once and for all than possessing empty titles of freedom, to have to ransom ourselves every year.[1]

In other words, it's better to be a chattel slave than a tax slave.

The Tax Foundation in Washington is best known for its calculation of "Tax Freedom Day," the day each year after which Americans' earnings are all their own. (However, for the average working husband and wife, it is not at all improbable that one of them works full time, all year long, for the tax man.)

The Tax Freedom day in 1902 was January 31,

in 1922 was February 17,
in 1948 was March 28,
in 1958 was April 10,
in 1968 was April 24,
in 1978 was April 30,
in 1988 was May 2,
in 1998 was May 10.

All indications are that tax freedom day will continually be delayed until we become a nation half-free and half-slave. Slavery is, after all, forced labor with no compensation. Tolstoy gave it this definition:

> The essence of all slavery consists in taking the produce of another's labor by force. It is immaterial whether this force be founded upon ownership of the slave or ownership of the money that he must get to live. (*What Shall We Do?*, 1891)

Those favoring big taxes and big spending would object to the slavery label. After all, they point out, we tax slaves benefit from all this slave labor. But isn't this like the planter in our slave economy in the South who provided for the slave from cradle to grave? We now get public services that do about the same thing. This, however, misses the point. Once the taxes are paid, it is the government, not the taxpayer, who determines who gets what. In all slave economies it is the master who selects the deserving among the enslaved. That some slaves are well-provided for (as Southern planters maintained in 1860) does not alter their status as slaves.

That we are fast moving toward a day when we will be half-slave and half-free should come as no surprise, and we are doing so with our consent. While we may not like big taxes, our representatives obviously do. And we are as much a culprit as they are by demanding and expecting governments to do all sorts of things, all of which require money, and money requires taxes. We noted how in Rome and in early Russia peasants gave up their freedom and became serfs to avoid taxes. They would rather be chattel slaves or land slaves, pure and simple, than be tax slaves to a powerful tax bureaucracy with its punitive powers, its confiscations, its brutality. Montesquieu tells us how so many Russians in Moscow chose to be slaves,[2] rather than face the Tsarists tax men. Hopefully, we may not be driven to that choice someday. But history is full of such examples, not just in Russia. The choice was what kind of slavery—tax or chattel? The fact that so many chose chattel slavery over tax slavery tells us just how oppressive and unbearable tax slavery can be.

Tax slavery was a great concern of the early Americans. British writers ridiculed the position taken by the Americans that any tax by the Crown was "a badge of slavery."[3] Again, we were not talking about a badge of chattel slavery. The leading underground organization that promoted the tax rebellions against the British in the 1760s and 1770s was called The Sons of Liberty. They tarred and feathered British tax agents, and when they paraded through the streets in the major cities, they sang a song with a chorus that went like this:

Parliament's voice has condemned us by law to be SLAVES,
Brave Boys!
Has condemned us by law to be SLAVES.[4]

Here we have the word "slaves" capitalized, and which obviously meant tax slaves.

When Montesquieu, in his great classic *The Spirit of Laws*, wrote that excessive taxes lead to slavery, and again that direct taxes are natural to slavery,[6] he was not talking about chattel slavery, but about tax slavery. And the Americans who looked upon Montesquieu as the great sage of

When word reached Boston in 1766 that the Stamp Act had been repealed, a monument was erected, which Paul Revere copied and preserved. The words above said in effect that it was better to die than be "SLAVES" (i.e., tax slaves)—a concept we have lost sight of.[5]

the Enlightenment were quick to focus on the tax slave issue in their dealings with Great Britain and at the Constitutional convention.

Lincoln used the words half-slave and half-free in his debates with Stephen Douglas in 1858, and he suggested that the nation could not survive this format. In substituting tax slavery for chattel slavery the same issue arises—can we survive as a free people if we are half-free and half-slave to the tax man?

Taxpayers who get fed up with the system can pick up their bags and leave the country, again like so many Romans who fled to the land of the barbarians, "to live as free men." But, unlike the Romans, they will be hounded for taxes in their foreign abode by IRS agents armed with summonses and ready for audit. Tens of thousands of people, from the Rolling Stones to Sean Connery to great athletes, have left their high-tax homelands for more gentler tax climes. This is a worldwide and historically lawful practice.

Direct taxes are a person's obligation to the country where they live. This country provides protection and services to its inhabitants. But if you don't live in that country, you are not receiving services and protection, hence there is no moral justification to tax you. Not so for Americans. They have to give up their citizenship to legally avoid being taxed. And now, if they do that, they can be banned from ever returning to the United States of America, like the Soviet writers who were expelled from the Soviet Union—they were criminals for "slander against the state." Solzenitzen was such a criminal. Americans who leave to avoid tax are a new type of criminal—traitors. Benedict Arnolds is what they are now called. If Americans are Benedict Arnolds, why aren't the Rolling Stones and William Joyces? (William Joyce was a notorious traitor to Britain in the war with Germany. His trial, a kind of trial of the century in the 1940s, centered on whether or not he was a citizen of Great Britain.)

Surprisingly, the Clinton administration opposed this new Benedict Arnold Law (passed in 1996), as the Congress has so proudly named it. How can such a law, so alien to Western civilization, be justified? Does it not really prove that Americans are more enslaved to the tax man than any other people on earth?

Today, Americans not wanting to take flight to avoid tax can join the modern underground railroad of the twentieth century—the underground economy. If caught, like fugitive slaves from the South they are punished and then returned to their servitude to the tax man.

When is a tax system a tax slave system? What would be the determinants? Surely we must have taxes in order to be a civilized society, and all taxes are not ipso facto slavery. But remember, we learned that in ancient times, until the Greeks came along, all civilization had been purchased with despotism. The Greeks concluded that civilization up until that time was not compatible with freedom. The culprit, according to the Greeks and the Romans, was direct taxation.

The test is, how much of your freedom has been surrendered to the tax man, to ensure the collection of taxes? That is the issue. If we have given up too much of our freedoms to the tax man—if the tax man intrudes into our lives excessively (like the scribes of the pharaohs), if the tax man punishes us excessively for tax disobedience, takes an excessive amount of the fruits of our labors and property, takes away our civil liberties, our Bill of Rights—if we are half-free and half-slave, are we not, as The Sons of Liberty proclaimed over two hundred years ago, subjects of a government that "Has condemned us by law to be SLAVES"?

Epilogue: The Foursquare

The history of various disciplines and professions is replete with revolutions of thought that had to be led by heretics, outsiders, and amateurs.
—Jeffrey Bell, *Populism and Elitism*, 1992

Over the years many readers and friends have asked me to summarize in a nutshell what I like to call the nuts and bolts of my thoughts about taxation and history. In these concluding paragraphs I will try and present some of the most important lessons from this study.

First is the glaring fact that all good tax systems tend to go bad. Unless restrained by the people in some effective way, governments are unable to live with a good working, moderate tax system. All governments tend to be spend-o-holics. Like immature consumers they will adjust their spending to their appetites, not their pocketbooks. History suggests that the best cure is to separate the power to spend from the power to tax.

Second, the most challenging problem of our age is whether or not civilization can extricate itself from its own tax self-destructiveness. If we don't address that problem, I believe our children in the next century will. Our tax destructiveness is on all fronts and we appear to be following the course of many great nations of the past—we are taxing ourselves to death, and not just economically. We have violated the tax rules our forefathers warned us about. Until recently, our system was excused because we need the money, and this is an efficient way to do the job. Now, that myth has been shattered. When the costs expended by taxpayers are added to those of the government, it has been quite properly called a "$600-Billion Tax Ripoff."[1] The so-called virtues of our income tax system are as phoney as the virtues of socialism.

The destructiveness is not just economic, it endangers more important matters of the human spirit. We are living in an age of liberty, not perfect, but certainly one of the better times in human history. The political philosopher Montesquieu, over two hundred years ago, warned us of the dangers a liberty-oriented society faces. Men living in a state of liberty will grant excessive taxing powers to their governments. These excessive powers, says Montesquieu, will require "extraordinary means of oppression," and when that happens, "the country is ruined."[2] It is not too difficult to apply Montesquieu's thesis to our times.

My personal optimism supports the belief that we will extricate ourselves from this gloomy conclusion. Just as Thomas Malthus's theory of population growth was full of doom, so is Montesquieu's prediction about liberty and taxes. Neither prediction has to bring disaster to civilization, but both require heroic efforts, for the natural course of events is leading us in the direction both of these men foresaw.

Third, the one common denominator of all good tax systems (before they went bad) has been moderation. This principle was given to us by the ancients as the ideal of the good life and of good government. It was especially dominant as an ethical ideal with the ancient Greeks; Aristotle formalized it in his *Ethics*, as the doctrine of the "golden mean."[3] It was the foundation of the ethics of Adam Smith.[4] Aristotle arranged a long list of moral qualities in triads. Virtue was a middle ground between extremes, called vices. Courage was the golden mean between cowardice and rashness. Applying the principle of the golden mean to taxation, how often are we at a vicious extreme rather than the virtuous middle in such matters as *rates*, *equality*, *intrusions*, and *penalties*? A well-balanced system, consistent with the concept of a moderate government, can be likened unto a foursquare, which Tennyson expressed as: "That tower of strength, Which stood foursquare to all winds that blew."

How near a foursquare is our present system? Today, our income tax (not capital gains) looks somewhat like the first illustration below. Today's figure is grotesque because the intrusions and punitive provisions are out of step with the spirit of a free society. No matter how lopsided it is now, we can make it foursquare, like the second illustration on the next page.

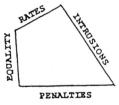

For the income tax

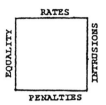

The true "foursquare"

Rates should be moderate. If too low, the lives and property of the people cannot be protected. If too high, the economy will drag. Do the rates encourage evasion, emigration, and rebellion? Are they on the negative or positive side of the Laffer curve?

Equality is the virtue. It means the absence of any discrimination against any class of citizens with respect to rates, exemptions, privileges, and burdens. The vices are the regressive or the progressive extremes. Regressive systems unfairly burden the poor; progressive systems, if extreme, steal from the wealthy. Taxes which touch a broad range of economic activities, even with equal rates, will inevitably be mildly progressive, the golden mean.

Intrusions. Whatever is taxed must be surveyed, but how extensive should that be? Are we sacrificing too much of our liberty for tax compliance? Is ours an honor system or a spy system?

Penalties. How punitive are we? Or, as Montesquieu said, are people who cannot be considered as bad men punished as villains?[5]

To have a foursquare, where do we start? With the legislatures, of course, but in practice the "experts" make the decisions. They would be the Treasury, Congressional Committees, and sub-rosa, super-elites, whose members are sworn to secrecy, such as the Eagle Lodge group.[6] For the average, even well-informed, congressman, the tax law is unintelligible. To start, we should get rid of these "experts." They are as entrenched in tax making as the Communist party was entrenched in the Soviet Union. They will pile reason upon reason why we have to have an over-complicated, grotesque tax system. They were supposed to give us much more simplicity in the Reagan reforms of 1986 and ten years later in 1997. They ended up increasing the complexity dramatically, making themselves increasingly indispensable. Tax practitioners were shocked at the new reforms which were now getting beyond the comprehension of even the experts.[7] The experts weren't satisfied with just decimating the intelligibility of the tax code, they have also turned tax concepts such as equality and fairness into a morass of philosophical gobbledygook,[8] like the "separate but equal" doctrine that justified segregation.

We need to start with new energetic minds and give the old experts a rest from their labors. When Henry Ford wanted to protect lives and prevent injuries from shattered auto glass, he asked the glass experts to make unbreakable glass for his new models. The world's glass experts said it couldn't be done. They knew too many reasons why it couldn't be done. Henry said, "Bring me eager young fellows who do not know the reasons why unbreakable glass cannot be made. Give the problem to ambitious young fellows who think nothing is impossible." He got the unbreakable glass.[9]

It is not the heavy taxed realm that executes great deeds, but the moderately taxed one.

—Ancient Asian Proverb

Notes

Introduction

1. A. H. M. Jones, *The Roman Economy* (Oxford, 1974), p. 86.
2. Adrienne Koch and William Peder, eds., *The Selected Works of John and John Quincy Adams* (New York, 1946), pp. 24–27.
3. John Stuart Mill, *Principles of Political Economy* (New York, 1961, reprint of 1885 edition), p. 808, n.2.

Part I

1. Samuel Karmer, *History Begins at Sumer* (New York, 1959), ch. 7.
2. M. Davidson, L. Cottrel, eds., *Lost Worlds* (New York, 1962), p. 154.

Chapter 1

1. A. Erman, *Literature of the Ancient Egyptians* (London, 1927), p. 244.
2. M. Rostovtzeff, *The Social and Economic History of the Hellenistic World*, vol. 2 (Oxford, 1967), p. 1094.
3. Alan Gardiner, "Ramesside Tests Relating to Taxation of Corn," *Journal of Egyptian Archeology*, vol. 27 (London, 1941), pp. 19–21.
4. Cyril Aldren, *The Egyptians* (New York, 1963), p. 180.
5. Victor Ehrenberg, *The Greek State* (New York, 1960), p. 153.
6. James Baikie, *A History of Egypt*, vol. 2 (London, 1929), p. 313.
7. Baikie, *History of Egypt* 2, p. 299.
8. Charles Eliot, ed., *The Harvard Classics*, vol. 33, Herodotus, "*Histories, Bk. II*," trans. G. C. Macaulay, p. 85.
9. James Baikie, *The Amarna Age, A Study of the Crises of the Ancient World* (London, 1926), p. 428.
10. Diogenes, *The April Game* (Chicago, 1973), p. 122.

Chapter 2

1. Rostovtzeff, *Hellenistic World* 2, p. 901.
2. Ibid., pp. 705–36.
3. Ibid., p. 914.
4. Edwyn Bevan, *A History of Egypt Under the Ptolemaic Dynasty* (London, 1927), chs. VIII-XIII.
5. Suetonius, *The Lives of the Ceasars*, Bk. II, XVIII, vol. 1, trans. J. C. Rolfe (London, 1979), p. 149.
6. Jack Lindsay, *Daily Life in Roman Egypt* (London, 1963), p. 253.
7. Flavius Josephus, *The Wars of the Jews*, Bk. II, trans. William Winston (Philadelphia, 1936), ch. XVI, para. 4, p. 692.

Chapter 3

1. Exodus 1:7–11.
2. Flavius Josephus, *The Antiquities of the Jews*, Bk. 2, ch. 14, para. 1.
3. H. Graetz, *History of the Jews*, vol. 3 (Phila. 1895) p. 108; Hugo Grotius, *The Law of Peace and War* (Oxford, 1925), Bk. 2, ch. 5, xxxii, 1625 edition, p. 259; *Encyclopedia of Religion and Ethics*, ed. James Hastings, vol. 11, pp. 595–631; C. H. W. Johns, *Babylonian and Assyrian Laws, Contracts and Letters* (Edinburgh, 1904), passim.
4. Hosea 8:10; Amos 5:11; Isaiah 13:1; Ezekiel 12:10; 2 Chronicles 10; 1 Kings 12:4; Josephus, *Antiquities*, Bk. 8, ch. 8. Then compare with the text on the Egyptian "burdens" in Josephus, *Antiquities*, Bk. 2, ch. 9; Exodus 6:6.
5. Samuel 8:11–17.
6. Josephus, *Antiquities*, Bk. 8, ch. 7, para. 5.
7. Ecclesiastes 7:28.
8. Josephus, *Antiquities*, Bk. 8, ch. 7, para. 5.
9. E. W. Heath, *Solomon's New Men* (New York, 1974), p. 55.
10. II Chron. 16:17.
11. Ibid., Bk. 8, ch. 8, para. 3.
12. Josephus, *Antiquities*, Bk. 8, ch. 8, v. 3.
13. 2 Chronicles 10:18.
14. Josephus, *Antiquities*, Bk. 8, ch. 8, v. 3.
15. Isaiah 30:15.
16. Isaiah 37:33.
17. Recent translations of Assyrian records by a University of Toronto scholar indicate just how barbaric these rulers were. See A. Kirk Grayson, *Assyrian Rulers of the Early First Millennium BC I (1114–859 BC)* (Toronto, 1991), passim.
18. Max I. Dimont, *Jews, God and History* (New York, 1962), pp. 66–68.

Chapter 4

1. Josephus, *Antiquities*, Bk. 12, ch. 4, para. 1–2.
2. Ibid.
3. Ibid., para. 10.

4. 1 Maccabees 11:34; M. Rostovtzeff, *The Social and Economic History of the Hellenistic World*, vol. 1 (Oxford, 1967), p. 467.

5. Flavius Josephus, *The Wars of the Jews*, Bk. 2, ch. 16, para. 4.

6. Moses Hadas, "Roman Allusions in Rabbinic Literature," *Philological Quarterly* 8 (1929), p. 373.

Chapter 5

1. *The Sayings of Mencius*, Trans. James R. Ware (New York, 1960), p. 55.

2. Ibid., p. 68.

3. Fung Yu-Lan, *A Short History of Chinese Philosophy* (New York, 1948), p. 75.

4. Ni, Hua-Ching, *Stepping Stones for Spiritual Success* (Los Angeles, 1989), p. 66.

5. Fung yu-Lan, p. 102.

6. Tzo Te Ching, trans. Stephen Mitchell (New York, 1985), No. 75.

7. Ibid., No. 60.

Chapter 6

1. Gustave Glotz, *Ancient Greece at Work* (New York, 1967), p. 154.

2. M. I. Finley, *The Ancient Economy* (Berkeley, 1973), p. 95.

3. Polybus, *The Rise of the Roman Empire*, Bk. II, 56; trans. Ian Scott-Kilvert (London, 1979), p. 169.

4. Victor Ehrenberg, *The Greek State* (New York, 1964), passim; Gustave Glotz, *The Greek City and Its Inhabitants* (London, 1929), pp. 113-16.

5. A. R. Burns, *A Pelican History of Rome* (New York, 1987), p. 124.

6. Rostovtzeff, *Hellenistic World* 2, p. 620.

7. The author's translation. See Charles Eliot, *The Harvard Classics*, vol. 12, p. 105, "Plutarch's Lives," trans. Arthur Clough (New York, 1909).

8. Thucydides, *History of the Peloponnesian War*, trans. Rex Warner (New York, 1972) pp. 79–80, Bk. 1, 75.

9. Ibid., p. 198, Bk. 3, 10.

Chapter 7

1. Xenophon, *Oeconomicus* II, 5–8, recorded in M. M. Austin and P. Vidal-Nagaet, *Economic and Social History of Ancient Greece* (London, 1977), note 97, p. 320.

2. Ibid.

3. Thucydides, *Peloponnesian War*, pp. 145–48.

4. Carolyn Webber, Aaron Wildavsky, *A History of Taxation and Expenditure in the Western World* (New York, 1985), pp. 57–59.

5. Ibid., pp. 128–31.
6. Rostovtzeff, *Hellenistic World* 1, pp. 243–44.
7. Ibid. 2, p. 818.
8. Ehrenberg, *Greek State*, p. 178.

Part II

1. M. Rostovtzeff, *The Social and Economic History of the Roman Empire*, vol. 1 (Oxford, 1971), pp. 419, 515, 530; Ferdinand Lot, *The End of the Ancient World* (New York, 1961), pp. 70, 174–76.
2. Tacitus, *The Annals of Imperial Rome*, trans. Michael Grant (New York, 1977), p. 308.

Chapter 8

1. Hugo Grotius, *Law of Peace and War*, p. 259.
2. Livy, "History of Rome" 39.11.44, *Roman Civilization, Sourcebook I: The Republic* (New York, 1966), p. 405. (Hereafter cited as *Sourcebook I.*)
3. Cicero, "On Duties II," from Cicero, *On the Good Life*, trans. Michael Grant (New York, 1971), p. 162. For a different translation, see Naphtali Lewis and Meyer Reinhold, *Sourcebook I*, pp. 254–55.
4. Cicero, "Second Speech against Verres," See *Sourcebook I*, p. 347.
5. Ibid.
6. Ibid., p. 349.
7. P. A. Brunt, *Social Conflicts in the Roman Republic* (London 1971), p. 115.
8. Livy, "History of Rome" XXV.iii.9, *Sourcebook I*, p. 226.

Chapter 9

1. Rostovtzeff, *Hellenistic World* 2, p. 965.
2. H. H. Scullard, *From the Gracchi to Nero* (London, 1976), p. 270.
3. Cicero, "Letters to his Brother Quintus," *Sourcebook I*, p. 353; Rostovtzeff, *Hellenistic World* 2, p. 965.
4. Polybius, *The Histories*, Bk. 30.30, trans. W. R. Paton, vol. vi (Cambridge, 1927), p. 156.
5. See Brunt, *Social Conflicts in the Roman Republic*, p. 38.
6. Appian, "Roman History" XII.IX, 61-63; *Sourcebook I*, p. 203.
7. Rostovtzeff, *Hellenistic World* 2, p. 963, 994. Special agents were also used by Mark Anthony when he fleeced the Asiatic provinces, p. 1006.
8. Cicero,*On Duties* III, "Is Honesty Always Necessary?," *Cicero's Selected Works*, trans. Michael Grant (New York, 1966), p. 193.
9. 2 *Tax Notes International*, 687, 1130 (July, November 1990).
10. Rostovtzeff, *Hellenistic World* 2, pp. 982–83.

11. Cicero, *On Duties* II, 8.

12. Rostovtzeff, *Hellenistic World* 2, p. 995.

13. Josephus, *Antiquities*, Bk. 14, ch. 10, para. 5.

14. Charles W. Eliot, ed., *The Harvard Classics*, vol. 10, Adam Smith, *The Wealth of Nations* (New York, 1909), p. 532 (referring to the invention of stamp taxes in the early eighteenth century that were quickly adopted by all nations).

15. Rostovtzeff, *Hellenistic World* 2, pp. 1006–7.

Chapter 10

1. Rostovtzeff, *Roman Empire* 1, p. 388; see also Rostovtzeff, *Hellenistic World* 2, pp. 1016–17.

2. Tacitus, *Annals*, pp. 308–9.

3. Ibid.

4. The maltreatment of taxpayers by tax agents was a long-standing abuse throughout Roman history. See Ch. 11, and Ch. 38, notes 1 and 4.

5. Suetonius, *The Lives of the Caesars*, Bk. III, ch. XXXII, vol.1, trans. John Rolfe (London: Loeb Classics, 1979), p. 341

6. S. M. Rostovtzeff, *Journal of Economic and Business History* 1 (1928–29), pp. 353–55; *Sourcebook II*, p. 399.

7. Edict of Hadnan, *Sourcebook II: The Empire* (New York, 1966), pp. 396–97.

8. Oxyrhynchus Papyrus No. 252, *Sourcebook II*, p. 397.

9. Dio Cassius, *Roman History* LXII.iii, *Sourcebook II*, p. 415. Compare with Tacitus, *Annals of Rome* XIV, pp. 34–38.

10. Tacitus, *The Histories* Bk. IV, LXXXIV, vol. 2, trans. W. H. Fyfe (Oxford, 1912), pp. 187–88.

11. Dio Cassius, *Roman History* LXXI.III.3: Rostovtzeff, *Roman Empire* 1, p. 373.

12. Rostovtzeff, *Roman Empire* 1, p. 392.

Chapter 11

1. Dio Cassius, *Roman History* LXXVI.xv.2, *Sourcebook II*, p. 419.

2. "Inflation by the Bushel," *Horizon* (Summer 1976), p. 20.

3. Stephen Williams, *Diocletian and the Roman Recovery* (New York, 1985), p. 30.

4. Rostovtzeff, *Roman Empire* 1, p. 518.

5. Lactantius, "On the Death of Persecutors," vii, *Sourcebook II*, p. 459.

6. Ibid.

7. Egyptian Papyrus, trans. H. C. Youfe, University of Michigan, *Sourcebook II*, p. 461.

8. D. Saunders, ed., *The Portable Gibbon, The Decline and Fall of the Roman Empire* (New York, 1973), p. 378.

9. C. Pharr, ed., *Theodosian Code*, XI 7, 3; A.D. 320 (Princeton, 1952); *Sourcebook II*, p. 477.

10. J. Stevenson, ed., *A New Eusebius, Documents Illustrative of the History of the Christians to A.D. 337* (London, 1968), pp. 295, 302–3.

11. Rostovtzeff, *Roman Empire* 1, pp. 531–32.

Chapter 12

1. Montesquieu, *Considerations*, p. 169.

2. Ferdinand Lot, *The End of the Ancient World and the Beginnings of the Middle Ages* (New York, 1961), p. 174.

3. *Theodosian Code* XI.28.1-17 (Tax remissions A.D. 363–436).

4. Salvian, *On the Government of God, A Treatise*, ed. and trans. Eva M. Sanford (New York, 1930), pp. 141–49.

5. Theodosian Code XI.7.3, p. 299, *Sourcebook II*, p. 477.

6. *Theodosian Code* XI.28.2.

7. *Ammianus Marcellinus*, Bk. XVII.3.5, trans. John C. Wolfe (London, 1963), pp. 315–17.

8. Lot, *End of the Ancient World*, p. 175.

9. Aurelio Bernardi, "The Economic Problems of the Roman Empire at the Time of its Decline," in Carlo Cippola, ed., *Economic Decline of Empires* (London, 1970), p. 72.

10. Tacitus, *The Histories*, Bk. II, LXIX, trans. C. H. Moore (Cambridge, 1980), p. 271.

11. M. I. Finley, "Manpower and the Fall of Rome," in Cipolla, ed., *Economic Decline of Empires*, p. 90.

12. A. H. M. Jones, *The Roman Economy* (Oxford, 1974), pp. 82–89.

13. Rostovtzeff, *Roman Empire* 1, p. 398; Salvian, *On the Government of God*, pp. 141–49.

14. Bernardi, "Economic Problems of the Roman Empire," p. 66.

15. Ibid., pp. 81-83.

16. Jones, *Roman Economy*, pp. 134–35; see for other theories, D. Kagan, ed., *Decline and Fall of the Roman Empire: Why Did It Collapse?* (Boston, 1962).

17. *Justinian Digest* L.XVII, Paulus on Edict II, *Sourcebook II*, p. 539.

18. Ibid., Gaius on Provincial Edict V.

19. Livy, xxiv.16.19; Ovid, *Fasti*, iv.623; Dio Cassius xxxviii.xvii.6, reports how a Temple of Liberty was erected on the spot where Cicero's house was destroyed after his banishment by Clodius. A Temple of Liberty was erected by the Senate after Caesar's defeat of Pompey, and later by Tiberius after he put down the revolt of Sejanus: Dio Cassius, xliii.44.1; lviii.12.5. The last reference to this goddess is in the restored Temple of Jupiter, in which Augustus set aside a special hall in her honor.

20. Montesquieu, *Considerations*, last chapter.

Part III

1. Ferdinand H. H. Grapperhaus, *Taxes, Liberty and Property* (Amsterdam, 1989), p. 35.

Chapter 13

1. Daniel C. Dennett, Jr., *Conversion and the Poll Tax in Early Islam* (Harvard, 1950), ch. II.

2. Ibid., p. 10, citing *History of the Patriarchs of the Coptic Church of Alexandria*, ed. Evetts (1910), pp. 189–90.

3. Ibid.

4. Abu Yusuf, "Advice to a Caliiph," *Islam from the Prophet Muhammad to the Capture of Constantinople*, vol. 1, trans. Bernard Lewis (New York, 1974), pp. 167–68.

5. M. A. Shaban, *Islamic History, a New Interpretation* (Cambridge, 1971), p. 39.

6. The author cannot locate his original source for this quotation; however, the event is confirmed in Dennett, *Conversion*, pp. 55–57, citing Moslem sources. The poll tax was protection money; when the protection could not be provided a refund was required. See "Islam and the Jews," Jacob. R. Marcus, ed. *The Jews in the Medieval World, A Sourcebook* (New York, 1975) pp. 13-19.

7. Ibid.

8. Desmond Stewart, *Early Islam* (New York, 1967), p. 63.

9. Lewis, *Islam from the Prophet Muhammad* 1, pp. 234–35.

10. Abu Uboyd, "Tiflis (A.D. 642–643)," *Islam from the Prophet Muhammad*, vol. 1, pp. 239–40.

11. al-Tahari, "On Collecting Taxes, (A.D. 739)," *Islam from the Prophet Muhammad*, vol. 2, p. 133.

12. Abu Yusuf, "The Conquest of Mesopotamia (A.D. 631–634)," *Islam from the Prophet Muhammad*, vol. 1, p. 230.

13. Ibid., pp. 231–32.

14. Al Turtushi, "On Taxation and Its Effects (Ninth to the Twelfth Centuries)," *Islam from the Prophet Muhammad*, vol. 1, pp. 134–35.

15. Bernard Lewis, *The Arabs in History* (1960), found in Cipolla, *Economic Decline of Empires*, p. 114.

16. Malise Ruthven, "1001 Arabian Years," *The Wilson Quarterly* (Washington, D.C., Summer 1991), p. 97.

17. Salo W. Baron, Arcadius Kahan, et al., *Economic History of the Jews*, ed. Nachum Gross (New York, 1975), p. 26.

18. Lewis, *Arabs in History*, p. 113.

Chapter 14

1. Roy Cave and Herbert Coulson, *A Source Book for Medieval Economic History* (New York, 1965), p. 355.

2. Kunwar Deo Prasad, *Taxation in Ancient India* (Delhi, 1987), pp. 30–31.

3. Grapperhaus, *Taxes, Liberty and Property*, p. 46.

4. Ibid., p. 47.

5. Baron de Montesquieu, *The Spirit of Laws* (Dublin, 1751), vol. 2, Bk. 28, pp. 204 et seq.

6. Grapperhaus, *Taxes, Liberty and Property*, p. 38.

7. Ibid., p. 56.

8. Stephen Dowell, *A History of Taxation and Taxes in England*, vol. 1 (London, 1965, reprint of 1884 edition), p. 22.

9. Ibid.

10. Ibid., p. 26.

Chapter 15

1. Dimont, *Jews, God and History*, p. 256; Werner Sombart, *The Jews and Modern Capitalism*, trans. M. Epstein (New York, 1962), passim, pp. 42–43, 97; but see Fernand Braudel, *Civilization and Capitalism*, vol. 2 (New York, 1986), pp. 159–69. Philippe Merlin, a leading scholar on French law during the Napoleonic era, "attributes the invention of bills of exchange to the Jews." See James Kent, *Commentaries on American Law,* vol. 3 (New York, 1828, reprint 1986), p. 44, note a. Bills of exchange are what make modern international commerce work, and are what make ancient capitalism differ from modern capitalism.

2. Jacob R. Marcus, ed., *The Jew in the Medieval World, A Source Book*: *315–1791* (New York, 1975), pp. 8–9.

3. Israel Abrahams, *Jewish Life in the Middle Ages* (New York, 1975), p. 40.

4. Salo W. Baron et al., *Economic History of the Jews* (New York, 1975), pp. 26–27.

5. Sombart, *Jews and Modern Capitalism*, p. 16.

6. Dimont, *Jews, God and History*, p. 225; the strange legal status of the Jews as the king's property is explained in Pollack and Maitland, *The History of English Law*, vol. 1 (Cambridge, 1899), pp. 468–75.

7. Heinrich Graetz, *The History of the Jews,* vol. 3 (Philadelphia, 1894), p. 645; Leon Poliakov, *The History of Anti-Semitism*, vol.1 (New York, 1965), p. 78.

8. Poliakov, *History of Anti-Semitism*, pp. 99–100.

9. Baron, *Economic History of the Jews*, p. 43.

Chapter 16

1. David C. Douglas, *William the Conqueror* (London 1964), pp. 348–49

2. Found under "Tallage" in *Oxford English Dictionary*, vol. XVII (Oxford, 1989), p. 588.

3. Ibid.

4. Sydney Knox Mitchell, *Taxation in Medieval England* (New Haven, 1951), p. 329.

5. Magna Carta XLII.

6. Gaines Post, *Studies in Medieval Legal Thought* (Princeton, 1964), pp. 262–302.

Part IV

1. Ian Grey, *The Horizon History of Russia* (New York, 1970), p. 6.

Chapter 17

1. Grey, *History of Russia*, p. 25.
2. Arthur Koestler, *The Thirteenth Tribe* (New York, 1976), p. 113.
3. Bernard Pares, *A History of Russia* (London, 1926), p. 52.
4. Ibid., ch. 6.
5. Crane Brinton, John B. Christopher, Robert Lee Wolff, *A History of Civilization*, vol. 1 (Englewood Cliffs, N.J., 1971), p. 335.
6. James Mavor, *An Economic History of Russia*, vol. 1 (New York, 1965), p. 82; note 10.
7. Ibid., p. 116.
8. See B. H. Sumner, *Peter the Great and the Emergence of Russia* (London, 1964), p. 124; Ian Grey, *Peter the Great* (London, 1960), p. 314, note 17; N. A. Voskveseusky, ed., *Legislative Acts of Peter I* (Moscow, 1945), Nos. 242–244; V. O. Kluchevsky, *A History of Russia*, vol. 4 (New York, 1960), p. 128.
9. Mavor, *An Economic History*, pp. 192–245; see Henry Sumner Maine, *Ancient Law* (London, 1861, reprint 1982), pp. 266–67.
10. Maxime Kovalevsky, *Modern Customs and Ancient Laws of Russia*, Lecture VI (London, 1891), pp. 209–50. See also August von Haxthausen, *Studies on the Interior of Russia*, S. F. Starr, ed., E. Schmidt, trans. (Chicago, 1977, 1852 Berlin ed.), ch. 13.
11. Leonid Lipilin, "Historians Should Be Kind," *Soviet Life* (Washington, D.C., July 1991), pp. 28–29, 58.

Chapter 18

1. Ch. 32, note 11.
2. The hypercritical view of Swiss privacy by the United States was well expressed by the editor and staff of *Tax Notes International*, December 1990, pp. 1227, 1235. The editor calls the Swiss a "spider" nation for its financial privacy and suggests the United States limit its tax treaty to the "Bare Bones." The real issue deals with the fundamental relation between taxes and liberty. With the United States, in any contest between liberty and taxes, taxes win. The Swiss take the opposite position.
3. Wilhelm Ropke "The Right of Privacy," *Switzerland, Image of a People* (Berne, 1971), p. 93.

Chapter 19

1. R. Trevor Davies, *The Golden Century of Spain* (London, 1937), p. 3.
2. Jean Hippoly te Mariejal, *The Spain of Ferdinand and Isabella* (New Brunswick, 1961), p. 213.
3. Ibid.

4. Davies, *The Golden Century*, p. 79.

5. See Martin A. S. Hume, *Spain its Greatness and Decay (1479-1788)* (Cambridge, 1898), p. 221; Henry Kamen, *Spain 1469-1714, A Society of Conflict* (London, 1983), p. 224.

6. R. Trevor Davies, *Spain in Decline 1621-1700* (London, 1957), p. 159.

7. Davies, *The Golden Century*, p. 265.

8. Davies, *Spain in Decline*, p. 93.

9. Edward Gibbon, *The Portable Gibbon,* Dero A. Saunders, ed. (New YOrk, 1952), p. 621.

10. From a sixteenth-century novel, *Lazarillo de Tormes*, quoted in Jaime Vicens Vives, *An Economic History of Spain* (Princeton, 1969), p. 416.

11. This quotation can be found in an early English account of the Dutch Revolt over the tenth penny in the Library at the Univ. of Leyden, The Netherlands.

12. Grapperhaus, *Taxes, Liberty and Property*, p. 133.

13. See Jaime Vicens Vives in Davies, *Spain in Decline*, pp. 405–6;

14. Davies, *Spain in Decline*, p. 105.

15. Thomas Jefferson, "Letter to James Madison, Jan. 30, 1787," *The Papers of Thomas Jefferson*, vol. 11, ed. Julian Boyd (Princeton, N.J., 1955), pp. 92–97.

16. Memorial de la Politics, p. 24, found in Cipolla, *Economic Decline of Empires*, p. 186.

Chapter 20

1. Eric Wolf, *Sons of the Shaking Earth* (Chicago, 1962), p. 149.

2. Nigel Davies, *The Aztecs, A History* (London, 1973), p. 101.

3. *Bernard Diaz Chronicles*, trans. Albert Idell (New York, 1956), pp. 73–74.

4. Michael D. Coe, *Mexico* (New York, 1962), p. 169; Wolf, *Shaking Earth*, p. 141.

5. Davies, *The Aztecs*, p. 285.

Chapter 21

1. Preserved Smith, *The Life and Letters of Martin Luther* (Boston, 1911), p. 159.

2. Martin Luther, *Against the Murdering and Robbing Band of the Peasants*, found in Hartmann Grisar, *Luther*, trans. E. M. Lamond, vol. 2 (London, 1915), 199n, 201–2n.

3. Brinton et al., *History of Civilization* 2, p. 597.

4. Nancy Mitford, *Frederick the Great* (London, 1973), p. 291.

5. On file in my memory from a lecture in European history by Dr. Harry Nerhood, professor of history at Whittier College. As happened with so many of his students, my love affair with history developed from the spellbinding lectures he delivered, filled with anecdotes, stories, and worldly wisdom. The inspiration for this book, to make tax history alive, fun to read, and filled with wisdom, came from this remarkable teacher.

6. Mitford, *Frederick*, p. 251.

7. See S. Fischer-Fabian, *Prussia's Glory* (New York, 1981), p. 267, for a watered-down translation.

Chapter 22

1. G. R. R. Treasure, *Seventeenth Century France* (London, 1966), p. 296.

2. Ambrose Saricks, *Pierre Samuel du Pont de Nemours* (Lawrence, Ks., 1965), passim.

3. J. W. Goethe, "Conversations with Eckermann, November 24, 1824," in H. L. Mencken, ed., *A New Dictionary of Quotations* (New York, 1987), p. 428.

Chapter 23

1. Roland Mousnier, *Peasant Uprisings in Seventeenth Century France, Russia and China*, trans. Brian Pearce (London, 1971), p. 137.

2. Jude Wanniski, *The Way the World Works* (New York, 1978), p. 190.

3. Moote, *Revolt of the Judges*, p. 123.

4. Mousnier, *Peasant Uprisings*, p. 107.

5. Treasure, *Seventeenth Century France*, p. 190.

Part VI

1. Sinclair, *Public Revenues of the British Empire* l, p. 130.

2. Dowell, *History of Taxation* 1, pp. 124–25.

3. Pollock and Maitland, vol. 1, *History of English Law*, pp. 615–16.

4. Act II, Scene 5; A. L. Rowse, *The England of Elizabeth* (London, 1964), p. 335.

5. Dowell, *History of Taxation* 1, p. 150.

6. Preamble to the Act of Parliament, in Dowell, *History of Taxation* 1, p. 133; 25 Henry VIII, c. 21.

Chapter 24

1. Conyers Read, "Good Queen Bess," *American Historical Review*, XXXI, No. 4, July 1926, p. 647.

2. Dowell, *History of Taxation* 1, p. 148.

3. Rowse, *England of Elizabeth*, p. 339.

4. Ibid., p. 158.

5. R. B. Wernham, *Before the Armada* (London, 1966), pp. 296–97; Sinclair, *Public Revenues of the British Empire*, vol. 1, p. 217.

6. Dowell, *History of Taxation* 1, p. 148.

7. Read, "Good Queen Bess," p. 661.

8. Rowse, *England of Elizabeth*, p. 338.

Chapter 26

1. Stephen Dowell, *A History of Taxation and Taxes in England,* vol. 2 (London, 1965, reprint of 1884 edition), p. 39.

2. Ibid., p. 40.

3. William Kennedy, *English Taxation 1640-1799* (London, 1913, reprint 1964), p. 42.

4. Dowell, *History of Taxation* 2, p. 8.

5. Sinclair, *Public Revenues of the British Empire* 1, p. 283.

6. Ibid., p. 316.

7. J. H. Plumb, *Sir Robert Walpole*, vol. 2 (Clifton, N. J., 1973), p. 239.

8. Kennedy, *English Taxation*, pp. 99–109.

9. Edward Hughes, *Studies in Administration and Finance 1558–1825* (Manchester, 1934), pp. 291–304. Excellent discussion of the salt tax debates, harshly critical of Walpole.

10. Report of Sir John Cope's committee regarding the frauds committed in the revenue, dated June 7, 1732. See Dowell, *History of Taxation* 2, p. 97.

11. Plumb, *Sir Robert Walpole* 2, p. 238. Military forces were actually used in Suffolk.

12. Ibid., p. 252; Raymond Turner, "The Excise Scheme of 1733," *The English Historical Review* (London, 1927, reprint 1971), pp. 34–57.

13. Plumb, *Sir Robert Walpole* 2, p. 46.

14. Ibid., p. 269 (different version of quote); see also Turner, "Excise Scheme."

15. Turner, "Excise Scheme," p. 46.

16. Plumb, *Sir Robert Walpole* 2, pp. 241, 247.

17. David Burnham, *A Law Unto Itself* (New York, 1989), pp. 228–30, 236–38. See also Joseph P. Lash, *Eleanor and Franklin* (New York, 1970), p. 120.

18. Plumb, *Sir Robert Walpole* 2, p. 246.

19. John Brewer, "The English State and Fiscal Appropriations, 1688–1789," *Politics and Society*, vol. 16, nos. 2–3 (1988), pp. 335–85.

20. Ibid., p. 357.

21. William Blackstone, *Commentaries on the Laws of England, Bk. I* (London, 1765), ch. 8, p. 308. This chapter in the *Commentaries* contains an excellent summary and critique of English taxation up to the time of the American Revolution.

22. Brewer, "The English State," p. 357.

23. Stephen Dowell, *A History of Taxation and Taxes in England,* vol. 4 (London, 1965, reprint of 1884 edition), pp. 306–10.

24. Ibid. 2, p. 105.

25. Ibid., p. 122.

Chapter 27

1. Sombart, *Jews and Modern Capitalism*, pp. 37, 41.
2. Charles Wilson, *The Dutch Republic and the Civilization of the Seventeenth Century* (London, 1968), p. 232.
3. K. H. D. Haley, *The Dutch in the Seventeenth Century* (London, 1972), p. 154.
4. Brewer, "The English State," pp. 335–85.
5. Dowell, *History of Taxation* 2, p. 89.
6. C. R. Boxer, *The Dutch Seaborne Empire, 1600–1800* (London, 1965), pp. 64–65.
7. Ibid.
8. Wilson, *The Dutch Republic*, pp. 234–35.

Chapter 28

1. George Seldes, ed., *The Great Thoughts* (New York, 1985), p. 319.
2. Thomas Paine, *The Rights of Man* (New York, 1969), p. 206. Found in Thomas Paine, *Common Sense*, ed. Isaac Kramnick (New York, 1987), pp. 49–57.
3. *The Writings of Thomas Paine*, vol. III (New York, 1906), p. 204.
4. Ibid., p. 55.
5. Ibid., pp. 81, 183, 189.
6. Paine, *Rights of Man*, p. 165.
7. Montesquieu, *Spirit of Laws*, vol. 1, Bk. 13, ch. l, p. 255.
8. "The War Within," *New York Times Magazine*, Aug. 21, 1988, pp. 34–38; "A Huge Leap into Unreason," *Newsweek*, Sept. 5, 1988, p. 70.
9. Adam Smith, *The Wealth of Nations*, p. 491.
10. Montesquieu, *Spirit of Laws*, vol. 1, p. 267.
11. Ibid., p. 261.
12. Ibid., p. 266.
13. John Locke, "Second Treatise on Civil Government," *On Politics and Education* (New York, 1947), ch. XI, para. 135, p. 145.
14. Montesquieu, *Spirit of Laws*, vol. 1, p. 261.
15. Ibid.
16. Blackstone, *Commentaries* 1: 307.
17. Smith, *Wealth of Nations*, p. 563.
18. Albert Jay Nock, *Our Enemy the State* (New York, 1989), pp. 94–95
19. David Hume, *The Philosophical Works*, vol. 3, eds. Thomas Green and Thomas Grose (London, 1882, reprint 1964), pp. 356–60.
20. John Phillip Reid, *The Constitutional History of the American Revolution, The Authority to Tax* (Madison, Wisc., 1986), p. 145
21. Ibid.
22. Ibid., p. 86.

23. Ibid., p. 88; Page Smith, *A New Age Begins*, vol. 1 (New York, 1976), p. 242.

24. Ibid., p. 112.

25. Blackstone, *Commentaries* 1: 135–36.

26. Reid, *Constitutional History of the American Revolution*, p. 113.

27. Harold Syrett, ed., *The Papers of Alexander Hamilton*, vol. III (New York, 1962), p. 104.

28. Thomas M. Cooley, *The Constitutional Principles of the Constitutional Law of the United States of America* (Boston, 1880), pp. 55–56.

29. Hume, *Philosophical Works*, pp. 356–60.

30. Smith, *Wealth of Nations*, p. 498.

31. Locke, "Second Treatise," ch. XI, para. 135–40, pp. 147–48.

32. Thomas M. Cooley, *Constitutional Limitation* (Boston, 1868, reprint, Birmingham, Ala., 1987), ch. XI4.

33. Friedrich A. Hayek, *The Constitution of Liberty* (Chicago, 1960), p. 313.

34. *New and Old Principles of Trade Compared; or a Treatise on the Principles of Commerce between Nations* (London, 1788), p. 20, found in *A Selected Collection of Scarce and Valuable Tracts on Commerce*, ed. John R. McCulloch (1859) (New York, reprint 1966), p. 582.

35. Montesquieu, *Spirit of Laws*, vol. 1, p. 256.

36. Josiah Tucker, *A Brief Essay on . . . Trade* (London, 1753), pp. 104–5, found in McCulloch, *Selected Collection*, pp. 412–13.

37. Smith, *Wealth of Nations*, pp. 561–64.

38. William Paley, *The Principles of Moral and Political Philosophy*, vol. II (London, 1788), pp. 204–5, 388–96.

39. Lord Henry Home Kames, *Sketches in the History of Man* (Dublin, 3rd. ed., 1769), pp. 486–513, at pp. 512–13.

40. Maynard Mack, *Alexander Pope, A Life* (New Haven, Conn., 1985), p. 266.

41. Henry David Thoreau, *Walden and Civil Disobedience*, ed. S. Paul (Cambridge, 1960), p. 248.

42. John Stuart Mill, *Principles of Political Economy*, Book V (London, 1885, 9th ed., reprint New York, 1961), Ch. II, pp. 802–72.

43. McCulloch, *Selected Collection*, pp. 170, 417.

44. *Boyd v. United States*, 116 U.S. 616, 631.

45. Friedrich A. Hayek, *The Road to Serfdom* (Chicago, 1972), p. 43.

Chapter 29

1. P. Smith, *A New Age* 1, p. 121.

2. Charles Francis Adams, *The Works of John Adams*, vol. 2 (Boston, 1850), p. 525.

3. Richard Harris, "Annals of Law [Fourth Amendment II]," *The New Yorker*, November 10, 1975. See P. Smith, *A New Age*, vol. 1, pp. 179–88.

4. Ibid.

5. Thomas Andrew Green, *Verdict According to Conscience* (Chicago, 1985), p. xviii.

6. L. W. Labaree, ed., *The Papers of Benjamin Franklin*, vol. 13 (New Haven, Conn., 1969), pp. 129–58.

7. Benjamin Franklin, "Rules by which a Great Nation May be Reduced to a Small One," *American Issues*, vol. l, Willard Thorp et al., eds. (Chicago, 1944), p. 79.

8. Brinton et al., *History of Civilization*, vol. 2, p. 649.

9. P. Smith, *A New Age*, vol. l (New York, 1976), pt. II, ch. l; pt. III, ch. l.

10. Franklin, "Rules," pp. 80–81.

11. See *Burke Selected Works*, ed. E. J. Payne (Oxford, 1881), pp. 95 et seq.

12. Reid, *Constitutional History of the American Revolution*, pp. 282–83.

Chapter 30

1. See Ellis Paxson Oberholtzer, *Robert Morris, Patriot and Financier* (London, 1903).

2. Max Farrand, *The Records of the Federal Convention of 1767*, vol. 2 (New Haven, Conn., 1966), pp. 143, 181, 418, 594 note 13, 614; vol. 3, pp. 205, 365.

3. Cooley, *Constitutional Limitations*, p. 495.

4. Paul L. Ford, ed., *Pamphlets on the Constitution of the United States 1787-1788* (Brooklyn, 1888), p. 50.

5. "The Third Speech of June 28, 1788," *The Papers of Alexander Hamilton, 1788-1789*, vol. 5 (New York, 1962), p. 123.

6. Benjamin Oliver, *The Rights of an American Citizen* (New York, 1832), p. 95.

7. *U.S. v. Singer*, 15 Wall:lll,121; 21 L.ed. 49, 51 (c. 1873).

8. Cooley, *Constitutional Limitations*, p. 493. Cooley set forth the meaning of uniformity in his many texts on constitutional law. In his *Treatise on the Law of Taxation* (Chicago, 1876), p. 138, he takes the position that a tax is not uniform in character when it discriminates between individuals or classes in the same trade or business. There are reprints and new editions up until the 1920s. Thus equality of burdens constituted the very substance designed to be secured by the rule [uniformity].

9. Ibid.

10. Comment, "The Uniformity Clause," 51 *U. of Chicago Law Review*, 1193 (1984), 44 *Tax Law Review* 588–601 (1989).

11. B. E. J. Sabine, *A History of the Income Tax* (New York, 1966), p. 103.

12. Mill, *Principles of Political Economy*, Bk. V, ch. III, s.1.

13. Mercy Otis Warren, *History of the Rise, Progress and Termination of the American Revolution*, vol. II (Boston, 1805, reprint Indianapolis, 1988), p. 660. This remark has been questioned by some scholars. See Warren, p. 660n.

14. New Hampshire Constitution, Article X.

15. *The Oxford English Dictionary.* Thirteen Volumes. London, 1928, Reissued in Compact Edition, 1971. Volume 4 (E), p. 379, "Excise" 26.

16. Hugh Henry Brackenridge, *Incidents of the Insurrection,* Daniel Marder, ed. (New Haven, 1972), p. 17.

17. Henry Adams, ed., *The Writings of Albert Gallatin,* vol. 1 (New York, 1960), p. 3.

18. Leland D. Baldwin, *Whiskey Rebels* (Pittsburgh, 1968), pp. 102–3.

19. Thomas P. Slaughter, *The Whiskey Rebellion: Frontier Epilogue to the American Revolution* (Oxford, 1986), pp. 199–228.

20. Bernard A. Weisberger, "Seeking a Real Tax Revolt," *American Heritage,* vol. 42, no. 3 (New York, May/June, 1991), p. 24.

21. See N. Kittrie and E. Wedlock, Jr., eds., *The Tree of Liberty, A Documentary History of Rebellion and Political Crime in America* (Baltimore, 1968), pp. 91–97, for a full account of the court opinions, petitions for pardon and Hamilton's objections.

22. *Papers of Thomas Jefferson,* vol. II (Princeton, 1955), p. 93.

Chapter 31

1. Paul M. Angle, ed., *The Lincoln Reader* (New Brunswick, N.J., 1947), p. 407. The Emancipation Proclamation was not the glorious human rights document it was held up to be. One historian observed: "The famous document, to be so celebrated and misunderstood by later generations . . . declared free the slaves in the rebellious states . . . controlled by Union forces and hence the only areas where military emancipation could be made a reality." Editors blasted Lincoln for its illusory scope. The army, which was strongly anti-abolition, was demoralized. "Fighting Joe Hooker," the Union commander at the time, said: "A large element of the army had taken sides antagonistic to it, declaring that they would never have embarked in the war had they anticipated this action of the government." See T. Harry Williams, *Lincoln and the Radicals* (Madison, Wis., 1960), pp. 215–16, 240–41.

2. Edmund Ruffin, *Anticipations of the Future to Serve as Lessons for the Present Time* (Richomnd, Va., 1860), Appendix. A. O. Craven, *Edmund Ruffin, Southerner, A Study in Secession* (New York, 1932).

3. John C. Calhoun, "Speech on the Slavery Question," March 4, 1850, in Edwin Rozweus, ed., *The Causes of the Civil War* (Boston, 1961), p. 4.

4. Edward Pollard, *The Lost Cause* (New York, 1866; reprint 1970), pp. 61–62.

5. Ruffin, *Anticipating the Future*, Appendix.

6. George Fitzhugh, *Sociology for the South on the Failure of Free Society* (Richmond, Va., 1854), ch. V; William J. Grayson, "The Hireling and the Slave" (1854), in *Selected Poems by William J. Grayson*, comp. Mrs. William Armstrong (New York and Washington, D.C., 1907); By a White Republican, "Negros and Slavery in the United States," *Fraser's Magazine* (London, February 1863), pp. 192 et seq.

7. Clement Laird Vallandigham, "Speech before the Democratic Union Association," New York, March 7, 1863, *Speeches, Arguments, Addresses and Letters of Clement L. Vallandigham* (New York, 1864); also found in *American Issues*, vol. 1, pp. 553–60.

8. George Eggleston, *A Rebel's Recollection* (New York, 1897), pp. 193–94.

9. John Ford Rhodes, *Lectures on the American Civil War* (New York, 1913), pp. 2-16.

10. *Collected Works of John Stuart Mill*, vols. 22–25, *Newspaper Writings*, eds. Ann and John Robson (Toronto, 1986), pp. 1204–5; *Fraser's Magazine* (London, February 1862), pp. 258–68; F. A. Hayek, *The Life of John Stuart Mill* (New York, 1954), p. 423.

11. By a White Republican, "Negros and Slavery in the United States," pp. 192 et seq. There was considerable support from Christian churches for slavery. Negros were believed to be the descendants of Ham, the son of Noah, who was cursed by his father to be a slave, "a servant of servants," Gen. 9:25. See Thomas T. Smiley, *Sacred Geography* (Philadelphia, 1924); Alexis de Tocqueville's account of the plight of Negros in the North, and of their rights and the attitude of Northern Whites, is devastating to those who believe the Negros had many friends in the North. See *Democracy in America* (New York, 1838), pp. 336–61. The abolitionists of the North found no favor with the majority of citizens. Prudence Crandall was a Quaker who set up a little school for Negro children in Connecticut. It was against the law of that state to have a school for blacks. Miss Crandall was convicted and went to jail. The leader of the abolitionists in the North was William Garrison, who had to flee from Boston to avoid a lynching for his abolitionist publication, *The Liberator*. In Illinois another abolitionist newspaper was published by a man named Elijah Lovejoy. Four times his newspaper was attacked and his presses destroyed. Finally, a mob not only finished his abolitionist newspaper, but murdered him in the process. There is little doubt that abolitionists were a small and despised reform movement that had no political clout whatsoever.

12. *Boston Transcript*, 18 March 1861, found in Kenneth M. Stampp, *The Causes of the Civil War* (Englewood, N.J., 1959), p. 80. There were other editorials in the North calling for war because tax-free ports in the South would bring economic ruin to the Northern economy: *New York Evening Post*, March 12, 1861; *Newark Daily Advertiser*, April 2, 1861; found in Howard Cecil Perkins, ed., *Northern Editorials on Secession*, vol. II (New York, 1942).

13. *Fraser's Magazine*, April 1861, pp. 403–14.

14. See notes 6, 11, and 14. Besides the works of cartoonists, propagandists in the North and South produced innumerable patriotic covers for the mails. An examination of scores of these covers by the author and the librarian at the American Philatelic Society library has unearthed only one anti-slavery cover. See Robert Grant, *Handbook of Civil War Patriotic Covers and Postal History*, 2 vols. (Hanover, Mass., 1977).

15. Lysander Spooner, "No Treason," *American Issues*, p. 573.

16. Charles A. and Mary R. Beard, *The Rise of American Civilization*, vol. 2 (New York, 1927), pp. 39–40.

Part VIII

1. *Historia Anglicana* (London, 1422, trans. 1864), pp. 369–70.
2. Sinclair, *Public Revenues of the British Empire* 1, p. 139.
3. Smith, *Wealth of Nations*, p. 532.

Chapter 32

1. Sabine, *A History of the Income Tax*, pp. 42–43.
2. James Coffield, *A Popular History of Taxation* (London, 1970), p. 108. See Charles Mackay, *Life and Times of Sir Robert Peel*, 4 vols (London, 1850), vol. 4., pp. 305–42.
3. Francis W. Hirst, *Gladstone as Financier and Economist* (London, 1931), p. 148; see also Edwin Seligman, *The Income Tax* (New York, 1970, reprint of 1914 edition), p. 153.
4. Seligman, *The Income Tax*, p. 216.
5. Ibid., pp. 271–72.

Chapter 33

1. Parliamentary Debates, 16 April 1894, 4th series, vol. 23; James Coffield, *A History of Taxation* (London, 1960), pp. 140–41.
2. Seligman, *The Income Tax*, pp. 210–11.
3. 157 U.S. 429, 543 (1894).
4. 157 U.S. 429, 596.
5. 158 U.S. 675.
6. Nancy Shepherdson, "The First 1040," *American Heritage* (New York, March 1989), pp. 101–5.
7. J. R. McCulloch, *Taxation and the Funding System* (London, 1845), pp. 141–43.
8. Coffield, *History of Taxation*, p. 251.
9. Ibid.
10. Randolph E. Paul, *Taxation in the United States* (Boston, 1954), p. 26.
11. *Knowlton v. Moore*, 178 U.S. 41, 109 (1899). This comment runs counter to what the most respected scholars on American society had been saying in the nineteenth century. Alexis de Tocqueville's *Democracy in America* (New York, 1838) saw the "Tyranny of the Majority" as our greatest weak spot. Fifty years later, James Bryce's *The American Commonwealth* (London and New York, 1888) agreed, even pinpointed taxation as one of the areas where this tyranny would most likely occur (ch. XV). These books were in print then and still are.
12. N. H. Carter, W. L. Stone, and M. Gould, *Reports of the Proceedings and Debates of the Constitution of 1821* (Albany, N.Y., 1821), found in *American Issues*, vol. 1, pp. 198–201.
13. *The Federalist*, No. 10.

14. *Magoun v. Illinois Trust and Savings Bank*, 170 U.S. 283, 301–3 (1898).

15. *Brushaber v. Union Pacific R. Co.*, 240 U.S. 1 (1916).

16. Frank Warren Hackett, "The Constitutionality of the Graduated Income Tax Law," *Yale Law Journal* 25 (1916), p. 427.

17. Cooley, *Constitutional Limitations*, ch. XIV.

18. 25 *Yale Law Journal*, p. 438.

19. 157 U.S. 607 (1894).

20. *Budd v. New York*, 143 U.S. 517, 551 (1891).

Chapter 34

1. *Washington Post Magazine*, Dec. 29, 1991, p. 23.

2. Karl Hess, *Dear America* (New York, 1975), p. 92.

3. Mike Bryan, "Profile: Karl Hess," *Gallery* (New York, December 1981), pp. 38 et seq., at p. 41.

4. Martin A. Larson, *Tax Revolt, the Battle for the Constitution* (Greenich, Conn., 1985), passim. This book is filled with the accounts of tax resisters and their triumphs and defeats.

5. Judith Rehak, *International Herald Tribune* (Paris, August 24, 1991), p. 15.

6. Gerald Carson, *The Golden Egg* (Boston, 1977), p. 252.

7. Jerome R. Hellerstein, *Taxes, Loopholes, and Morals* (New York, 1963), p. 231.

8. Richard Neely, "The Politics of the Crime," *The Atlantic* (August 1982), at p. 28.

9. Sinclair, *Public Revenues of the British Empire* 1, pp. 282–83, 316.

10. Andrew Mellon, *Taxation, The People's Business* (New York, 1924), pp. 220–21, table p. 193.

11. *Burke Selected Works*, vol. 1, "Thoughts on the Present Discontents, Two Speeches on America," ed. E. J. Payne (Oxford, 1881), pp. 178–89.

12. Blackstone, *Commentaries* 1:307.

13. David Shipler, *Russia* (New York, 1983), pp. 224–26.

14. Diogenes, *April Game*, p. 124.

15. "Lamsdorff, 20 others found guilty," *International Herald Tribune* (Paris, 17 Feb. 1987), pp. 1, 6.

16. Confidential source, U.S. Attorney's office, Washington, D.C. See *Wall Street Journal*, May 9, 1988.

17. Montesquieu, *Spirit of Laws*, vol. 1, Bk. 8, ch. 8, p. 261; Blackstone, *Commentaries* 1:307.

18. Natalia Milchakova, "New Soviet Income Tax," *Tax Notes International* (March 1991), p. 242.

19. Art Harris, "The Tax Man and the Big Sting," *Washington Post* (April 16, 1989), pp. F1–5.

20. Floyd Rogers, "Fighting the IRS," *Winston-Salem Journal* (October 22, 1989); "One Death, Taxes and a Callous IRS," *Newsday* (May 19, 1992).

21. Wilhelm Ropke, "The Right of Privacy," *Switzerland Image of a People*, ed. Alfred Vetter (Bern, 1971), p. 92. Ropke was a key architect of Germany's economic miracle. See Johannes Overbeek, ed., *2 Essays by Wilhelm Ropke* (New York, 1987).

22. 416 U.S. 21, 845 (1974).

23. 116 U.S. 616, 631–32.

24. *Olmstead v. U.S.*, 277 U.S. 438, 474 (1927).

25. *U.S. v. Doe*, 465 U.S. 606, 618 (1984).

26. See William H. Rehnquist, *The Supreme Court, How It Was, How It Works* (New York, 1987), p. 313. Rehnquist calls the commands of the 14th Amendment "fuzzy generalities," p. 180. See also Sue Davis, *Justice Rehnquist and the Constitution* (Princeton, 1989).

27. Diogenes, *April Game*, pp. 120–21.

28. "Swedes may smite a 'terrible tax giant' at polls tomorrow," *The Toronto Star* (Sept. 18, 1976).

29. *American Scholar* (Washington, D.C., Spring 1989), p. 292.

30. Kittrie and Wedlock, Jr., eds., *The Tree of Liberty*, ch. 7.

Chapter 35

1. Duncan Fraser, *The Smugglers* (Montrose, Scotland, 1971); Henry Shore, *Smuggling Days and Smuggling Ways* (London, 1971).

2. "Tax Evasion Rampant in China," *Cayman Compass,* Beijing, AP, Friday 10 March 1989.

3. See Chapter 38.

4. Shepherdson, "The First 1040," pp. 101–5.

5. Wanniski, *The Way the World Works*, p. 259.

6. J. Harvard Perry, *Taxes, Tariffs, and Subsidies*, vol. 1 (Toronto, 1955), p. 287.

7. L. White, ed., *Democratick Editorials* (Indianapolis, 1984), p. 4.

8. *Budd v. New York*, 143 U.S. 517, 551 (1891).

9. Art Wortman, ed., *Will Rogers, Wise and Witty Sayings of a Great American Humorist* (Claremore, Okla., 1969), pp. 14–15.

10. Lord Clyde in *Ayrshire Pullman Services Ltd. v. C.I.R.*, 14 TC 263–64.

11. John Blosser, "Howard Hughes paid no income taxes for 15 years," *National Enquirer* (February 7, 1978). A photocopy of Hughes's return is in the article, showing payments of $57,300 to Jane Russell.

Chapter 36

1. Mellon, *Taxation*, pp. 216–27. See Wanniski, *The Way the World Works*, pp. 120–21.

2. Paul, *Taxation in the United States*, p. 201.

3. Confidential comment to the author.

4. Richard Harrington, "Stone Free," *Washington Post* (November 11, 1988).

5. There are many writings on the Laffer curve. The easiest to understand can be found in John Galt, *Dreams Come Due* (New York, 1986), pp. 177–79; or Wanniski, *The Way the World Works*, ch. 6.

6. Melanie S. Tammen, "Kleptocracy—Capitalism in the Soviet 'Second Economy,' " *Journal of Economic Growth*, vol. 4, no. 3 (Washington, D.C., December 1990), pp. 3–13.

Chapter 37

1. Jon Woronoff, *Asia's 'Miracle' Economies* (New York, 1986), ch. 5.

2. Marcus Gee, "The real end of Japan, Inc.," *The Globe and Mail*, Toronto (April 18, 1998), p. D4.

3. Pepper, Jarow, Wheeler, *The Competition: Dealing with Japan* (New York, 1985), p. 91, n. 36.

4. Hiromitsu Ishi, *The Japanese Tax System* (Oxford, 1989), p. 16.

5. Pepper et al., *The Competition*, p. 91, n. 35.

6. Hugh Borton, *Peasant Uprising in Japan of the Tokugawa Period* (New York, 1968, reprint 1938 edition), passim.

7. James K. Glassman et al., "Curiing the Asian Flu," *Reason* (Los Angeles, May 1998), pp. 18–27.

8. Woronoff, *'Miracle' Economies*, p. 132.

9. Gracula Ortez, ed., *Journal of Economic Growth*, vol. 3, no. 1, p. 2.

10. Gee, "Real end of Japan, Inc.," p. D4.

11. Tom Bethell, "Is the Kibbutz Kaput?" *Reason* (October 1990).

12. "Israel's War Against Capitalism," *Journal of Economic Growth*, vol. 3, no. 3 (Washington, D.C., 1989), pp. 49–57.

13. Ibid., p. 50.

14. Mellon, *Taxation*, pp. 74–75.

Chapter 38

1. *The Federalist,* No. 10.

2. Cecilia M. Kenyon, ed., *The Anti Federalist* (Indianapolis, 1966), p. lxiii.

3. Benjamin Oliver, *The Rights of an American Citizen* (New York, 1832), p. 95.

4. Randolph Paul, *Taxation in the United States* (Boston, 1954), p. 654.

5. Comment, 51 *University of Chicago Law Review*, 1193 (1984).

6. *Chicago Tribune,* January 17, 1926.

7. "Speech of Edmund Burke, March 22, 1775," *Burke Selected Works* 1, pp. 178–89; see also Ch. 26, notes 20–24.

8. *Hylton v. United States*, 3 Dall 171, 175–183 (1796).

9. *U.S. v. Ptasynski*, 1035 S.Ct. 2239 (1983); it is interesting that under the federal rules of procedure there is an automatic appeal to the Supreme Court whenever a federal tax statute is declared unconstitutional. Hmmm?

10. See Thomas M. Cooley, *Constitutional Limitations*, ch. XIV; Walter Blum and Henry Kalvern Jr., *The Uneasy Case for Progressive Taxation* (Chicago, 1953); *Pollock v. Farmers Loan and Trust*, 157 U.S. 429, 607 (J. Field), 614 (J. White and Harlan), 158 U.S. 675 (J. Harlan) 1984; *Magoun v. Illinois Trust* 1898; "The Uniformity Clause," 51 *U. of Chicago Law Review* 1193 (1984); Lawrence Zelenak "Are Rifle Shot Transition Rules and Other Ad Hoc Tax Legislation Constitutional?" 44 *Tax Law Review* 563 (1989); also see Chapters 28, 31, 32 *infra*.

11. Grappenhaus, *Taxes, Liberty and Property*, p. 134.

12. Post, *Medieval Legal Thought*, p. 252.

13. Ibid., p. 250.

14. *Wisconsin State Journal*, editorial, 27 Aug. 1959.

15. H. L. Mencken, ed., *A New Dictionary of Quotations* (New York, 1987), p. 213.

16. John-Rogers and Peter McWilliams, *You Can't Afford the Luxury of a Negative Thought* (Los Angeles, 1989), p. 211.

Chapter 39

1. Polybius, *The Rise of the Roman Empire*, trans. Scott-Kilvert (New York, 1979), p. 41.

2. Paul Kennedy, *The Rise and Fall of the Great Powers* (New York, 1987), pp. 514–40.

3. James S. Eustice, "Tax Complexity and the Tax Practitioner," 45 *Tax Law Review* 8 (1989).

4. Grapperhaus, *Taxes, Liberty and Property*, p. 129.

5. Swedish author Astrid Lindgren charged, in an open letter to the tax bureau, that there were hundreds of thousands of Swedes having heart attacks or turning into alcoholics wondering how they could survive Sweden's crushing tax system (*Toronto Star*, Sept. 18, 1976, Assoc. Press release).

6. This is not an overstatement. To demonstrate just how pro-government and pro-IRS the Supreme Court is, follow the case of *U.S. v. Kilpatrick*, 594 F.Supp. 1328 (1984); 821 F.2d 1456 (1986); 108 S.Ct. 2369 (1988), through the trial courts to the Supreme Court and then back again. Here is the case of a criminal indictment (tax) obtained by deceit, lies, fraud, intimidation, and subordination of perjury, which was thrown out of court by the federal trial judiciary after lengthy hearings in which these acts of misconduct were fully revealed and are in print, 594 F.Supp. 1328 (1984). Thereafter, the Supreme Court reversed the trial court and let the fraudulently obtained indictment stand (the "rubber stamp" indictments as the lower court described them). The Supreme Court gave its blessing, *sub-silento*, to this misconduct the same as it did for the felonies IRS agents committed in *U.S. v. Paynor*, 434 F.Supp. 113 (1977); reversed 100 S.Ct. 2349 (1980). When the *Kilpatrick* case was finally back in the trial court, the federal judge wasted little time throwing the case out of court on its facts. There never was any evasion in the first place.

7. *The Portable Gibbon*, p. 375.

Chapter 40

1. Theodosian Code 11.7.1, pp. 301–2, 317.
2. Prasad, *Taxation in Ancient India*, p. 31.
3. St. Thomas Aquinas, *On Law and Justice, Excerpts from Summa Theologica*, Q. 66, Art. 8 (Birmingham, Ala., 1988), pp. 1480–81.
4. Tacitus, *Annals*, p. 309.
5. *Dollars and Sense* (Washington, D.C., Aug.–Sept. 1988), p. 12.
6. Burnham, *Law Unto Itself*, passim.
7. Hess, *Dear America*, p. 90.
8. *Washington Post*, June 4, 1991.
9. Burnham, *Law Unto Itself*, pp. 296–302. Congressman George Hansen had similar trouble. See his book, *To Harass Our People* (Washington, D.C., 1984), pp. 78–81; also Martin Larson, *Tax Revolt, The Battle for the Constitution* (Greenwich, Conn., 1985), pp. 75–80.
10. Judge Fred Winner's opinion in William A. Kilpatrick, *The Big Tax Lie* (New York, 1986), pp. 274–75; also found in *U.S. v. Kilpatrick*, 575 F. Supp. 325 (1983).
11. I was on the committee.
12. *Peter Buchanan Ltd. v. McVey* (1955) A.C. 516, 529.
13. James L. Payne, "Unhappy Returns, The $600-Billion Tax Ripoff," *Policy Review,* vol. 59 (Washington, D.C., Winter 1992), p. 21.
14. *Selected Works of John and John Quincy Adams*, pp. 24–27.
15. *U.S. v. DeTar*, 832 F.2d l110 (9th Cir., 1987), reversed on appeal.
16. Michel de Montaigne, *Essays III* (1588), found in Mencken, p. 656.
17. See *Saratoga News*, "Saratoga tax man calls IRS a 'monster,' " August 13, 1986, p. 10; WSJ, 10/6/75; WSJ, 7/26/77; WSJ. 10/4/77.
18. Kilpatrick, *Big Tax Lie*, pp. 259–61, note; 575 F. Supp. 325 (1983); Marshall's dissent is 108 S.Ct. 2369, 2379 (1988).
19. Senator David Pryor, "Time to Rein in the IRS," *Reader's Digest* (April, 1992), pp. 122–26.
20. Hansen, *To Harass Our People*.
21. Martin A. Larson, *Tax Revolt, The Battle for the Constitution* (Greenwich, Conn., 1985), pp. 75–80.
22. Bernard Wolfman et al., *Dissent Without Opinion* (Philadelphia, 1975).
23. Burnham, *Law Unto Itself*, pp. 247–49.
24. 45 *Tax Law Review* 7–8 (1989).
25. Mellon, *Taxation*, p. 83.
26. *Wall Street Journal* (Dec. 10, 1981), p. 30.
27. James L. Payne, *Costly Returns*, S.F. 1993.
28. A.B.A. Section of Taxation Newsletter, vol. v, no. 3 (Spring 1993), pp. 56–68.
29. Jefferson P. Vandenwolk, "Opinion," Tax Notes Int'l., vol. 5, no. 13 (Washington, D.C., Sept. 28, 1992), pp. 660–61.
30. Amity Shlaes, "Rein in the Revenue Hounds," *Wall Street Journal* (March 24, 1998).

Chapter 41

1. Dio Cassius, *Roman History*, LXII, iii; compare with Tacitus *Annals of Rome*, XIV, pp. 34–38.
2. Baron de Montesquieu, *The Spirit of Laws*, vol. 1, Bk. XV, ch. VI, p. 296.
3. Charles Adams, *For Good and Evil* (New York, 1993), p. 295.
4. Charles Adams, *Those Dirty Rotten Taxes* (New York, 1998), pp. 38–39.
5. *The American Heritage History of the Thirteen Colonies*, Ed. Richard Blow (New York, 1967), pp. 348–49.
6. Montesquieu, *Spirit of Laws*, vol. 1, Bk. XIII, ch. 14, pp. 266–67.

Epilogue

1. Payne, "Unhappy Returns," p. 18.
2. Montesquieu, *Spirit of Laws*, vol. 1, Bk. XIII, ch. 8.
3. Aristotle, *Nicomachean Ethics*, Bk. III, ch. 6–9; Bk. IV, ch. 1–2.
4. Charles L. Griswold, Jr., "Conscience of Capitalism," *The Wilson Quarterly* (Washington, D.C., Summer 1991), pp. 53–61.
5. Montesquieu, *Spirit of Laws*, Bk. XIII, ch. 8.
6. Robert D. Hershey, Jr., "Elite Gathering Opens Up a Little," *New York Times* (February 8, 1992), p. 36.
7. Crenshaw, "A Tax System in Trouble," *Washington Post*, April 16, 1989, H1–9. For some impressive academic treatises on complexity see a remarkable series of articles in 45 *Tax Law Review* (1989–90); also, "Why Are Taxes So Complex and Who Benefits?" *Tax Notes* 341 (April 16, 1990). This author blames the tax professionals (CPAs and lawyers), plus the IRS.
8. Harold M. Groves, *Tax Philosophers*, Donald Curran, ed. (Madison, Wis., 1974), passim; Charles M. Allan, *The Theory of Taxation* (Middlesex, England, 1971), passim. A recent wordy and unintelligible treatise on the concept of "income" can be found in sixty pages of gobbledygook by professor Victor Thuronyi, "The Concept of Income" (46 *Tax Law Review* 45–105 [1991]). After plowing through this philosophical esoterica, I have more sympathy for the tax resisters who insist that wages are not income. The struggles tax academics have over "income" quickly moves into the realm of "deductions," which also has produced an extensive philosophical debate. Stanley A. Koppelman, "Personal Deductions Under an Ideal Income Tax" (*Tax Law Review* 43 679 [1988–89]).
9. I am indebted to a delightful little book by William Danforth, *I Dare You* (St. Louis, 1945), pp. 21–23, which was given to me by my grandfather when I was sixteen. The ideal of a foursquare relative to a well-balanced life is set forth in that little book, which I have adapted here.

Selected Bibliography

General

Adams, Charles. *Fight, Flight, Fraud.* Curacao, 1983.

Cipolla, Carlo M., ed. *The Economic Decline of Empires.* London, 1970.

Coffield, James. *A Popular History of Taxation.* London, 1980.

Grapperhaus, Ferdinand H.H. *Taxes, Liberty and Property.* Amsterdam, 1989.

Montesquieu, Baron de. *Spirit of Laws.* 1751. Reprint. Birmingham, Ala., 1984.

Webber, Carolyn and Aaron Wildavsky. *A History of Taxation and Expenditure in the Western World.* New York, 1986.

The Ancient Egyptians

Aldren, Cyril. *The Egyptians.* London, 1961.

———. *Akhenaten.* London, 1968.

Baikie, J. *The Amarna Age, A Study in the Crises of the Ancient World.* London, 1926.

———. *A History of Egypt.* 2 vols. London, 1929.

Breasted, James. *A History of Egypt.* New York, 1937.

Budge, Sir Wallace. *The Rosetta Stone.* London, 1928.

Bullock, Michael. *Daily Life in Egypt.* New York, 1964.

Erman, Adolf. *Life in Ancient Egypt.* New York, 1894.

Gardiner, Alan. "Ramesside Texts Relating to Taxation of Corn," *The Journal of Egyptian Archaeology* 27 (1941): 19–73.

Grenfell, B. P. *Revenue Laws of Ptolemy Philadelphus.* Oxford, 1896.

Maspero, G. *History of Egypt.* Vol. 2. London, 1903.

Packman, Zola. *The Taxes in Grain in Ptolemaic Egypt.* New Haven, 1958.

Rostovtzeff, M. *Social and Economic History of the Hellenistic World.* 3 vols. Oxford, 1967.

Wallace, Sherman. *Taxation in Egypt from Augustus to Diocletian.* Princeton, 1938.

Ward, William. *The Spirit of Ancient Egypt.* Beirut, 1965.

Ancient Israel, Assyria, and Babylon

The Bible. Exodus 1; II Kings 17–20; II Chronicles 10, 32, 36.

Contenau, George. *Everyday Life in Babylon and Assyria.* London, 1954.

Baron, Solo. *Ancient and Medieval Jewish History.* Rutgers, 1972.

———. *Economic History of the Jews.* New York, 1969.

Flavius Josephus. *Antiquities of the Jews,* Books IX, X, XII; *Wars of the Jews,* Book IV. Translated by William Whiston. Philadelphia, 1936.

Grayson, A. Kirk. *Assyrian Rulers of the Early First Millenium BC.* Toronto, 1991.

Graetz, Heinrich. *History of the Jews.* Philadelphia, 1898.

Grayson, A. Kirk. *The Assyrian Rulers of the Early First Millenium B.C.I (1114–859 B.C.).* Toronto, 1991.

Koestler, Arthur. *The Thirteenth Tribe.* New York, 1976.

Kramer, Samuel. *History Begins at Sumer.* New York, 1959.

Rostovzeff, M. *Social and Economic History of the Hellenistic World.* 3 vols. Oxford, 1967.

Ancient Greece

Austin, M. M., and P. Vidal-Naquet. *Economic and Social History of Ancient Greece: An Introduction.* London, 1977.

Eliot, Charles, ed. "Plutarch's Lives, Aristides." *The Harvard Classics.* Vol. 12. New York, 1909.

Ehrenberg, Victor. *The Greek State.* New York, 1964.

Ferguson, W. S. *Hellenistic Athens.* London, 1911.

Finley, M. I. *The Ancient Economy.* Berkeley, 1973.

Glotz, Gustave. *Ancient Greece at Work.* New York, 1967.

Meritt, Benjamin. *Documents on Athenian Tribute.* Harvard, 1937.

Thomsen, Rudi. *A Study of Direct Taxation in Ancient Athens.* Copenhagen, 1964.

Rome

Badian, E. *Publicans and Sinners.* Cornell, 1972.

Browning, Robert. *The Emperor Julian.* London, 1975.

Brunt, P. A. *Social Conflict in the Roman Republic.* London, 1971.

Cicero. "Is Honesty Always Necessary?" *On Duties III.* In *Cicero's Selected Works.* Ed. Michael Grant. New York, 1960.

———. "On the Good Life," *On Duties II,* 21:73. Ed. Michael Grant. New York, 1971.

Cipolla, Carlo M., ed. *The Economic Decline of Empires.* London, 1970.

Gibbon, Edward. *The Decline and Fall of the Roman Empire.* London, 1776.

Goffard, Walter. *Caput and Colonate.* Toronto, 1974.

Jones, A. H. M. *The Roman Economy.* Oxford, 1974.

Katz, Solomon. *Decline of Rome.* Cornell, 1955.

Lewis, Naphtali, and Meyer Reinhold. *Life in Egypt under Roman Rule*. Oxford, 1983.

Lewis, Naphtali, and Meyer Reinhold, eds. *Sourcebook I: The Republic*. New York, 1966.

———, eds. *Sourcebook II: The Empire*. New York, 1966.

Lot, Ferdinand. *The End of the Ancient World*. New York, 1961.

Montesquieu, Baron de. *Consideration on the causes of the greatness of the Romans and their decline*. Translated by David Lowenthal. New York, 1965.

Polybius. *The Rise of the Roman Empire*, trans. Ian Scott-Kilvert. New York, 1979.

Rostovtzeff, M. *The Social and Economic History of the Roman Empire*. 2 vols. Oxford, 1971.

Smith, Charles. *Tiberius and the Roman Empire*. Baton Rouge, 1942.

Tenney, Frank, ed. *An Economic Survey of Ancient Rome*. 6 vols. Paterson, N.J., 1959.

The Theodosian Code. Edited by Clyde Pharr. New York, 1969.

Tranquillus, Gaius Suetonius [Suetonius]. *Lives of the Caesars*. Translated by J. C. Rolfe. Cambridge, 1979.

Walbank, F. W. *The Awful Revolution*. Toronto, 1976.

———. *The Decline of the Roman Empire in the West*. London, 1946.

Wallace, Sherman. *Taxation in Egypt from Augustus to Diocletian*. Princeton, N.J., 1938.

Islam

Abbas, al 'Azzai. *History of Taxation in Iraq*. Baghdad, 1959.

Aghnicles, Nicolas P. *Mohammedian Theories of Finance*. New York, 1916.

Ashtor, Eliyahu. *A Social and Economic History of the Near East in the Middle Ages*. London, 1976.

Dennett, Daniel. *Conversion and the Poll Tax in Early Islam*. Cambridge, 1950.

Imamuddin, S. M. *The Economic History of Spain Under the Umayyads: 711–1031*. Dacca, 1963.

Lapidas, Ira. *Muslim Cities in the Late Middle Ages*. Cambridge, 1967.

Lokkegaard, Frede. *Islamic Taxation in the Classical Period*. Philadelphia, 1978.

Lewis, Bernard, ed. *Islam from the Prophet Muhammad to the Capture of Constantinople*. 2 vols. New York, 1974.

Shaban, M. A. *Islamic History, A New Interpretation*. Cambridge, 1971.

Shemesh, A. Ben. *Taxation in Islam*. 2 vols. London, 1958, 1965.

Stewart, Desmond. *Early Islam*. New York, 1967.

The Middle Ages

Abrahams, Israel. *Jewish Life in the Middle Ages*. New York, 1969.

Baron, Solo. *A Social and Religious History of the Jews*. 8 vols. New York, 1960.

Cave, Roy, and Herbert Coulson. *A Source Book for Medieval Economic History*. New York, 1965.

Harriss, G. L. *King, Parliament and Public Finance in Medieval England*. Oxford, 1975.

Henneman, John. *Royal Taxation in Fourteenth Century France*. Princeton, 1971.

Hodgett, Gerald. *A Social and Economic History of Medieval Europe*. London, 1972.

Marcus, Jacob. *The Jew in the Medieval World*. New York, 1975.

Mitchell, Sydney. *Taxation in Medieval England*. Yale, 1951.

Morgan, Shepard. *History of Parliamentary Taxation in England*. New York, 1911.

Post, Gaines. *Studies in Medieval Legal Thought*. Princeton, 1964.

Prasad, Kunwar Deo. *Taxation in Ancient India*. Delhi, 1987.

Strayer, Joseph. *Studies in Early French Taxation*. Camabridge, Mass., 1939.

Russia

Blum, J. *Lord and Peasant in Russia from the 9th to the 19th Century*. Princeton, N.J., 1961.

Dmytryshyn, B., ed. *Medieval Russia: A Source Book 900–1700*. New York, 1967.

Fennell, John. *The Emergence of Moscow 1304-1359*. London, 1968.

Grey, Ian. *The Horizon History of Russia*. New York, 1970.

Klyuchevsky, Vasili. *Peter the Great*. New York, 1958.

Mavor, James. *An Economic History of Russia*. 2 vols. New York, 1965.

Oliva, L. Jay, ed. *Catherine the Great*. Englewood Cliffs, N.J., 1971.

Pares, Bernard. *A History of Russia*. New York, 1964.

Prawdin, M. *The Mongol Empire, Its Rise and Legacy*. London, 1967.

Riasanovsky, Nicholas. *A History of Russia*. Oxford, 1969.

Vernadsky, George. *The Mongols in Russia*. Boston, 1980.

———. *A History of Russia*. New Haven, 1966.

Switzerland

Marchi, Otto. *Schweitzes Geschichte*. Zurich, 1971.

Ikle, Max. *Switzerland: An International Banking and Financial Center*. Stroudsburg, Pa., 1972.

Vetter, Alfred, ed. *Switzerland, Image of a People*. Berne, 1971.

Vickers, Roy. *Those Swiss Money Men*. New York, 1973.

Germany

Benecke, G. *Society and Politics in Germany: 1500-1750*. London, 1974.

Dawson, William Harbrett. *The Evolution of Modern Germany*. New York, 1908.

Ergang, Robert. *The Potsdam Fuhrer.* New York, 1941.
Grunberger, Richard. *A Social History of the Third Reich.* Middlesex, England, 1971.
Holborn, Hajo. *A Modern History of Germany, 1648-1840.* New Haven, 1964.
Johnson, Hubert. *Frederick the Great and His Officials.* New Haven, 1975.
Palmer, Alan. *Frederick the Great.* London, 1974.
Seligman, Edwin R. *The Income Tax.* New York, 1914.
Stolpher, Gustav. *German Economy 1870-1940.* New York, 1940.

Spain and Mexico
Coe, Michael. *Mexico.* New York, 1962.
Davies, Nigel. *The Aztecs.* London, 1973.
Davies, R. Trevor. *The Golden Century of Spain.* London, 1937.
———. *Spain in Decline.* London, 1957.
———. *The Decline of Spain, 1598-1640.* Cambridge, 1963.
Elliott, J. H. "The Decline of Spain," *Past and Present* No. 20, 1961: 169–95. Also found in *The Economic Decline of Empires*, edited by Carlo Cipolla. London, 1970.
Grice-Hutchinson, Marjorie. *Early Economic Thought in Spain.* London, 1978.
Hamilton, Earl J. *American Treasures and the Price Revolution in Spain, 1501-1650.* Cambridge, 1965.
———. "The Decline of Spain." *Economic History Review* 8 (1938):168–79.
Highfield, Roger, ed. *Spain in the 15th Century.* London, 1972.
Hippoly te Mariegal, Jean. *The Spain of Ferdinand and Isabella.* New Brunswick, N.J., 1961.
Hume, Martin A. S. *Spain its Greatness and Decay.* Cambridge, 1898.
Imamuddin, S. M. *The Economic History of Spain Under the Umayyads: 711-1031.* Dacca, 1963.
Kamen, Harry. *Spain 1469-1714, A Society of Conflict.* London, 1983.
Kennedy, Paul. *The Rise and Fall of the Great Powers.* New York, 1987.
Klein, Julius. *The Mesta, A Study in Spanish Economic History.* Cambridge, 1920.
Ortez, Antonio. *The Golden Age of Spain.* London, 1971.
Ross, Kurt, ed. *Codex Mendoza.* Fribourg, Switz., 1978.
Vicens, Jaime. *An Economic History of Spain.* Princeton, N.J., 1969.
Wolf, Eric. *Sons of the Shaking Earth.* Chicago, 1962.

The Netherlands
Boxer, C. R. *The Dutch Seaborne Empire, 1600-1800.* London, 1965.
Geyl, Pieter. *The Netherlands in the 17th Century.* London, 1961.
———. *Revolt in the Netherlands.* London, 1966.
Grapperhaus, Ferdinand. *Alva en de Tiende Penning.* Deventer, 1982.
———. *Taxes, Liberty and Property.* Amsterdam, 1989.
Haley, K. H. D. *The Dutch in the Seventeenth Century.* London, 1968.

Motley, John. *The Rise of the Dutch Republic.* New York, 1901.
Parker, Geoffrey. *The Dutch Revolt.* London, 1977.
Schama, Simon. *Embarrassment of Riches.* London, 1977.
Schiller, Johann. *The History of the Revolt in the Netherlands, 1788.* Translated by E.B. Eastwick. New York, 1847.
Schoffer, Ivo. *A Short History of the Netherlands.* Amsterdam, 1973.
Wilson, Charles. *The Dutch Republic and the Civilization of the Seventeenth Century.* London, 1968.

France

Bercé, Yves-Marie. *History of Peasant Revolts.* Ithaca, N.Y., 1990.
Bosher, J. F. *French Finances, 1720-1795.* Cambridge, 1970.
Brinton, Crane. *A Decade of Revolution, 1789-1799.* New York, 1934.
Brunn, Geoffrey. *Europe and the French Imperium: 1799-1813.* New York, 1938.
Carswell, John. *The South Sea Bubble.* London, 1961.
Church, William. *Richelieu and Reason of State.* Princeton, N.J., 1972.
Cole, Arthur. *The Great Mirror of Folly.* Cambridge, 1949.
Collins, James B. *The Fiscal Limits of Absolutism.* Berkeley, 1988.
Dakin, Douglas. *Turgot and the Ancien Régime in France.* London, 1939.
Dent, Julian. *Crises in France, Crown Finances and Society in 17th Century France.* New York, 1973.
Ebeling, Richard M. "Inflation and Controls in Revolutionary France: The Political Economy of the French Revolution." In *Reflections on the French Revolution, A Hillsdale College Symposium*, ed. Stephen Tonsor. Washington, D.C., 1990.
Funck-Brentano, Frantz. *The Old Regime in France.* New York, 1920.
Goubert, Pierre. *The Ancien Régime.* New York, 1974.
Hampson, N. *The French Revolution.* London, 1969.
Higgins, Earl Leroy. *The French Revolution as Told by Contemporaries.* New York, 1975.
Lewis, W. H. *The Splendid Century.* London, 1962.
Lodge, Eleanor C. *Sully, Colbert, and Turgot: A Chapter in French Economic History.* London, 1931.
Lough, John. *An Introduction of Eighteenth Century France.* London, 1960.
Matthews, George. *Royal Farms in 18th Century France.* New York, 1958.
Moote, Lloyd. *The Revolt of the Judges.* Princeton, 1971.
Mousnier, Roland. *Peasant Uprisings.* London, 1971.
Padover, Saul. *The Life and Death of Louis XVI.* New York, 1963.
Seligman, Edwin R. *The Income Tax.* New York, 1914.
Seward, Desmond. *The Prince of the Renaissance.* London, 1974.
Tocqueville, Alexis de. *The Ancient Regime and the French Revolution.* Translated by M. W. Patterson. Oxford, 1962.
Wheeler, Harold. *The French Revolution.* London, 1913.
Wolfe, Martin. *The Fiscal System of Renaissance France.* New Haven, 1972.

Britain

Beresford, Maurice. *The Poll Taxes of 1377, 1379 and 1381.* Canterbury, 1963.

Brewer, John. "The English State and Fiscal Appropriations, 1688-1789." *Politics and Society* 16 (1988): 335–85.

Camden, William. *The History of Princess Elizabeth.* 1688. Reprint, Chicago, 1920.

Caswell's Illustrated History of England. London, 1903.

Coffield, James. *A Popular History of Taxation.* London, 1970.

Davis, R. *The Rise of the English Shipping Industry in the Seventeenth and Eighteenth Centuries.* London, 1962.

Dowell, Stephen. *A History of Taxation and Taxes in England.* 1884. Reprint. 4 vols. New York, 1965.

Farnsworth, A. *Addington, Author of the Modern Income Tax.* London, 1951.

Fraser, Duncan. *The Smugglers.* Montrose, Scotland, 1971.

Grappenhaus, Ferdinand. *Taxes, Liberty and Property.* Amsterdam, 1989.

Kames, Lord Henry. *Sketches in the History of Man.* Dublin, 1769.

Kennedy, William. *English Taxation 1649-1799.* London, 1964.

Lacey, R. *Henry VIII.* London, 1972.

Mathias, Peter. *The Brewing Industry in England, 1700-1800.* Cambridge, 1965.

McCulloch, J. R. *Taxation and the Funding System.* London, 1845.

———, ed. *A Collection of Scarce and Valuable Tracts on Commerce* [1859]. Reprint. New York, 1966.

Mill, John Stuart. *Principles of Political Economy.* New York, 1961.

Morley, John. *Life of Gladstone.* 3 vols. London, 1903.

Plumb, J. H. *Sir Robert Walpole.* 2 vols. New Jersey, 1973.

Read, Conyers, "Good Queen Bess," *The American Historical Review* (July, 1926).

———, *Mr. Secretary Walsinghem and the Policy of Quen Elizabeth.* 3 vol. Cambridge, Mass., 1925.

Ricardo, David. *The Principles of Political Economy and Taxation.* Ed. L. Reynolds and W. Fellner. New Haven, 1963.

Sabine, B. E. J. *A History of Income Tax.* London, 1966.

Shore, Henry. *Smuggling Days and Smuggling Ways.* London, 1971.

Shoup, Carl. *Ricardo on Taxation.* New York, 1960.

Sinclair, John. *A History of the Public Revenues of the British Empire.* 1803. Reprint. 3 vols. New York, 1966.

Smith, Adam. *The Wealth of Nations.* London, 1776.

Stone, Lawrence. *The Crisis of the Aristocracy 1558–1641.* Oxford, 1965.

Teignmouth, Lord, et al. *The Smugglers.* 2 vols. London, 1923.

Ward, W. R. "The Administration of the Window and Assessed Taxes, 1696-1798." *English Historical Review* 67 (October 1952): 522–42.

Wiener, Joel H. *The War of the Unstamped: The Movement to Repeal the British Newspaper Tax, 1830–1836.* Ithaca, N.Y., 1969.

British cases on tax avoidance

Ayrshire Pullman Services, Ltd. v. I.R.C., (1929) 14 T.C. 754, 763–64.

Howard de Walden v. I.R.C., (1942) 25 T.C. 121, 134.

Latilla v. I.R.C., (1943) 25 T.C. 107, 117.
Vestey's Executors v. I.R.C, (1949) 31 T.C. l, 90.
Peter Buchanan v. McVey, (1951) (1955) A.C. 516, 529.

Japan and the Tigers

Borton, Hugh. *Peasant Uprisings in Japan of the Tokugawa Period.* New York, 1968.
Duus, Peter. *Feudalism in Japan.* New York, 1976.
Glassman, Lindsey, Lifau, Mallaby and Miltzer. "Is the Asian Flu Fatal." *Reason* (Los Angeles, May 1998).
Gee, Marcus, "The Real End of Japan, Inc." *Globe and Mail* (Toronto, April 18, 1998).
Hall, John, and Marius Jansen, eds. *Studies in the Institutional History of Early Modern Japan.* Princeton, N.J., 1968.
Ishi, Hiromitsu. *The Japanese Tax System.* Oxford, 1989.
Noguchi, Yukio. "Tax Reform Debates in Japan." In *World Tax Reform*, ed. Michael Boskin and Charles McLure, Jr. San Francisco, 1990.
Pepper, Thomas P., Merit E. Jarow, and Jimmy Wheeler. *The Competition: Dealing with Japan.* New York, 1985.
Rabushka, Alvin. *Hong Kong, A Study in Economic Freedom.* Chicago, 1979.
———. "Tax Policy and Economic Growth in the Four Asian Tigers." *Journal of Economic Growth* 3 (1988): 11.
Scheiner I., and T. Nagita, eds. *Japanese Thought in the Tokugawa Period, 1600–1868.* Chicago, 1978.
Schell, Jonathan. "Speak Loudly, Carry a Small Stick." *Harper's* (March 1989).
Tsiang, S. C. "Taiwan's Economic Success Demystified." *Journal of Economic Growth* 3 (1988): 21.
Tsunoda, R., ed. *Sources of Japanese Tradition.* New York, 1958.
Woronoff, Jon. *Asia's 'Miracle' Economies.* New York, 1986.

Israel

Bethell, Tom. "Is the Kibbutz Kaput?" *Reason* (October 1988).
Friedman, Milton. "Capitalism and the Jews." *The Freeman* 38 (October 1988): 385–95.
Rabushka, Alvin. *Scorecard on the Israeli Economy, A Review of 1990.* Jerusalem, 1991.
Rabushka, Alvin, Steve H. Hanke, and Yakir Plessner, eds. *Toward Growth: A Blueprint for Economic Rebirth in Israel* 3 (Spring 1989): 49.
Sheshinski, Eytan. "The 1988 Tax Reform in Israel." In *World Tax Reform*, ed. Michael J. Boskin and Charles E. McLure, Jr. San Francisco, 1990.

United States

Adams, Charles. *Those Dirty Rotten Taxes.* New York, 1998.
Baldwin, Leland D. *Whiskey Rebels.* Pittsburgh, 1968.

Becker, Robert. *Revolution, Reform, and the Politics of American Taxation, 1763-1783*. Baton Rouge, La., 1980.

Bensel, Richard F. *Yankee Leviathan*. Cambridge, 1995.

Birnbaum, Jeffrey H. and Alan S. Murray. *Showdown at Gucci Gulch*. New York, 1987.

Blum, Walter, and Harry Kalvern, Jr. *The Uneasy Case for Progressive Income Taxation*. Chicago, 1953.

Brackenridge, Hugh Henry. *Incidents of the Insurrection*. 1795. Reprint. New Haven, 1972.

Brownlee, W. Ellliot. *Federal Taxation in America*. Cambridge, 1996.

Carson, Gerald. *The Golden Egg*. Boston, 1977.

Chambliss, Lauren. "The IRS, the gang that cannot shoot straight." *The Financial World* (March 21, 1989).

Conable, Barber B. *Congress and the Income Tax*. Norman, Okla., 1989.

Cooley, Thomas, M. *Constitutional Limitations*. 1868. Reprint. Birmingham, Ala., 1987.

Dalmetch, John. *Rebellion and Reconciliation*. London, 1975.

Davidson, Jim. "Punch Out the IRS," *Playboy Magazine* (April 1976). You might compare this with some articles written a decade earlier that created quite a strong response from the IRS. "Tyranny in the Internal Revenue Service," *The Reader's Digest* (August 1967). A few critics hide behind pseudonyms. See Diogenes and John Galt below.

Davis, Shelly. *Unbridled Power Inside the Secret Culture of the IRS*. New York, 1997.

Diogenes. *The April Game*. Chicago, 1973.

Eisenstein, Louis. *The Ideologies of Taxation*. New York, 1961. See interesting book review by Justice Douglas in *N.Y. Herald Tribune* (Sept. 24, 1961): 6 (Books).

Epstein, Daniel F. *The Political Thought of the Federalist*. Chicago, 1984.

Ferleger, Herbert. *David Wells and the American Revenue System*. Philadelphia, 1977.

Fleetwood, Blake. "The Tax Police." *Saturday Review of Literature* (May 1980).

Forsythe, Dall. *Taxation and Political Change in the Young Nation, 1781–1833*. New York, 1977.

Galt, John. *Dreams Come Due*. New York, 1986.

Grapperhaus, Ferdinand. *Taxes, Liberty and Property*. Amsterdam, 1989.

Groves, Harold M. *Tax Philosophers*. Madison, Wis., 1974.

Hall, Robert, and Alvin Rabushka. "A Proposal to Simplify Our Tax System." *Wall Street Journal* (December 10, 1981), p. 30.

Hansen, George. *To Harass Our People*. Washington, D.C., 1980.

Harris, Richard. "Annals of the Law (The Fourth Amendment II)," *The New Yorker* (November 10, 1975).

Hayek, Friedrich. *The Constitution of Liberty*. Chicago, 1978.

Hellerstein, Jerome. *Taxes, Loopholes and Morals*. Boston, 1977.

Hess, Karl. *Dear America*. New York, 1975.

Hummel, Jeffrey. *Emancipating Slaves, Enslaving Free Men.* Chicago, 1996.
Kellems, Vivian. *Toil, Taxes, and Trouble.* New York, 1952.
Ketchum, Richard. *Will Rogers.* New York, 1973.
Kilpatrick, William. *The Big Tax Lie.* New York, 1986.
Kittrie, Nicholas, and Eldon D. Wedlock, Jr., eds. *The Tree of Liberty, A Documentary History of Rebellion and Political Crimes in America.* Baltimore, 1986.
Knight, David. *The Whiskey Rebellion.* New York, 1968.
Kultner, Robert. *Revolt of the Haves.* New York, 1980.
Larson, Martin A. *Tax Revolt: The Battle for the Constitution.* Greenwich, Conn., 1983.
MacPherson, Donald W. *April 15th: The Most Pernicious Attack Upon English Liberty.* Phoenix, 1983.
Mellon, Andrew. *Taxation: The Peoples Business.* New York, 1924.
Nock, Albert J. *Our Enemy The State.* 1935. Reprint. New York, 1989.
Paul, Randolph. *Taxation in the United States.* Boston, 1954.
Payne, James L. *Costly Returns.* San Francisco, 1993.
————. *The Culture of Spending.* San Francisco, 1991.
Rabushka, Alvin. *The Flat Tax.* Stanford, 1985.
————. *The Tax Revolt.* Stanford, 1982.
Ratner, Sidney. *American Taxation.* New York, 1942.
————. *Taxation and Democracy in America.* New York, 1967.
Reid, John Phillip. *Constitutional History of the American Revolution.* Vol. 2, *The Authority to Tax.* Madison, Wis., 1987.
Seligman, Edwin. *The Income Tax.* 1914. Reprint. New York, 1970.
Senholz, Hans. *Taxes and Confiscation.* New York, 1993.
Sfeinmo, Sueu. *Taxation and Democracy.* New Haven, 1993.
Smith, Page. *A New Age Begins.* 2 vols. New York, 1976.
Stampp, Kenneth M. *The Causes of the Civil War.* Englewood, 1959.
Stern, Philip. *The Rape of the Taxpayer.* New York, 1973.
Strum, Phillip. *Louis D. Brandeis: Justice for the People.* Cambridge, Mass., 1984.
Surface, William. *Inside Internal Revenue.* New York, 1967.
Tait, Alan. *The Personal Wealth Tax.* Urbana, Ill., 1967.
Taylor, John. *Tyranny Umasked.* 1822. Reprint. Indianapolis, 1992.
Thomas, Peter. *British Politics and the Stamp Act Crises.* Oxford, 1975.
Throp, Willard, et al., eds. *American Issues.* Vol. 1: *The Social Record.* Chicago, 1944.
Wanniski, Jude. *The Way the World Works.* New York, 1978.
Warren, Mercy Otis. *History of the Rise, Progress and Termination of the American Revolution.* 1805. Reprint. Indianapolis, 1988.
Witte, John F. *The Politics and Development of the Federal Income Tax.* Madison, Wis., 1985.

Leading U.S. Tax Cases

Hylton v. United States (1796) 3 Dall. 171, 1 L.ed. 556.
United States v. Singer (1872) 15 Wall. 111, 21 L.ed 49.

Head Money Cases, (1884) 112 U.S. 580.

Pollock v. Farmers Loan and Trust Co. (1895) 157 U.S. 429.

Magoun v. Illinois Trust and Savings Bank, (1898) 170 U.S. 283.

Knowlton v. Moore, (1899) 178 U.S. 41.

United States v. Plasynski, (1982) 550 F.Supp. 549; reversed (1983) 462 U.S. 74, 103 S.Ct. 2239.

California Bankers Assn. v. Shultz (1974) 94 S.Ct. 1494.

Boyd v. United States (1885), 116 U.S. 616.

Fischer v. United States, (1976) 425 U.S. 391.

Selected Materials on the Offshore World

Chappel, Robert. *Secrets of Offshore Tax Havens.* Orlinda, Calif., 1985.

Clarke, Thurston, and John Tigue. *Dirty Money.* New York, 1975.

Fay, Stephen, et al. *Hoax, The Inside Story of the Howard Hughes-Clifford Irving Affair.* New York, 1972.

Frantz, Douglas. *Mr. Diamond.* London, 1987.

Kinsman, Robert. *Robert Kinsman Guide to Tax Havens.* Homewood, Ill., 1978.

———. *Your New Swiss Bank Book.* Homewood, Ill., 1979.

Kwitny, Jonathan. *The Fountain Pen Conspiracy.* New York, 1973.

Moffit, Donald, ed., and the staff reporters of the *Wall Street Journal. Swindled: Classical Business Frauds of the Seventies.* Princeton, 1976.

Naylor, R. T. *Hot Money.* Toronto, 1987.

Thomas, S. Clark. *How to Form Your Own Tax Haven Company Privately.* Fort Erie, Ontario, 1981.

United States v. Carver, et al. Court of Appeals, Jamaica (Cayman Islands Appeal No. 5, 1982).

Vicker, Ray. *Those Swiss Money Men.* New York, 1973.

U.S. Government Studies

Gordon, Richard. *Tax Havens and Their Use by American Taxpayers: An Overview.* U.S. Public Document 81-397. Washington, D.C., 1981.

Tax Havens in the Caribbean Basin. Department of the Treasury, U.S. Public Document 84–403. Washington, D.C., January 1984.

Leading U.S. Cases Involving Tax Haven Issues

U.S. v. Field, (1976) 532 F.2d 404; criticized in 17 *Virginia Journal of International Law* 328 (1977).

U.S. v. Paynor, (1977) 434 F.Supp. 113, reversed with dissenting opinions, (1980) 100 S.Ct. 24.

U.S. v. Bank of Nova Scotia (1984) 740 F.2d 817.

U.S. v. Kilpatrick (1984) 594 F.Supp. 1328; (1987) 821 F.2d 1456, (1988) 108 S.Ct. 2369.

Illustration Credits

American Heritage Publishing Co., Inc., *Horizon,* Summer 1876, 82
American Museum of Natural History, N.Y., 148
Assemblée Nationale, République Francaise, 166
Atlas van Stolk, Rotterdam, 140
Atwater Kent Museum, Philadelphia, 230

BBC Hulton Picture Library, London, 177
Bettmann Archive Inc., 38, 88, 149, 210, 218, 215–52, 283
Bibliothèque Nationale, Paris, 59, 158, 159, 169, 249
Bradford Barton Ltd., Cornwall, UK, 279
British Museum, 8, 18, 70, 114, 149, 184

Cartoon Features Syndicate, Boston, 265, 288
Chicago Tribune, 266
Collier Pictures, Inc., New York, 113, 260
Office of the Curator, United States Supreme Court, 263

Des Moines Register and Tribune Company, Copyright 1990, 261
George Dole, 265
Roy Doty, 292

Henry Elsevier Nederlands, B.V., Amsterdam, 100
Mary Evans Picture Library, London, 216, 220

Franceschi Librarie Athard, Paris, 51
Frankfurter Allgemeine, Frankfurt, 253

Institute of Advanced Studies, Princeton, 40

Koninklijke Bibliotheek, Pamflet 4000, The Hague, 290

The Mansell Collection, London, 69, 113, 114
Metropolitan Museum of Art, New York, 33
Museum für Deutsche Geschichte, 152

Newsweek, Inc., New York, copyright 1978, cover by Marvin Lichter, Lee Groos Associates, 312
New York Public Library, 123
Novosti Press Agency, London, 118

Pat Oliphant, courtesy Simon and Schuster, 268

Royal Library in the Hague, 141

Saturday Evening Post (reprinted with permission), 265
Schweizes Geschechte, Marchi, Switzerland, by Courtesy, Miklaus, Fleules, publisher, 130, 131
Swedish Embassy, Ottawa, 277

USSR embassy, Ottawa, 121
University of Marburg, Germany, 57

Vida Schreiber, London, 174

Sam Walker, ch. 1

Index

523

About the Author

Known as "the tax writer," Charles Adams entered the field of international taxation after ten years in private legal practice and became a certified specialist in taxation law. His writings have been published in magazines, newspapers, and periodicals with lead stories featured in the *New York Times, Washington Post,* and *Wall Street Journal.* Mr. Adams is also an adjunct scholar at both the Ludwig von Mises Institute at Auburn University and the Cato Institute and a visiting lecturer on U.S. tax history at the National Archives, George Mason University, University of Rochester, University of Toronto, and New York University.